The Best AMERICAN ESSAYS 1987

The Best
AMERICAN
ESSAYS
1987

Edited and with an Introduction
by GAY TALESE

ROBERT ATWAN,
Series Editor

TICKNOR & FIELDS   NEW YORK   1987

ISSN 0888-3742
ISBN 0-89919-468-0
ISBN 0-89919-533-4 (pbk.)

Printed in the United States of America

Q 10 9 8 7 6 5 4 3 2 1

"Teacher" by John Barth. First published in *Harper's Magazine*. Copyright ©
1986 by John Barth. Reprinted by permission of the author. "Teacher" also
appears in expanded form in *An Apple for My Teacher*, edited by Louis D. Rubin,
Jr., and published by Algonquin Books of Chapel Hill in 1987.

"What Do You Think of Ted Williams Now?" by Richard Ben Cramer. First
published in *Esquire*. Copyright © 1986 by Richard Ben Cramer. Reprinted by
permission of the author.

"On Writing a Novel" by John Gregory Dunne. First published in *Esquire*.
Copyright © 1986 by John Gregory Dunne. Reprinted by permission of the
author.

"Spring" by Gretel Ehrlich. First published in *Antaeus*. Copyright © 1986 by
Gretel Ehrlich. Reprinted by permission of the author. "Spring" also appears in
On Nature, edited by Daniel Halpern and published by North Point Press in
1987.

"The Case of Harry Houdini" by Daniel Mark Epstein. First published in *The
New Criterion*. Copyright © 1986 by Daniel Mark Epstein. "The Case of Harry
Houdini" also appears in the author's collection *Star of Wonder*, published by
The Overlook Press in 1986. Reprinted by permission of The Overlook Press.

"They Said You Was High Class" by Joseph Epstein. First published in *The
American Scholar*. Copyright © 1986 by Joseph Epstein. Reprinted by permission
of the author. "They Said You Was High Class" also appears in the author's
collection *Once More Around the Block*, published by W. W. Norton & Co. in 1987.

" 'This Guy Wouldn't Give You the Parsley off His Fish' " by Gary Giddins.
First published in *Grand Street*. Copyright © 1986 by Gary Giddins. Reprinted
by permission of the author.

"Winter" by Donald Hall. First published in the exhibition catalogue *Winter*,
published by the Hood Museum of Art, Dartmouth College. Copyright © 1986
by Donald Hall. Reprinted by permission of the author. "Winter" also appeared
in altered form in *Harper's Magazine*.

Contents

Foreword

FROM THE START, the essay was a gutsy form. To *essay:* Montaigne used the word to suggest intellectual experimentation as well as personal daring and risk — "The wisdom of my lesson is wholly in truth, in freedom, in reality." He wrote with a directness and candor that readers still find surprising, some even shocking. His essays introduced a new standard for honesty in human discourse, one that has never ceased to challenge the serious writer. The essay may be an open form, yet how *open* does the essayist dare to be?

This second volume of *The Best American Essays* shows that personal honesty and the frank disclosure of facts still rank high among the essayist's preoccupations. The personal essay for some time has been thought of as a dead form, permanently flattened by the one-two punch of news journalism and New Journalism. Yet what died was only the old-fashioned familiar essay, that genteel and whimsical item — whose writers always sounded vaguely British — which used to be a staple of highbrow magazines and sleepy freshman English courses.

The new personal essay is tougher-minded, more candid, less polite, takes greater emotional risks. Its practitioners aren't afraid of making enemies and are often as hard on themselves as they are on friends, lovers, and family. The new generation of essayists knows that if honesty is an occupational requirement, it is also an occupational hazard. Essayists don't usually invent fictional characters; they write about the people they know. Many times they must hope that those people will never see the essay.

Such hopes may not be entirely unrealistic, since most personal essays today first appear in literary periodicals with relatively small circulations. With few exceptions, the general magazines rarely publish the genuine personal essay; their main fare is journalism. Over fifty years ago critics and editors complained about this trend. In the midst of the Depression one of the hot literary issues revolved around the fate of the traditional essay. One writer reproached the quality magazines for "forsaking their literary habit" and becoming the "homes of journalism." In 1934, one could say journalism and mean *mere* journalism. Today, however, as William Zinsser aptly points out, journalism — or that brand of it we call literary nonfiction — has become "the New American Literature." Others call it "the Literature of Fact."

Magazine journalism regularly produces the "article" — a piece of nonfiction in which the timely topic takes precedence over everything else: style is subordinate to subject; craft to coverage. But when the writer's reflections on a topic become as compelling as the topic itself, when he searches for the larger theme behind an isolated issue or an event, or when his craft and handling of material reveal a keen sense of a subject's true complexity, then "essay" seems to be the most accurate literary designation. The especially well-crafted journalism of the past two decades — though it may have dealt the final blow to the old "familiar" essay — has in many ways given new life to the form, broadening the range of what an essay can be and do.

In this volume, readers will discover a remarkably diverse range of contemporary essays, a mixture of voices and styles that stretch the form so wide we can easily understand why no one has ever successfully defined it. These are essays of erotic and romantic reminiscence, of the pleasures and pains of family ties and the class system, of adventures on America's highways and in India's forests; essays on the serious difficulties of a self-employed intellectual, on no-holds-barred confrontations with the seasons, on tools of toil and tools of torture, on murder, sex and drugs, on makers of bridges and novels and ancient stone horses, and on four famous people — a great ballplayer, a great comedian, a great magician, and a great inventor.

Back in the 1930s, the debate over the death of the essay — or as one of the writers gracefully put it, "the desuetude of the essay" — was partly carried on in an annual series similar to the present one. What was clearly dying, however, was *belles-lettres*, not the essay. And what happened to the magazines that seemed in imminent danger of losing their literary identity and becoming "homes of journalism"? These are a few of the periodicals represented in the *1936 Essay Annual: Harper's, The Atlantic Monthly, The New Yorker, The Southern Review,* and *The American Scholar.* Fifty years later and here they are still.

The Best American Essays features a selection of the year's outstanding essays, essays of literary achievement that show an awareness of craft and a forcefulness of thought. Roughly 120 essays are screened from a wide variety of regional and national publications. These essays are turned over to a distinguished guest editor, who may add a few personal favorites to the list and who makes the final selections.

To qualify for selection, the essays must be works of respectable literary quality intended as fully developed, independent essays (not excerpts or reviews) on subjects of general interest (not specialized scholarship), originally written in English (or translated by the author) for first appearance in an American periodical during the calendar year. Publications that want to make sure their contributions will be considered each year should include the series on their subscription list (Robert Atwan, *The Best American Essays,* P.O. Box 1074, Maplewood, New Jersey 07040).

For this volume I'd like to thank Jack Roberts for generously helping me track down essays throughout the year. I'd like to thank, too, the many magazine editors who kept me informed about potential material and who kindly gave me advice and encouragement. Without their judgment and assistance this annual volume would hardly be possible. And then there is Gay Talese, whose writing has bridged the fields of journalism and literature, and whose own honesty, candor, and respect for fact can be felt throughout this volume.

R.A.

Introduction

As one who was identified in the 1960s with the popularization of a literary genre known best as the New Journalism — an innovation of uncertain origin that appeared prominently in *Esquire, Harper's, The New Yorker,* and other magazines, and was practiced by such writers as Norman Mailer and Lillian Ross, John McPhee, Tom Wolfe, and the late Truman Capote — I now find myself cheerlessly conceding that those impressive pieces of the past (exhaustively researched, creatively organized, distinctive in style and attitude) are now increasingly rare, victimized in part by the reluctance of today's magazine editors to subsidize the escalating financial cost of such efforts, and diminished also by the inclination of so many younger magazine writers to save time and energy by conducting interviews with the use of that expedient but somewhat benumbing literary device, the tape recorder.

I myself have been interviewed by writers carrying recorders, and as I sit answering their questions, I see them half-listening, nodding pleasantly, and relaxing in the knowledge that the little wheels are rolling. But what they are getting from me (and I assume from other people they talk to) is not the insight that comes from deep probing and perceptive analysis and old-fashioned legwork; it is rather the first-draft drift of my mind, a once-over-lightly dialogue that — while perhaps symptomatic of a society permeated by fast-food computerized bottom-line impersonalized workmanship — too frequently reduces the once-artful craft of magazine writing to the level of talk radio on paper.

Far from decrying this trend, most editors tacitly approve of it, because a taped interview that is faithfully transcribed can protect the periodical from those interviewees who might later claim that they had been damagingly misquoted — accusations that, in these times of impulsive litigation and soaring legal fees, cause much anxiety, and sometimes timidity, among even the most independent and courageous of editors.

Another reason editors are accepting of the tape recorder is that it enables them to obtain publishable articles from the influx of facile free-lancers at pay rates below what would be expected and deserved by writers of more deliberation and commitment. With one or two interviews and a few hours of tape, a relatively inexperienced journalist today can produce a three-thousand-word article that relies heavily on direct quotation and (depending largely on the promotional value of the subject at the newsstand) will gain a writer's fee of anywhere from approximately $500 to slightly more than $2,000 — which is fair payment, considering the time and skill involved, but it is less than what was being paid for articles of similar length and topicality when I began writing for some of these same magazines more than a quarter of a century ago.

In those days, however, the contemporary writers I admired usually devoted weeks and months to research and organization, writing and rewriting, before our articles were considered worthy of occupying the magazine space that today is filled by many of our successors in one tenth the time. And in the past, too, magazines seemed more liberal than now about research expenses.

During the winter of 1965 I recall being sent to Los Angeles by *Esquire* for an interview with Frank Sinatra, which the singer's publicist had arranged earlier with the magazine's editor. But after I had checked into the Beverly Wilshire, had reserved a rental car in the hotel garage, and had spent the evening of my arrival in a spacious room digesting a thick pack of background material on Sinatra, along with an equally thick steak accompanied by a fine bottle of California burgundy, I received a call from Sinatra's office saying that my scheduled interview the next afternoon would not take place.

Mr. Sinatra was very upset by the latest headlines in the press about his alleged Mafia connections, the caller explained, adding that Mr. Sinatra was also suffering from a head cold that threatened to postpone a recording date later in the week at a studio where I had hoped to observe the singer at work. Perhaps when Mr. Sinatra was feeling better, the caller went on, and perhaps if I would also submit my interview to the Sinatra office prior to its publication in *Esquire,* an interview could be rescheduled.

After commiserating about Mr. Sinatra's cold and the news items about the Mafia, I politely explained that I was obliged to honor my editor's right to being the first judge of my work; but I did ask if I might telephone the Sinatra office later in the week on the chance that his health and spirits might then be so improved that he would grant me a brief visit. I could call, Sinatra's representative said, but he could promise nothing.

For the rest of the week, after apprising Harold Hayes, the *Esquire* editor, of the situation, I arranged to interview a few actors and musicians, studio executives and record producers, restaurant owners and female acquaintances who had known Sinatra in one way or another through the years. From most of these people I got something: a tiny nugget of information here, a bit of color there, small pieces for a large mosaic that I hoped would reflect the man who for decades had commanded the spotlight and had cast long shadows across the fickle industry of entertainment and the American consciousness.

As I proceeded with my interviews — taking people out each day to lunch and dinner while amassing expenses that, including my hotel room and car, exceeded $1,300 after the first week — I rarely, if ever, removed a pen and pad from my pocket, and I certainly would not have considered using a tape recorder had I owned one. To have done so would have possibly inhibited these individuals' candor, or would have otherwise altered the relaxed, trusting, and forthcoming atmosphere that I believe was encouraged by my seemingly less assiduous research manner and the promise that, however retentive I considered my memory to be, I would not identifiably attribute or quote anything told me without first checking back with the source for confirmation and clarification.

Quoting people verbatim, to be sure, has rarely blended well with my narrative style of writing or with my wish to observe and describe people actively engaged in ordinary but revealing

situations rather than to confine them to a room and present
them in the passive posture of a monologist. Since my earliest
days in journalism, I was far less interested in the exact words
that came out of people's mouths than in the essence of their
meaning. More important than what people say is what they
think, even though the latter may initially be difficult for them
to articulate and may require much pondering and reworking
within the interviewee's mind — which is what I gently try to
prod and stimulate as I query, interrelate, and identify with my
subjects as I personally accompany them whenever possible, be
it on their errands, their appointments, their aimless peregri-
nations before dinner or after work. Wherever it is, I try physically to be there in my role as a curious confidant, a trustworthy
fellow traveler searching into their interior, seeking to discover,
clarify, and finally to describe in words (my words) what they
personify and how they think.

There are times, however, when I do take notes. Occasionally
there is a remark that one hears — a turn of phrase, a special
word, a personal revelation conveyed in an inimitable style —
that should be put on paper at once lest part of it be forgotten.
That is when I may take out a notepad and say, "That's wonderful! Let me get that down just as you said it"; and the person,
usually flattered, not only repeats it but expands upon it. On
such occasions there can emerge a heightened spirit of cooperation, almost of collaboration, as the person interviewed recog-
nizes that he has contributed something that the writer ap-
preciates to the point of wanting to preserve it in print.

At other times I make notes unobserved by the interviewee
— such as during those interruptions in our talks when the
person has temporarily left the room, thus allowing me moments in which to jot down what I believe to be the relevant
parts of our conversation. I also occasionally make notes immediately after the interview is completed, when things are still
very fresh in mind. Then, later in the evening, before I go to
bed, I sit at my typewriter and describe in detail (sometimes
filling four or five pages, single-spaced) my recollections of what
I had seen and heard that day — a chronicle to which I constantly add pages with each passing day of the entire period of
research.

This chronicle is kept in an ever-expanding series of cardboard folders containing such data as the places where I and my sources had breakfast, lunch, and dinner (restaurant receipts enclosed to document my expenses); the exact time, length, locale, and subject matter of every interview; together with the agreed-upon conditions of each meeting (i.e., am I free to identify the source, or am I obliged to contact that individual later for clarification and/or clearance?). And the pages of the chronicle also include my personal impressions of the people I interviewed, their mannerisms and physical description, my assessment of their credibility, and much about my own private feelings and concerns as I work my way through each day — an intimate addendum that now, after nearly thirty years of habit, is of use to a somewhat autobiographical book I am writing; but the original intent of such admissive writing was self-clarification, reaffirming my own voice on paper after hours of concentrated listening to others, and also, not infrequently, the venting of some of the frustration I felt when my research appeared to be going badly, as it certainly did in the winter of 1965 when I was unable to meet face to face with Frank Sinatra.

After trying without success to reschedule the Sinatra interview during my second week in Los Angeles (I was told that he still had a cold), I continued to meet with people who were variously employed in some of Sinatra's many business enterprises — his record company, his film company, his real estate operation, his missile parts firm, his airplane hangar — and I also saw people who were more personally associated with the singer, such as his overshadowed son, his favorite haberdasher in Beverly Hills, one of his bodyguards (an ex–pro lineman), and a little gray-haired lady who traveled with Sinatra around the country on concert tours, carrying in a satchel his sixty hairpieces.

From such people I collected an assortment of facts and comments, but what I gained at first from these interviews was no particular insight or eloquent summation of Sinatra's stature; it was rather the awareness that so many of these people, who lived and worked in so many separate places, were united in the knowledge that Frank Sinatra had a cold. When I would allude to this in conversations, citing it as the reason my interview with him was being postponed, they would nod and say yes, they were aware of his cold, and they also knew from their contacts within Sinatra's inner circle that he was a most difficult man to be around when his throat was sore and his nose was running. Some of the musicians and studio technicians were delayed from working in his recording studio because of the cold, while others among his personal staff of seventy-five were not only sensitive to the effects of his ailment but they revealed examples of how volatile and short-tempered he had been all week because he was unable to meet his singing standards. And one evening in my hotel, I wrote in the chronicle:

> . . . it is a few nights before Sinatra's recording session, but his voice is weak, sore and uncertain. Sinatra is ill. He is a victim of an ailment so common that most people would consider it trivial. But when it gets to Sinatra it can plunge him into a state of anguish, deep depression, panic, even rage. Frank Sinatra has a cold.
>
> Sinatra with a cold is Picasso without paint, Ferrari without fuel — only worse. For the common cold robs Sinatra of that uninsurable jewel, his voice, cutting into the core of his confidence, and it affects not only his own psyche but also seems to cause a kind of psychosomatic nasal drip within dozens of people who work for him, drink with him, love him, depend on him for their own welfare and stability.
>
> A Sinatra with a cold can, in a small way, send vibrations through the entertainment industry and beyond as surely as a President of the United States, suddenly sick, can shake the national economy . . .

The next morning I received a call from Frank Sinatra's public relations director.

"I hear you're all over town seeing Frank's friends, taking Frank's friends to dinner," he began, almost accusingly.

"I'm working," I said. "How's Frank's cold?" (We were suddenly on a familiar basis.)

"Much better, but he still won't talk to you. But you can come with me tomorrow afternoon to a television taping if you'd like. Frank's going to try to tape part of his NBC special . . . Be outside your hotel at three. I'll pick you up."

I suspected that Sinatra's publicist wanted to keep a closer eye on me, but I was nonetheless pleased to be invited to the taping of the first segment of the one-hour special that NBC-TV was scheduled to air in two weeks, entitled "Sinatra — The Man and His Music."

On the following afternoon, promptly and politely, I was picked up in a Mercedes convertible driven by Sinatra's dapper publicist, a square-jawed man with reddish hair and a deep tan who wore a three-piece gabardine suit that I favorably commented upon soon after getting into the car — prompting him to acknowledge, with a certain satisfaction, that he had obtained it at a special price from Frank's favorite haberdasher. As we drove, our conversation remained amiably centered around such subjects as clothes, sports, and the weather until we arrived at the NBC building and pulled into a white concrete parking lot in which there were about thirty other Mercedes convertibles as well as a number of limousines in which were slumped black-capped drivers trying to sleep.

Entering the building, I followed the publicist through a corridor into an enormous studio dominated by a white stage and white walls and dozens of lamps and lights dangling everywhere I looked. The place resembled a gigantic operating room. Gathered in one corner of the room behind the stage, awaiting the appearance of Sinatra, were about one hundred people — camera crews, technical advisers, Budweiser admen, attractive young women, Sinatra's bodyguards and hangers-on, and also the director of the show, a sandy-haired, cordial man named Dwight Hemion, whom I had known from New York because we had daughters who were preschool playmates. As I stood chatting with Hemion, and overhearing conversations all around me, and listening to the forty-three musicians, sitting in tuxedos on the bandstand, warming up their instruments, my mind was racing with ideas and impressions; and I would have liked to have taken out my notepad for a second or two. But I knew better.

And yet after two hours in the studio — during which time Sinatra's publicist never left my side, even when I went to the bathroom — I was able to recall later that night precise details about what I had seen and heard at the taping; and in my hotel I wrote in the chronicle:

> Frank finally arrived on stage, wearing a high-necked yellow pullover, and even from my distant vantage point his face looked pale, his eyes seemed watery. He cleared his throat a few times. Then the musicians, who had been sitting stiffly and silently in their seats ever

since Frank had joined them on the platform, began to play the opening song, "Don't Worry about Me." Then Frank sang through the whole song — a rehearsal prior to taping — and his voice sounded fine to me, and it apparently sounded fine to him, too, because after the rehearsal he suddenly wanted to get it on tape.

He looked up toward the director, Dwight Hemion, who sat in the glass-enclosed control booth overlooking the stage, and he yelled: "Why don't we tape this mother?"

Some people laughed in the background, and Frank stood there tapping a foot, waiting for some response from Hemion.

"Why don't we tape this mother?" Sinatra repeated, louder, but Hemion just sat up there with his headset around his ears, flanked by other men also wearing headsets, staring down at a table of knobs or something. Frank stood fidgeting on the white stage, glaring up at the booth, and finally the production stage manager — a man who stood to the left of Sinatra, and also wore a headset — repeated Frank's words exactly into his line to the control room: "Why don't we tape this mother?"

Maybe Hemion's switch was off up there, I don't know, and it was hard to see Hemion's face because of the obscuring reflections the lights made against the glass booth. But by this time Sinatra is clutching and stretching his yellow pullover out of shape and screaming up at Hemion: "Why don't we put on a coat and tie, and tape this . . . "

"Okay, Frank," Hemion cut in calmly, having apparently not been plugged into Sinatra's tantrum, "would you mind going back over . . ."

"Yes I *would* mind going back!" Sinatra snapped. "When we stop doing things around here the way we did them in 1950 maybe we . . ."

. . . Although Dwight Hemion later managed to calm Sinatra down, and in time to successfully tape the first song and a few others, Sinatra's voice became increasingly raspy as the show progressed — and on two occasions it cracked completely, causing Sinatra such anguish that in a fitful moment he decided to scrub the whole day's session. "Forget it, just forget it!" he told Hemion. "You're wasting your time. What you got there," he continued, nodding to the singing image of himself on the TV monitor, "is a man with a cold."

There was hardly a sound heard in the studio for a moment or two, except for the clacking heels of Sinatra as he left the stage and disappeared. Then the musicians put aside their instruments, and everybody else slowly turned toward the exit . . . In the car, coming back to the hotel, Frank's publicist said they'd try to retape the show within the week, he'd let me know when. He also said that in a few weeks he was going to Las Vegas for the Patterson-Clay heavyweight fight (Frank & friends would be there to watch it), and if I wanted to go he'd book me a room at the Sands and we could fly together. Sure, I said . . . but to myself I'm thinking: how long will *Esquire* continue to pay my expenses? By the end of this week, I'll have spent more than $3,000, have not yet talked to Sinatra, and, at the rate we're going, it's possible I never will . . .

Before going to bed that night, I telephoned Harold Hayes in New York, briefed him on all that was happening and not happening, and expressed concern about the expenses.

"Don't worry about the expenses as long as you're getting something out there," he said. "Are you getting something?"

"I'm getting something," I said, "but I don't exactly know what it is."

"Then stay out there until you find out."

I stayed another three weeks, ran up expenses close to $5,000, returned to New York, and then took another six weeks to organize and write a fifty-five-page article that was largely drawn from a two-hundred-page chronicle that represented interviews with more than one hundred people and described Sinatra in such places as a bar in Beverly Hills (where he got into a fight), a casino in Las Vegas (where he lost a small fortune at blackjack), and the NBC studio in Burbank (where, after recovering from the cold, he retaped the show and sang beautifully).

The *Esquire* editors titled the piece "Frank Sinatra Has a Cold," and it appeared in the April 1966 issue. It remains in print today in a Dell paperback collection of mine called *Fame and Obscurity*. While I was never given the opportunity to sit down and speak alone with Frank Sinatra, this fact is perhaps one of the strengths of the article. What could he or *would* he have said (being among the most guarded of public figures) that would have revealed him better than an observing writer watching him in action, seeing him in stressful situations, listening and lingering along the sidelines of his life?

This method of lingering and careful listening and describing scenes that offer insight into the individual's character and personality — a method that a generation ago came to be called the New Journalism — was, at its best, really fortified by the "Old

Journalism's" principles of tireless legwork and fidelity to factual accuracy. As time-consuming and financially costly as it was, it was this research that marked my Sinatra piece and dozens of other magazine articles that I published during the 1960s — and there were other writers during this period who were doing even more research than I was, particularly at *The New Yorker*, one of the few publications that could afford, and today still chooses to afford, the high cost of sending writers out on the road and allowing them whatever time it takes to write with depth and understanding about people and places. Among the writers of my generation at *The New Yorker* who personify this dedication to roadwork are Calvin Trillin and the aforementioned John McPhee; and the most recent example of it at *Esquire* was the piece about the former baseball star Ted Williams, written by Richard Ben Cramer, an old-fashioned legman of thirty-six whose keen capacity to *listen* has obviously not been dulled or otherwise corrupted by the plastic ear of a tape recorder.

But such examples in magazines are, as I mentioned earlier, becoming more and more rare in the 1980s, especially among free-lancers. The best of the nonfiction writers today — those unaffiliated with such solvent institutions as *The New Yorker* — are either having their research expenses underwritten by the book industry (and are excerpting parts of their books in magazines), or they are best-selling writers who can afford to do a well-researched magazine piece if they fancy the subject, or they are writers whose financial support comes mainly from faculty salaries and foundation grants. And what this latter group of writers are publishing today, mainly in modestly remunerative literary periodicals, are pieces that tell us more about themselves than about other people. They are opinioned pieces of intellectual or cultural content, or articles that are decidedly reflective and personal, and not dependent on costly time and travel. They are works researched out of a writer's own recollections. They are close to a writer's heart and place of dwelling. The road has become too expensive. The writer is home.

GAY TALESE

The Best
AMERICAN
ESSAYS
1987

JOHN BARTH

Teacher

FROM HARPER'S MAGAZINE

IN THE FEATURELESS, low-rise, glass-and-aluminum box in which, back in the early 1960s, I taught Humanities 1 (Truth, Goodness, and Beauty) at Pennsylvania State University, her hand was always up — usually first among those of the thirty undergraduates enrolled in my section. Many were seniors from the colleges of education, home economics, engineering, even agriculture, fulfilling their "non-tech elec"; Hum 1 was not a course particularly designed for liberal-arts majors, who would presumably pick up enough T G & B in their regular curriculum. But Miss Rosenberg of the bright brown eyes and high-voltage smile and upraised hand, very much a major in the liberal arts, was there (1) because it was her policy to study with as many members as possible of that university's huge faculty — almost regardless of their subject — who she had reason to believe were of particular interest or effectiveness; (2) because other of her English professors had given me O.K. notices; and (3) because the rest of my teaching load in those days was freshman composition (a requirement from which she'd easily been absolved) and the writing of fiction (an art for which she felt no vocation).

Hum 1, then:

What is Aristotle's distinction between involuntary and *non*-voluntary acts, and what are the moral implications of that distinction? Miss Rosenberg?

What does David Hume mean by the remark that the rules of art come not from reason but from experience? Anybody? Miss Rosenberg.

What are all those *bridges* for in *Crime and Punishment*? Let's
hear from somebody besides Miss Rosenberg this time. (No
hands.) Think of it this way: What are the three main things a
novelist can do with a character on a bridge? (No hands. Sigh.)
Miss Rosenberg?

Her responses were sound, thoughtful, based unfailingly
upon thorough preparation of the assigned material; and she
was always ready. If she was not the most brilliant student I'd
ever taught — I was already by then a dozen years into the
profession, with more than a thousand students behind me —
she was the best. Which is not to say that Miss R. (the sixties
weren't yet in high gear; in central Pennsylvania, at least, most
of us still lectured in jackets, white shirts, and neckties and
called our students Miss and Mr., as they called us Professor)
was docile: if she didn't understand a passage of Lucretius or
Machiavelli or Turgenev, she interrogated it and me until either
she understood it or I understood that I didn't understand it
either. Her combination of academic and moral seriousness,
her industry, energy, and animation — solid A, back when A
meant A.

The young woman was physically attractive, too: her skirt-
and-sweatered body trim and fit (from basketball, softball,
soccer, tennis, fencing), her brown hair neatly brushed, her
aforecited eyes and smile. Ten years out of my all-male alma
pater, I still found it mildly exciting — diverting, anyhow — to
have girls, as we yet thought of them, in my classroom. But
never mind that: as a student, for better or worse, I was never
personally close to my teachers; as a teacher, I've never been
personally close to my students. And on the matter of *physical*
intimacies between teacher and taught, I've always agreed with
Bernard Shaw's Henry Higgins: "What! That thing! Sacred, I
assure you. . . . Teaching would be impossible unless pupils
were sacred."

Now: What is the first rung on Plato's "ladder of love"? Nobody remembers? Miss Rosenberg.

All the same, it interested me to hear, from a friend and
senior colleague who knew her better, that my (and his) star
student was not immune to "crushes" on her favorite teachers,
who were to her as were the Beatles to many of her classmates:
crushes more or less innocent, I presumed, depending upon

their object. This same distinguished colleague I understood to
be currently one such object. She frequented his office between
classes; would bicycle across the town to drop in at his suburban
house. I idly wondered . . . but did not ask him, much less her.
Sacred, and none of my business.

I did however learn a few things further. That our Miss R.
was from Philadelphia, strictly brought up, an overachiever
(silly pejorative; let's say superachiever) who might well graduate first in her four-thousand-member class. That she was by
temperament and/or upbringing thirsty for attention and
praise, easily bruised, traumatically strung out by the term papers and examinations on which she scored so triumphantly.
That her emotional budget was high on both sides of the ledger:
she expended her feelings munificently; she demanded — at
least expected, anyhow hoped for — reciprocal munificence
from her friends and, presumably, from her crushees.

Mm hm. And the second rung, anybody? (No hands, except
of course . . .) Miss Rosenberg.

En route to her A in Hum 1 we had a couple of office conferences, but when she completed her baccalaureate (with, in fact,
the highest academic average in Penn State's hundred-year history, for which superachievement she was officially designated
the university's one hundred thousandth graduate at its centennial commencement exercises), I was still Mr. Barth; she was
still Miss Rosenberg. She would have prospered at the best colleges in our republic; circumstances, I was told, had constrained
her to her state university. What circumstances? I didn't ask.
Now (so my by-this-time-ex-crushee colleague reported) she had
several graduate fellowships to choose from; he believed she
was inclining to the University of Chicago.

I too, as it happened, was in the process of changing universities. I neither saw, nor heard from or about, nor to my recol-
lection thought of excellent Miss Rosenberg for the next four
years.

There is chalk dust on the sleeve of my soul. In the half century
since my kindergarten days, I have never been away from class-
rooms for longer than a few months. I am as at home among
blackboards, desks, lecterns, and seminar tables as among the
furniture of my writing room; both are the furniture of my

head. I believe I know my strengths and limitations as a teacher the way I know them as a writer: doubtful of my accomplishments in both métiers, I am not doubtful at all that they *are* my métiers, for good or ill.

Having learned by undergraduate trial and error that I was going to devote my adult life to writing fiction, I entered the teaching profession through a side door: by impassioned default, out of heartfelt lack of alternatives. I'd had everything to learn; the university had taught me some of it, and I guessed that teaching might teach me more. I needed time to clear my literary throat, but I was already a family man; college teaching (I scarcely cared where or what; I would improvise, invent if necessary) might pay landlord and grocer, if barely, and leave my faculties less abused and exhausted than would manual labor or routine office work, of both of which I'd had a taste. Teaching assistantships in graduate school at Johns Hopkins had taught me that while I was not a "natural" teacher, I was not an unnatural one, either. Some of my undergraduate students knew more about literature, even about the rules of grammar, syntax, and punctuation, than I did. I pushed to catch up. I accepted gratefully a $3,000-a-year instructorship in English composition at Penn State, where I taught four sections of freshman comp — six teaching days a week, twenty-five students per section, one composition per student per week, all papers to be corrected and graded by a rigorous system of symbols, rules, standards. That's three thousand freshman compositions a year, at a dollar per. It drove one of my predecessors, the poet Theodore Roethke, to drink. But there were occasional half days free, some evenings, the long academic holidays and summers. I stayed on there a dozen years, moving duly through the ranks and up the modest salary scale; got novels written and children raised; learned a great deal about English usage and abusage. And I had a number of quite good students among all those hundreds in my roll book . . . even a few superb ones.

My academic job changes happened to coincide with and correspond to major changes in society. As America moved into the High Sixties, I moved from Penn State's bucolic sprawl — still very 1950ish in 1965, with its big-time football, its pompommed cheerleaders, its more than half a hundred social fraternities, its fewer than that number of long-haired, pot-smoking counterculturals among the fifteen-thousand-plus undergraduates, its vast experimental farms and tidy livestock barns, through which I used to stroll with my three small children when not writing sentences or professing Truth, Goodness, and Beauty — moved to the State University of New York's edgy-urban new operation in Buffalo. The Berkeley of the East, its disruptivist students proudly called the place. The Ellis Island of Academe, we new-immigrant faculty called it, also with some pride; so many of us were intellectual heretics, refugees from constrained professional or domestic circumstances, academic fortune hunters in Governor Nelson Rockefeller's promising land.

Those next four years were eventful, in U.S. history and mine. Jetting once a month to guest-lecture at other universities, I literally saw the smoke rise from America's burning urban ghettos. More than once I returned from some tear-gassed campus to find my own "trashed," on strike, or cordoned off by gas-masked National Guardsmen. It was a jim-dandy place, SUNY/Buffalo, to work out the decade. My marriage came unglued; I finished *Giles Goat-Boy,* experimented with hashish and adultery, wrote *Lost in the Funhouse* and "The Literature of Exhaustion," began *Chimera.* Education, said Alfred North Whitehead, is the process of catching up with one's generation. The tuition can be considerable.

One afternoon in the sixties' final winter I took off from Buffalo in a snowstorm for my monthly off-campus lecture, this one at Boston College. The flight was late in arriving. My Jesuit host, who was to have taken me to a prelecture dinner, had his hands full just getting us across the snowed-in city to the BC campus, where most of my audience was kindly waiting. Promising dinner later, he hustled me onstage to do my number and then off to the obligatory reception (invited guests only) in a room above the auditorium. Since we were running late, we skipped the usual postlecture question period. Even so, as happens, people came forward to say hello, get their books signed, ask things.

Such as (her head cocked slightly, bright eyes, bright smile, nifty orange wool miniskirted dress, beige boots — but my host was virtually tugging at my sleeve; we'd agreed to cut short this ritual and get upstairs to that reception as quickly as courtesy allowed): "Remember me?"

For a superachiever in the U.S.A., public-school teaching is a curious choice of profession. Salaries are low. The criteria for employment in most districts are not notably high; neither is the schoolteacher's prestige in the community, especially in urban neighborhoods and among members of the other professions. The workload, on the other hand, is heavy, in particular for conscientious English teachers who demand a fair amount of writing as well as reading from the hundred or more students they meet five days a week. In most other professions, superior ability and dedication are rewarded with the five P's: promotion, power, prestige, perks, and pay. Assistant professors become associate professors, full professors, endowed-chair professors, emeritus professors. Junior law partners become senior law partners; middle managers become executives in chief; doctors get rich and are held in exalted regard by our society. Even able and ambitious priests may become monsignors, bishops, cardinals. But the best schoolteacher in the land, if she has no administrative ambitions (that is, no ambition to get out of the classroom), enters the profession with the rank of teacher and retires from it decades later with the rank of teacher, not remarkably better paid and perked than when she met her maiden class. Fine orchestral players and repertory actors may be union-scaled and virtually anonymous, but at least they get, as a group, public applause. Painters, sculptors, poets may labor in poverty and obscurity, but, as Milton acknowledged, "Fame is the spur." The condition of the true artisan, perhaps, is most nearly akin to the gifted schoolteacher's: an all but anonymous calling that allows for mastery, even for a sort of genius, but rarely for fame, applause, or wealth; whose chief reward must be the mere superlative doing of the thing. The maker of stained glass or fine jewelry, however, works only with platinum, gemstones, gold, not with young minds and spirits.

Sure, I remembered her, that snowy night: Penn State, Hum 1, hand raised. After a moment I even recalled her name, a feat I'm poor at in company. My sleeve was being tugged: the reception. So what was she doing there? She'd seen notice of my reading in the newspaper and hauled through the snow from

Brookline to catch her old teacher's act. No, I meant in Boston: Ph.D. work, I supposed, somewhere along the River Chuck, that cerebral cortex of America. Or maybe she'd finished her doctorate — I couldn't remember her specialty — and was already assistant professoring in the neighborhood? No: it was a long story, Ms. R. allowed, and there were others standing about, and my sleeve was being tugged. Well, then: Obliging of you to trek through the drifts to say hello to your old teach. Too bad we can't chat a bit more, catch up; but there's this reception I have to go to now, upstairs. You're looking fine indeed.

She was: not a coed now, but a city-looking smart young woman. Where was it she'd been going to go after Penn State? What interesting things had her ex-crushees among my ex-colleagues told me about her? Couldn't remember: only the hand invariably raised (sometimes before I'd reached my question mark) in Truth, Goodness, and Beauty, the lit-up smile, and maybe one serious office conference in her senior year. Was there a wedding ring on that hand now? Before I could think to look, I was Jesuited off to an elevator already filled with the invited.

As its doors closed, she caught them, caused them to reopen, and lightly asked, "May I come along?" Surprised, delighted, I answered for my host: former star student, haven't seen her in years, we did her out of her Q & A, of course she may come along.

No wedding ring. But at the reception, too, I was rightly pre-empted by the Boston Collegians whose guest I was. Ms. Rosenberg and I (but it was Shelly now, and please call me Jack) had time only to register a few former mutual acquaintances and the circumstance of my being in Buffalo these days (she'd read that) and of her having left Chicago (a long story, Jack) to teach in Boston. Aha. At Boston U? Tufts? Northeastern?

The incandescent smile. Nope: in the public schools. First at Quincy Junior High, then at Weston Junior High, currently at Wayland High. She was a public-school teacher of English. A schoolteacher is what she'd wanted to be from the beginning.

We supposed I ought to mingle with the invited. But as she'd already taken two initiatives — the first merely cordial, the second a touch audacious — I took the next four. My host, the kindly priest, meant to dine me informally after the reception, at some restaurant convenient to my motel, into which I'd not yet been checked. I urged her to join us, so that we could finish our catching up off company time. She agreed, the priest likewise. As she had her car with her and the weather was deep, they conferred upon likeliest roads and restaurants (one with oysters and champagne, the guest of honor suggested) and decided upon Tollino's on Route 9, not far from the Charterhouse Motel, where I was billeted. She'd meet us there.

My duty by the invited done, she did. Tollino's came through with half-shell Blue Points and bubbly; the priest had eaten, but he encouraged us to take our time (though the hour was late now) and to help ourselves. He even shared a glass with us. We tried politely to keep the conversation three-way; it was clear to all hands, however, that our patient host was ready to end his evening. Initiative two: The Charterhouse was just a few doors down the road; Ms. Rosenberg had her car. If she was agreeable . . .

Quite. The good father was excused; he would fetch me to the airport in the morning. Another round of oysters then, another glass of champagne to toast our reacquaintance. Here's to Penn State, to old mutual friends and ex-crushees, to Truth, to Goodness, to Beauty. Here's to lively Boston, bumptious Buffalo, and — where was it? Chicago, right. A long story, you said. On with it: long stories are my long suit.

A schoolteacher is what she'd wanted to be from the beginning. Though she'd used to weep at her difficulties with higher math, and was unnerved even back then by the prospect of examinations and term papers, she'd loved her Philadelphia public-school days. At the Pennypacker Elementary School and especially at the fast-track Philadelphia High School for Girls, Penn State's future academic superstar had regarded herself as no more than a well-above-average performer. But she'd relished each new school day; had spent the long summer breaks enthusiastically camp-counseling, the next-best thing to school.

Her resolution to "teach school" never wavered. At the urging of her professors at Penn State she'd gone on to graduate study in literature and art history in the University of Chicago's Division of the Humanities; she'd done excellent work there with Edward Wasiolek, Elder Olson, Edward Rosenheim. She'd even

charmed her way into one of Saul Bellow's courses, to check
that famous fellow out. But she had no ambition for a doctorate:
her objective was *schoolteaching!* (she said it always with excla-
mation mark and megawatt smile), and she wanted to get to it
as soon as possible. On the other hand, she'd had no truck with
"education" courses: Mickey Mouse stuff, in her opinion, except
for the history and philosophy of education, which she'd found
engrossing. Her baccalaureate was in English, her M.A. was to
have been in the humanities. Neither had she been a teaching
assistant; hers was a no-strings fellowship.

I pricked up my ears. *Was to have been?*

Yes: she'd left Chicago abruptly after a year and a half, for
nonacademic reasons, without completing the degree. This ir-
regularity, together with the absence of education courses on
her transcripts, had made it necessary for her first employer, in
Quincy, to diddle benignly with her credentials for certification
to teach in the commonwealth's public schools, especially as
she'd come to Boston in midacademic year. She was hired and
was being paid as "M.A. equivalent," which she certainly was.

Abruptly, you said? For nonacademic reasons?

Yup. A love trauma, only recently recovered from. Long
story, Jack.

Tollino's was closing. Initiative three: I supposed there was a
bar of some sort in or near my motel, where we could have a
nightcap and go on with our stories (I too had one to tell).
Should we go check me into the Charterhouse and have a look?

Sure. We made the short change of *mise-en-scènes* down the
snowplowed highway in her silver-blue Impala convertible, behind the wheel whereof my grown-up and, it would seem, now
seasoned former student looked quite terrific in those beige
boots and that orange miniskirted dress under that winter coat.
And in the motel's all-but-empty lounge I was told at last the
long story and some shorter ones, and I told mine and some
shorter ones, and presently I took Initiative four.

Plato has Socrates teach in *The Symposium* that the apprehension
of Very Beauty, as distinct from any beautiful thing or class of
things, is arrived at by commencing with the love of, even the
lust for, some particular beautiful object or person. Thence one
may proceed to loving beautiful objects and persons in general,

the shared quality that transcends their individual differences
— may learn even to admire that shared quality without lusting
after it: "Platonic love." Thereby one may learn to love the
beauty of nonmaterial things as well: beautiful actions, beautiful
ideas (a philosopher colleague back at Penn State, remarking to
me that he could not read without tears the beautiful scene near
the end of Turgenev's *Fathers and Children* where Bazarov's old
parents visit their nihilist son's grave, added, "But I weep at the
Pythagorean theorem, too"). Whence the initiate, the elect, the
platonically invited, may take the ultimate elevator to Beauty
Bare: the quality abstracted even from beautiful abstractions.
This is the celebrated "ladder of love," as I understood and
taught it in Humanities 1 at Penn State, Miss Rosenberg's hand
raised at every rung. Our relationship began at the top of that
ladder, with those lofty abstractions: Truth, Goodness, Beauty.
Now my (former) student taught her (former) teacher that that
process is reversible, anyhow coaxial; that ladder a two-way
street; that ultimate elevator — May I come along? — a not-bad
place to begin.

She was (and is) the natural teacher I've never been. Distraught by the termination of her first adult love affair, she'd
abruptly left Chicago and her almost completed graduate degree and found asylum in Boston with a Girls' High classmate,
now a Harvard doctoral candidate. In the midst of this turmoil
— and in midyear — she entered the profession she'd known
since first grade to be her calling; and with no prior training or
direct experience, from day one on the chair side of the teacher's desk she was as entirely in her element as she'd known she
would be. M.A. or no M.A., she was a master of the art; personal
crisis or no personal crisis, she improvised for the Quincy Junior
High fast-trackers, later for the whiz kids at Weston and Wayland, a course in literature and art history as high-powered and
high-spirited as its teacher. She flourished under the staggering
workload of a brand-new full-time superconscientious public-
school English teacher. She throve in the life of her new city:
new friends, apartment mates, parties, sports, explorations,
dates, liaisons — all worked in between the long hours of preparing lesson plans and study questions, assembling films and
organizing projector slides, critiquing papers, grading quizzes

and exams, and teaching, teaching, teaching her enthusiastic
students, who knew a winner when they learned from one.

In subsequent Boston visits (No need to fetch me to the airport this morning, Father; I have a ride, thanks) I would meet
various of her colleagues — most of them likewise energetic,
dedicated, and attractive young men and women — and a few
of her students, bound for advanced placement in the Ivy
League. I would come to see just how good "good" public
schooling can be, how mediocre mine was, how barely better
had been my children's. Alas, I was unable to witness my former
student's teacherly performances as she'd witnessed a semester's
worth of mine. Public schools are not open to the public; anyhow, my presence would have been intrusive. By all accounts
they were superlative, virtuoso. From what I knew of her as a
student, I could not imagine otherwise.

Yet she came truly into her professional own when, after our
marriage, we moved to Buffalo — returned to Buffalo in my
case, from a honeymoon year as a visiting professor at Boston
University — and, beginning to feel the burden of full-time
public-school teaching, she took with misgivings a half-time job
in a private girls' high school, the old Buffalo Seminary. Its non-
coed aspect gave her no trouble; much as she'd enjoyed her
male students in Boston, she'd enjoyed even more the atmosphere of the Philadelphia High School for Girls. But the notion
of private schools — "independent schools," they call themselves — ran counter to her liberal-democratic principles. Buff
Sem's exclusiveness was not academic, as had been that of Girls'
High and the Wayland fast track; she feared it would be social,
perhaps racist: a finishing school for the daughters of well-to-
do Buffalonians who didn't want their kids in the racially and
economically integrated city system.

Her apprehensions were not foundationless. Despite generous scholarship programs and sincere attempts at "balance,"
good U.S. private schools are far more homogeneous — racially, economically, socially, academically — than our public
schools are, especially our urban public schools. But her misgivings evaporated within a week in the sunny company of her new
charges. The girls as a group were no brighter than those at
Quincy, Weston, Wayland; *less* bright, as a group, than her fast-

trackers in those public schools or her own high school classmates back in Philadelphia. But they were entirely likable, not
at all snobbish, and wondrously educable. There are next to no
disciplinary problems in a good private girls' school, at least not
in the classroom. And with only twelve or so students per class,
and with only two classes, and without the powerfully distracting sexual voltage of coeducation at the high school level —
what teaching could get done!

We stayed for only one academic year. But more than a dozen
years later she is still remembered with respect and affection by
her seminary headmaster and by her students from that *Wun-
derjahr*. She had become Mrs. Barth in two respects: It pleased
her to append her husband's last name to her own (to be called
Mrs. *John* Barth, however, rightly rankles her; she is herself, not
Mrs. Me), and she had become the pedagogical phenomenon
her students refer to among themselves as "Barth." One does
not speak of taking "Mrs. Barth's course" in myth and fantasy,
or in the short story, or in the nineteenth-century Russian novel,
or in the literature of alienation; one speaks of "taking Barth."
For along with large infusions of the curricular subject matter,
what one gets from "taking Barth" is a massive (but always high-
spirited, high-energy) education in moral-intellectual responsibility: responsibility to the text, to the author, to the language,
to the muses of Truth, Goodness, and Beauty . . . and, along
the way, responsibility to the school, to one's teachers and classmates, to oneself.

Very little of this came via her husband. I don't doubt that
"Barth" learned a few things from her undergraduate professor
about the texts in Hum 1 — texts on which, however, I was no
authority. No doubt too her daily life with a working novelist
and writing coach sharpened her understanding of how fiction
is put together, how it manages its effects. But she is a closer
reader than I, both of literary texts and of student essays, and a
vastly more painstaking critic of the latter, upon which she frequently spends more time than their authors. The Barth who
writes this sentence involves himself not at all with the extracur-
ricular lives and extraliterary values of the apprentice writers in
his charge. My concern is with their dramaturgy, not with the
drama of their personal lives, and seriously as I take my academic commitments, they unquestionably rank second to my

commitments to the muse. The Barth "taken" by the girls at the Buffalo Seminary, and thereafter (since 1973, when we moved from Buffalo to Baltimore) at Saint Timothy's School, gives them 100 percent of her professional attention: an attention that drives her to work time and a half at her "half-time" job, and that is directed at her charges' characters and values as well as at their thought processes, their written articulateness, and their literary perceptivity. I'm at my best with the best of my students, the ones en route to joining our next literary generation, and am at my weakest with the weakest. She works her wonders broadcast; the testimonial letters — I should get such reviews! — pile in from her C and D students as well as from the high achievers, and from their parents. Often those letters come from college (wimpy, the girls complain, compared to taking Barth; we thought college would be *serious!*); sometimes they come years later, from the strong young urban professionals many of those students have become: You opened my eyes. You changed my life.

This she has done for more than a dozen years now at Saint Tim's, a fairly aristocratic, Episcopal-flavored boarding school in the horse-and-mansion country north of Baltimore. It has proved a virtually ideal place for the exercise of her gifts. She has her complaints about it (as I do about my dear once-deadly-serious Johns Hopkins). She worries about grade inflation, about the risk of softening performance standards, about the unquestioning conservatism of many of her students. She freely admires, however, the general fineness of the girls themselves, who wear their privileges lightly and who strive so, once their eyes have been opened, to measure up to her elevated standards, to deserve her praise. (I have met numbers of the best of these girls and am every time reminded of Anton Chekhov's remark to his brother: "What the aristocrats take for granted, we paid for with our youth." Encircled by a garland of them at a party at our house, Donald Barthelme once asked my wife, "Can't I take a few of them home in my briefcase?")

She hopes to go on with this wonder working . . . oh, for a while yet. She doubts she has the metabolism for a full-length career, sometimes wonders whether she has it for a full-length life. As her habits of relentless self-criticism and superprepara-tion have required a half-time situation on which to expend more than full-time energy, so — like some poets and fictionists — she will accomplish, perhaps must accomplish, a full professional life in fewer than the usual number of years. We feel similarly, with the same mix of emotions, about our late-started marriage, consoling ourselves with the reflection that, as two teachers who do most of our work at home, we are together more in one year than most working couples are in two. At the front end of her forties, unlike some other high-energy schoolteachers, she has no interest in "moving up" or moving on to some other aspect of education. For her there is only the crucible of the classroom — those astonishing fifty-minute bursts for which, like a human satellite transmitter, she spends hours and hours preparing — and the long, patient, hugely therapeutic individual conferences with her girls, and the hours and hours more of annotating their essays: word by word, sentence by sentence, idea by idea, value by value, with a professional attention that puts to shame any doctor's or lawyer's I've known. How I wish my children had had such a high school teacher. How I wish *I* had!

So: for a while yet. A few years from now, if all goes well, I myself mean to retire from teaching, which I'll have been at for four decades, and — not without some trepidation — we'll see. An unfortunate side effect of the single-mindedness behind my best former student's teaching is that, like many another inspired workaholic, she's short on extraprofessional interests and satisfactions. And both of us are socially impaired persons, so enwrapped in our work and each other that our life is a kind of solipsism *à deux*. We'll see.

My university's loss will easily be made up. Talented apprentice writers doubtless learn things from the sympathetic and knowledgeable coach in a well-run writing program; I surely did. But they acquire their art mainly as writers always have done: from reading, from practice, from aesthetic argument with their impassioned peers, from experience of the world and of themselves. Where the talent in the room is abundant, it scarcely matters who sits at the head of the seminar table, though it matters some. The Johns Hopkins Writing Seminarians will readily find another coach.

But if when I go she goes too — from schooling her girls in art and life, nudging them through the stage of romance, as

Whitehead calls it, toward the stage of precision — *there's* a loss can nowise be made good. Writers publish; scholars, critics publish. In a few cases, what they publish outlives them, by much or little. But a first-rate teacher's immortality is neither more nor less than the words (spoken even decades later by her former students to their own students, spouses, children, friends): "Mrs. Barth used to tell us . . ."

I like to imagine one of hers meeting one of mine, some sufficient distance down the road. *He* has become (as I'd long predicted) one of the established writers of his generation; *she* is a hotshot young whatever, who's nevertheless still much interested in literature, so exciting did her old high school English teacher make that subject. They're in an elevator somewhere, upward bound to a reception for the invited, and they're quickly discovering, indeed busily seeking, additional common ground. Somehow the city of Baltimore gets mentioned: Hey, they both went to school there! Later, over oysters and champagne, they circle back to that subject. She'd been in high school, he in graduate school: Saint Timothy's, Johns Hopkins. Hopkins, did he say, in the mid-eighties? She supposes then (knowledgeably, indeed, for a young international banker) that he must have worked with her old English teacher's husband, the novelist . . .

Sure, we all had Barth.

What a smile she smiles! You think *you* had Barth, she declares (it's late; the place is closing; they bet there's a nightcappery somewhere near his motel). Never mind *that* one: Out at Saint Timothy's, we had *Barth!* Talk about teachers!

Let's.

RICHARD BEN CRAMER

What Do You Think of Ted Williams Now?

FROM ESQUIRE

FEW MEN TRY for best ever, and Ted Williams is one of those. There's a story about him I think of now. This is not about baseball but fishing. He meant to be the best there, too. One day he says to a Boston writer: "Ain't no one in heaven or earth ever knew more about fishing."

"Sure there is," says the scribe.

"Oh, yeah? Who?"

"Well, God made the fish."

"Yeah, awright," Ted says. "But you had to go pretty far back."

It was forty-five years ago, when achievements with a bat first brought him to the nation's notice, that Ted Williams began work on his defense. He wanted fame, and wanted it with a pure, hot eagerness that would have been embarrassing in a smaller man. But he could not stand celebrity. This is a bitch of a line to draw in America's dust.

Ted was never the kind to quail. In this epic battle, as in the million smaller face-offs that are his history, his instinct called for exertion, for a show of force that would *shut those bastards up*. That was always his method as he fought opposing pitchers, and fielders who bunched up on him, eight on one half of the field; as he fought off the few fans who booed him and thousands who thought he ought to love them, too; as he fought through, alas, three marriages; as he fought to a bloody stand-off a Boston press that covered, with comment, his every sneeze and snort. He meant to *dominate,* and to an amazing extent, he did. But he came to know, better than most men, the value of his time. So over the years, Ted Williams learned to avoid annoyance. Now in his seventh decade, he has girded his penchants for privacy and ease with a bristle of dos and don'ts that defeat casual intrusion. He is a hard man to meet.

This is not to paint him as a hermit or a shrinking flower, Garbo with a baseball bat. No, in his home town of Islamorada, on the Florida Keys, Ted is not hard to *see.* He's out every day, out early and out loud. You might spot him at a coffee bar where the guides breakfast, quizzing them on their catches and telling them what *he* thinks of fishing here lately, which is, "IT'S HORSESHIT." Or you might notice him in a crowded but quiet tackle shop, poking at a reel that he's seen before, opining that it's not been sold because "THE PRICE IS TOO DAMN HIGH," after which Ted advises his friend, the proprietor, across the room: "YOU MIGHT AS WELL QUIT USING THAT HAIR DYE. YOU'RE GOING BALD ANYWAY."

He's always first, 8:00 A.M., at the tennis club. He's been up for hours, he's ready. He fidgets, awaiting appearance by some other, any other, man with a racket, whereupon Ted bellows, before the newcomer can say hello: "WELL, YOU WANNA PLAY?" Ted's voice normally emanates with gale force, even at close range. Apologists attribute this to the ear injury that sent him home from Korea and ended his combat flying career. But Ted can speak softly and hear himself fine, if it's only one friend around. The roar with which he speaks in a public place, or to anyone else, has nothing to do with his hearing. It's your hearing he's worried about.

Ted Williams can hush a room just by entering. There is a force that boils up from him and commands attention. This he has come to accept as his destiny and his due, just as he came to accept the maddening, if respectful, way that opponents pitched around him (he always seemed to be leading the league in bases on balls), or the way every fan in the ball park seemed always to watch (and comment upon) T. Williams's every move. It was often said Ted would rather play ball in a lab, where fans couldn't see. But he never blamed fans for watching him. His hate was for those who couldn't or wouldn't *feel* with him, his effort, his exultation, pride, rage, or sorrow. If they wouldn't share those, then there was his scorn, and he'd make them feel that, by God. These days, there are no crowds, but Ted is watched, and why not? What other match could draw a kibitzer's eye when Ted, on the near court, pounds toward the net, slashing the air with his big racket, laughing in triumphant derision as he scores with his killer drop shot, or smacking the ball twenty feet long and roaring, "SYPHILITIC SONOFABITCH!" as he hurls his racket to the clay at his feet?

And who could say Ted does not mean to be seen when he stops in front of the kibitzers as he and his opponent change sides? "YOU OKAY?" Ted wheezes as he yells at his foe. "HOW D'YA FEEL? . . . HOW OLD ARE YOU? . . . JUST WORRIED ABOUT YOUR HEART HA HA HAW." Ted turns and winks, mops his face. A kibitzer says mildly: "How are you, Ted?" And Ted drops the towel, swells with Florida air, grins gloriously, and booms back: "WELL, HOW DO I LOOK? . . . HUH? . . . *WHAT DO YOU THINK OF TED WILLIAMS NOW?*"

It is another matter, though, to interrupt his tour of life and force yourself on his attention. This is where the dos and don'ts come in. The dos fall to you. They concern your conduct, habits, schedule, attitude, and grooming. It's too long a list to go into, but suffice it to recall the one thing Ted liked about managing the Washington Senators: "I was in a position where people had to by God *listen.*"

The don'ts, on the other hand, pertain to Ted, and they are probably summed up best by Jimmy Albright, the famous fishing guide, Ted's friend since 1947 and Islamorada neighbor. "Ted don't do," Jimmy says, "mucha anything he don't want to."

He does not wait or bend his schedule: "I haven't got my whole career to screw around with you, bush!" He does not screw around with anything for long, unless it's hunting fish, and then he'll spend all day with perfect equanimity. He does not reminisce, except in rare moods of ease. He does not talk about his personal life. "Why the hell should I?"

His standing in the worlds of baseball and fishing would net him an invitation a night, but he does not go to dinners. One reason is he does not wear ties, and probably hasn't suffered one five times in a quarter century. Neither does he go to parties, where he'd have to stand around with a drink in his hand, "listening to a lot of bullshit." No, he'd rather watch TV.

He does not go to restaurants, and the reasons are several: They make a fuss, and the owner or cook's on his neck like a gnat. Or worse, it's a stream of *sportsfans* (still Ted's worst epithet) with napkins to sign. At restaurants you wait, wait, *wait*. Restaurants have little chairs and tables, no place for elbows, arms, knees, feet. At restaurants there's never enough food. Lastly, restaurants charge a lot, and Ted doesn't toss money around. (A few years ago he decided $2.38 was top price for a pound of beef. For more than a year, he honed his technique on chuck roast and stew meat. Only an incipient boycott by his friends, frequent dinner guests, finally shook his resolve.)

The last reason is seized upon unkindly by restaurateurs in Islamorada and nearby Keys: "No, he doesn't come in. He's too cheap. He'd go all over town, sonofabitch, and he'd pay by check, hoping they wouldn't cash the check, they'd put it on the wall."

But this is resentment speaking, and it is Ted's lot in life to be misunderstood. Some are put off, for instance, by the unlisted phone, by the steel fence, the burglar alarm, and KEEP OUT signs that stud his gates when he swings them shut with the carbon-steel chain and the padlock. But friends think nothing of it. A few have his number, but they don't call, as they know he's got the phone off the hook. No, they'll cruise by; if the gates are unchained, if they see his faded blue truck with the bumper sign IF GUNS ARE OUTLAWED ONLY OUTLAWS WILL HAVE GUNS, if it's not mealtime and not too late and there's nothing they know of that's pissing Ted off, well, then . . . they drive right in.

And this is the way to meet Ted: by introduction of an old friend, like Jimmy Albright. It's Jimmy who knows where to park the car so it won't annoy Ted. It's Jimmy who cautions, as we throw away our cigarettes, that Ted won't allow any smoke in his house. It's Jimmy who starts the ball rolling, calls out "Hiya, Ted!" as the big guy launches himself from his chair and stalks across the living room, muttering in the stentorian growl that passes with him as sotto voce: "Now who the hell is THIS?"

He fills the door. "Awright, come on in. WELL, GET THE HELL IN HERE." He sticks out a hand, but his nose twitches, lip curls at a lingering scent of smoke. Ted's got my hand now, but he says to Jimmy: "S'that you who stinks, or this other one, too? Jesus! Awright, sit down. Sit over there."

Ted wants to keep this short and sweet. He's in the kitchen filling tumblers with fresh lemonade. Still, his voice rattles the living room: "D'YOU READ THE BOOK?" He means his memoir, *My Turn at Bat.* "Anything you're gonna ask, I guarantee it's in the goddamn book . . . Yeah, awright. I only got one copy myself.

"Where's the BOOK?" he yells to Louise Kaufman, his mate. Ted thinks that Lou knows the location of everything he wants. "HEY SWEETIE, WHERE'S THAT GODDAMN BOOK?"

Lou has raised three sons, so no man, not even Ted, is going to fluster her. She comes downstairs bearing the book, which she hands to Ted, and which he throws to the floor at my feet. He growls: "Now, I want you to read that. And then I'm gonna ask you a *key question.*"

I ask: "Tomorrow? Should I call?"

"HELL NO."

Jimmy says he'll arrange a meeting.

Ted says: "HOW'S THAT LEMONADE?"

"Good."

"HUH? IS IT? . . . WELL, WHAT DO YOU THINK OF ME?"

In the car, minutes later, Jimmy explains that Ted won't talk on the phone. "Ted gimme his number twenty-five years ago," Jimmy says. "And I never give it yet to any asshole." We both nod solemnly as this fact settles, and we muse on the subject of trust. I'm thinking of the fine camaraderie between sportsmen and . . . wait a minute. Jimmy and Ted have been friends forty years now.

Does that make fifteen years Ted *didn't* give him the number?

I'm glad it's over. Before anything else, understand that I am glad it's over. . . . I wouldn't go back to being eighteen or nineteen years old knowing what was in store, the sourness and the bitterness, knowing how I thought the weight of the damn world was always on my neck, grinding on me. I wouldn't go back to that for anything. I wouldn't *want* to go back. . . . I wanted to be the greatest hitter who ever lived.

                            — Ted Williams, with John Underwood: *My Turn at Bat*

*

San Diego was a small town, and the Williams house was a small
box of wood, one story like the rest on Utah Street. It was a
workingman's neighborhood, but at the bottom of the Great
Depression a lot of men weren't working. Ted's father was a
photographer with a little shop downtown. Later he got a U.S.
marshal's job, in gratitude for some election favors he'd done
for Governor Merriam, and that remained his claim to fame.
Ted never saw much of him. His mother was the strength in the
family, a small woman with a will of steel who gave her life to
the Salvation Army. She was always out on the streets, San Diego
or south of the border, the Angel of Tijuana, out fighting the
devil drink, selling the *War Cry* or playing on a cornet, and God-
blessing those who vouchsafed a nickel. Sometimes she'd take
along her elder boy, and Ted hated it, but he didn't disobey. He
was a scrawny kid and shy, and he tried to shrink behind the
bass drum so none of his friends would see. There was school,
but he wasn't much good there. History was the only part he
liked. And then he'd come home, and his mother was out, and
sometimes it was ten at night, and Ted and his brother, Danny,
were still on the porch on Utah Street, waiting for someone to
let them in.

Soon home lost its place at the center of Ted's life. There
wasn't much in the little house that could make him feel special.
It wasn't the place where he could be the Ted Williams he
wanted to be. North Park playground was a block away, and
there, with one friend, a bat, and a ball, Ted could be the biggest
man in the majors. The game he played was called Big League:
one kid pitched, the other hit to a backstop screen. "O.K., here's
the great Charlie Gehringer," Ted would announce as he took
his stance. Or sometimes it was Bill Terry, Hack Wilson, or
another great man he'd never seen. "Last of the ninth, two men
on, two out, here's the pitch . . . *Gehringer swings!*" Ted swung.
Crack! Another game-winning shot for the great . . . *the Great
Ted Williams.*

They were just the dreams of a kid, that's all. But Ted went
back to the playground every day. First it was with a friend his
own age, then the playground director, Rod Luscomb, a grown
man, a two-hundred-pounder who'd made it to the Cal State
League. Ted pitched to Luscomb, Luscomb to Ted. At first
they'd always tell each other when they were going to throw

a curve. But then Ted started calling out: "Don't tell me, just see if I can hit it." *Crack!* Ted could hit it. "Listen, Lusk," Ted used to say. "Someday I'm going to build myself a ball park with cardboard fences. Then, I'm going to knock 'em all down, every darn one, with home runs." But Ted wasn't hitting homers with his scrawny chest, those skinny arms. Luscomb set him to push-ups, twenty, then forty, fifty, then a hundred, then fingertip push-ups. Ted did them at home on Utah Street. He picked his high school, Herbert Hoover High, because it was new and he'd have a better chance to make the team. When he made it, he came to school with his glove hung like a badge on his belt. He carried a bat to class. And after his last class (or before), it was back to the playground. Then in darkness, home for dinner, the push-ups, and the dreams.

There were no major leagues in San Diego. There was no TV. He had no more idea of the life he sought than we have of life on the moon. Maybe less, for we've seen the replays. Ted had to dream it all himself. And how could he measure what he'd give up? He wasn't interested in school, didn't care about cars, or money, or girls. He felt so awkward, except on the field. There, he'd show what Ted Williams could do. Now Hoover High went to the state tourney, traveled all the way to Pomona for a double-header, and Ted pitched the first game, played outfield in the second, and hit and hit, and Hoover won, and wasn't it great? There was an ice cream cart, and Ted ate eighteen Popsicles. His teammates started counting when he got to ten. But Ted didn't mind them making fun. That's how good he felt: him hitting, and Hoover winning, and the big crowd. Gee, that's the governor! And Ted found himself in the governor's path, the man who'd tossed his father a job, and he had to say something, and the awkwardness came flooding back, he felt the red in his face. So Ted grabbed tighter on his bat and he barked at Merriam: "HIYA, GOV!"

Of course people called him cocky. But he only wondered: was he good enough? At seventeen, as high school closed, he signed with the local team, the Coast League Padres. They offered $150 a month and said they'd pay for the whole month of June, even though this was already June 20. So that was Ted's bonus — twenty days' pay. He didn't care: he was a step closer, and each day was a new wonder.

He rode the trains, farther from home than he'd ever been. He stayed in hotels with big mirrors, and Ted would stand at a mirror with a bat or a rolled-up paper, anything — just to see his swing, how he looked: he had to look good. He got balls from the club, so many that his manager, Frank Shellenback, thought Ted must be selling them. No, Ted took them to his playground, got Lusk and maybe a kid to shag flies, and hit the covers off those balls.

Best of all, there were major leaguers, real ones, to see. They were old by the time they came to the Coast League, but Ted watched them, almost ate them with his eyes, measured himself against their size. Lefty O'Doul was managing the San Francisco Seals, and he was one of the greats. Ted stopped Lefty on the field one day. He had to know: "Mr. O'Doul, please . . . What should I do to be a good hitter?" And Lefty said: "Kid, best advice I can give you is don't let anybody change you." Ted walked around on air. After that, in bad times, he'd hear O'Doul's voice telling him he'd be O.K. The bad times were slumps. If Ted couldn't hit, the world went gray. In his second year with San Diego, Ted hit a stretch of oh-for-eighteen. He hung around the hotel in San Francisco, moping. He didn't know what to do with himself. He got a paper and turned to the sports. There was an interview with O'Doul. The headline said: WILLIAMS GREATEST HITTER SINCE WANER. And Ted thought: I wonder who this Williams is?

It was a newspaper that told him, too, about Boston buying his contract. The Red Sox! Ted's heart sank. It was a fifth-place club and as far away as any team could be: cold, northerly, foreign. Still, it was big league, wasn't it?

He had to borrow $200 for the trip east; there were floods that spring of 1938. He got to Sarasota, Florida, about a week late. And when he walked into the clubhouse, all the players were on the field.

"Well, so you're the kid."

It was Johnny Orlando, clubhouse boy. The way Johnny told it, he'd been waiting for this Williams. "Then, one morning, this Li'l Abner walks into the clubhouse. He's got a red sweater on, his shirt open at the neck, a raggedy duffle bag. His hair's on end like he's attached to an electric switch . . . 'Where you been, Kid?' I asked him. 'Don't you know we been working out almost a whole week? Who you supposed to be, Ronald Colman or somebody you can't get here in time?" Johnny gave Ted a uniform, the biggest he had in stock. But as Ted grabbed a couple of bats, his arms and legs stuck out, the shirttail wouldn't stay in the pants.

"Well, come on, Kid," Johnny said, and he led the bean pole out to the field. From the first-base stands, a voice yelled: "Hey, busher, tuck your shirt in! You're in the big leagues now."

Ted wheeled around, face red. "Who's that wise guy up in the stands?" Johnny told him: "That's Joe Cronin, Kid, your manager." Ted put his head down and made for the outfield. It wasn't the reception he'd expected, but at least he had his nickname. Everyone heard Johnny show him around: "Look here, Kid. Go over there, Kid." It stuck right away; it was a role, he knew. And soon Joe Cronin would fill the spot Rod Luscomb had held in Ted's life. Cronin was only thirty-one, but that was old enough. He was a hitter and a teacher, a manager, a counselor, and Ted was ever the Kid.

Cronin had come from Washington, one of the Red Sox's imported stars. The owner, Tom Yawkey, was buying a contender. Along with Cronin, the Hall of Fame shortstop, Yawkey raided Washington for Ben Chapman, a speedy right fielder and .300 hitter. From the Browns, Yawkey got Joe Vosmik, a left fielder who would hit .324. From the A's, Yawkey bought two old greats, Lefty Grove and Jimmy Foxx, along with Doc Cramer, another .300 hitter, for center field.

These were the finest hitters Ted had seen. He couldn't take his eyes off the batter's box. But the presence of all those hitters in camp meant one thing of terrible import to Ted: no nineteen-year-old outfielder was breaking in, not that year, and the veterans let Ted know it. Vosmik, Chapman, and Cramer, rough old boys all of them, made sure he had his share of insults. He lasted about a week, until the club broke camp for the first game in Tampa.

Ted wasn't going to Tampa. He was headed to Daytona Beach, where the Minneapolis farm team trained. Ted saw the list and the shame welled up, turned to rage. He yelled to the veteran outfielders: *"I'll be back. And I'll make more money in this fucking game than all three of you combined."* When he walked to the bus stop with Johnny Orlando, he asked: "How much you think those guys make?" And Johnny said: "I don't know, maybe fifteen thousand apiece." Ted nodded, his mouth set in a grim line. He had his salary goal now. Then he borrowed $2.50 from Johnny for the bus trip to the minors.

In Minneapolis, Ted led the league in everything: average, home runs, runs batted in, screwball stunts . . . There were tales of his conduct in the outfield, where he'd sit down between batters or practice swinging an imaginary bat, watching his leg-stride, watching his wrist-break, watching everything except balls hit to him. If he did notice a fly ball, he'd gallop after it, slapping his ass and yelling, "HI HO SILVER!" He was nineteen, and fans loved him. But if there was one boo, the Kid would hear it, and he'd try to shut that sonofabitch up for good. Once, when a heckler got on him, Ted fired a ball into the stands — and hit the wrong guy. That was more than the manager, poor old Donie Bush, could stand. He went to the owner, Mike Kelley, and announced: "That's it. One of us goes. Him or me." Kelley replied, quick and firm: "Well, then, Donie, it'll have to be you."

By the time Ted came back to Sarasota, the Red Sox were banking on him, too. They traded Ben Chapman, the right fielder who'd hit .340 the year before. Ted told himself: "I guess that shows what they think of ME." It was like he had to convince himself he was really big league now. Even after a good day, three-for-four, he'd sit alone in the hotel with the canker of one failure eating at him. If he screwed up, or looked bad, the awkwardness turned to shame, the shame to rage. As the team headed north, Ted was hitting a ton, but it wasn't enough. At the first stop, Atlanta, Johnny Orlando pointed out the strange right-field wall — three parallel fences, one behind the other. Johnny said: "I saw Babe Ruth hit one over that last fence . . ." Ted vowed right there he'd do it, too. But next day, he couldn't clear one fence. Worse still, he made an error. In the seventh, he put the Sox up with a three-run triple, but it wasn't enough. He had to show what Ted Williams could do! When he struck out in the eighth, he went to right field seeth-

ing. Then a pop-up twisted toward his foul line. He ran and
ran, dropped the ball, then booted it trying to pick it up. Rage
was pounding in him. He grabbed the ball and fired it over
those right-field walls. By the time the ball hit Ponce de Leon
Avenue and bounced up at a Sears store, Cronin had yanked
Ted out of the game.

Even Ted couldn't understand what that rage was to him,
why he fed it, wouldn't let it go. He only knew that the next day
in Atlanta he smashed a ball over those three walls and trotted
to the bench with a hard stare that asked Johnny Orlando and
anyone else who cared to look: Well, what do you think of the
Kid now?

He had a great first year in the bigs. On his first Sunday at
Fenway Park, he was four-for-five with his first home run,
a shot to the bleachers in right-center, where only five balls
had landed the whole year before. There were nine Boston
dailies that vied in hyperbole on the new hero. TED WILLIAMS
REVIVES FEATS OF BABE RUTH, said the *Globe* after Ted's fourth
game.

From every town he wrote a letter to Rod Luscomb with a
layout of the ball park and a proud X where his homer hit. He
was always first to the stadium and last to leave after a game. He
took his bats to the post office to make sure they were the proper
weight. He quizzed the veterans mercilessly about the pitchers
coming up. "What does Newsom throw in a jam? How about
Ruffing's curve?" It was as if he meant to ingest the game. He
only thought baseball. On trains, he'd never join the older guys
in poker games or drinking bouts. At hotels, it was always room
service, and Ted in his shorts, with a bat, at a mirror.

His roomie was Broadway Charlie Wagner, a pitcher with a
taste for fancy suits and an occasional night on the town. One
night, at four A.M., Wagner was sleeping the sleep of the just
when, *wham, CRASH*, he's on the floor with the bed around his
ears, and he figures it's the end. He opens his eyes to see the
bean-pole legs, then the shorts, and then the bat. Ted's been
practicing and he hit the bedpost. Does he say he's sorry? No,
doesn't say a damn thing to Wagner. He's got a little dream-
child smile on his face and he murmurs to himself: "Boy, what
power!"

He ended up hitting .327 and leading the league in runs batted in, the first time a rookie ever won that crown. He finished with thirty-one home runs, at least one in each American League park. There was no Rookie of the Year award, but Babe Ruth himself put the title on Ted, and that seemed good enough.

And after the season, he didn't go home. San Diego had lost its hold. His parents were getting a divorce, and that was pain he didn't want to face. He didn't want to see his troubled brother. He didn't want to see the crummy little house with the stained carpet and the chair with the hole where the mice ate through. He had a car now, a green Buick worth a thousand bucks. He went to Minnesota. There was a girl there he might want to see. Her dad was a hunting guide, and he could talk to her. And there was duck to hunt. As many as he wanted. And he could go where he wanted. And do what he wanted. He was twenty-one. And Big League.

Everybody knew 1940 would be a great year. Ted knew he'd be better: now he'd seen the pitchers, he knew he could do it. Tom Yawkey sent him a contract for $10,000, double his rookie pay. "I guess that shows what they think of ME."

No one thought about this, but pitchers had seen Ted, too. And this time around, no one was going to try to blow a fastball by him. Cronin was having an off year and Double-X Foxx was getting old and would never again be batting champ. So the pressure fell to Ted. If they pitched around him and he got a walk, that wasn't enough; the Sox needed hits. If he got a hit, it should have been a homer. A coven of bleacherites started riding Ted. And why not? They could always get a rise. Sometimes he'd yell back. Or he'd tell the writers: "I'm gonna take raw hamburger out to feed those wolves." The papers rode the story hard: O Unhappy Star! Then he told the writers: "Aw, Boston's a shitty town. Fans are lousy." Now the papers added commentary, pious truths about the Boston fans as the source of Ted's fine income. So Ted let them have it again: "My salary is peanuts. I'd rather be traded to New York." That did it. Now it wasn't just a left-field crowd riding Ted. It was civic sport: *He doesn't like Boston, huh? Who does he think he is?*

Writers worked the clubhouse, trying to *explain* the Kid. Big

Jimmy Foxx, a hero to Ted, said: "Aw, he's just bein' a spoiled boy." The great Lefty Grove said if Williams didn't hustle, he'd punch him in the nose. Of course, all that made the papers. Now when writers came to his locker, Ted didn't wait for questions. "HEY, WHAT STINKS?" he'd yell in their faces. "HEY! SOMETHING STINK IN HERE? OH, IT'S YOU. WELL, NO WONDER WITH THAT SHIT YOU WROTE." So they made new nicknames for him: Terrible Ted, the Screwball, the Problem Child. Fans picked it up and gave him hell. It didn't seem to matter what he *did* anymore. And Ted read the stories in his hotel room and knew he was alone. Sure, he read the papers, though he always said he didn't. He read the stories twenty times, he'd recite them word for word. He'd pace the room and seethe, want to shut them up, want to hit them back. But he didn't know how.

And Ted would sit alone in the locker room boning his bats, not just the handle, like other guys did, but the whole bat, grinding down on the wood, compressing the fiber tighter, making it tougher, harder, tighter. He would sting the ball. He'd show them. He'd shut them up. Jesus, he was trying. And he was hitting. Wasn't his average up? Wasn't he leading the league in runs? He was doing it like he'd taught himself, like he'd dreamed. Wasn't that enough? What the hell did they want him to be?

What else could he be? Some players tried to help, to ease him up a bit. Once, Ted gave Doc Cramer a ride, and they were talking hitting, as Ted always did. It was at Kenmore Square that Cramer said: "You know who's the best, don't you? You know who's the best in the league? You are." And Ted never forgot those words. But neither could he forget what was written, just as he couldn't forget one boo, just as he'd never forget the curve that struck him out a year before. Why didn't they understand? He could never forget.

And one day he made an error, and then struck out, and it sounded like all of Fenway was booing, and he ran to the bench with his head down, the red rising in his face, the shame in his belly, and the rage. Ted thought: These are the ones who cheered, the fans I waved my cap to? Well, never again. He vowed to himself: Never again. And he could not forget that either.

*

Lou is in a Miami hospital for heart tests. Ted says I can drive up with him. He figures we'll talk, and he'll have me out of his hair. We start from his house and I wait for him on the porch, where a weary woman irons. The woman is trying to fill in for Lou and she's been ironing for hours. Ted may wear a T-shirt until it's half holes and no color at all, but he wants it just so. The woman casts a look of despair at the pile and announces: "She irons his *underpants.*"

Ted blows through the back door and makes for the car, Lou's Ford, which he proclaims "a honey of a little car, boys!" When Ted puts his seal of judgment on a thing or person, by habit he alerts the whole dugout. We are out of Islamorada on the crowded highway, U.S. 1, the only road that perseveres to these islets off the corner of the country, when Ted springs his key question. "You read the book? Awright. Now we're going to see how smart YOU are. What would YOU do to start, I mean, the first goddamn thing now, the first thing you see when you're sitting in the seats and the lights go off, how would YOU start the movie?"

Ted is considering a film deal for *My Turn at Bat.* He is working the topic of moviedom, as he does anything he wants to know. Now as he pilots the Ford through Key Largo, he listens with a grave frown to some possible first scenes. "Awright. Now I'll tell you how it's supposed to start, I mean how the guy's doing it said . . . It's in a fighter plane, see, flying, from the pilot's eye, over KOREA, Seoul. And it's flying, slow and sunny and then *bang* WHAM BOOOOMMM *the biggest god-damn explosion ever on the screen,* I mean BOOOOOMMM. And the screen goes dark. DARK. For maybe ten seconds there's NOTHING. *NOTHING.* And then when it comes back, there's the ball park and the crowd ROARING . . . and that's the beginning."

"Sounds great, Ted."

"Does it? LOOKIT THIS NOW. I wonder where he's goin'. Well, O.K., he's gonna do *that.* Well, O.K. — I'm passing too. Fuck it." Ted is pushing traffic hard to be at the hospital by two, when Lou's doctors have promised results from the heart tests. He is trying to be helpful, but he's edgy.

"How long have you and Lou been together?"

"Oh, I've known Lou for thirty-five years. You shouldn't put any of that shit in there. Say I have a wonderful friend, that's all."

"Yeah, but it makes a difference in how a man lives, Ted, whether he's got a woman or not —"

"Boy, that Sylvester Stallone, he's really made something out of that Rocky, hasn't he? . . ."

"So Ted, let me ask you what —"

"LOOK, I don't wanta go through my personal life with YOU, for Christ's sake. I won't talk to you about Lou, I won't talk to you about any of it. You came down here and you're talkin' about me, as I'm supposed to be different and all that . . ."

"Do you think you're different?"

"NO, not a damn bit. I'm in a little bit different POSITION. I mean, I've had things happen to me that have, uh, made it possible for me to be different. DAMN DIFFERENT in some ways. Everybody's not a big league ball player, everybody doesn't have, uh, coupla hitches in the service, everybody hasn't had, uh, as much notoriety about 'em as I had ALL MY LIFE, so . . ."

"So . . ."

"I wanna go NORTH. I'm gonna go up here and go farther down. I made a mistake there, GODDAMNIT, HOW THE HELL DO I GET ON THE FUCKIN' THING? I'll make a U-turn . . ."

"Ted, I think you were more serious about living life on your own terms . . ."

"Well, I wanted to be alone at times. It was the hustle and the bustle of the crowd for seven months a year. So sure, I wanted a little more privacy, a little more quiet, a little more tranquility. This is the fucking left we wanted."

"Yeah, but it's not just privacy, Ted. I'm not trying to make it seem unnatural. But what you toss off as a little more privacy led you *off* the continent, so far off in a corner that —"

"Well, lemme tell you about Koufax. He got through playin' baseball, he went to a fuckin' little shitty remote town in Maine, and that's where he was for five years. Everybody thought he was a recluse, he wasn't very popular just 'cause he wanted to be alone and he finally moved out. Lemme tell you about Sterling Hayward, Hayden. HELL of an actor. And still he wanted to be ALONE, he wanted to TRAVEL, he wanted to be on his

BOAT GOIN' TO THE SOUTH SEAS. So, see, that's not way
outa line! . . . I guess I'll take a right, that oughta do it. Eight
seventy-four, do you see eight seventy-four anyplace? Go down
here till I get to Gilliam Road, or some goddamn thing . . . Fuck,
eight seventy-four's where I wanted to go, but looked like it was
puttin' me back on the fuckin' turnpike, shit. So, you know,
seeking privacy and, uh, seeking that kind of thing . . . what
road is this?"

"We're on Killian . . . So privacy, you don't think that's what?"

"*Unusual*, for Christ's sake. Shit."

"I don't think it's unusual either."

"WELL, YOU'RE MAKIN' A PROJECT OUT OF IT!"

"No, I don't think it's unusual . . . You don't think you're ex-
ceptionally combative?

"Nahh, me? Not a bit. Hell, no. THAT SAY KENDALL?
Does it? Well, I made a hell of a move here. HELL of a move!
See, eight seventy-four is right off there, hospital's down
here . . ."

"You're a half-hour early, too."

"Here it is, right here, too. Best hospital in Miami. Expensive
sonofabitch, boy. Christ. I'm all for Medicare. And I've always
thought that, ALWAYS thought that. Shit. WELL, WHERE
ARE YOU GOING? Where ARE you going, lady? *Cunt!*" Ted
takes the parking space vacated by the lady and tells me he'll be
back in an hour.

When he comes back he has good news about Lou: all tests are
negative, her heart is fine. "Gee, I met the big cardiovascular
man, he came in and I met him." Ted sounds twenty years
younger.

He's walking to the car when a nurse passes. "GEE, WASN'T
IT A SHAME," Ted suddenly booms. "THAT ALLIGATOR
BIT THAT LITTLE GIRL'S LEG OFF?" He casts a sly side-
ward glance at the nurse to see if she's fallen for his favorite
joke.

"Honey of a little shittin' car!" he sings out as we hit the road.
Now there is no fretting with traffic. Ted makes all the turns.
Along the way, he sings forth a monologue about cars, this car,
this road, this town of Homestead, that house, his house, the
new house he's planning in central Florida, up on a hill, just

about the highest point in the whole goddamn state, what a deal
he's getting there, Citrus Hills, HELL of a deal; about his hopes
for his kids, his daughter Claudia, only fourteen, who lives in
Vermont with her mother, Ted's third wife, who was too much
of a pain in the ass to live with, but gee, she's done a hell of a
job with those kids, HELL of a job, the little girl is an actress,
she had the lead in the Christmas play and she was so good, the
papers up there all said she bears watching, SHE BEARS
WATCHING, and her brother, Ted's boy, John Henry, he's
picking colleges now, he's a good boy and Ted's critical, but he
can't see too much wrong with that boy, and even the big daughter, Bobby Jo, she's thirty-eight already, still can bust Ted's
chops pretty good, boys, but she's straightening out now; and
these islands, there's bonefish here, used to be wonderful, years
ago, there was NOTHING, NOTHING except a few of the best
fishermen God ever made, and a narrow road between bay and
sea, just a little shittin' road, and some women who weren't
half bad on the water or off it either, and the world here was
empty and the water was clear and you could have a few pops
of rum, maybe get a little horny, go see friends, that's all there
was here, a few friends, thirty, thirty-five years ago, when this
place was young, when he first fished with Jimmy and he met
Lou . . .

"Gee, I'm so fuckin' happy about Louise," Ted says. "Goddamn, she's a great person. Have more fun with her than . . .
Goddamn."

They booed in Boston? Well, not in Detroit, the 1941 All-Star
Game, with all the nation listening in. Ted doubled in a run in
the fourth, but the National League still led, 5–3, going into the
ninth. Then an infield hit, a single, a walk, a botched double
play, and here it was: two out, two on, bottom of the ninth.
Here's the great Ted Williams. Claude Passeau, the Cubbie on the
mound, sends a mean fastball in on his fists. *Williams swings!*
When the ball made the seats, Ted started jumping on the base
path. DiMaggio met him at home plate, Bob Feller ran out in
street clothes, Cronin jumped the box-seat rail, the dugout emptied. The manager, Del Baker, kissed him on the forehead.
They carried the Kid off the field.

He was showing them all now: after the All-Star break, Ted

was still hitting more than .400. Sure, guys hit like that for a month, but then tailed off. No one in the league hit like that for a year, not since the twenties, and each day the whole country watched. Writers from New York joined the Sox. *Life* brought its new strobe-light camera to photograph Ted in his shorts, swinging like he did in front of the mirror. Ted was on national radio: "Can you keep it up, Kid?" It was murderous pressure. By September, he was slipping, almost a point a day. On the last day, the Sox would have two games in Philadelphia. Ted had slipped to .39955. The way they round off averages, that's still .400. Cronin came to Ted on the eve of the twin bill and offered: "You could sit it out, Kid, have it made." But Ted said he'd play.

That night, he and Johnny Orlando walked Philadelphia. Ted stopped for milk shakes, Johnny for whiskey. Ten thousand people came to Shibe Park, though the games meant nothing. Connie Mack, the dour and penurious owner of the A's, threatened his men with fines if they eased up on Williams. But Ted didn't need help. First game, he got a single, then a home run, then two more singles. Second game, two more hits: one a screaming double that hit Mr. Mack's right-field loudspeaker so hard that the old man had to buy a new horn. In all, Ted went six-for-eight, and .406 for his third season. That night, he went out for chocolate ice cream.

Who could tell what he'd do the next year: maybe .450, the best *ever*, or break the Babe's record of sixty homers. He got a contract for $30,000, and he meant to fix up his mother's house. He'd have more money than he'd ever expected. He was the toast of the nation. But then the nation went to war.

Ted wanted to play. He'd read where some admiral said we'd kick the Japs back to Tokyo in six months. What was that compared to hitting? A lawyer in Minnesota drew up a plea for deferment, and Ted O.K.'d the request: he was entitled, as his mother's support. When the local board refused deferment, the lawyer sent it up for review by the presidential board. That's when the papers got it. In headlines the size of howitzer shells, they said Ted didn't want to fight for his country. Teddy Ballgame just wanted to play.

Tom Yawkey called to say he could be making the mistake of

his life. The league president told Ted to go ahead and play. Papers ran man-on-the-street polls. In Boston, Ted was bigger news than war in the Pacific. At spring training, Joe Cronin said he'd be on his own with fans. "To hell with them," Ted spat. "I've heard plenty of boos." Still, he remembered the venomous letters that said he was an ingrate or a traitor. The one that hurt most said nothing at all: it was just a blank sheet of paper, *yellow* paper.

Opening day in Boston, reporters sat in the left-field stands, out there with soldiers and sailors, to record reaction to Ted. The Kid treated the day as a personal challenge. His first time up, two on, two strikes, he got a waist-high fast ball and drilled it into the bleachers. All the fans rose to cheer, servicemen among them. The Kid was back, and Fenway was with him. "Yeah, ninety-eight percent were for me," Ted said later as he scraped his bat. A writer said: "You mean one hundred percent. I didn't hear a boo." Ted said: "Yeah, they were for me, except a couple of kids in the left-field stand, and a guy out in right. I could hear them."

In May, he enlisted for Navy wings and that shut up most of the hecklers. Still, he was always in a stew of contempt for some joker who said something unfair. It seemed Ted courted the rage now, used it to bone his own fiber. Now there was no awkwardness, no blushing before he blew. It was automatic, a switch in his gut that snapped on and then, watch out for the Kid. One day in July, a fan in left was riding Ted pretty hard. Ted came to bat in the fifth: he took a strange stance and swung late, hit a line drive, but well foul into the left-field seats. Next pitch, again he swung late, hit another liner, but this stayed fair — and Ted didn't run, barely made it to second. Cronin yanked him out of the game, fined him $250 for loafing. But Ted wasn't loafing; the hit caught him by surprise. He'd been trying to kill the heckler with a line drive foul.

Ted loved the service, its certainty and ease. He never had a problem with authority. It was drawing his own lines that gave him fits. He had his fears about the mathematics, navigation problems, and instrument work. But at Amherst College, where the Navy started training, he found his mind was able, and he was pleased. And he loved the feel of an airplane. He was good, right from the start. There was coordination in it, and care: those were natural to him. And he was a constant student, always learning in the air. But he was proudest of his gunnery, the way he could hold back until the last pass, then pour out the lead and shred the sleeve. That wasn't study, that was art. He got his wings near the top of his class and signed on as an instructor at Pensacola, Florida. He was happy, and good at his job. Strangely, in uniform, he was freer than before.

On the day he was commissioned (second lieutenant, U.S. Marines), he married that daughter of the hunting guide, Doris Soule from Minnesota. Now, for the first time, he'd have a house, a place on the coast near the base. And now, on off days, he'd scrape up some gas stamps, grab his fly rod, find a lonesome canal, and lose himself in a hunt for snook. Back at the base, Ted would grab a cadet and take him up in his SNJ, and the new guy of course was goggle-eyed, flying with *Ted Williams,* and Ted would make his plane dance over the coast, then he'd dive and point, and yell to the cadet: *"That's where the Kid fished yesterday."*

Orders came through slowly for him. What base commander would give him up as ornament and outfielder? At last he got combat training and packed up for the Pacific. But Ted was just getting to Hawaii when Japan folded. So he packed up again for Boston, and now he felt he was going to war.

He came back like he owned the game. Opening day, Washington, after a three-year layoff: *crack,* a four-hundred-foot home run. And then another and another, all around the league. By the All-Star break in 1946, he was hitting .365, with twenty-seven home runs. In the All-Star Game, Ted alone ruined the National League: four straight hits, two homers, and five runs batted in.

And the Red Sox were burying the American League. Tom Yawkey's millions were paying off. The team as a whole was hitting .300, and Ted was hammering the right-field walls. In the first game of two in Cleveland, he hit three homers, one a grand slam when the Sox were behind, the second with two on to tie, the third in the bottom of the ninth to win, 11–10. As Ted came up in the second game, Cleveland's manager, Lou Boudreau, started moving men: the right fielder backed toward the corner; the center fielder played the wall in right-center; the third baseman moved behind second; and Boudreau, the shortstop, played a deep second base; the second baseman stood in short right; the first baseman stood behind his bag. There were eight men on one half of the field (the left fielder was alone on the other), and Ted stood at home plate and laughed out loud.

There never had been anything like it. He had bent the nature of the game. But he would not bend his own and slap the ball for singles to left. He hit into the teeth of the Shift (soon copied around the league), and when he slumped, and the Sox with him, the papers started hammering Ted again, his pride, his "attitude." At last, against the Shift in Cleveland, Ted sliced a drive to left-center, and slid across the plate with an inside-the-park home run, first and last of his career. The Sox had their first pennant since 1918. But the headlines didn't say, SOX CLINCH. Instead, eight-column banners cried that Ted stayed away from the champagne party. "Ted Williams," Dave Egan wrote in the *Record,* "is not a team man." And when St. Louis pulled the Shift in the Series and held Ted to singles, five-for-twenty-five, a new banner read: WILLIAMS BUNTS. And the Red Sox lost the Series, first and last of his career, and after the seventh game, in St. Louis, Ted went to the train, closed his compartment, hung his head, and cried. When he looked up, he saw a crowd watching him through the window. The papers wrote: "Ted Williams cannot win the big ones." The Associated Press voted him number two in a poll for Flop of the Year.

It seemed like Ted couldn't laugh anymore, not in a ball park. He said he was going to Florida to fish. He didn't want to see a bat for months. Soon that was a pattern: one year, before spring training, he tucked in a week in the Everglades. Next year, it was a month. Year after that, longer. In early 1948, the papers discovered that Doris was in a Boston hospital to deliver Ted's first child. But where was the big guy? In Florida? FISHING? The mothers of Boston pelted the press with angry letters. "To hell with them," Ted said. He didn't come north for two days. And two days later, he was back fishing. In two years, he'd moved Doris and his daughter, Barbara Joyce, to a house in

Miami, the first he'd ever owned. But he never stayed home there either. He heard about some men in the Keys catching bonefish with light fly tackle. When Ted tried this new sport, he found a love that would last longer than any of his marriages.

The Keys were empty, their railroad wrecked by a hurricane in 1935. There were only a few thousand souls on one road that ran for a hundred miles; the rest was just mangrove and mosquitoes, crushed coral islands, and shining water. In Islamorada — a town of one store, a bar, a restaurant, one gas pump — a few fishing guides, led by Jimmy Albright, were poling their skiffs over shallows that only they knew, hunting bonefish and inventing an art as they went along. These were Ted's kind of men, who'd sneer or scream at a chairman of the stock exchange if he made a lousy cast. Islamorada was a strange meritocracy: if you could not play a fish, tie a fly, cast a line through the wind, you were no one in this town.

Ted could do it all brilliantly. The guides didn't make much fuss about his fame, but they loved his fishing. His meticulous detail work, always an oddity at Fenway Park, was respected here as the mark of a fine angler. Ted had the best tackle, best reels, best rods, the perfect line, his lures were impeccable. He'd work for hours at a bench in his house, implanting balsa plugs with lead so they'd sail off a spinning rod just so, then settle in the water slowly like a fly. He could stand on the bow of a skiff all day, watching the water for signs of fish, and soon he was seeing them before the guides. His casts were quick and long, his power was immense. He never seemed to snap a line, never tangled up, his knots were sure, his knowledge grew, and he always wanted to know *more*. He'd question Jimmy relentlessly and argue every point. But if you showed him something once, he never needed showing again. He fished with Jimmy week after week, and one afternoon as he stood on the bow, he asked without turning his head: "Who's the best you ever fished?" Jimmy said a name, Al Mathers. Ted nodded, "Uh-huh," and asked another question, but he vowed to himself: "He don't know it yet, but the best angler he's had is me."

Every winter, he'd fish the flats, then head north to make his appearance at the Boston Sportsmen's Show. He'd spend a few days doing fly-casting stunts and then take a couple of hours, at

most, to tell Tom Yawkey what he wanted for a contract. His
salary was enormous. He was the first to break Babe Ruth's
$80,000. Ted didn't care for the money as much as the record.
It was history now that was the burr on his back. The joy was
gone, but not the dream.

Every day, every season, he was still first to the ball park,
where he'd strip to shorts and bone his bats; still first out to the
cage, where he'd bark his imaginary play-by-play: "Awright,
Detroit, top of the ninth . . ." Then back to his locker for a clean
shirt and up at a trot to the dugout, to clap a hostile eye on the
pitcher warming up, to pick apart his delivery, hunting for any
weakness. No, Ted would not give up on one game, one time at
bat, a single pitch. No one since Ruth had hit so many home
runs per times at bat. No one in the league hit like Ted, year
after year: .342, .343, .369, .343 . . . It seemed he never broke a
bat at the plate, but he broke a hundred in the clubhouse runway. If he failed at the plate he'd scream at himself, "YOU
GODDAMN FOOL!" and bash the cement while the Sox in the
dugout stared ahead with mute smiles. Once, after a third
strike, he smashed the water pipe to the cooler with his bare
fists. No one could believe it until the flood began. And on
each opening day, Ted would listen to the national anthem
and he'd feel the hair rise on the back of his neck, and his
hands would clench, and he'd vow to himself: "This year, the
best *ever*."

In the 1950 All-Star Game, he crashed the outfield wall to
catch a drive by Ralph Kiner. His elbow was broken, with thirteen chips off the radius. Surgeons thought he was through, but
Ted returned in two months. His first game back, once again:
home run, and four-for-four. But Ted could tell as weeks went
by that the elbow was not the same. The ball didn't jump off his
bat. So all next winter, Ted stayed in the Keys, where he poled
a skiff, hunting bonefish and rebuilding his arm. He was pushing thirty-three now, just coming to know how short was his
time. But then, after the 1951 season, he was called back to the
Marines, drafted for a two-year hitch in Korea. It seemed his
time was up.

Ted's living room has a wide white armchair, into and out of
which he heaves himself twenty times a day; the chair has a wide

white ottoman onto which he'll flop, as whim dictates, one or
both of his big legs. From this chair, he roars commands and
inquiries, administering the house and grounds. Across the
room, a big TV shows his *National Geographic* specials. At his
side, a table holds his reading and correspondence. At the moment, these piles are topped by *Yeager: An Autobiography,* and
teachers' reports on his son, John Henry. To Ted's right, ten
feet away, there's a doorway to the kitchen, through which Lou
can supply him and let him know who that was on the phone.
To his left and behind, a grand window affords a view of a
patio, his dock, some mangrove, and some Florida Bay. Finally,
ahead and to the right, in a distant semicircle, there are chairs
and a couch for visitors.

"NOW WE'RE GONNA SEE HOW MUCH *YOU* KNOW,
SONOFABITCH," Ted is shouting at Jack Brothers. Jimmy
Albright is there, too. The shouting is ritual.

"Ru-mer. R-U-M-E-R." Brothers contends he is spelling the
name of the first spinning reel. But Ted has hurled himself up
to fetch a fishing encyclopedia, and now he's back in the chair,
digging through to the section on spinning. Just so things don't
get dull, he says: "Where'd you get that HAIRCUT? D'you have
to PAY FOR IT?"

Ted and Jimmy began this colloquy in the early Truman
years. Jack helped heat it up when he drifted down from Brooklyn a few years after the war, before Islamorada got its second
restaurant or first motel, not to mention the other ten motels,
the condos, gift shops, Burger King, or the billboard to proclaim
this place: SPORTFISHING CAPITAL OF THE WORLD. These elders
are responsible for a lot of the history here, as they helped
create flats fishing and turn it into a sport/industry (which they
now quietly deplore). Jimmy and Jack were teachers of the first
generation of salt-water anglers. Ted is the star of that generation, and its most ferocious pupil.

"Here. HERE! 'Mr. Brown began importing SPINNERS,
starting with the LUXAR . . .' THE *LUXAR*. WANNA SEE? GO
AHEAD, SONOFABITCH!"

"Yeah, but that don't say the first spinning reel *manufactured*,"
Brothers grins in triumph. "Sonofabitch, with your books!"

"This is the goddamn HISTORY, Brothers. Not a FUCKING
THING about RUMOR, RHEUMER, RHOOOMAN . . . I

GUESS YOU DIDN'T KNOW MUCH ABOUT SPINNING REELS, DID YOU?"

Ted is always the one with the books. He wants *answers,* not a lot of bullshit. Ted is always reading history, biography, fact of all kinds. He doesn't like much made of this, as he's tender on the subject of his education. Once in a camp in Africa, while he and his coauthor, John Underwood, gazed at the night sky, Ted turned from the stars and sighed: "Jeez, I wish I was smart like you."

Now he reports to his friends on his college tours with his son, John Henry: "So we get to Babson and I like it. Babson's a pretty good school, boys. HELL of a school, but, uh, they got dorms, boys and girls all in one dorm, see, and I look on the walls and they're written all over, fuck this and fuck that. I'm thinking, gee, right out there on the walls, it just seemed, you know . . ."

"Liberal?" Jimmy suggests.

"Well, I like to see a place with a little more standards than *that.* So we get to Bates. We got this German girl to show us around, see? And she was a smart little shit, two languages, and she's telling us what she's studying, *aw,* a smart little shit! She give us the tour, see, and John Henry loved Bates, LOVED it. We get back to the office and she goes out. I don't know, she musta told someone, told some of her friends, who she just showed around, see? Then somebody *told* her. She didn't know, see . . .

"Well, a minute later, she's back with some kid and he says, OH, Mr. Williams! and OH this and OH that. And *then* we start talking. And how about *this,* how about *that,* and how would John Henry like to come for a *weekend,* get the feel of the place, you know . . ."

Ted stops for a moment and thinks to himself. He doesn't really have to finish the thought for his friends, who can see him beaming in his big chair. So he just trails off, to himself: ". . . boy mighta thought the old man wasn't gonna . . . you know, around a college . . . Well!"

The mayor and the Red Sox held a day for Ted when he left for flight school. Three weeks into the 1952 season, at Fenway, they gave him a Cadillac and made a donation to the Jimmy

Fund, a charity for sick children that Ted supported. They gave him a *Ted Williams Memory Book*, with signatures of four hundred thousand fans. For his last at bat, bottom of the seventh, he gave them a three-run homer to win the game, 5–3. He threw a party that night at his Boston hotel. The crowd was mostly cooks and firemen, bellhops, cabbies, ice cream men. Ted never liked a smart crowd. Smart people too often asked: "Oh, was your father a ball player?" "Oh, what did your mother do?" Ted didn't like to talk about that.

He was just Captain Williams, U.S. Marines, at his flight base at Pohang, Korea. He had a shed for a home and a cot with inner-tube strips for springs. The base was a sea of mud, the air was misty and cold, and he was always sick. He was flying close air support, low strafing, and bombing runs. His plane was a jet now, an F-9 Panther, but he couldn't take much joy from flying. He was in and out of sick bay. Doctors called it a virus, then pneumonia, but his squadron was short of pilots, so he always flew.

On a bombing run, north of the thirty-eighth parallel, Ted lost sight of the plane ahead. He dropped through clouds, and when he came out, he was much too low. North Koreans sent up a hail of bullets. Ted's plane was hit and set afire. The stick stiffened and shook in his hand; his hydraulics were gone. Every warning light was red. The radio quit. A Marine in a nearby F-9 was pointing wildly at Ted's plane. He was trying to signal: "Fire! Bail out!" But Ted's biggest fear was ejecting; at six three, wedged in as he was, he'd leave his kneecaps under his gauges. So the other pilot led him to a base. Ted hauled his plane into a turn and he felt a shudder of explosion. One of his wheel doors had blown out. Now he was burning below, too. He made for a runway with fire streaming thirty feet behind. Koreans in a village saw his plane and ran for their lives. Only one wheel came down; he had no dive breaks, air flaps, nothing to slow the plane. He hit the concrete at 225 miles an hour and slid for almost a mile while he mashed the useless brakes and screamed, *"STOP YOU DIRTY SONOFABITCH STOP STOP STOP."* When the F-9 stopped skidding, he somersaulted out the hatch and slammed his helmet to the ground. Two Marines grabbed him on the tarmac and walked him away as the plane burned to char.

He was flying the next day, and the day after. There weren't enough pilots to rest a man. Ted was sicker, weak and gaunt. Soon his ears were so bad he couldn't hear the radio. He had flown thirty-seven missions and won three air medals when they sent him to a hospital ship. Doctors sent him on to Hawaii and then to Bethesda, Maryland, where at last they gave him a discharge. His thirty-fifth birthday was coming up; he was tired and ill. He didn't want to do anything, much less suit up to play. But Ford Frick, the commissioner, asked him to the 1953 All-Star Game, just to throw out the first ball.

So Ted went to Cincinnati, sat in a sport coat in the dugout. Players greeted him like a lost brother; even Ted couldn't hear a boo in the stands. Tom Yawkey was there, and Joe Cronin; they worked on the Kid. The league president asked him to come back; the National League president, too. Branch Rickey sat him down for a talk; Casey Stengel put in a plea. Ted went to Bethesda to ask the doctors, and then he told the waiting press to send a message to the fans at Fenway: "Warm up your lungs." He took ten days of batting practice and returned with the Red Sox to Boston. First game, Fenway Park, bottom of the seventh: pinch-hit home run.

Ted Williams was the greatest old hitter. In two months, upon return from Korea, he batted .407 and hit a home run once in every seven at bats. For the next two years, he led the league (.345 and .356), but injuries and walks robbed him of the titles: he didn't get the minimum four hundred at bats. In 1956, he lost the title in the season's last week to twenty-four-year-old Mickey Mantle (who finished with .353 to Ted's .345). The next year, Mantle had an even better season, but Ted, at age thirty-nine, pulled away and won, at .388, more than twenty points ahead of Mantle, more than sixty points ahead of anyone else. With five more hits (say, the leg hits that a younger man would get), it would have been .400. As it was, it stood as the highest average since his own .406, sixteen years before. In 1958, Ted battled for the crown again, this time with a teammate, Pete Runnels. They were even in September, but then, once again, Ted pulled away to win at .328. For the final fifty-five games (including one on his fortieth birthday), he batted .403.

He accomplished these prodigies despite troubles that would

have made most men quit. In 1954, he made spring training for the first time in three years, but he wasn't on the field a minute before he fell and broke his collarbone. He was out six weeks and had a steel bar wired into his clavicle. (First day back, twin bill in Detroit: two home runs, eight-for-nine, seven RBIs.) In 1955, Doris alleged in divorce court that he'd treated her with "extreme cruelty" and constant profane abuse. Boston papers ran the story under two-inch headlines: TED GETS DIVORCE, with a "box score" on the money, the house, the car, and "Mrs. Ted's" custody of Bobby Jo. In 1956, Ted came forth with his Great Expectorations. In a scoreless game with the Yankees, in front of Fenway's biggest crowd since World War II, he was booed for an error, and he let fans know what he thought of them: he spat toward the right-field stands and spat toward the left, and when fans rained more boos on his head, he leaped out of the dugout and sprayed all around. "Oh, no, this is a bad scene," Curt Gowdy, the Sox broadcaster, mourned to his microphone. Tom Yawkey heard the game on radio, and Ted got a $5,000 fine (tying another Babe Ruth record). Boston writers said Ted ought to quit. But Ted was in the next game, on Family Night, and at his appearance, fans gave him a five-minute ovation. (He then hit a home run in the bottom of the eighth and clapped his hand over his mouth as he scored the winning run.) In 1957, grippe knocked him flat and stuck him in his hotel for seventeen days in September. He came back to hit four consecutive home runs. In 1958, ptomaine from bad oysters wrecked opening day, then he injured an ankle, pulled a muscle in his side, and hurt his wrist twice. In September, after a called third strike, Ted threw his bat and watched in horror as it sailed to the stands and clonked a gray-haired lady on the head. Ted sat in tears in the dugout and had to be ordered to his place in left field. But over the next twenty at bats, he hit .500.

Now the switch in his gut was always on. The Red Sox gave him a single room and barred the press from the clubhouse for two hours before each game. But it wasn't outside annoyance that was fueling Ted's rage. He'd wake up in the middle of the night, screaming obscenities in the dark. He kept himself alone and pushed away affection. There were plenty of women who would have loved to help. But Ted would say: "WOMEN?" and then he'd grab his crotch. "ALL THEY WANT IS WHAT I

GOT RIGHT HERE." Now the press didn't cover just explo-
sions on the field. The *American* wrote him up for shredding a
telephone book all over the floor when a hotel maid failed to
clean his room. "Now tell me some more," wrote Austen Lake,
"about Ted's big, charitable, long-suffering spirit." Roger Kahn
reported a scene when Ted was asked about Billy Klaus, the
shortstop who was coming back after a bad year. "You're asking
ME about a BAD YEAR? . . . OLD T.S.W., HE DON'T HAVE
BAD YEARS."

But old Ted had a terrible year in 1959. A pain in his neck
turned to stiffness, and he was in traction for three weeks.
When he came out, he could barely look at the pitcher. His
average languished below .300 for the first time in his career.
For the first time, he was benched for not hitting. The sight of
the Kid at the plate was pathetic; even the papers softened.
They started summing up his career, treating him like an old
building menaced by the wrecking ball. He finished at .254 and
went to see Tom Yawkey. "Why don't you just wrap it up?"
Yawkey said, and Ted started to boil. No one was going to make
him retire. Ted said he meant to play, and Yawkey, who loved
the Kid, offered to renew his contract: $125,000, the high-
est ever. No, Ted said, he'd had a lousy year and he wanted
a cut. So Ted signed for $90,000 and came back one more
time.

Opening day, Washington: a five-hundred-foot home run.
Next day, another. He slammed his five hundredth in Cleveland, passed Lou Gehrig and then Mel Ott. Only Foxx and Ruth
would top him on the all-time list. At forty-two, Ted finished his
year with twenty-nine homers and .316. Talk revived that Ted
might be back. But this was really quits. On his last day at Fenway, a headline cried: WHAT WILL WE DO WITHOUT TED? And
though the day was dreary and the season without hope, ten
thousand came out to cheer him and hear him say goodbye.
There was another check for the Jimmy Fund and, this time, a
silver bowl. And Ted made a speech that said, despite all, he
felt lucky to play for these fans. And when he came up in the
eighth and they stood to cheer, he showed them what Ted
Williams could do. He hit a Jack Fisher fast ball into the bull-
pen in right field. And he thought about tipping his cap as he

rounded first but he couldn't, even then, couldn't forget, so
he ran it straight into the dugout, and wouldn't come out for
a bow.

Now it was no hobby: Ted fished harder and fished more than
any man around. After his divorce from Doris, he'd made his
home in Islamorada, bought a little place on the ocean side,
with no phone and just room for one man and gear. He'd wake
before dawn and spend the day in his boat, then come in, maybe
cook a steak, maybe drive off to a Cuban or Italian joint where
they served big portions and left him alone. Then, back home,
he'd tie a few flies and be in bed by ten. He kept it very spare.
He didn't even have a TV. That's how he met Louise. He
wanted to see a Joe Louis fight, so Jimmy took him to Lou's big
house. Her husband was a businessman from Ohio, and they
had a TV, they had everything. Lou had her five kids, the best
home, best furniture, best car, and best guides. Though she
wasn't a woman of leisure, she was a pretty good angler, too.
She could talk fishing with Ted. Yes, they could talk. And soon,
Lou would have a little money of her own, an inheritance that
she'd use to buy a divorce. She wanted to do for herself, she
said. And there was something else, too. "I met Ted Williams,"
Louise said. "And he was the most gorgeous thing I ever saw in
my life."

Now Ted's life was his to make, too. He signed a six-figure
deal with Sears, to lend his name to their line of tackle, hunting gear, and sporting goods. Now, when Hurricane Donna
wrecked his little house on the ocean, he bought his three-bed-
room place on the bay, near Louise's house. Now he bought a
salmon pool on the Miramichi, in New Brunswick, Canada, and
he fished the summer season there. In Islamorada, he was out
every day, fall, winter, spring. He wanted the most and the
biggest — bonefish, tarpon, salmon — he called them the Big
Three. He wanted a thousand of each, and kept books on his
progress. He thought fishing and talked fishing and taught fishing at shows for Sears. He felt the joy of the sport, still. But now
there was something else: the switch that clicked when he'd get
a hot fish that ran and broke off his lure. Ted would slam his
rod to the deck or break it in half on the boat. "HERE, YOU

LOUSY SONOFABITCH . . ." He'd hurl the rod into the bay. "TAKE THAT, TOO."

He married again in 1961, a tall blond model from Chicago, Lee Howard. They'd both been divorced, and they thought they'd make a go. Ted brought her down to the Keys. But he still wasn't staying home: he'd be out at dawn without a word on where he'd go or what he planned, and then he'd come home, sometimes still without words. Sometimes there was only rage, and Lee found she was no match. After two years, she couldn't take it. She said: "I couldn't do anything right. If we went fishing, he would scream at me, call me a —— and kick the tackle box."

So Ted found another woman, one to meet him, fire with fire. Her name was Dolores Wettach, a tall, large-eyed former Miss Vermont. He spotted her across the aisle on a long plane flight. He was coming from fishing in New Zealand. Dolores had been in Australia, on modeling assignment for *Vogue.* He wrote a note: "Who are you?" He wadded it up, tossed it at her. She looked him over, tossed one back: "Who are *you?*" He tossed: "Mr. Williams, a fisherman," and later told her his first name was Sam. It wasn't until their third date that she found out he'd done anything but fish. When he found out she was a farm girl who loved the outdoors as much as he, he figured he'd met his match. In a way, he had. She learned to fish, she could hunt, could drink, could curse like a guide. And when they fought, it was toe to toe and Ted who slammed out of the house. They had a son, John Henry, and daughter, Claudia. But that didn't stop the fights, just as it hadn't with Bobby Jo, the daughter he'd had with Doris. Ted would tell his friends he wasn't cut out for family. He was sick at heart when Bobby Jo left school and didn't go to college. He would seethe when any woman let him know that he'd have to change. What the hell did they want? When Dolores became his third divorce, Ted was through with marriage.

Ted made the Hall of Fame in 1966. His old enemies, the writers, gave him the largest vote ever. So Ted went north to Cooperstown and gave a short speech outside the hall. Then he went back to Florida. He never went inside. They gave him a copy of his plaque. It listed his .406 year, his batting titles, slugging titles, total bases, walks, home runs. It didn't say anything about the wars, the dream, the rage, the cost. But how much can a plaque say?

There are no statistics on fans, how they felt, what they took from the game. How many of their days did Ted turn around? How many days did he turn to occasions? And not just with hits: there was a special sound from a crowd when Ted got his pitch, turned on the ball, whipped his bat in that perfect arc — and missed. It was a murmurous rustle, as thousands at once let breath escape, gathered themselves, and leaned forward again. To see Ted suffer a *third* strike was an event four times more rare, and more remarkable, than seeing him get a hit. When Ted retired, some owners feared for attendance in the *league*. In Boston, where millions came through the years to cheer, to boo, to care what he did, there was an accretion of memory so bright, bittersweet, and strong that when he left, the light was gone. And Fenway was left with a lesser game.

And what was Ted left with? Well, there was pride. He'd done, he felt, the hardest thing in sport: by God, he hit the ball. And there was pride in his new life: he had his name on more rods and reels, hunting guns, tackle boxes, jackets, boots, and bats than any man in the world. He studied fishing like no other man, and lent to it his fame and grace, his discerning eye. He had his tournament wins and trophies, a fishing book and fishing movies, and he got his thousand of the Big Three. Jimmy Albright says to this day: "Best all around, the best is Ted." But soon there were scores of boats on the bay, and not so many fish. And even the Miramichi had no pools with salmon wall to wall. And Ted walked away from the tournaments. There wasn't the feeling of sport in them, or respect for the fish anymore. Somehow it had changed. Or maybe it was Ted.

Last year, Ted and Lou went up to Cooperstown together. This was for the unveiling of a statue of the Kid. There are many plaques in the Hall of Fame, but only two statues: just the Babe and him. And Ted went into the hall this time, pulled the sheet off his statue and looked at his young self in the finish of that perfect swing. He looked and he looked while the crowd got quiet and the strobes stopped flashing. And when he tried to speak, he wept.

*

"HEY, WHERE THE HELL IS HE?" It's after four and Ted's getting hungry. "I'M GONNA CALL HIM."

Lou says, "Don't be ugly."

"I'm not ugly," Ted insists, but quietly. He dials and bends to look at me. "Hey, if this guy doesn't come, you can eat. You wanna eat here?" Then to the phone: "WHERE THE HELL ARE YOU?"

"Ted, don't be mean."

"I'm not. YEAH, TOMORROW? WELL, O.K., BUDDY." Ted has had a successful phone conversation. Quick and to the point.

"Awright, you can eat. Hey, sweetie, take him up so he can see."

There are no mementos in the living room, but Lou has put a few special things in a little room upstairs. Most of the pictures have to do with Ted, but the warmth of the room, and its character, have to do with Louise. This is no shrine. It is a room for right now, a room they walk through every day, and a handsome little place, too. Now it is filled with her quiet energy. "Here's Ted Williams when I met him," she says. "And if that isn't gorgeous, I'll eat my hat." And here's an old photo of Lou in shorts, with a fly rod, looking fragile next to a tarpon she pulled from Florida Bay. She does not seem fragile now. She is spry and able. She has been with Ted ten years straight, and that speaks volumes for her strength and agility. She gets angry sometimes that people do not credit Ted with tenderness — "You don't know him," she says, and her voice has a surprising edge — but she also knows he'll seldom show it. So here she shows a lonely young Ted with a little suitcase, off to flight school. Here's Ted and Tom Yawkey, and look: Mr. Yawkey has pictures of Ted behind him, too. "Here he is in Korea," says Louise. "You know, when he landed that plane, the blood was pouring from his ears. I have to tell people that . . . because he's *so* loud. Big, too." Lou picks up a cushion of a window seat. There are pictures beneath. "See, he's done so many things . . ."

"Hey, you want a drink?" Ted is calling. "TED WILLIAMS IS GONNA HAVE A DRINK."

Soon he flops into his chair with a tumbler and hands over a videotape. He wants it in the VCR. He says: "This is the most wonderful guy. Hell of a guy. Bill Ziegler. I got him into the majors . . ." That was when Ted came back in 1969 to manage the Senators. Bill Ziegler was the trainer.

"So he had a son and he named him Ted Williams Ziegler. You're gonna see him now. IS IT IN? HEY, YOU LISTEN-ING?" The tape shows Ziegler's two sons batting. Ziegler sends the tapes for analysis. The sound track sends out a steady per-cussion: *thwack . . . thwack . . . thwack.* Both boys get wood on the ball. "I'm gonna show you the first tape he sent, and I'm gonna ask what's the difference. See this kid, I told him his hips, he's got to get them OPEN."

From the kitchen, Lou protests: "Ted! Not now. Wait for me!"

"SEE? . . ." *Thwack.* "Ground ball. A little slow with his hands."

From Lou: "O.K., O.K., I don't know nothin'."

"HANDS THROUGH!" *Thwack.* "Center field, always to cen-ter, see where his hips are pointed? He's got to [*thwack*] OPEN 'EM UP."

From Lou, coming in, wiping her hands as she watches: "He doesn't step into it like Ted Williams."

Ted pretends he doesn't hear. "Hips come through OPEN . . ."

"He doesn't bring his hands around like you do, honey."

"Yeah, he's got to, GROUND BALL! See, when I'M up" — and now Ted takes his stance in the living room — "I'm grind-in' . . ." Now his hands are working. "I got the hands cocked. *COCKED!*" And here's the pitch. "*BAMMMM!*" says Ted as he takes his cut and asks: "We got Bill Ziegler's number? WHERE'S HIS NUMBER?"

Ted is yelling on the phone in the kitchen, and Lou is in the living room, fitting her thoughts to small silences. "When Ted talks [*thwack*] it's always right now . . ."

"BILL, I WANNA SEE HIM ON HIS FRONT FOOT MORE, AND THE HANDS QUICK, *QUICK* . . ."

"You know, the baseball players . . . it's not macho, they're just . . . athletes, just beautiful boys . . ."

Ted hangs up and throws himself into his chair: "AWRIGHT, MAJOR LEAGUE! LET'S SET IT UP." That means dinner. Lou's cooking Chinese. Ted's still watching Ziegler's kids. "Ground ball. You don't make history hittin' 'em on the ground,

boys." Now he pulls away from the TV. "Sweetie," he sings
playfully. "We got any sake-o?" Lou sings: "Not tonight-eo."
Ted sings: "Well, where's the wine-o?"

Lou says grace while all hold hands. Then we set to food, and
Ted is major league. "It's good, huh?" he says between mouth-
fuls. "Well, isn't it? HEY! Aren't you gonna finish that rice?"

He's finished fast and back in his chair. "We got any sweets?"

A little album on the coffee table has pictures from Christmas.
John Henry gave his letter of acceptance from Bates as his present to Ted. It's got Ted thinking now about the car he's got to
buy so John Henry can take a car to school. "Got to have a
car . . ." He's thinking aloud so Louise can check this out.
"Course, there's gonna have to be rules . . ." He's working it
over in his mind, and he muses: "Maybe say that other than
school . . . he can't take the car if his mother says no . . ." Lou is
in a chair across the room. She's nodding. "HAVE to be rules,"
Ted says, "so he doesn't just slam out of the house . . . slam out
and JUMP IN THE CAR . . ."

Something has turned in his gut, and his face is working,
growing harder. There's a mean glitter in his eye, and he's
thinking of his elder daughter, walking away from him . . .

"SLAM OUT . . . LIKE MY DAUGHTER USED TO . . ." .

His teeth are clenched and the words are spat. It's like he's
turned inward to face something we cannot see. It is a fearsome
sight, this big man, forward, stiff in his chair, hurling ugly
words at his vision of pain . . . I feel I should leave the room,
but too late.

". . . *THAT BURNED ME . . .*"

The switch is on. Lou calls it the Devil in him.

". . . *A PAIN IN MY HAIRY RECTUM!*"

"Nice," says Lou. She is fighting for him. She has not flinched.

"Well, DID," he says through clenched teeth. "*AND MAKES
YOU HATE BROADS! . . .*"

"Ted. Stop." But Ted is gone.

". . . *HATE GOD! . . .*"

"TED!"

". . . *HATE LIFE!*"

"TED! . . . JUST . . . STOP!"

"DON'T YOU TELL ME TO STOP. DON'T YOU *EVER*
TELL ME TO STOP."

Lou's mouth twists up slightly, and she snorts: "HAH!"

And that does it. They've beaten it, or Lou has, or it's just gone away. Ted sinks back in his chair. His jaw is unclenched. He grins shyly. "You know, I love this girl like I never . . ."

Lou sits back, too, and laughs.

"SHE'S IN TRAINING," Ted says. "I'M TEACHIN' HER . . ."

"He sure is," Lou says, like it's banter, but her voice is limp. She heads back to the kitchen, and Ted follows her with his eyes.

Then he finds me on his couch, and he tries to sneer through his grin: "WHEN ARE YOU LEAVING? HUH?

". . . JESUS, YOU'RE LIKE THE GODDAMN RUSSIAN SE-CRET POLICE!

". . . O.K., BYE! YEAH, SURE, GOODBYE!"

Ted walks me out to the driveway. As I start the car, Lou's face is a smile in the window, and Ted is bent at his belly, grabbing their new Dalmatian puppy, tickling it with his big hands while the dog rolls and paws the air. And as I ease the car into gear, I hear Ted's voice behind, cooing, very quiet now: "Do I love this little dog, huh? . . . Yes, this little shittin' dog . . . Yes, yes I love you . . . Yes, I do."

JOHN GREGORY DUNNE

On Writing a Novel

FROM ESQUIRE

ON JUNE 6, 1982, the *New York Times Book Review* asked a number of writers to describe their work in progress. I did not have a work in progress, only a contract for a work in progress, but no matter: if a writer is asked to describe a work in progress, perhaps the work in progress might actually progress. And so for the *Times* I wrote: "This summer I am going to Central America and will be working on a novel called *The Red, White and Blue.* The trip and the novel are not related, but who knows? . . . All I know about *The Red, White and Blue* is that Scott Fitzgerald considered a similar title for *The Great Gatsby.* What will it be about? About 600 pages, I hope."

The result of this fabrication was that my publisher invited me to lunch at The Four Seasons to discuss the work in progress, and the progress I was making on it. The night before the lunch, I sat down at my typewriter in a suite at the Carlyle Hotel that a movie company was picking up the tab for in the misplaced hope that I was paying more attention to the screenplay I was allegedly writing than I was to the novel the producers did not know I allegedly had in progress. In a spasm of fear, I wrote the following sentence: "When the trial began, we left the country." An hour or so later I had reached the point where I could note in my diary the next day, "Lunch w/ JE [my publisher] — showed her 1st 3–4 pp RWB." And thus began four years at the factory.

What civilians do not understand — and to a writer anyone not a writer is a civilian — is that writing is manual labor of the mind: a job, like laying pipe. Although I had not written a word,

I had in fact thought a great deal about the novel over the course of the preceding year. I knew what the first sentence was going to be, and I also knew the last — it is a peculiarity of mine that I always know the last sentence of a book before I begin. That last sentence I intended to be a line of dialogue, either "No" or "Yes," with the penultimate line its reverse, either Yes or No, not in dialogue. It was the six or seven hundred pages between "When the trial began, we left the country" and "No" (or "Yes") that seemed a desert I could not irrigate.

I also knew the book would have a first-person narrator, largely because I had never used one before. The narrator I had in mind was the narrator of Ford Madox Ford's *The Good Soldier,* a commentator on events and actions that had taken place years before the book actually begins, events and actions at times not even witnessed and at best only dimly understood, events and actions that in my case the narrator would have to reconstruct through letters and diaries and videotapes and sec- ondhand accounts and Freedom of Information files and what- ever else came to mind. "You'll be sorry," my wife, who is also a novelist, said when I told her my plan, and how right she was.

That summer of 1982 I did go to Central America, and I saw the possibilities for a section of the book I would not address for another three and a half years; my notes for the trip were twice as long as the section that eventually appeared in the manuscript. In September, I cleared away all other commit- ments and began concentrating on the book full time. By the summer of 1983, I had completed 262 pages — and none of it seemed to work. Individual scenes played, but the narrative did not hold together. Narrative, I should explain, is not plot. Plot is, "The queen died, the king died"; narrative is, "The queen died, the king died of a broken heart." (I would like to claim that definition as my own, but it is a free translation of E. M. Forster, from *Aspects of the Novel.*) Because one has written other books does not mean the next becomes any easier. Each book in fact is a tabula rasa; from book to book I seem to forget how to get characters in and out of rooms — a far more difficult task than the nonwriter might think. Still I went to my office every day. That is the difference between the professional and the amateur. The professional guts a book through this period, in full knowledge that what he is doing is not very good. Not to work is to exhibit a failure of nerve, and a failure of nerve is the best definition I know for writer's block.

In August 1983, I put the manuscript aside and traveled to France and England, armed with my tattered copy of *The Good Soldier,* which by then went everywhere with me, not so much a book to read as a talisman to hold and touch. I was also accompanied by a photocopy of an interview Philip Roth had given the *New York Times* in 1977. "My own way," Roth had said, "seems to be to write six months of trash — heterosexual trash usually — and then to give up in despair, filing away a hundred pages or so that I can't stand, to find ten pages or so that are actually alive. . . ." The despair of another writer is enormously reassuring to one who thinks his own despair is unique.

Back home, I started all over again on page 1, circling the 262 pages like a vulture looking for live flesh to scavenge. I knew the problem. The narrative was too constricted; it was like a fetus strangling on its own umbilical cord. Knowing the problem, however, is not the same as solving it. The second draft, which I began in euphoria in the fall of 1983, I abandoned seventy-two pages later, again on the outskirts of despair.

I was now in 1984, having worked steadily for nearly two years with almost nothing to show for it except a file box full of pages with typing on them. To clear my head I wrote a long piece for *The New York Review of Books* about a septuagenarian former Hollywood Communist who had come out of the closet of his past, as it were, disguised as a prizewinning young Mexican novelist. I also needed money if I was ever going to finish this damn book, and I agreed to write the screen adaptation of Norman Mailer's novel *The Deer Park.* The fee was simply too high to pass up; with taxes and the commissions of agents, lawyer, and accountants deducted, my wife and I would have enough to keep us for approximately another two years.

The cruelties of life had also intervened. "When the trial began, we left the country," I had written that spring of 1982. Five months later my niece was murdered, and when her killer came to trial in Los Angeles the following summer, my wife and I indeed did leave the country. "I do not understand people who attend the trials of those accused of murdering their loved ones," I had continued in those three or four pages I had shown my publisher at The Four Seasons, half a year before any of this

happened. "You see them on the local newscasts. . . . I watch
them kiss the prosecutor when the guilty verdict is brought
in or scream at those jurors who were not convinced that the
pimply-faced defendant was the buggerer of Jimmy and the
dismemberer of Johnny." I wondered for several years if I
should retain those lines in the final manuscript, should I ever
complete it; in a slightly altered version I did. There, with all its
emotional baggage, was the obscenity of coincidence.

Then in the summer of 1984, when my wife and I were in
East Hampton working on the screenplay of *The Deer Park* with
Sidney Lumet, my closest friend suffered in rapid succession a
stroke and a massive heart attack. His name was Barry Farrell,
and for the last six months of his life he lay semicomatose in a
Veterans Administration hospital not five minutes from my
house in Los Angeles. Writers do not make easy friends of one
another; they are professional carpers, too competitive, mean-
spirited, and envious for the demands of lasting friendship.
With occasional lapses from grace, Barry and I were an exception to this rule. I had known him for twenty-five years, since
we both worked at *Time* — through the accidental death of his
son and through a divorce. His youngest child was named Joan
Didion Farrell after my wife. Every morning at nine-fifteen, he
and I would talk on the telephone; a natter, he would call it.
The New York and Los Angeles newspapers would be read by
then, and with ribald shrewdness he would give me a close tex-
tual exegesis of the morning's news. Barry was one of those rare
people who talked in complete sentences, every sentence perfectly parsed, plural predicates for plural subjects, no dangling
participles, every clause modifying what it was supposed to
modify, "that" never confused with "which." I would often tell
him I wished a tape recording device could be implanted under
his skin to record his conversation, throwing out its tape at the
end of the day. That, I said, would solve his writing block. His
private life was untidy: he could not write and drank; he drank
and could not write. His death shattered me. I cannot hear the
telephone ring at nine-fifteen anymore without a frisson. It will
not be Barry.

On New Year's Day, 1985, two weeks after Barry's funeral, I
began *The Red, White and Blue* for the third time. This time it
went well from the start. The two failed previous drafts yielded

nuggets I had not been able to find before. Those first three or four pages I had written in the spring of 1982 became, in the spring of 1986, the last five pages of a 710-page novel; pages 44–46 in the second draft became pages 304–307 in the third. Slowly the book began to open up. In a churchyard in the Cotswolds, I found the name of a nineteenth-century church warden — Bentley Innocent; I immediately gave his surname to a character of my own. On that same trip, an English novelist told me about a *papeterie* on rue de l'Ancienne Comédie that was the only place in Paris that sold the notebooks he and I favored; I set a scene there. In Barry Farrell's papers I found an instruction sheet from the Nevada Department of Prisons on how to operate "a lethal gas chamber" for an execution and how to clean it when the job was completed ("After each execution, sinks, plugs, pot and entire inside of cabinet should be washed down with warm water and a detergent; add two ounces of agua ammonia to each gallon of water . . ."). Here was a perfect example of bureaucracy gone mad; it went into the manuscript. "He has an enthusiasm for tragedy," I remember Barry once saying about someone; it went into the manuscript. "Let's get the cows to Abilene," the producer of *The Deer Park* had said when the delivery of the screenplay was delayed — into the manuscript.

I devised stratagems and inside jokes to relieve the clock-punching tedium of a book that was building by only a page or a page and a half a day. I named someone after a character in one of my wife's earlier novels; a corpse received a name I have now used in four books. Because I believe scores are made to be settled, I settled a couple of scores in a way that only the person against whom the score is being settled would ever recognize, if indeed that person ever read the book. In my last novel, I had some gratuitous sport with Peter Jennings, the ABC anchor-man, and when a friend of his asked how I could be beastly about someone I did not know, I replied, "Never be rude to a stranger, because the stranger may turn out to be a novelist with a long memory."

January 5, 1986, the first Monday of the new year: I now had 493 pages of *The Red, White and Blue* completed. In the next three months, I worked seven days a week, taking only one day off during that entire stretch, seldom going out at night. This was the magic time that made up for the previous three and a half years of toil and anxiety and suicidal depression. It is like a dream sexual experience. Everything seems to work; the chance encounter, the overheard remark in a restaurant, feed into the next day's material, opening up possibilities you had never considered. In three months I wrote 230 pages; in the last two weeks alone, 92. On Sunday, April 6, at 2:19 in the afternoon, I wrote the last sentence: "No."

The book took two months short of four years to write, with another year spent taking notes and thinking about it. In the course of those four years, this is what I also did: I wrote three pieces for *The New York Review of Books* and a second screenplay, an adaptation of Carlos Fuentes's *The Old Gringo,* a meditation by Carlos (a good friend) on what happened to Ambrose Bierce when he went down to Mexico to die. The screenplay, without me, is in another stage of development, but from a biography of Bierce I would not otherwise have read I did get the book's epigraph: "History is an account, mostly false, of events, mostly unimportant, which are brought about by rulers, mostly knaves, and soldiers, mostly fools." Other than these interruptions, only the book. Four years, 1,400 days, 710 pages; prorated, it amounts to half a page, 125 words, a day. Put that way, not much to show for four years. But that is the writer's life. You write. You finish. You start over again.

Spring

FROM ANTAEUS

WE HAVE A nine-acre lake on our ranch and a warm spring that feeds it all winter. By mid-March the lake ice begins to melt where the spring feeds in, and every year the same pair of mallards come ahead of the others and wait. Though there is very little open water they seem content. They glide back and forth through a thin estuary, brushing watercress with their elegant folded wings, then tip end-up to eat and, after, clamber onto the lip of ice that retreats, hardens forward, and retreats again.

Mornings, a transparent pane of ice lies over the meltwater. I peer through and see some kind of waterbug — perhaps a leech — paddling like a sea turtle between green ladders of lakeweed. Cattails and sweetgrass from the previous summer are bone dry, marked with black mold spots, and bend like elbows into the ice. They are swords that cut away the hard tenancy of winter. At the wide end a mat of dead waterplants has rolled back into a thick, impregnable breakwater. Near it, bubbles trapped under the ice are lenses focused straight up to catch the coming season.

It's spring again and I wasn't finished with winter. That's what I said at the end of summer too. I stood on the twenty-foot-high haystack and yelled "No!" as the first snow fell. We had been up since four in the morning picking the last bales of hay from the oatfield by hand, slipping under the weight of them in the mud, and by the time we finished the stack, six inches of snow had fallen.

It's spring but I was still cataloguing the different kinds of snow: snow that falls dry but is rained on; snow that melts down

into hard crusts; wind-driven snow that looks blue; powder
snow on hardpack on powder — a Linzertorte of snow. I look
up. The troposphere is the seven-to-ten-mile-wide sleeve of air
out of which all our weather shakes. A bank of clouds drives in
from the south. Where in it, I wonder, does a snowflake take on
its thumbprint uniqueness? Inside the cloud where schools of
flakes are flung this way and that like schools of fish? What gives
the snowflake its needle, plate, column, branching shapes — the
battering wind or the dust particles around which water vapor
clings?

Near town the river ice breaks up and lies stacked in indus-
trial-sized hunks — big as railway cars — on the banks, and is
flecked black by wheeling hurricanes of newly plowed topsoil.
That's how I feel when winter breaks up inside me: heavy, oner-
ous, upended, inert against the flow of water. I had thought
about ice during the cold months too. How it is movement betrayed, water seized in the moment of falling. In November, ice
thickened over the lake like a cataract, and from the air looked
like a Cyclops, one bad eye. Under its milky spans over irrigation ditches, the sound of water running south was muffled.
One solitary spire of ice hung noiselessly against dark rock at
the Falls as if mocking or mirroring the broom-tail comet on the
horizon. Then, in February, I tried for words not about ice, but
words hacked from it — the ice at the end of the mind, so to
speak — and failed.

Those were winter things and now it is spring, though one
name can't describe what, in Wyoming, is a three-part affair:
false spring, the vernal equinox, and the spring when flowers
come and the grass grows.

Spring means restlessness. The physicist I've been talking to
all winter says if I look more widely, deeply, and microscopically
all at once I might see how springlike the whole cosmos is. What
I see as order and stillness — the robust, time-bound determi-
nacy of my life — is really a mirage suspended above chaos.
"There's a lot of random jiggling going on all the time, everywhere," he tells me. Winter's tight sky hovers. Under it, the
hayfields are green, then white, then green growing under
white. The confinement I've felt since November resembles the
confinement of subatomic particles, I'm told. A natural velocity
finally shows itself. The particle moves; it becomes a wave.

The sap rises in trees and in me and the hard knot of perseverance I cultivated to meet winter dissipates; I walk away from the obsidian of bitter nights. Now, when snow comes, it is wet and heavy, but the air it traverses feels light. I sleep less and dream not of human entanglements, but of animals I've never seen: a caterpillar fat as a man's thumb, made of linked silver tubes, has two heads — one human, one a butterfly's.

Last spring at this time I was coming out of a bout with pneumonia. I went to bed on January first and didn't get up until the end of February. Winter was a cocoon in which my gagging, basso cough shook the dark figures at the end of my bed. Had I read too much Hemingway? Or was I dying? I'd lie on my stomach and look out. Nothing close up interested me. All engagements of mind — the circumlocutions of love interests and internal gossip — appeared false. Only my body was true. And my body was trying to close down, go out the window without me.

I saw things out there. Our ranch faces south down a long treeless valley whose vanishing point is two gray hills, folded one in front of the other like two hands, and after that — space, cerulean air, clouds like pleated skirts, and red mesas standing up like breaching whales in a valley three thousand feet below. Afternoons, our young horses played, rearing up on back legs and pawing oh so carefully at each other, reaching around, ears flat back, nipping manes and withers. One of those times their falsetto squeals looped across the pasture and hung on frozen currents of air. But when I tried to ingest their sounds of delight, I found my lungs had no air.

It was thirty-five below zero that night. Our plumbing froze, and because I was very weak my husband had to bundle me up and help me to the outhouse. Nothing close at hand seemed to register with me: neither the cold nor the semicoziness of an uninsulated house. But the stars were lurid. For a while I thought I saw the horses, dead now, and eating each other, and spinning round and round in the ice of the air.

My scientist friends talk with relish about how insignificant we humans are when placed against the time-scale of geology and the cosmos. I had heard it a hundred times, but never felt it truly. As I lay in bed, the black room was a screen through which some part of my body traveled, leaving the rest behind. I thought I was a sun flying over a barge whose iron holds soaked me up until I became rust floating on a bright river.

A ferocious loneliness took hold of me. I felt spring-inspired desire, a sense of trajectory, but no interception was in sight. In fact, I wanted none. My body was a parenthetical dash laid against a landscape so spacious it defied space as we know it — space as a membrane — and curved out of time. That night a luscious, creamy fog rolled in, like a roll of fat, hugging me, but it was snow.

Recuperation is like spring: dormancy and vitality collide. In any year I'm like a bear, a partial hibernator. During January thaws I stick my nose out and peruse the frozen desolation as if reading a book whose language I don't know. In March I'm ramshackle, weak in the knees, giddy, dazzled by broken-backed clouds, the passing of Halley's comet, the on-and-off strobe of sun. Like a sheepherder I X out each calendar day as if time were a forest through which I could clear-cut a way to the future. My physicist friend straightens me out on this point too. The notion of "time passing," like a train through a landscape, is an illusion, he says. I hold the Big Ben clock taken from a dead sheepherder's wagon and look at it. The clock measures intervals of time, not the speed of time, and the calendar is a scaffolding we hang as if time were rushing water we could harness. Time-bound, I hinge myself to a linear bias — cause and effect all laid out in a neat row — and in this we learn two things: blame and shame.

Julius Caesar had a sense of humor about time. The Roman calendar with its calends, nones, and ides — counting days — changed according to who was in power. Caesar serendipitously added days, changed the names of certain months, and when he was through, the calendar was so skewed that January fell in autumn.

Einsteinian time is too big for even Julius Caesar to touch. It stretches and shrinks and dilates. In fact, it is the antithesis of the mechanistic concept we've imposed on it. Time, indecipherable from space, is not one thing but an infinity of space-times, overlapping, interfering, wavelike. There is no future that is not now, no past that is not now. Time includes every moment.

It's the ides of March today.

I've walked to a hill a mile from the house. It's not really a hill but a mountain slope that heaves up, turns sideways, and comes down again, straight down to a foot-wide creek. Everything I can see from here used to be a flatland covered with shallow water. "Used to be" means several hundred million years ago, and the land itself was not really "here" at all, but part of a continent floating near Bermuda. On top is a fin of rock, a marine deposition created during Jurassic times by small waves moving in and out slapping the shore.

I've come here for peace and quiet and to see what's going on in this secluded valley, away from ranch work and sorting corrals, but what I get is a slap on the ass by a prehistoric wave, gains and losses in altitude and aridity, outcrops of mud composed of rotting volcanic ash that fell continuously for ten thousand years a hundred million years ago. The soils are a geologic flag — red, white, green, and gray. On one side of the hill, mountain mahogany gives off a scent like orange blossoms; on the other, colonies of sagebrush root wide in ground the color of Spanish roof tiles. And it still looks like the ocean to me. "How much truth can a man stand, sitting by the ocean, all that perpetual motion," Mose Allison, the jazz singer, sings.

The wind picks up and blusters. Its fat underbelly scrapes the uneven ground, twisting like taffy toward me, slips up over the mountain, and showers out across the Great Plains. The sea smell it carried all the way from Seattle has long since been absorbed by pink gruss — the rotting granite that spills down the slopes of the Rockies. Somewhere over the Midwest the wind slows, tangling in the hair of hardwood forests, and finally drops into the corridors of the cities, past Manhattan's World Trade Center, ripping free again as it crosses the Atlantic's green swell.

Spring jitterbugs inside me. Spring *is* wind, symphonic and billowing. A dark cloud pops like a blood blister over me, letting hail down. It comes on a piece of wind that seems to have widened the sky, comes so the birds have something to fly on.

A message reports to my brain but I can't believe my eyes. The sheet of wind had a hole in it: an eagle just fell out of the sky. It fell as if down the chute of a troubled airplane. Landed, falling to one side as if a leg were broken. I was standing on the hill overlooking the narrow valley that had been a seashore 170 million years ago, whose sides had lifted like a medic's litter to catch up this eagle now.

She hops and flaps seven feet of wing and closes them down and sways. She had come down (on purpose?) near a dead fawn whose carcass had recently been feasted upon. When I walked closer, all I could see of the animal was a ribcage rubbed red with fine tissue and the decapitated head lying peacefully against sagebrush, eyes closed.

At twenty yards the eagle opened her wings halfway and rose up, her whole back lengthening and growing stiff. At forty feet she looked as big as a small person. She craned her neck, first to one side, then the other, and stared hard. She's giving me the eagle eye, I thought.

Friends who have investigated eagles' nests have literally feared for their lives. It's not that they were in danger of being pecked to death but, rather, grabbed. An eagle's talons are a powerful jaw. Their grip is so strong the talons can slice down through flesh to bone in one motion.

But I had come close only to see what was wrong, to see what I could do. An eagle with a bum leg will starve to death. Was it broken, bruised, or sprained? How could I get close enough to know? I approached again. She hopped up in the air, dashing the critical distance between us with her great wings. Best to leave her alone, I decided. My husband dragged a road-killed deer up the mountain slope so she could eat, and I brought a bucket of water. Then we turned toward home.

A golden eagle is not golden but black with yellow spots on the neck and wings. Looking at her, I had wondered how feathers came to be, how their construction — the rachis, vane, and quill — is unlike anything else in nature.

Birds are glorified flying lizards. The remarkable feathers that, positioned together, are like hundreds of smaller wings, evolved from reptilian scales. Ancestral birds had thirteen pairs of cone-shaped teeth that grew in separate sockets like a snake's, rounded ribs, and bony tails. Archaeopteryx was half bird, half dinosaur who glided instead of flying; ichthyornis was a fishbird, a relative of the pelican; diatryma was a giant, seven feet tall with a huge beak and wings so absurdly small they must have been useless, though later the wingbone sprouted from them. *Aquila chrysaëtos*, the modern golden eagle, has seven thousand contour feathers, no teeth, and weighs about eight pounds.

I think about the eagle. How big she was, how each time she spread her wings it was like a thought stretching between two seasons.

Back at the house I relax with a beer. At 5:03 the vernal equinox occurs. I go outside and stand in the middle of a hayfield with my eyes closed. The universe is restless but I want to feel celestial equipoise: twelve hours of daylight, twelve of dark, and the earth ramrod straight on its axis. In celebration I straighten my posture in an effort to resist the magnetic tilt back into dormancy, spiritual and emotional reticence. Far to the south I imagine the equatorial sash, now nose to nose with the sun, sizzling like a piece of bacon, then the earth slowly tilting again.

In the morning I walk up to the valley again. I glass both hillsides, back and forth through the sagebrush, but the eagle isn't there. The hindquarters of the road-killed deer have been eaten. Coyote tracks circle the carcass. Did they have eagle for dinner too?

Afternoon. I return. Far up on the opposite hill I see her, flapping and hopping to the top. When I stop, she stops and turns her head. Her neck is the plumbline on which earth revolves. Even at two hundred yards, I can feel her binocular vision zeroing in; I can feel the heat of her stare.

Later, I look through my binoculars at all sorts of things. I'm seeing the world with an eagle eye. I glass the crescent moon. How jaded I've become, taking the moon at face value only, forgetting the charcoal, shaded backside, as if it weren't there at all.

That night I dream about two moons. One is pink and spins fast; the other is an eagle's head, farther away and spinning in the opposite direction. Slowly, both moons descend and then it is day.

At first light I clamber up the hill. Now the dead deer my husband brought is only a hoop of ribs, two forelegs, and hair. The eagle is not here or along the creek or on either hill. I go to the hill and sit. After a long time an eagle careens out from the narrow slit of the red-walled canyon whose creek drains into this valley. Surely it's the same bird. She flies by. I can hear the bone-creak and whoosh of air under her wings. She cocks her head and looks at me. I smile. What is a smile to her? Now she is not so much flying as lifting above the planet, far from me.

Late March. The emerald of the hayfields brightens. A flock of gray-capped rosy finches who overwintered here swarms a leaf-less apple tree, then falls from the smooth boughs like cut grass. The tree was planted by the Texan who homesteaded this ranch. As I walk past, one of the boughs, shaped like an undulating dragon, splits off from the trunk and falls.

Space is an arena in which the rowdy particles that are the building blocks of life perform their antics. All spring, things fall; the general law of increasing disorder is on the take. I try to think of what it is to be a cause without an effect, an effect without a cause. To abandon time-bound thinking, the use of tenses, the temporally related emotions of impatience, expectation, hope, and fear. But I can't. I go to the edge of the lake and watch the ducks. Like them, my thinking rises and falls on the same water.

Another day. Sometimes when I'm feeling small-minded I take a plane ride over Wyoming. As we take off I feel the plane's resistance to accepting air under its wings. Is this how an eagle feels? Ernst Mach's principle tells me that an object's resistance against being accelerated is not the intrinsic property of matter, but a measure of its interaction with the universe; that matter has inertia only because it exists in relation to other matter.

Airborne, then, I'm not aloof but in relation to everything — like Wallace Stevens's floating eagle for whom the whole, intricate Alps is a nest. We fly southeast from Heart Mountain across the Big Horn River, over the long red wall where Butch Cassidy trailed stolen horses, across the high plains to Laramie. Coming home the next day, we hit clouds. Turbulence, like many forms of trouble, cannot always be seen. We bounce so hard my arms sail helplessly above my head. In evolution, wingbones became arms and hands; perhaps I'm de-evolving.

From ten thousand feet I can see that spring is only half here: the southern part of the state is white, the northern half is green. Land is also time. The greening of time is a clock whose hands are blades of grass moving vertically, up through the fringe of numbers, spreading across the middle of the face, sinking again as the sun moves from one horizon to the other. Time doesn't go anywhere; the shadow of the plane, my shadow, moves across it.

To sit on a plane is to sit on the edge of sleep where the mind's forge brightens into incongruities. Down there I see disparate wholenesses strung together and the string dissolving. Mountains run like rivers; I fly through waves and waves of chiaroscuro light. The land looks bare but is articulate. The body of the plane is my body, pressing into spring, pressing matter into relation with matter. Is it even necessary to say the obvious? That spring brings on surges of desire? From this disinterested height I say out loud what Saint Augustine wrote: "My love is my weight. Because of it I move."

Directly below us now is the fine old Wyoming ranch where Joel, Mart, Dave, Hughy, and I have moved thousands of head of cattle. Joel's father, Smokey, was one of two brothers who put the outfit together. They worked hard, lived frugally, and even after Fred died, Smokey did not marry until his late fifties. As testimony to a long bachelorhood, there is no kitchen in the main house. The cookhouse stands separate from all the other buildings. In back is a bedroom and bath, which have housed a list of itinerant cooks ten pages long.

Over the years I've helped during roundup and branding. We'd rise at four. Smokey, now in his eighties, cooked flapjacks and boiled coffee on the wood cookstove. There was a long table. Joel and Smokey always sat at one end. They were look-alikes, both skin-and-bones tall with tipped-up dark eyes set in narrow faces. Stern and vigilant, Smokey once threw a young hired hand out of the cookhouse because he hadn't grained his saddle horse after a long day's ride. "On this outfit we take care of our animals first," he said. "Then if there's time, we eat."

Even in his early twenties, Joel had his father's dignity and razor-sharp wit. They both wore white Stetsons identically shaped. Only their hands were different: Joel had eight fingers and one thumb — the other he lost while roping.

Eight summers ago my parents visited their ranch. We ate a hearty meal of homemade whiskey left over from Prohibition days, steaks cut from an Angus bull, four kinds of vegetables, watermelon, ice cream, and pie. Despite a thirteen-year difference in our ages, Smokey wanted Joel and me to marry. As we rose from the meal, he shook my father's hand. "I guess you'll be my son's father-in-law," he said. That was news to all of us. Joel's face turned crimson. My father threw me an astonished look, cleared his throat, and thanked his host for the fine meal.

One night Joel did come to my house and asked me if I would take him into my bed. It was a gentlemanly proposition — doffed hat, moist eyes, a smile almost grimacing with loneliness. "You're an older woman. Think of all you could teach me," he said jauntily, but with a blush. He stood ramrod straight waiting for an answer. My silence turned him away like a rolling wave and he drove to the home ranch, spread out across the Emblem Bench thirty-five miles away.

The night Joel died I was staying at a writer's farm in Missouri. I had fallen asleep early, then awakened suddenly, feeling claustrophobic. I jumped out of bed and stood in the dark. I wanted to get out of there, drive home to Wyoming, and I didn't know why. Finally, at seven in the morning, I was able to sleep. I dreamed about a bird landing, then lifting out of a tree along a river bank. That was the night Joel's pickup rolled. He was found five hours after the accident occurred — just about daylight — and died on the way to the hospital.

Now I'm sitting on a fin of Gypsum Springs rock looking west. The sun is setting. What I see are three gray cloud towers letting rain down at the horizon. The sky behind these massifs is gilded gold, and long fingers of land — benches where the Hunt Oil Company's Charolais cattle graze — are pink. Somewhere over Joel's grave the sky is bright. The road where he died shines like a dash in a Paul Klee painting. Over my head, it is still winter: snow so dry it feels like Styrofoam when squeezed together, tumbles into my lap. I think about flying and falling.

The place in the sky where the eagle fell is dark, as if its shadow had burned into the backdrop of rock — Hiroshima style. Why does a wounded eagle get well and fly away; why do the head wounds of a young man cut him down? Useless questions.

Sex and death are the riddles thrown into the hopper, thrown down on the planet like hailstones. Where one hits the earth, it makes a crater and melts, perhaps a seed germinates, perhaps not. If I dice life down into atoms, the trajectories I find are so wild, so random, anything could happen: life or nonlife. But once we have a body, who can give it up easily? Our own or others'? We check our clocks and build our beautiful narratives, under which indeterminacy seethes.

Sometimes, lying in bed, I feel like a flounder with its two eyes on one side pointing upward into nothingness. The casings of thought rattle. Then I realize there are no casings at all. Is it possible that the mind, like space, is finite, but has no boundaries, no center or edge? I sit cross-legged on old blankets. My bare feet strain against the crotch of my knees. Time is between my toes, it seems. Just as morning comes and the indigo lifts, the leaflessness of the old apple tree looks ornate. Nothing in this world is plain.

"Every atom in your body was once inside a star," another physicist says, but he's only trying to humor me. Not all atoms in all kinds of matter are shared. But who wouldn't find that idea appealing? Outside, shadows trade places with a sliver of sun that trades places with shadow. Finally the lake ice goes and the water — pale and slate blue — wears its coat of diamonds all day. The mallards number twenty-six pairs now. They nest on two tiny islands and squabble amicably among themselves. A Pacific storm blows in from the south like a jibsail reaching far out, backhanding me with a gust of something tropical. It snows into my mouth, between my breasts, against my shins. Spring teaches me what space and time teach me: that I am a random multiple; that the many fit together like waves; that my swell is a collision of particles. Spring is a kind of music, a seething minor, a twelve-tone scale. Even the odd harmonies amassed only lift up to dissolve.

Spring passes harder and harder and is feral. The first thunder cracks the sky into a larger domain. Sap rises in obdurateness. For the first time in seven months, rain slants down in a slow pavane — sharp but soft — like desire, like the laying on of hands. I drive the highway that crosses the wild-horse range. Near Emblem I watch a black studhorse trot across the range all alone. He travels north, then turns in my direction as if trotting to me. Now, when I dream of Joel, he is riding that horse and he knows he is dead. One night he rides to my house, all smiles and shyness. I let him in.

DANIEL MARK EPSTEIN

The Case of Harry Houdini

FROM THE NEW CRITERION

WHEN MY GRANDFATHER was a boy he saw the wild-haired magician escape from a riveted boiler. He would remember that image as long as he lived, and how Harry Houdini, the rabbi's son, defeated the German Imperial Police at the beginning of the twentieth century. Hearing those tales and others even more incredible, sixty years after the magician's death we cannot help but wonder: what did the historical Houdini *really* do? And how on earth did he do it?

The newspaper accounts are voluminous, and consistent. The mere cataloguing of Houdini's escapes soon grows tedious, which they were not, to be sure, in the flesh. But quickly: the police stripped him naked and searched him thoroughly before binding his wrists and ankles with five pairs of irons. Then they would slam him into a cell and turn the key of a three-bond burglar-proof lock. He escaped, hundreds of times, from the most secure prisons in the world. He hung upside down in a straitjacket from the tallest buildings in America, and escaped in full view of the populace. He was chained hand and foot and nailed into a packing case weighted with lead; the packing case was dropped from a tugboat into New York's East River and ninety seconds later Houdini surfaced. The packing case was hauled up intact, with the manacles inside, still fastened. He was sealed into a paper bag and got out without disturbing the seal. He was sewn into a huge football, into the belly of a whale, and escaped. In California he was buried six feet underground, and clawed his way out. He did this, he did that. These are facts that cannot be exaggerated, for they were conceived as exaggerations. We know he did these things because his actions were more public than the proceedings of Congress, and most of them he performed over and over, so no one would miss the point.

How did he do such things? For all rational people who are curious, sixty years after the magician's death, there is good news and bad news. The good news is that we know how the vast majority of Houdini's tricks were done, and the explanations are as fascinating as the mystery was. Much of our knowledge comes from the magician's writings, for Houdini kept ahead of his imitators by exposing his cast-off tricks. We have additional information from technicians and theater historians. No magician will reveal Houdini's secrets — their code forbids it. But so much controversy has arisen concerning his powers — so much conjecture they may have been supernatural — that extraordinary measures have been taken to assure us Houdini was a *mortal* genius. Many secrets have leaked out, and others have been discovered from examining the props. So at last we know more about Houdini's technique than any other magician's.

The disturbing news is that, sixty years after his last performance, some of his more spectacular escapes remain unexplained. And while magicians such as Doug Henning are bound not to expose their colleagues, they are free to admit what mystifies them. They know how Houdini walked through the brick wall at Hammerstein's Roof Garden, in 1914, but they do not know how he made the elephant disappear in 1918. This trick he performed only for a few months in New York. And when people asked him why he did not continue he told them that Teddy Roosevelt, a great hunter, had begged him to stop before he exhausted the world's supply of pachyderms.

But before we grapple with the mysteries, let us begin with what we can understand. Let us begin with my grandfather's favorite story, the case of Harry Houdini versus the German police. Houdini's first tour of Europe depended upon the good will and cooperation of the law. When he arrived in London in 1900 the twenty-six-year-old magician did not have a single booking. His news clippings eventually inspired an English agent, who had Houdini manacled to a pillar in Scotland Yard. Seeing that Houdini was securely fastened, Superintendent

Melville of the Criminal Investigation Department said he would return in a couple of hours, when the escapist had worn himself out. By the time Melville got to the door the magician was free to open it for him.

The publicity surrounding his escape from the most prestigious police force in the world opened up many another door for the young magician. Booked at the Alhambra Theater in London, he performed his "Challenge" handcuff act, which had made him famous on the vaudeville circuit. After some card tricks and standard illusions, Houdini would stand before the proscenium and challenge the world to restrain him with ropes, straitjackets, handcuffs, whatever they could bring on, from lockshops, prisons, and museums. A single failure might have ruined him. There is no evidence that he ever failed, though in several cases he nearly died from the effort required to escape from sadistic shackles. The "Challenge" act filled the Alhambra Theater for two months. Houdini might have stayed there if Germany had not already booked him; the Germans could hardly wait to get a look at Houdini.

As he had done in America and England, Houdini began his tour of Germany with a visit to police headquarters. The Dresden officers were not enthusiastic, yet they could hardly refuse the magician's invitation to lock him up. That might suggest a crisis of confidence. And like their colleagues the world over, the Dresden police viewed Houdini's news clippings as so much paper in the balance with their locks and chains. Of course the Dresden police had no more success than those of Kansas City, or San Francisco, or Scotland Yard. Their manacles were paper to him. The police chief reluctantly signed the certificate Houdini demanded, but the newspapers gave him little coverage.

So on his opening night at Dresden's Central Theater, Houdini arranged to be fettered in the leg irons and manacles of the Mathildegasse Prison. Some of the locks weighed forty pounds. The audience, packed to the walls, went wild over his escape, and the fact that he spoke their language further endeared him. If anything could have held him captive it would have been the adoring burghers of Dresden, who mobbed the theater for weeks. The manager wanted to buy out Houdini's contract with the Wintergarten of Berlin, so as to hold him over in Dresden, but the people of Berlin could not wait to see the magician.

Houdini arrived in Berlin in October of 1900. The first thing he did was march into the police station, strip stark naked, and challenge the jailors. They could not hold him. This time Count von Windheim, the highest ranking policeman in Germany, signed the certificate of Houdini's escape. The Wintergarten was overrun. The management appealed to the theater of Houdini's next engagement, in Vienna, so they might hold him over an extra month in Berlin. The Viennese finally yielded, demanding an indemnity equal to Houdini's salary for one month. When the magician, at long last, opened at the Olympic Theater in Paris, in December of 1901, he was the highest paid foreign entertainer in French history.

But meanwhile there was big trouble brewing in Germany. It seems the police there had little sense of humor about Houdini's peculiar gifts, and the Jew had quickly exhausted what little there was. In Dortmund he escaped from the irons that had bound Glowisky, a notorious murderer, beheaded three days before. At Hanover the police chief, Count von Schwerin, plotted to disgrace Houdini, challenging him to escape from a special straitjacket reinforced with thick leather. Houdini agonized for one and a half hours while von Schwerin looked on, his jubilant smile melting in wonder, then rage, as the magician worked himself free.

The cumulative anger of the German police went public in July of 1901. Inspector Werner Graff witnessed Houdini's escape from all the manacles at the Cologne police station and vowed to end the humiliation. It was not a simple matter of pride. Graff, along with von Schwerin and other officials, feared Houdini was weakening their authority and inviting jailbreaks, if not other kinds of antisocial behavior. So Graff wrote a letter to Cologne's newspaper, the *Rheinische Zeitung*. The letter stated that Houdini had escaped from simple restraints at the police headquarters, by trickery; but his publicity boasted he could escape from restraints *of any kind*. Such a claim, Graff wrote, was a lie, and Houdini ought to be prosecuted for fraud.

Though he knew the letter was nonsense, the magician could not ignore it, for it was dangerous nonsense. If the police began calling him a fraud in every town he visited, Houdini would lose his audience. So he demanded that Graff apologize and the newspaper publish a retraction. Graff refused, and other Ger-

man dailies reprinted his letter. Should Harry Houdini sue the
German policeman for libel? Consider the circumstances. Germany, even in 1901, was one of the most authoritarian states in
the world. Houdini was an American, a Jew who embarrassed
the police. A libel case against Graff would turn upon the magician's claim that he could escape from *any* restraint, and the
courtroom would become an international theater. There a German judge and jury would try his skill, and, should they find it
wanting, Houdini would be washed up, exiled to play beer halls
and dime museums. Only an artist with colossal pride and total
confidence in his methods would act as Houdini did. He hired
the most prominent trial lawyer in Cologne, and ordered him
to sue Werner Graff and the Imperial Police of Germany for
criminal libel.

There was standing room only in the Cologne *Schöffengericht.*
The judge allowed Werner Graff to seek out the most stubborn
locks and chains he could find, and tangle Houdini in them, in
full view of everyone. Here was a hitch, for Houdini did not
wish to show the crowd his technique. He asked the judge to
clear the courtroom, and in the ensuing turmoil the magician
released himself so quickly no one knew how he had done it.
The *Schöffengericht* fined the astonished policeman and ordered
a public apology. So Graff's lawyer appealed the case.

Two months later Graff was better prepared. In the *Strafkammer,* or court of appeals, he presented thirty letters from legal
authorities declaring that the escape artist could not justify his
advertisements. And Graff had a shiny new pair of handcuffs.
The premier locksmith of Germany had engineered the cuffs
especially for the occasion. Werner Graff explained to the judge
that the lock, once closed, could never be opened, even with its
own key. Let Houdini try to get out of these.

This time the court permitted Houdini to work in privacy,
and a guard led the magician to an adjacent chamber. Everyone
else settled down for a long wait, in a chatter of anticipation.
They were interrupted four minutes later by the entrance of
Houdini, who tossed the manacles on the judge's bench. So the
Strafkammer upheld the lower court's decision, as did the *Ober-
landesgericht* in a "paper" appeal. The court fined Werner Graff
thirty marks and ordered him to pay for the trials as well as a
published apology. Houdini's next poster showed him in eve-

ning dress, his hands manacled, standing before the judge, jurors, and a battery of mustachioed policemen. Looking down on the scene was a bust of the Kaiser against a crimson background, and a scroll that read: "The Imperial Police of Cologne slandered Harry Houdini . . . were compelled to advertise 'An Honorary Apology' and pay costs of the trials. By command of Kaiser Wilhelm II, Emperor of Germany."

Now this is surely a wondrous tale, like something out of the *Arabian Nights,* and it will seem no less wonderful when we understand the technique that made it come true. In 1901, when Houdini took on the Imperial Police, he was not whistling in the dark. By the time he left America at the end of the nineteenth century he had dissected every kind of lock he could find in the New World, and whatever he could import from the old one. Arriving in London, Houdini could write that there were only a few kinds of British handcuffs, "seven or eight at the utmost," and these were some of the simplest he had ever seen. He searched the markets, antique shops, and locksmiths, buying up all the European locks he could find so he could dismantle and study them.

Then during his Berlin engagement he worked up to ten hours a day at Mueller's locksmith on the Mittelstrasse, studying restraints. He was the Bobby Fischer of locks. With a chessmaster's foresight Houdini devised a set of picks to release every lock in existence, as well as *any he could imagine.* Such tireless ingenuity produced the incandescent light bulb and the atom bomb. Houdini's creation of a theatrical metaphor made a comparable impact on the human spirit. He had a message that he delivered so forcefully that it goes without mentioning in theater courses: humankind cannot be held in chains. The European middle class had reached an impressionable age, and the meaning of Houdini's theater was not lost upon them. Nor was he mistaken by the aristocracy, who stayed away in droves. The spectacle of this American Jew bursting from chains by dint of ingenuity did not amuse the rich. They wanted desperately to demythologize him.

It was not about to happen in the German courtroom. When Werner Graff snapped the "new" handcuffs on Houdini, they were not strange to the magician. He had already invented them, so to speak, as well as the pick to open them, and the pick was in his pocket. Only a locksmith whose knowledge surpassed Houdini's could stop him; diligent study assured him that, as of 1901, there could be no such locksmith on the face of the earth.

What else can we understand about the methods of Harry Houdini, born Ehrich Weiss? We know he was a superbly conditioned athlete who did not smoke or take a drop of alcohol. His straitjacket escapes he performed in full view of the world so they could see it was by main force and flexibility that he freed himself. He may or may not have been able to dislocate his shoulders at will — he said he could, and it seems no more marvelous than certain other skills he demonstrated. Friends reported that his toes could untie knots most of us could not manage with our fingers. And routinely the magician would hold his breath for as long as four minutes to work underwater escapes. To cheapen the supernatural claims of the fakir Rahman Bey, Houdini remained underwater in an iron box for ninety minutes, as against the Egyptian's sixty. Examining Houdini, a physician testified that the fifty-year-old wizard had halved his blood pressure while doubling his pulse. Of course, more wonderful than any of these skills was the courage allowing him to employ them, in predicaments where any normal person would panic.

These things are known about Houdini. The same tireless ingenuity, when applied to locks and jails, packing cases and riveted boilers; the same athletic prowess, when applied at the bottom of the East River, or while dangling from a rope attached to the cornice of the *Sun* building in Baltimore — these talents account for the vast majority of Houdini's exploits. As we have mentioned, theater historians, notably Raymund Fitzsimons in his *Death and the Magician,* have carefully exposed Houdini's ingenuity, knowing that nothing can tarnish the miracle of the man's existence. Their accounts are technical and we need not dwell on them, except to say they *mostly* support Houdini's oath that his effects were achieved by natural, or mechanical, means. The Houdini problem arises from certain outrageous effects no one has ever been able to explain, though capable technicians have been trying for more than sixty years.

Let us briefly recall those effects. We have mentioned the disappearing elephant. On January 7, 1918, Houdini had a ten-thousand-pound elephant led onto the bright stage of the Hippodrome in New York City. A trainer marched the elephant around a cabinet large enough for an elephant, proving there was space behind. There was no trap door in the floor of the Hippodrome, and the elephant could not fly. Houdini ushered the pachyderm into the cabinet and closed the curtains. Then he opened them, and where the elephant had stood there was nothing but empty space. Houdini went on with his program, which might have been making the Hippodrome disappear, for all the audience knew. A reporter for the *Brooklyn Eagle* noted: "The program says that the elephant vanished into thin air. The trick is performed fifteen feet from the backdrop and the cabinet is slightly elevated. That explanation is as good as any." After Houdini stopped making elephants disappear, nineteen weeks later, the trick would never be precisely duplicated.

That is the single "conventional" illusion of Houdini's repertoire that remains unexplained. He was not the greatest illusionist of his time, though he was among the better ones. His expertise was the escape act, that specialty of magic furthest removed from theater, for its challenges are quite real and sometimes beyond the magician's control. It was the escapes, as his wife later wrote, that were truly dangerous, and Houdini privately admitted some anxieties about them. Give a wizard twenty years to build a cabinet that snuffs an elephant, and you will applaud his cleverness if he succeeds, in the controlled environment of his theater. But surrender the same man, stark naked, to the Russian police, who stake their honor upon detaining him in a convict van, and you may well suspect the intercession of angels should he get out.

And that is exactly what Houdini did, in one of the strangest and most celebrated escapes of his career. Strange, because it was Houdini's habit to escape only from barred jail cells where the locks were within easy reach, and then only after inspection, so he might hide picks in crannies, or excuse himself if he foresaw failure. But the Siberian transport cell made his blood boil. On May 11, 1903, the chief of the Russian secret police searched the naked Houdini inside and out. The revolt of 1905 was in its planning stages and the Imperial Police were understandably touchy. The magician's wrists were padlocked and his ankles fettered before the police locked him into the *carette*. Mounted

on a wagon, the zinc-lined steel cell stood in the prison courtyard in view of Chief Lebedoeff, his staff, and a number of
civilians. Twenty-eight minutes later Houdini was walking
around the courtyard, stretching. Nobody saw him get out, but
he was out. The police ran to the door of the *carette*. The door
was still locked and the shackles lay on the floor of the undam-
aged van. The police were so furious they would not sign the
certificate of escape, but so many people had witnessed the
event that the news was soon being shouted all over Moscow.
Doug Henning has written: "It remains one of his escapes about
which the real method is pure conjecture."

In the Houdini Museum at Niagara Falls, Canada, you may
view the famous *Mirror* handcuffs. If you are a scholar you can
inspect them. In March of 1904 the London *Daily Mirror* discovered a blacksmith who had been working for five years to build
a set of handcuffs no mortal man could pick. Examining the
cuffs, the best locksmiths in London agreed they had never seen
such an ingenious mechanism. The newspaper challenged Houdini to escape from them. On March 17, before a house of four
thousand in the London Hippodrome, a journalist fastened the
cuffs on Houdini's wrists and turned the key six times. The
magician retired to his cabinet onstage, and the band struck up
a march. He did not emerge for twenty minutes. When he did,
it was to hold the lock up to the light. Remember that most
"Challenge" handcuffs were regulation, and familiar to Houdini. He studied the lock in the light, and then went back into
the cabinet as the band played a waltz.

Ten minutes later Houdini stuck his head out, asking if he
could have a cushion to kneel on. He was denied. After almost
an hour Houdini came out of the cabinet again, obviously worn
out, and his audience groaned. He wanted the handcuffs to be
unlocked for a moment so he could take off his coat, as he was
sweating profusely. The journalist denied the request, since
Houdini had never before seen the handcuffs unlocked, and
that might give him an advantage. Whereupon Houdini, in full
view of the four thousand, extracted a penknife from his pocket
and opened it with his teeth. Turning the coat inside out over
his head, he shredded it loose with the penknife and returned
to the cabinet. Someone called out that Houdini had been handcuffed for more than an hour. As the band played on, the

journalists of the *Daily Mirror* could taste the greatest scoop of the twentieth century. But ten minutes later there was a cry from the cabinet and Houdini leaped out of it, free, waving the handcuffs high in the air. While the crowd roared, several men from the audience carried Houdini on their shoulders around the theater. He was crying as if his heart would break.

For all his other talents, Houdini was a notoriously wooden actor, and we may assume the rare tears were altogether real, the product of an uncounterfeitable emotion. It is as if the man himself had been overwhelmed by his escape. Eighty years of technological progress have shed no light upon it. We know how Houdini got out of other handcuffs, but not these. As far as anyone can tell, the *Mirror* handcuffs remain as the blacksmith described them — a set of handcuffs no mortal man could pick. One is tempted to dismiss the whole affair as mass hypnosis.

In the same Canadian museum you may view the Chinese water torture cell, in which the magician was hung upside down in water, his ankles padlocked to the riveted roof. His escape from this cell was the crowning achievement of his stage career, and though he performed it on tour during the last ten years of his life, no one has the slightest notion of how he did it. The gifted Doug Henning revived the act in 1975 on television. But he would be the first to tell you his was *not* Houdini's version but his own, and he would not do it onstage before a live audience seven nights a week, with matinees on Wednesday and Saturday, because the trick would be unspeakably dangerous even if he could perform it there. When Houdini died he willed the contraption to his brother Hardeen, a fine magician in his own right. But Hardeen would not get in it either, and the instructions were to be burned upon his death. Again, as with the vanishing elephant, we are reviewing a stage illusion under controlled conditions, and may bow to a master's technical superiority without fretting that he has used supernatural powers.

But the *Mirror* handcuffs and the Siberian van escape are troublesome, as are certain of Houdini's escapes from reinforced straitjackets and packing cases under water. So is the fact that he was buried six feet underground and clawed his way out. He only tried it once, and nearly died in the struggle, but the feat was attested, and you do not need a degree in physics to know it is as preposterous as rising from the dead. The weight of the earth is so crushing you could not lift it in the open air. Try doing this with no oxygen. The maestro himself misjudged the weight and, realizing his folly, tried to signal his crew when the grave was not yet full. They could not hear him and kept right on shoveling as fast as they could, so as not to keep him waiting. Then they stood back to watch. A while later they saw his bleeding hands appear above the ground.

If we find Houdini's record unsettling, imagine what our grandparents must have thought of him. They knew almost nothing of his technique. Where we remain troubled by a few of his illusions and escapes, our ancestors were horrified by most of them. The European journalists thought he was some kind of hobgoblin, a shapeshifter who could crawl through keyholes or dematerialize and reappear at will. One can hardly blame them. Despite his constant reassurances that his effects were technical, and natural, the practical-minded layman could not believe it, and even fellow magicians were disturbed by his behavior.

So we come to the central issue in the case of Harry Houdini. It is an issue he carefully avoided in public while studying it diligently in private. To wit: Can a magician, by the ultimate perfection of a technique, generate a force that, at critical moments, will achieve a supernatural result? Houdini's writings show this was the abiding concern of his intellectual life. It is, of course, the essential mystery of classical magic since before the Babylonians. Yet it remained a private and professional concern until Houdini's career forced it upon the public.

With the same determination that opened the world's locks, Houdini searched for an answer. His own technique was so highly evolved that its practice might have satisfied him, but his curiosity was unquenchable. He amassed the world's largest collection of books pertaining to magic and the occult, and no less a scholar than Edmund Wilson honored Houdini's authority. The son of a rabbi, Houdini pursued his studies with rabbinic thoroughness. And, from the beginning of his career, he sought out the living legends of magic and badgered them in retirement, sometimes with tragicomic results.

As far back as 1895 it seemed to Houdini something peculiar was going on when he performed the metamorphosis with his

wife, Beatrice, who was known as Bess. You have probably seen
this classic illusion. Two friends of mine once acted it in my
living room as a birthday present. When the Houdinis performed the metamorphosis, Bess would handcuff Harry, tie
him in a sack, and lock him in a trunk. She would draw a curtain
hiding the trunk, and then it would open, showing Houdini free
upon the stage. Where was Bess? Inside the trunk, inside the
sack, handcuffed — there was Bess. The method of this trick is
only mysterious if you cannot pay for it. But the Houdinis'
timing of the metamorphosis got very mysterious indeed. They
polished the act until it happened in less than three seconds —
three rather blurred seconds in their own minds. Believe me,
you cannot get *into* the trunk in less than three seconds. So when
the Houdinis had done the trick they were often as stunned as
their audience. It seemed a sure case of technique unleashing a
supernatural force. Perplexed, Houdini planned to interview
Hermann the Great, the pre-eminent conjuror in America in
1895, and ask Hermann what was up. But Hermann died as
Houdini was about to ask him the question.

And Houdini shadowed the marvelous Harry Kellar, cross-
examining him, and Alexander Heimburger, and the decrepit
Ira Davenport, who had been a medium as well as a magician.
But the great magicians flatly denied the psychic possibility, and
Davenport would not answer to Houdini's satisfaction. In 1903
he discovered that Wiljalba Frikell, a seemingly mythic wizard
of the nineteenth century, was still alive, in retirement near
Dresden. When the ancient mage would not acknowledge his
letters, Houdini grew convinced Wiljalba Frikell was the man to
answer his question. He took the train to Dresden and knocked
on Frikell's door. His wife sent Houdini away. On the road in
Germany and Russia, Houdini continued to send letters and
gifts to Frikell. And at last, six months after he had been turned
away from Frikell's door, the reclusive magician agreed to see
him.

Houdini rang the doorbell at two P.M. on October 8, 1903, the
exact hour of his appointment. The door swung open. An hour
earlier, Wiljalba Frikell had dressed in his best suit and laid out
his scrapbooks, programs, and medals for Houdini to view.
Houdini excitedly followed Frikell's wife into the room where
the master sat surrounded by the mementos of his glorious

career. But he would not be answering any of the questions that buzzed in Houdini's brain. The old man was stone dead.

Throughout his life Houdini categorically denied that any of his effects were achieved by supernatural means. He crusaded against mediums, clairvoyants, and all who claimed psychic power, advertising that he would reproduce any of their manifestations by mechanical means. In the face of spiritualists who accused *him* of being a physical medium, he protested that all his escapes and illusions were tricks. He was probably telling the truth as he understood it. But Rabbi Drachman, who spoke at Houdini's funeral and had been in a position to receive confidences, said: "Houdini possessed a wondrous power that he never understood, and which he never revealed to anyone in life."

Houdini was not Solomon; he was a vaudeville specialist. If he ever experienced a psychic power, it surely humbled his understanding. And to admit such a power, in his position, would have been a monumental stupidity. Why? If for no other reason, Talmudic law forbids the performance of miracles, and Houdini was the obedient son of Rabbi Weiss. Also, in case he should forget the Jewish law, it is strictly against the magician's code to claim a supernatural power, for reasons impossible to ignore. Mediums made such claims at their own risk. Two of the more famous mediums of the nineteenth century, Ira and William Davenport, achieved manifestations similar to Houdini's. Audiences in Liverpool, Leeds, and Paris rioted, stormed the stage, and ran the mediums out of town, crying their performances were an outrage against God and a danger to man. Whether or not the acts were supernatural is beside the point — billing them as such was bad business and hazardous to life and limb. Yet the Davenports were no more than a sideshow compared to Houdini. The man was blinding. There had not been such a public display of apparent miracles in nearly two thousand years. Had the Jew so much as hinted his powers were spiritual, he might have expected no better treatment than the renegade Hebrew of Nazareth.

Houdini was the self-proclaimed avatar of nothing but good old American know-how, and that is how he wished to be remembered. Bess, his wife of thirty years, was loyal to him in this, as in all other things. Pestered for revelations about Houdini's magic long after his death, the widow swore by her husband's account. But against her best intentions, Bess clouded the issue by saying just a little more than was necessary. It was in a letter to Sir Arthur Conan Doyle, who had been a close friend of hers and Houdini's.

The friendship was an odd one. The author of Sherlock Holmes believed in spiritualism, and championed the séance with all the fervor with which Houdini opposed it. There were two great mysteries in Doyle's life: the powers of Sherlock Holmes and Harry Houdini. Doyle knew the Houdinis intimately, and nothing the magician said could shake Sir Arthur's conviction that certain of Houdini's escapes were supernatural. Doyle never stopped trying to get Houdini to confess. In 1922 it was more than a personal issue. The séance had become big business in America, with millions of bereaved relatives paying to communicate with their dear departed. Spiritualism was a home-grown, persuasive religious movement, a bizarre reaction to American science and pragmatism. The great critic Edmund Wilson, who admired Houdini and understood his gifts, recognized that the magician had appeared at a critical moment in the history of spiritualism. Houdini was the only man living who had the authority, and the competence, to expose the predatory mediums, and his success was decisive.

Yet Houdini's lecture-demonstrations, and exposures of false mediums, only fueled Doyle's suspicions that his friend was the real thing, a physical medium. In all fairness, Sir Arthur Conan Doyle was a credulous old gentleman who knew nothing of Houdini's techniques. But his instinct was sound. Two months after Houdini died, Sir Arthur wrote to Bess in despair of ever learning the truth from the magician's lips, and she wrote Doyle a long letter. What concerns us here are a few sentences that, coming from the woman who shared his life and work and who maintained her loyalty to Houdini alive and dead, we must regard as altogether startling.

> I will never be offended by anything you say for him or about him, but that he possessed psychic powers — he never knew it. As I told Lady Doyle often he would get a difficult lock, I stood by the cabinet and I would hear him say, "This is beyond me," and after many

minutes when the audience became restless I nervously would say,
"Harry, if there is anything in this belief in Spiritism, — why don't
you call on them to assist you," and before many minutes had passed
Houdini had mastered the lock.

We never attributed this to psychic help. We just knew that that
particular instrument was the one to open that lock, and so did all
his tricks.

The tone of this letter penned so soon after her husband's
death is somber throughout, painfully sincere. This was not a
subject for levity, this being the central issue in the life of Harry
Houdini. So what on earth is Bess trying to tell Sir Arthur when
she testifies to the invocation of spirits in one sentence and
repudiates psychic help in the next? What kind of double-talk is
this, when the widow refers to the summoning of spiritual aid
as "that particular instrument," as if a spirit were no different
from any other skeleton key? It sounds like sheer euphemism;
it sounds like the Houdinis' lifetime of work had uncovered a
power so terrifying they would not admit it to each other, let
alone the world. Would that Albert Einstein had been so dis-
creet in 1905.

So what if Harry Houdini, once in a while, "spirited" himself
out of a Siberian van, or a pair of *Mirror* handcuffs, or a packing
case at the bottom of the East River? It is perhaps no more
remarkable than that an American Jew won a verdict against
the German police for criminal libel in 1901, or reversed a religious movement in America in 1922. Houdini died in Detroit
on Halloween in 1926, of acute appendicitis. He was born in
Budapest on March 24, 1874, but told the world he was born in
Appleton, Wisconsin, on April 6. Not until after World War II
did Americans discover that their greatest magician was an
alien. Houdini's work was no more miraculous than his life. His
life was no more miraculous than the opening and closing of a
flower.

JOSEPH EPSTEIN

They Said You Was High Class

FROM THE AMERICAN SCHOLAR

"Look, I know it's a dodgy topic, but you are lower class, aren't you, darling? Just between ourselves, naturally."
  "I was before I came up in the world, true, but lower-middle class, not working class. Very important distinction. My old dad got really wild if you said he was working class. Worse than calling him a Jew."
  — Kingsley Amis, *Stanley and the Women*

KARL, FRIEDRICH, forgive me, fellas, for never having taken much interest in your class struggle, but the truth is that for the better part of my life I have been a bit unclear about what class I myself belong to. If the phrase didn't imply that I was of a higher social class than I am — and make me sound like an Englishman into the bargain — I should call the whole thing a frightful muddle. More than a mite confusing it is, though. How nice to be able to say with confidence, as George Orwell once did, that one is "lower-upper-middle class." Yet, unless I am quite wrong, such terms have now lost much of their descriptive power. The social pace has quickened; nowadays people move in and out of social classes with greater rapidity than ever before. Sometimes I wonder if today social class, at least as we used to think of it in this country, has about as much relevance as an electric salad fork and as bright a future as a cha-cha instructor in Montana.

  Social mobility — the jumping or, more commonly, sliding from one class to another — is scarcely a new phenomenon. Chekhov, to cite an interesting instance, had a grandfather who bought himself out of serfdom and a nephew who became a

Hollywood producer. I myself have a cousin, ten years older than I, named Moe and a niece, thirty years younger than I, named Nicole; and to go from Moe to Nicole in only forty years is in some respects to travel farther than the Chekhovs did from Voronezh Province to Beverly Hills. Other evidence of our whirring social flux can readily be adduced. The janitor of the apartment building I live in has published a book; it is not, granted, a slender little volume on the poetry of the Comte Robert de Montesquiou but instead a book about the martial arts; yet the same man is a janitor and a published author. The other day, in Manhattan, I had the bite put on me by a panhandler wearing a rumpled but still a real Ralph Lauren shirt; and it occurred to me shortly afterward that, should I ever hit the skids, I may not have the wardrobe to go on the bum. Just when you begin to think you understand a thing or two about the drama of life, they change the scenery and send in a whole new cast of characters.

Cracks, major fault lines, in the class system, may be a worldwide phenomenon. Peregrine Worsthorne, the British political writer, recently noted in *The Spectator* that "the class system has changed out of all recognition in my lifetime." Certainly, social distinctions in America have become vastly less clear in my own. When does a child first notice such distinctions? My own first realization that the world was a place filled with social differences might have been the gross recognition that some people lived rather better than we and others rather worse. It might have been the woman, whose name was Emma, who came in to clean for us on Tuesdays, for I seem to recall thinking it peculiar that someone would clean a place not her own. It might have had to do with automobiles, for we lived on a street that was a thoroughfare, and the first organized knowledge I acquired as a child had to do with telling the difference between cars; and it could not have been long before I also learned that some cars (Cadillacs, Packards, Lincolns) were held in higher regard than others (Fords, Studebakers, Plymouths). These were the years of World War II, during which my father drove a green 1942 Dodge sedan.

If our family had a crest, that green 1942 Dodge sedan ought to be at its center. That car placed us — socially, financially, and stylistically — and where it placed us was slam-bang in the middle. Our family was not so much socially uninteresting as socially uninterested. If life is in some sense a status race, my parents never noticed the flag drop. While we owned possessions roughly comparable to those owned by our neighbors, we showed no passion for the subtleties of social life. Even when the money was there to do so, it would never have occurred to my parents to join a city club or country club or to move to a fashionable address — a residence with social resonance. Their notion of the good life was to live comfortably, always well within their means, and insofar as possible never to pay for pretension. Then as now that seems to me quite sensible — though I must add, I myself have not had the character to live up to it.

I have omitted a social fact of no small significance and even greater complication. The fact is that I am Jewish. I was born thus, and thus I shall remain; and it is exceedingly difficult to be Jewish and not have a somewhat heightened sense of social and class distinctions. Not for nothing was the keenest modern observer of such distinctions, Marcel Proust, half Jewish and fully homosexual; after all, a man who is in danger of being despised from two different directions learns to devise sensitive antennae. Another sharp observer of social gradations, Anton Chekhov, was neither Jewish nor homosexual; but he was low born, the son of a bankrupt grocer, the grandson of a serf, and that put the antennae permanently on his roof. In a famous letter to his friend and publisher, Alexey Suvorin, Chekhov explained his own social unease when he wrote that "what aristocratic writers take from nature gratis, the less privileged must pay for with their youth," adding that he had had to squeeze "the slave out of himself drop by drop" before he "finds that the blood coursing through his veins is no longer the blood of a slave, but that of a real human being."

Let me hasten to insert that I never for a moment felt the least like a slave. Doubtless this was in large part owing to having a father who was successful yet in no way tyrannical or crushing, on the model, say, of Papa Kafka. My father, along with giving me the reassuring sense that I was working with a net under me, encouraged me to believe that I came of a family capable of serious achievement. But my father also alerted me early to the alarming fact that people might detest me for reasons having nothing to do with my character or conduct and everything to do with my religion. I must have been four or five years old when the potential social consequences of being Jewish were thus impinged upon me. In the 1940s and early 1950s the word — the euphemism, really — for de facto anti-Semitic arrangements was "restricted"; and in those years many neighborhoods and suburbs, clubs and resorts, fraternities and sororities were restricted.

I would be a liar if I said that knowledge of such things didn't bother me. But I would be an even greater liar if I said that it bothered me very much. When I was growing up, we lived in neighborhoods that tended to be at least 50 percent Jewish, and the same was true of the public schools I attended. If anything, this encouraged me in the belief that Jews were rather superior — a belief based, unknowingly, on social class. What I didn't know was that the non-Jews who remained in the neighborhoods we lived in were mainly people who for one reason or another were probably unable to depart them. In other words, most of the non-Jews I went to grade school and high school with were the sons and daughters of the working class or the lower white-collar classes, while the Jews tended to be among the newly surging middle classes, still very much on the make.

Although so far as I know I have never been the victim of any serious anti-Semitic acts, the first time I recall feeling rather out of the social mainstream because I was Jewish was during a year I spent as a freshman student at the University of Illinois in the middle 1950s. Illinois was very much a school of fraternities and sororities — a "Greek campus," as it was called — and I, who had not yet developed socially to the point of knowing there was something in the world called nonconformity, accepted an invitation to join what was thought to be the best of the Jewish fraternities. (All non-Jewish fraternities and sororities at Illinois were then "restricted.") The reigning spirit at the university in those days, far from being the Jewish and metropolitan one I was used to, was Protestant and small town — a midwestern, somewhat more yokelish version of the muscular Christianity that George Santayana found several decades earlier prevailing at Yale. The student who seemed to me best to represent this spirit was a young man from Peoria named Hiles Stout. Stout was a Sigma Chi and played three major sports for the university and resembled e. e. cummings's conscientious objector Olaf only in being "more brave than me:more blond than you" — though perhaps it would be more accurate to say that he was "more Hiles than me:more Stout than you."

I did not so much feel outclassed or declassed at the University of Illinois as I felt myself on the outside of a house I had no particular desire to enter. For while attending the University of Illinois, I had informally enrolled at good old Mencken-Lewis-Dreiser University, where I learned a haughty if not especially original disdain for the middle class, that inartistic and uninspired group also known as the booboisie — that is to say, a disdain for the social class and culture from which, apart from being Jewish, I myself had derived. From MLDU, beloved alma mater, I learned not to join the class struggle but instead to disassociate myself, insofar as possible, from my own class.

As a step in that direction, I transferred to the University of Chicago, which was perhaps as close as I have ever come to living in a classless society — I refer to the student segment of university society — and rather closer than I ever again care to come. A few fraternities remained at the University of Chicago at that time, but far from being thought in any way admirable, the chief attitude toward them was a mixture of mild contempt and apathy. Wealth and genteel birth counted for naught at the University of Chicago; apart from books and classical records, material possessions were thought the sign of a cramped spirit. Physical beauty and social graces were held to be beside the point, and the standard joke of the day had it that a panty raid on one of the women's dormitories netted a fatigue jacket and a single combat boot. A passionate bohemianism was what the University of Chicago student body aspired to; a grim scruffiness was what it often achieved.

Intellectually, the University of Chicago strove much higher, holding four tasks in life to be worthwhile: to be an artist, to be a scientist, to be a statesman, or to be a teacher of artists, scientists, or statesmen. In this regard the University of Chicago was not anti–middle class in the abrasive manner of Sinclair Lewis and H. L. Mencken; it was para–middle class by its tacit implication that there were higher things in life than getting a good job, earning a living, raising a family, and getting on. Chamfort once said that society was divided between those who had more

dinners than appetite and those who had more appetite than
dinners, but at the University of Chicago the division was between those who loved art and learning and those who did not,
and those who loved it were thought better.

If the University of Chicago was relatively free of conventional social-class considerations, the United States Army, the
institution in which I was to spend the next two years of my
life, was, at least formally, as class-bound as any society I have
ever lived in. The first — and chief — class distinction was the
patent one between officers and enlisted men. Officers ate,
slept, dressed, and were paid better. Obeisance needed to be
paid them in the form of salutes and in addressing them as "sir."
Theirs was a strikingly better deal; one didn't have to be Alexis
de Tocqueville to notice that. As an enlisted man who as a boy
was never required to learn the habits of obeisance, I could not
help marveling at the vast social discrepancies between officers
and enlisted men. I did not so much resent them as wonder how
career noncommissioned officers managed to tolerate them, especially in a peacetime army, when an officer's responsibilities
were less and the call on his bravery nonexistent. Confronted
for the first time with a codified class system, I found myself
more of a democrat than I had imagined.

At the same time that the U.S. Army was rigidly hierarchical
and held together by the idea of rank, no American institution
was, at its core, more democratic. Well in advance of the larger
society of which it was a part, the U.S. Army had integrated its
facilities and was color-blind in its promotions and other procedures. As an enlisted man, one was really thrown into the stew
of American life. In my own basic-training platoon I lived with
Missouri farmers, Appalachian miners, an American Indian
auto mechanic, a black car salesman from Detroit, a Jewish lawyer from Chicago, a fundamentalist high school teacher from
Kansas, and others no less varied but now lost to memory. It
felt, at moments, like living in a badly directed screen version of
Leaves of Grass. Although I groaned and cursed, questioning the
heavens for putting me through the torture in tedium that I
then took my time in the Army to be, I have since come to view
that time as one of the most interesting interludes in my life —
among other reasons because it jerked me free, if only for a few
years, from the social classes in which I have otherwise spent

nearly all my days. It jerked everyone free from his social class, however high or low that class may have been, and yet somehow, despite the jolt, it seemed to work.

Or at least it seemed to work most of the time. A case where it didn't was that of Samuel Schuyler III, whom I worked with as a fellow enlisted man in the Public Information Office at Fort Hood, Texas. The Third, as I always thought of him, had gone to the Wharton School of Business, hungered for the country-club ease he was missing while in the Army, and drove a black Cadillac convertible, the current year's model. Despite the numeral affixed to his name, the Third was without social pretensions; he was a simple hedonist and a straight money man. How he had come to own that Cadillac convertible at the age of twenty-three I never discovered — my own social-class manners, I now suppose, prevented me from asking — but he played the stock market fairly often, calling his broker in Pittsburgh to place his orders.

What was not difficult to discover was the Third's contempt for everyone around him, officers and enlisted men both. (Only a few acquaintances, of whom for some reason I was one, were spared.) Forms through which to express this contempt were not wanting to him. The Third had developed a salute that, while formally correct, made every officer to whom he tendered it think at least twice about it; there was about this salute the faint yet almost unmistakable suggestion that its recipient go forth to exercise an anatomical impossibility upon himself. Driving on the post in his black Cadillac, the Third was everywhere taken for the post commander — who himself drove a more modest car, a Buick — and everyone, even up to the rank of bird colonel, dropped everything to salute him, only to receive in turn the Third's own extraordinary salute. The Third even dressed with contempt. If there is a word that is the antonym of "panache," I should avail myself of it to describe the deliberately slovenly way that he wore his uniform. In mufti, meanwhile, no muted Ivy League dresser, the Third preferred draped trousers, alligator shoes, and in shirts showed an unfortunate penchant for the color known as dubonnet. Toward the close of his enlistment, the Third was promoted from Pfc. to Sp4c. but refused the promotion on the grounds that the additional money wasn't worth the trouble of sewing new patches on his uniforms.

No gesture better summed up his refusal to partake of military class arrangements; he scoffed at them every chance he got, making clear that, short of doing anything that could land him in the stockade, he chose not to play the game. His lofty contempt earned him a great deal of not-so-lofty-hatred. The Third knew he was hated and felt about this much as he did about his promotion — he could not, that is, have cared less.

I cared rather more, in the Army and elsewhere, because social class has always seemed to me intrinsically fascinating. I have inevitably been interested in attempting to take the measure of any class system in which I found myself, though when young I must often have been, as Henry James might have put it, destitute of the materials requisite for measurement. A fantasy about social class said to be common among children, especially children fed ample rations of fairy tales, is that one's parents are not one's real parents but instead that one is much higher born — and is probably, as will surely one day be revealed, a prince or princess. My fantasy, taken up in early adolescence and not quite dropped to this day, is that I can roam freely from social class to social class, comfortable everywhere and everywhere welcome. Sometimes I think it would be more realistic to believe that one is the last of the Romanovs.

Not that I am a proletarian fancier, the American equivalent of a Narodnik or a Slavophile. There is something inherently condescending in assigning special qualities to the lower class. Dorothy Parker, after being told that Clare Boothe Luce was always kind to her inferiors, is supposed to have asked, "And where does she find them?" But I like to view myself as being able to slip from class to class because I detest the notion of one's destiny being absolutely determined by birth and social upbringing; I readily grant the importance of both but not their decisiveness. I myself dislike being labeled too easily, being understood too quickly. Neither a strict Marxist nor a straight Freudian be — such is the advice of this old Polonius. Accept the possibility of all influences; reject the fiats of all absolute determinants.

The old, received wisdom about social class is that one is supposed to dislike the class just below one's own and gaze yearningly upon those above one's own. But I find that the only class whose members can sometimes get me worked up are the upper classes, or what is left of them after taxes and the Zeitgeist have done their work. A plummy upper-class English accent with nothing behind it but enormous self-satisfaction can, in the proper mood, still bring out the residual Red in me. My Anglophilia, which may have had behind it a certain social-class longing, seems to have slipped badly in recent years; today, apart from being somewhat regretful about not having gone to an Oxbridge college when a boy, I have only one regret about not being English, which is that, because I am not, I cannot be permitted to use the word "whilst" without seeming affected. The upper class of my own country now seems to me, when it is not sad, mostly comic. The traditional WASP-ocracy seems to have left the field without firing a shot; they resemble nothing so much as white Russians, with the serious proviso that they appear to have been forced into exile without actually leaving their own country. One reads about them nowadays at play in Newport or in Charleston, or in repose at the Somerset Club in Boston, or sees them decked out for a photographer from *Town & Country*, but they seem rather desiccated and plain tuckered out.

It is a bit difficult to have a serious class system when, as in this country at present, you don't have a convincing upper class. So long as there is a convincing upper class, other classes in the society at least know what to imitate, however absurd the imitation. I can attest to this when I recall that, in 1950, as a boy of thirteen growing up in a middle-class, mostly Jewish neighborhood, I and several of my pals attended a class in ballroom dancing called Fortnightly. It was held at the field house of a public park, was taught by a couple of very correct posture and general deportment whom I now think would be best described as "shabby genteel," and, despite the name Fortnightly, met every Saturday afternoon. What we did in this class was, in effect, prepare for a cotillion none of us would ever attend. Young ladies sat on one side of the room, young gentlemen on the other; young gentlemen crossed the room to ask young ladies to dance, and to dance waltzes, fox trots, and other, rather intricate dances and steps that this young gentleman, aging fast, has still never had to press into service.

The decisive moment in the defeat of upper-class, capital-*S* Society may have come when, in newspapers all over the nation, what used to be called the Society page was replaced by the Style section. The old Society page, with its accounts of engagements and weddings, charity balls and coming-out parties, tended to be boring and silly; while the new Style section, with its accounts of designer clothing, gourmandizing, and the trend of the moment, tends to be lively and silly. The Society page, like Society itself, began to go under sometime in the middle 1960s, which was not exactly a felicitous time for establishments of many kinds. Not that the sixties did away with class consciousness; it attempted instead to reorient such consciousness in favor of other classes. The animus of the sixties generation, expressed in its popular culture, was against both upper- and middle-class life. In their place it wished to substitute ethnic pride and, as expressed by such groups as the Beatles and the Rolling Stones, something of a working-class ethos, with sexual freedom and drug use added. Even in England, that most traditional of class-bound countries, according to the English journalist Jilly Cooper, "working-class became beautiful and everyone from Princess Anne downwards spat the plums out of their mouths, embraced the flat 'a' and talked with a working-class accent."

Not many people outside of it are likely to have been sorry to see the old upper class in this country pushed rudely to the sidelines. The upper class had a lot to apologize for, and in many ways it is still apologizing. In wealthy Fairfield County, Connecticut, in the town of Darien (the setting for Laura Hobson's novel about genteel anti-Semitism, *Gentleman's Agreement*), a local newspaper, according to the *New York Times*, ran an article by a high school girl attacking the town for its lack of social diversity. "I am," this girl wrote, "a white Protestant living in a basically white Protestant community. I lack the richness and cultural background gained from a diversified environment. What are you, the townspeople, going to do about it?" Few things so lower the morale, and raise the gorge, as being lectured to by one's own children. One of these things may be being lectured to on the same grounds by the clergymen of one's church, and no church in America has gone at this task more relentlessly than the Episcopalian church, once *the* church of the old upper classes if there is truth in the one-sentence sociology of religion that holds: A Methodist is a Baptist with shoes, a Presbyterian is a Methodist who has gone to college, and an Episcopalian is a Presbyterian living off his investments.

Although much that was once thought to represent upper-class life appears to have been routed, much more lives on, often in attenuated and snobbish form. Contemned the old upper class may be, yet the line of people hopefully awaiting their children's enrollment in such formerly exclusively upper-class prep schools as Choate, Groton, Exeter, and Saint Paul's has not, my guess is, in any serious way diminished. Most middle-class students who have a wide choice will tend to choose universities favored by the old upper classes; and most university professors, given a similar choice in institutions, will do the same — a tenured professor who has left Princeton for Purdue, or Harvard for Hofstra, or Yale for Ypsilanti Community College is a fit candidate for the television show called "That's Incredible."

Freud said that it was better to be an ancestor, which he turns out to have been, than to have ancestors, which he lacked. But surely better still is both to be an ancestor and to have ancestors. In literary life I can think of at least three living writers whose careers owe more than a little to upper-class cachet: Gore Vidal, who at every opportunity brings his family connections into his writing; William F. Buckley, who attempts to live like an aristocrat, though without much in the way of aristocratic leisure; and George Plimpton, whose many autobiographical books on the subject of sports have about them something of the aura of slumming. (I do not count Louis Auchincloss, a novelist whose subject is often the eclipse of the upper class in which he grew up.) All three men are, in accent, neither chummy nor unplummy.

If he were still alive, I should most certainly count in Robert Lowell, whose ancestors were reputed to speak only to God and who, before his death, was generally conceded to be this country's first poet. Without for a moment claiming that Lowell set out to exploit his upper-class genealogy, neither can one for another moment disclaim the importance of that genealogy to Lowell's poetry. Elizabeth Bishop once told Lowell: "All you have to do is put down the names! And the fact that it seems significant, illustrative, American, etc., gives you, I think, the confidence you display about tackling any idea or theme, *seriously*, in both writing and conversation. In some ways you are the luckiest poet I know." Was Elizabeth Bishop correct? Let us change some of those names she claimed Lowell had only to mention. What if Lowell's poem "My Last Afternoon with Uncle Devereux Winslow" were instead entitled "My Last Afternoon with Uncle Morris Shapiro," or his "Terminal Days at Beverly Farms" were instead entitled "Terminal Days at Grossinger's"? (Actually, given that resort's famously rich provender, any day at Grossinger's could be terminal.) Not quite the same, perhaps you will agree.

But then neither is anti-Semitism in the United States quite the same as it once was, or else I could not make the kind of easy joke that I just did about the titles of Robert Lowell's poems, at least not in print. Whether anti-Semitism is today less, whether racism has greatly diminished, cannot be known with certainty; my sense is that they both are much reduced. But what can be known is that neither is any longer officially recognized in restricted or segregated arrangements, and this, along with marking impressive progress, has made for significant changes in the American class system. Whereas the retreat of the old upper class has blown the roof off the system, the demise of official and quasi-official discrimination has uprooted the basement. The metaphor I seem to be building toward here is a class system that resembles an open-air ranch house. Strange edifice, this, but then socially many strange things appear to have taken place in recent years. In many industries union wages have placed many union workers, financially at least, into the upper reaches of the middle class, while attending college, once the ultimate rite of passage into solid middle-class respectability, no longer inevitably accomplishes this task — owing doubtless to the spread and watering down of higher education. There is a great deal of senseless and haphazard luxury in the land. Athletes and rock stars, many of them made millionaires before they are thirty, are removed from the financial wars for all their days. Meanwhile a servant class has all but disappeared. A daughter from the working class uses part of her wages from working at the supermarket to buy designer jeans, while a son of Scarsdale comes into Manhattan to acquire his duds at a

Salvation Army thrift shop. The other day, in a parking lot near where I live, I noted a rather dingy Saab automobile, with an antenna for a telephone on its roof, an Oberlin College decal on its back window, and bumper stickers reading "National Computer Camp" and "I Support Greenpeace." Now there is a vehicle with a lot of class — and, symbolic of our time, a lot of class confusions.

If that car isn't owned by someone from what today passes for the upper-middle class, I'll buy you a salmon mousse and a manual on how your children can raise their SAT scores fully thirty points. "The upper-middle classes," writes Jilly Cooper, "are the most intelligent and highly educated of all the classes, and therefore the silliest and most sensitive to every new trend: radical chic, health food, ethnic clothes, bra-lessness, gifted children, French cooking." The members of the upper-middle class that Miss Cooper has in mind are mostly newly risen and, not always sure where they are, insecure about where they are headed. This upper-middle class is not to be confused with the nouveau riche. The former tends to be rather better educated, immensely concerned with what it understands to be good taste, and serious if also a little worried about culture — very little that one could think of, in fact, would be more wounding to members of this upper-middle class than to be taken for nouveau riche. I think I know what I am talking about here; this upper-middle class is my milieu — or, as the writer Josephine Herbst used to call it, my "maloo."

When I say that the upper-middle class is my maloo, I do not mean that I am quite of that class. Strictly speaking, I am fairly sure that I do not qualify financially. I do not drive a BMW, a Mercedes, or a Jaguar; I do not dream of driving such cars, and if I leave the earth without owning one or the other of them, I shall not, for that reason, die with a frown on my face (I cannot otherwise promise to depart smiling). I own no works of art, nor do I aspire to own anything above the level of an unnumbered print. No espresso machine sits on the counter of my kitchen, no mousse molds sit upon the shelves of my cabinets. From the tax standpoint, I do not earn enough money now, nor do I soon expect to earn enough, to cry out, in the words of the rock 'n' roll song, "Gimme shelter." Do not get me wrong. I should not in the least mind driving off in a Mercedes 380 SL, a Turner watercolor locked in its trunk, on my way to have a cappuccino with my tax lawyer. But my mind, the great wanderer, does not linger long on such things. Expensive good taste, that sine qua non of the new upper-middle class, is not my sine qua non. I do not despise it; I am not in the least uncomfortable around it; but I do not live for it.

What, then, do I live for? Apart from love for my family and friends, I live for words. I live for the delights of talking and reading and writing. I am content when talking with people I adore or admire or at least feel I can learn a little something from; I am happy when I am reading something fine or subtle or powerful; and I am delirious when I am writing something of which I am not altogether ashamed. If one's social class is defined, at least in part, by one's wishes, then I ought perhaps to be defined as a member of what I think of as the verbal class — someone, that is, who both earns his livelihood and derives his greatest pleasure from words. Membership in the verbal class has its advantages and its disadvantages: the hours are a bit crazy, but, like the village idiot posted at the town gates to await the arrival of the messiah, at least you are never out of work.

The term "verbal class" is meant to be almost purely descriptive; nothing, certainly, honorific is intended by it. Orwell, who did not use the term "verbal class," did once refer to "the new aristocracy" of professors, publicists, and journalists who in large part comprise the verbal class; he did so in the portion of *1984* that purports to be from Emmanuel Goldstein's manuscript, where this new aristocracy is described as "less tempted by luxury, hungrier for pure power" than their opposite numbers in past ages. In Chekhov's time the verbal class of our day and the new aristocracy of *1984* would have been described as the intelligentsia. This is the same intelligentsia of whom Chekhov, in a letter to a friend, writes: "I have no faith in our intelligentsia; it is hypocritical, dishonest, hysterical, ill-bred, and lazy." Which made them, in Chekhov's view, quite as wretched as any other social class, though perhaps a bit worse because the pretensions of the intelligentsia were more extravagant and its complaints better formulated and more insistently expressed. Read Chekhov and, in questions of social class, one soon becomes a Chekhovian. "I have faith in individuals," he wrote. "I see salvation in individuals scattered here and there . . . be they intellectuals or peasants, for they're the ones who really matter, though they are few."

Yet my sense is that the verbal class has risen slightly in recent years. It has not done so, near as I can make out, because of any improvement in its members' general mental acuity or civic valor. The verbal class appears instead to be rising by default. Members of the verbal class, odd fish that they are, seem able to swim easily through a fluid social scene — and the American social scene at present seems extremely fluid. John Adams spoke of his studying "politics and war that my sons may have the liberty to study mathematics and philosophy," but what would he have thought of men who studied real estate and the stock market that their daughters may have the liberty to study Marxist historiography and their sons become, through downward mobility, carpenters in Vancouver? He would probably think his wife, Abigail, very clever for describing the American people as "the mobility."

"Classless Soviet Is Far Off, Siberian Scholar Says." So read a recent headline in the *New York Times*. It is difficult to doubt such authority, for surely one of the quickest ways of telling that a classless society is far off is merely to live in Siberia. My guess is that a classless society is roughly as near completion in the Soviet Union as it is in the United States — which isn't very near at all. Not that this even remotely suggests the need for intensifying the class struggle. Take it from a member of the verbal class: in a real class struggle one is lucky to end up with a draw, except that it inevitably turns out to have been a very bloody draw.

I see the serious class struggle as that of men and women singly fighting off being entirely shaped by the social class into which they were born. Insularity, unimaginativeness, self-satisfaction — each social class has its own special drawbacks, blindnesses, vices. "Vices" reminds me of a story a friend of mine, a man born into the English working class, used to tell about a shop class he was required to take at a grammar school in London. It was taught by a flinty little Scotsman who, when he wanted the class's attention in order to make an announcement, used to cry out, "Stand by your vices, boys!" When we think too exclusively as members of our social class, we all, essentially, stand by our vices. I should have thought the trick of becoming a human being is to stand away from them.

GARY GIDDINS

"This Guy Wouldn't Give You the Parsley off His Fish"

FROM GRAND STREET

I BECAME INTERESTED in Jack Benny in the early 1970s, when I saw him live. The occasion was a New York concert appearance by George Burns, who, after several years of relative inactivity, was embarking on his highly successful comeback. Benny came along to introduce him. It took him about ten minutes, and I don't remember a word he said. But I've never forgotten that as soon as he walked out — body flouncing, arms swinging to breast-pocket level, eyes glazed with stoic chagrin — I was convulsed with laughter, an effect his TV appearances had never had on me. If Burns was good, Benny was magical. During the past year my impressions of that evening have been confirmed almost nightly, thanks to the Christian Broadcasting Network. CBN harvests souls by day, but by night it lures prospective recruits with back-to-back reruns of old programs by those same wily Jewish comedians, Burns and Benny. After a year of late-night viewing, often of shows that I recalled from childhood with a rather indifferent fondness, I've become a Jack Benny zealot, recounting bits and anecdotes, hoarding pregnant pauses and martyred stares, and even composing this tract. Here was a radiantly funny man, whose humor stands up against all odds.

The fact that I can't recall anything Benny said in concert is germane, since he may be the only great comedian in history who isn't associated with a single witticism. He got his biggest laughs with two exclamations — "Now cut that out!" and "Well!"

— and impeccably timed silences. When he died in 1974, I
watched the news stories for samples of his jokes. There weren't
any. The one bit they frequently played came from radio:
Benny, out for a stroll, hears footsteps behind him. A holdup
man says, "Your money or your life." Benny says . . . nothing,
for a very long time. That's the joke. But it isn't the topper. The
holdup man repeats his threat and Benny shouts, "I'm thinking
it over!" On the original radio broadcast, he followed through
with yet a third variation on the theme: the holdup man gets
abusive and Benny, a model of agitated innocence, responds,
"If you wanted money, why didn't you just ask for it?" Needless
to say, none of this is funny if you don't know the character
of Jack Benny. What an arduous exercise it would be to try
and explain Benny's unprecedented and unequaled success in
American comedy to an audience unfamiliar with the sound of
his voice or the pan on his face. Happily, that task is not yet
necessary.

Everyone I know knows Benny, though the degree of knowledge depends on age. Those under forty remember him from
TV; those over forty remember him chiefly from radio (specifi-
cally, a Sunday-night-at-seven ritual so widespread that in 1943
NBC declared the time slot his no matter what sponsor bought
it). Benny was a comic institution for about forty years and
apparently had no detractors — though Benny wouldn't have
been too sure. In his later years, an insurance group eager to
use him in its newspaper ads hired a marketing researcher to
measure his popularity. The company was elated by the results:
he was loved by 97 percent of the American public — a higher
number than for anyone else. "What did I do to that three
percent?" Benny wanted to know.

  Yet the character he created and developed with inspired
tenacity all those years — certainly one of the longest runs ever
by an actor in the same role — was that of a mean, vainglorious
skinflint: a pompous ass at best, a tiresome bore at near best. To
find his equal, you have to leave the realm of monologists and
delve into the novel for a recipe that combines Micawber and
Scrooge, with perhaps a dash of Lady Catherine de Bourgh and
a soupçon of Chichikov; or, better still, a serial character like
Sherlock Holmes, who proved so resilient that not even Conan

Doyle could knock him off. The Benny character was no less fully rounded — an obsessed fan, armed with hundreds of broadcasts, might construct a reasonably detailed biography of him. On the other hand, no one believed Doyle was Holmes, while many people believed Benny was "Benny," a phenomenon that amazed the actor as much as a literary parallel would later distress Philip Roth. A lawyer once dunned him with outraged letters for refusing to pay Rochester his piddling back wages (a plot contrivance on radio); the exasperated Benny finally wrote him, "I only hope you're making in one year what Rochester makes in one month."

Many of the veteran entertainers who pioneered on radio, exchanging a string of vaudeville theaters for millions of living rooms, were surprised by the new audience's credulity and the implications. A fan once asked Gracie Allen if Benny was really cheap; she responded, "Am I stupid?" Yet Benny, like Roth, courted trouble by injecting just enough reality into his work to confuse the issue, and by sustaining his conceit — this, perhaps, was his greatest achievement — through all the fashions that attended the Depression, the Second World War, the affluent society, and the switch to television. Once he established his image, he remained intransigently loyal to it. No but-seriously-folks closers or nice-guy apologias for him. Unlike every other comedian you can name, he never stepped out of character. He seems to have sensed early on the new medium's potential as a mirror for the more commonplace foibles of a mass audience. In any case, he emerged over the decades as a comic staple who could bind the sensibilities of several generations.

Meredith wrote of Molière that he "did not paint in raw realism [but] seized his characters firmly for the purpose of the play, stamped them in the idea, and, by slightly raising and softening the object of his study . . . generalized upon it so as to make it permanently human." Benny's fictions evolved so humanly that the actors who incarnated them ended up adopting the names of their roles. Eddie Anderson had many credits before he joined the Benny crew, but was thereafter known in private life as Rochester. Owen Patrick McNulty legally changed his name to Dennis Day after his first four years with Benny; his family convinced him to change it back, but he performed exclusively as Day. Sayde Marks, Benny's wife, assumed the name of the

dumb gentile shopgirl she played and remained Mary Livingstone Benny even after retirement. Benny also underwent
a name change, though not to suit a script. During his apprentice years in vaudeville, his real name, Benjamin Kubelsky,
prompted two law suits — the first from a violinist named Ku-
belik who thought a violin-playing Kubelsky would confuse people; the second from Ben Bernie, who complained that the
resulting pseudonym, Benny K. Benny, was a deception designed to cash in on Bernie's fame. ("Now Jack Osterman is
suing me," Benny used to tell friends, referring to a comic of
the day.)

If the Benny character looms as a kind of metafiction, it isn't in
Victorian novels that its genesis is to be found. Benny virtually
invented situation comedy, and like most significant innovations, his was a natural outgrowth of local traditions: the American stereotypes and modes of entertainment predominant at
the turn of the century. When Benny came along, minstrelsy's
ritualistic subordination of individual performers to a faceless
— or blackfaceless — group was on the wane, but the idiom's
conventions had a lasting influence. The minstrel olio was the
first American variety show, typifying theatrical fragmentation
and creating such enduring specialties as the Irish tenor (who
traditionally sang the first solo), the stout announcer and buf-
foon (Mr. Interlocutor), sketch dialogues (Mr. Tambo and Mr.
Bones), and grotesque caricatures of every racial and ethnic
group.
    Vaudeville, its immediate heir, freed the specialty acts from
an oppressive scheme, not to mention blackface, and forced the
performers to assume more individual identities. Still, nostalgia
for the old minstrel troupes lingered. The first variety show ever
broadcast was a 1924 performance by Dailey Paskman's Radio
Minstrels, and tributes to minstrel stars regularly turned up on
radio and in movies through the mid-1940s. During the broadcast première for the 1940 film *Love Thy Neighbor*, the banter
between Benny and Fred Allen turned into a kind of minstrel
badinage, which prompted Benny to ad lib (and fluff!) a reference to Mr. Tambo: "We'll go right into a black routine," he
said, imitating the endmen laugh. "Yuk, yuk, yuk." He had a
right to patronize the old style. The best of the untethered,

unmasked comics on the vaudeville circuit had long since origi-
nated more precise and inventive personae, often working in
pairs — a straight man with a laugh getter. Sketch humor had
come into its own.

Into that world, enter Benjamin Kubelsky, a very young and
eager violinist manqué. He was born on Saint Valentine's Day,
1894, in Waukegan, Illinois, the son of Russian immigrants and
Orthodox Jews. At six he began violin lessons and at eight was
acclaimed a local prodigy; at twelve he persuaded a friend to
get him a job in a theater and worked his way up from ticket
taker to usher to musician in the pit orchestra. He must have
been pretty good, because Minnie Marx tried to hire him as
music director when her sons played the theater, an offer his
parents made him decline. In 1912 Benny was expelled from
high school and went on the road with a flashy pianist and
veteran performer named Cora Salisbury. When she retired
after the season, he teamed with another pianist and in 1916
the act of Benny and Lyman played the Palace theater at $250
a week. They did eleven minutes of musical parody, and although *Variety* called it a "pleasing turn for an early spot," they
flopped. Benny returned home when he learned his mother was
dying; a year later he joined the Navy, where he devised a
routine with the famous novelty composer and pianist Zez Con-
frey. More significantly, he also did his first monologue in a
Navy show that eventually toured the Midwest. By the time he
returned to the civilian circuit, Benny was concentrating on
getting laughs while holding on to the violin as a prop. He
was billed as "Benny K. Benny: Fiddle Funology," then "Jack
Benny: Fun with a Fiddle," and finally "A Few Minutes with
Jack Benny."

Robert Benchley praised his cool bravado and subtlety when
Benny returned to the Palace in 1924, but others panned him
for what they construed as egotism and aloofness. Benny was
studying other comics to learn how to sustain narratives and
raiding joke books for one-liners, including occasional "cheap
jokes" — for example, "I took my girl to dinner, and she
laughed so hard at one of my jokes that she dropped her tray."
Nevertheless, he was regularly employed. Nora Bayes hired and
romanced him, and the Shuberts installed him in the revue
Great Temptations, on which tour he courted and married eight-

een-year-old Sadye Marks. Never a major vaudeville star, Benny appeared in three unsuccessful movies and worked mostly as an emcee during the next few years. Yet he was making good money in 1930 — at least $1,500 a week — as the comic in *Earl Carroll's Vanities,* when he faced up to the fact that vaudeville was through and began looking beyond it.

Ed Sullivan gave Benny his first radio shot in 1931; he opened with, "Ladies and gentlemen, this is Jack Benny talking. There will be a slight pause while you say, 'Who cares?' " No one did, but the following summer his agent got him a job as emcee on a show featuring George Olson's band. Benny experimented with topical humor, and began kidding movies and the sponsor ("I was driving across the Sahara desert when I came across a party of people . . . ready to perish from lack of liquid. I gave them each a glass of Canada Dry Ginger Ale, and not one of them said it was a bad drink"). By summer's end, he had made a terrifying discovery. Radio consumed material faster than he could get it. A joke that might have worked for a whole season in vaud was good for only one night on radio.

In 1934, at age forty, Benny saw the promised land. His guide was a writer George Burns had introduced him to named Harry Conn, who seems to have played Herman Mankiewicz to Benny's Orson Welles. Accounts differ about Conn's contribution, since they parted bitterly a few years later, but there is no doubt — Benny himself was emphatic about it — that Conn was instrumental in conceiving the brainstorm that revolutionized radio: situation comedy based on the lives of the performers, complete with sophisticated sound effects. Instead of revue skits and strings of jokes, each show would be a variation on a constant theme: life with Jack Benny. It was Conn's misfortune to underestimate the importance of Benny's delivery, timing, personality, and script editing in making the initial concept work. Once the idea was established, writers could be replaced, as Conn was when his demands grew unreasonable. But before that happened, he and Benny came up with many of the motifs that would become the star's trademarks: the scenes set in his home, the Irish tenor, the cheerful announcer, the dumb girlfriend, the obnoxious band leader, and the *reductio ad absurdum* of shows that depicted only a mock rehearsal for the show on the air. It was not an immediate hit; in 1934, the *New York World*

Telegram named Benny the most popular comedian on radio, but two sponsors dropped him. Not until 1936 and 1937, when Rochester and Phil Harris joined the cast, did the Benny phenomenon take hold.

When Benny surpassed Eddie Cantor in the ratings in 1937 as the most popular star on radio — a position he maintained for most of the next fifteen years — he rang the death knell, symbolic and real, for vaudeville. Cantor later remarked, "He made all the other comics throw away their joke files." His popularity had no equal in radio, then or ever. Utterly stymied by Benny's success on NBC, CBS produced an ambitious series of topical dramas for the Sunday-at-seven slot, because no sponsor would buy the time. (The notion of combating popularity with quality seems rather quaint today: CBS, which bought Benny's radio show in 1948 and made a fortune with it, canceled him on TV in 1964, when "Gomer Pyle" beat him in the ratings.) As Fred Allen told Maurice Zolotow in 1950, "Practically all comedy shows on the radio today owe their structure to Benny's conceptions. He was the first to realize that the listener is not in a theater with a thousand other people but is in a small circle at home. . . . Benny also was the first comedian in radio to realize that you could get big laughs by ridiculing yourself instead of your stooges. Benny became a fall guy for everybody else on the show." Or as Benny put it, "The whole humor of Jack Benny is — here's a guy with plenty of money, he's got a valet, he's always traveling around, and yet he's strictly a jerk."

Some jerk. Everyone knows a few things about radio's Jack Benny: he was eternally thirty-nine, cheap, bald, self-admiring, drove a dilapidated Maxwell (is there any other kind?), lived alone with a valet named Rochester, and had irresistably blue eyes. With the possible exception of the last, none of this was true of the real Jack Benny; in fact, he had to eliminate the bald jokes when he moved to television. Henri Bergson wrote, "The comic comes into being just when society and the individual, freed from the worry of self-preservation, begin to regard themselves as works of art." Benny honed that generalization to a lunatic specificity: he made himself a clown by acting the part of an artwork. No matter how many humiliations he had to endure, his self-esteem remained untouched; like cartoon characters who fall off cliffs, are momentarily flattened, and quickly restored, Benny and his vanity were emboldened by adversity. The better the audience knew that, the less he had to do for a laugh. *He* was the laugh. All he had to do was trigger a few buzzwords. A carnival pitchman bets him a quarter that he can correctly guess Benny's age, and guesses thirty-nine. Benny simply gazes helplessly, and the audience is right with him, agonizing over his hopeless choice between the quarter and his vanity.

He opened one television show by striding center stage and calmly announcing, "Well, here I am again, standing in front of millions of viewers, completely relaxed, and not a worry in the world. Now, some critics will attribute this to my years of experience; others will say it's the temperament of a true artist. Personally, I feel that it's nauseating confidence." Right away, the audience likes him. Yet he continues in a mode of fake candor, as though he were stepping out of character: "My psychology in starting out with a remark like that is to get you people to dislike me immediately. Then when you realize you're disliking a nice, harmless, elderly man, this gives you a guilt complex. Guilt leads to sympathy, sympathy leads to laughter, and laughter leads to applause. And then when the applause is over, you go home and I go to the bank. That's when I laugh."

Money, and Benny's affection for it, was his most successful leitmotif, one that required some courage to pursue, since it underscored the most persistent of negative Jewish stereotypes (and yet another convention of minstrelsy). Of course, by carrying it off so well, Benny helped to dispel penuriousness as an anti-Jewish barb. Still, this was a matter of concern to him. In 1945, at the height of the fad for radio contests, his show offered a prize to the listener who could best explain "Why I Hate Jack Benny" in twenty-five words or less. Benny approved the idea, but worried about inviting anti-Semitic responses and asked that they be pulled. Of 270,000 entries, only three were offensive. Benny's Jewishness, in the context of his comedy, is a rather complicated issue, and the manner in which he broached it suggests the degree to which the Jews of his generation felt, in Bergson's phrase, "freed from the worry of self-preservation."

Before 1900 Jewish grotesquerie was a familiar ingredient in the entertainment world, but Jewish humor that wasn't self-deflating simply didn't exist on the American stage. "There were plenty of excellent Jewish performers," according to vaudeville's chronicler Douglas Gilbert, "but they were doing Dutch, blackface, or singing and dancing acts. Some of them were good Irish comedians. Indeed, Weber and Fields at one time did a neat Irish act." Gilbert traces the emergence of Jewish humor to the Mauve Decade success of one Frank Bush, whose doggerel included:

> Oh, my name is Solomon Moses I'm a bully Sheeny man,
> I always treat my customers the very best what I can.
> I keep a clothing store 'way down on Baxter Street,
> Where you can get your clothing I sell so awful cheap.

But no single performer can liberate a people's pragmatic instinct to keep their ethnicity under cover. Something more, a confident sense of assimilation, is necessary. Years later, Al Jolson seemed to personify and answer that need: first he Anglicized his name and hid behind blackface, then he wiped it off to emerge as a celebrity whose renown in the Jazz Age was rivaled only by that of Babe Ruth and Charles Lindbergh. As Jack Robin (in *The Jazz Singer*), he was the Augie March of his time — a fast-talking all-American hustler who could discard or employ his Jewish roots with equal facility. Which isn't to say that Jewish entertainers weren't apprehensive about their gradual acceptance as Jews; even in the Hollywood of the thirties and forties, Jewish producers avoided Jewish subjects, and Jewish actors played Italians.

Benny's ambivalence about Jewish humor runs throughout his program. Mary Livingstone, who variously turned up as his wife, girlfriend, or just another prickly opponent, had no Jewish characteristics. Benny drew directly on his own Jewishness only rarely. In a TV episode, he auditions actors to play his father in a movie to be based on his life. One actor identifies himself, with a thick burr, as Kevin O'Houlihan. Benny stares haplessly into the camera before blurting, "NEXT!" On a radio show, guest star Bing Crosby told of how he'd been rejected by a country club for being an actor. Benny ad-libbed, "How would you like to be an actor *and* a Jew?" To his friends, he was the quintessential Jewish monologist. The harmonica virtuoso Larry Adler,

who toured with him and considered himself a disciple, told me
that Benny "not only epitomized Jewish storytelling and intonation, but showed everyone else how to do it." That intonation
comes across more clearly in off-camera interviews and, oddly
enough, his highly amusing letters — some of which are collected in Irving A. Fein's *Jack Benny: An Intimate Biography* —
than on the air. Nevertheless, the Benny program employed
two Jewish dialecticians — Sam Hearn in the early years, and
later the more enduring Mr. Kitzel (played by Artie Auerbach).

A harmless middle-aged man who speaks with a chirpy Ellis
Island twang and wears a glassy-eyed smile, Mr. Kitzel is the
only recurring character who doesn't treat Benny like a jerk. No
matter how harassed he is, Benny is always delighted to hear
Mr. Kitzel's "Hallo, Mr. Benny," and to play straight man for
his corny jokes. Mr. Kitzel isn't nearly as funny as the other cast
members (especially Frank Nelson as a maddening repertory
character with prim mustache and uniquely chromatic way of
saying "Ye-e-e-e-s?"), but for Benny he represents one bright
moment amid a regimen of humiliations. On an early TV show,
Benny takes the Beverly Hills Beavers, a boys' club, to the carnival. Mr. Kitzel plays a utility man who keeps turning up in
different guises — first selling hot dogs, then in a gorilla suit,
and so forth. The show ends when the boys want to see the belly
dancer, and Benny says he doesn't think it would be right. We
zoom in on the dancer's face, and hear Mr. Kitzel's voice as she
lip-synchs, "It's all right, Mr. Benny, it's only me." Benny turns
an amazed smile to the camera, shrugs his shoulders, and leads
the pack into her tent.

Benny was probably wise not to make too many direct Jewish
allusions. After all, his alter ego embodied enough standard
Jewish stereotypes not only to effect the anti-Semitic backlash
he feared but to intimate the self-denigrating humor of early
vaud. He toted a violin, ogled himself like a girl, mistreated the
help, and hid his money in a dungeon surrounded by a moat.
Yet he played the role with such originality and brio that his
failings seemed at once too particularized and too broad to represent an ethnic group. His moot sexuality is a good example of
his restraint. In a TV episode, he explains to Rochester why the
studio wants to film his life: "I wasn't exactly the first choice, but
they found out mine was the only life they wouldn't have to

GARY GIDDINS   111

censor. [Intent pause.] Darn it!" Though he was eternally youthful (else the age jokes wouldn't have seemed quite so crafty)
and, at least in his early years, a great success with women,
Benny so convincingly embodied the ineffectual fop that he
became a professional neuter — sexless even when playing opposite Carole Lombard in his best film, *To Be or Not to Be.*

On radio, Benny was sexually anchored by Mary; on TV, he
became slightly hysterical (floozy Barbara Nichols played his
occasional date). He was surrounded by sexuality that was vulgar (Phil Harris), sly (Rochester), and placid (guest couples such
as the Ronald Colmans on radio or the Jimmy Stewarts on TV).
But Benny remained a naïf, a momma's boy without a momma,
or, more precisely and odd, a momma's boy with a black male
servant for a momma. Yet unlike Johnny Carson, who, for all
Benny's obvious influence on him, is sexually cold and untouch-
able, Benny was warm and intensely physical — constantly pat-
ting the hands of his female guests and wrapping his arms
around the shoulders of his male friends. (Benny prefigured
the "Tonight" show host in his movie *The Big Broadcast of 1937.*
He played a radio host named Jack Carson, who boosts his
ratings by having a couple get married on the air, à la Tiny
Tim.)
    Most of Benny's character traits evolved accidentally. If a cer-
tain joke worked one week, he played a variation on it the next.
The age jokes, for example, didn't start until he was fifty-five,
and a nurse in a sketch asked him his age; he paused and said
thirty-six. It got a big laugh, so he remained thirty-six for the
rest of the season. The following year, he was thirty-seven; in
the next, thirty-eight. He decided to freeze at thirty-nine because it's a funnier number than forty. Of course, his most
fertile subject was his stinginess, an angle that produced count-
less variants. Here is a small garland of them:

    He pays his agent 9 percent.
    He keeps Mary's fur in his refrigerator: it's "a better deal than the
        storage company."
    He plays a one-hundred-dollar Stradivarius — "one of the few *ever*
        made in Japan."
    For fifteen years, he drove a 1927 Maxwell — sound effects by Mel

Blanc — which he reluctantly sacrificed to the wartime need for scrap metal. Reborn as a bomber, it made the same sputtering noises.

When traveling, he pawns his parrot rather than leave it at the pet shop at seventy-five cents a day.

He stays at the Acme Plaza in New York — the basement suite, which "underlooks the park."

The act of pulling a dime out of his pocket produces suction.

He discovers his tux is stained. Rochester: "That's what you get when you rent a dress suit." Benny: "Well, let's be careful who we rent it out to."

When Fred Allen visits him in the 1945 movie *It's in the Bag*, Allen finds a hat-check girl in the closet and a cigarette machine in the living room. "This guy wouldn't give you the parsley off his fish," Allen mutters.

Benny's secretary calls a cab for him, and is told it'll take two hours. "Are they that busy?" he asks. "No, they say they'd like time to think it over."

A terrorist throws a rock through Benny's window with a note that warns, "Get out of town before it's too late." "Hmmm," Benny muses, "just a note, no ticket."

At the race track, Benny says, "I hope I win. I can sure use the money." Mary: "Why? You've never used any before."

On TV, Benny lives in characteristic middle-class, sit-com modesty — his house and those of his movie-star neighbors could easily be exchanged for the dwellings on "Father Knows Best" or "Leave It to Beaver." On radio, however, his vault is somehow located in a subterranean passage, protected by a drawbridge, a moat, a creaking door, a guard who hasn't seen daylight since the Civil War, and finally a combination safe. "You must have a million dollars in the vault," Mary assures him when he worries about money. "I know," he says, "but I hate to break up the serial numbers."

Benny's cast of characters was fine-tuned by the same hit-and-miss system that produced his most enduring conceits. Some performers remained with him for decades. The most celebrated was Eddie Anderson, a vaudeville star whose appearance as a Pullman porter in a 1937 episode was so successful that he was brought back as Benny's valet. He continued as Benny's long-suffering but shrewd and frequently impertinent sidekick until he retired twenty-one years later. As Rochester Van Jones,

Anderson delivered a brazenly hoarse counterpoint to Benny's spry chatter, and usually got the best lines. On his day off, Rochester might don an outrageously gaudy smoking jacket, sprawl on a chaise sipping mint julep and smoking a cigar, refusing even to answer the phone. But he earned those days. Rochester had to dip his typewriter ribbon in grape juice because Benny wouldn't replace it. When Benny tried to talk him out of installing his own phone, assuring him he could use his, Rochester said, "I know, boss, but look at it this way. Suppose the house is burning down and I haven't got any change?" They didn't quite love each other; but they were thoroughly at home in each other's company. One Christmas, Rochester asked a department store clerk to help him choose a gift.

Clerk: What kind of man is your boss? Is he the athletic type?
Rochester: No.
C: The intellectual type?
R: Well, no.
C: The executive type?
R: Hmmm, no.
C: Perhaps the outdoor type?
R: NO!
C: Well, perhaps he's the playboy type.
R: (Laughs.)
C: I'm afraid there isn't very much left.
R: That's him!

It was a source of pride to Benny and his staff that when the NAACP and other groups condemned the portrayal of blacks in the media in the 1950s, there was no protest about Rochester. Nor could anyone doubt Benny's personal feelings: in 1940 he refused to perform or board in segregated establishments, and in 1968 he returned $17,000 rather than fulfill a touring contract that would have taken him to South Africa. Yet his public image was utterly nonpolitical. Indeed, his refusal to link his comedy to serious issues made him especially valuable in the 1960s, when everyone else made a show of taking sides. Benny continued to fulfill the comedian's contract to focus on manners rather than morals. I've been able to find only one instance of his making a political statement: "I am neither a Democrat nor a Republican. I'm a registered Whig. If it was good enough for

President Fillmore, it's good enough for me. Now don't laugh about President Fillmore. After all, he kept us out of Vietnam."

I don't imagine there will ever be another generation of entertainers who can sustain the loyalties of successive generations as Benny and a handful of his contemporaries did. President Kennedy is said to have been eager to meet Benny because he recalled the Sunday evening ritual in the 1930s when his father made the whole family sit around the radio. The tempo of life, the dissolution of family entertainment, and the increasing disposability of popular culture have imposed new imperatives and standards. Does this mean that Benny himself will simply fade away? Will the very character-induced economy that enabled him to get laughs simply by staring into the camera undermine the effectiveness of his programs when the character is no longer widely known? One innovative cultural critic, John A. Kouwenhoven, has suggested that the strengths of American art lie in its open-endedness, in its fulfillment of Emerson's dictum that man is great "not in his goals but in his transitions." Situation comedies, like other American variations in high and low culture — including skyscrapers, jazz, *Leaves of Grass,* comic strips, the Constitution, and soap operas (to use some of Kouwenhoven's examples) — derive their integrity not from a notion of finalization but from process and continuity. They are designed with interchangeable parts, to be altered and disposed. What survives is the motivating idea, the germinal core.

Benny himself was a remarkably adaptable figure in the entertainment world, taking every technological twist and popular fashion in stride and refusing to wallow in sentimentality and nostalgia. Yet his radio shows are largely inaccessible to contemporary tastes, as are virtually all radio shows from the pre-TV era — except to satisfy those same maudlin longings Benny rejected. The TV shows are another story, chiefly because we still live in a television age. Ironically, despite the visual humor and the irresistible physical presence of Benny, they are not as richly made as the radio series. But they will suffice to keep Benny from becoming primarily a show business metaphor — much as films kept Will Rogers and W. C. Fields from becoming mere metaphors respectively of cracker-barrel wisdom and inebriated impudence. In the relaxed ambiance of Benny's TV skits, a singular clown holds his ground — "completely relaxed, and

not a worry in the world." The viewer who hasn't been primed
on the fine points of Benny's world will pick them up soon
enough; though even a naïve viewer may find Benny's preposterous carriage and delivery sufficient to evoke a deeply, and
perhaps unexpectedly, satisfied smile. It's not the situations in
Benny's comedy that compel attention; it's Benny himself — or,
more accurately, Benny qua "Benny" — a peculiarly durable
character.

DONALD HALL

Winter

FROM HOOD MUSEUM OF ART EXHIBITION CATALOGUE*

IN NEW HAMPSHIRE we know ourselves by winter — in snow, in cold, in darkness. For some of us the first true snow begins it; for others winter begins with the first bruising assault of zero weather; there is yet another sort, light-lovers, for whom winter begins with dark's onset in mid-August. If we wake as we ought to at 5:30, we begin waking in darkness; and dawn turns throaty with the ululations of photophiliacs, noctophobics, some of whom are fanatical enough to begin lamentation late in the month of June — when dawn arrives at 4:32 A.M. and yesterday it arrived at 4:31:30. On June 22 my wife exchanges postcards of commiseration with a fellow in Michigan who is another amorist of light. Fortunately this mountain has an upside as well as a downside. When in January daylight lasts half a minute longer every day, Jane's faint green leaves take on color, she leans south toward Kearsarge and the low, brief but lengthening pale winter sun; an observer can spy the faint buds that will burst into snowdrops in April, daffodils in April, tulips in May . . .

Some of us, on the other hand, are darkness-lovers. We do not *dislike* the early and late daylight of June, whippoorwill's graytime, but we cherish the gradually increasing dark of November, which we wrap around ourselves in the prosperous warmth of woodstove, oil, electric blanket, storm window, and insulation. We are partly tuber, partly bear. Inside our warmth we fold ourselves in the dark and the cold — around us, outside

* A version of this essay also appeared in *Harper's Magazine*.

us, safely away from us; we tuck ourselves up in the long sleep and comfort of cold's opposite, warming ourselves by thought of the cold, lighting ourselves by darkness's idea. Or we are Persephone gone underground again, cozy in the amenities of Hell. Sheltered between stove and electric light, we hollow islands of safety within the cold and dark. As light grows less each day, our fur grows thicker. By December 22 we are cozy as a cat hunkered under a Glenwood.

Often October has shown one snow flurry, sometimes even September. For that matter, it once snowed in New Hampshire every month of the year. In 1816, it snowed and froze in June, in July, in August — the Poverty Year, season of continuous winter when farmers planted over and over again, over and over again ripped out frozen shoots of corn and pumpkin. A volcanic eruption in the South Seas two years earlier did it, though at the time our preachers thought the source more local and divine wrath explicit.

Winter starts in November, whatever the calendar says, with gray of granite, with russet and brown of used leaves. In November stillness our stonewalls wait, attentive, and gaunt revenant trunks of maple and oak settle down for winter's stasis, which annually mimics and presages death for each of us and for the planet. November's palette, Braque's analytic cubism, static and squared with fieldstones, interrupts itself briefly with the bright-flapped caps of deer hunters and their orange jackets. Always it is modified by the black-green fir, enduring, hinting at permanence. Serious snow begins one November afternoon. Gradually Mount Kearsarge, south of us, disappears into white gauzy cloud, vanishing mountain, weather-sign for all of us to its north. For one hundred and eighty years the people of this house have looked south at dawn's light and again at sunset to tell the coming weather, reliable in 1802 when the first builder put in the south windows, reliable still. When Kearsarge disappears, the storm comes closer. Birds gather at the feeder, squabbling, gobbling their weight. When they are full they look for shelter, and we do the same, or at least we bring wood from the shed to stack beside the old Glenwoods and the new Jøtul.

Every year the first snow sets us dreaming. By March it will only bring the grumps, but November snow is revenance, a dreamy restitution of childhood or even infancy. Tighten the door and settle a cloth snake against the breeze from the door's bottom; make sure the storms are firmly shut; add logs to the stove and widen the draft. Sit in a chair looking south into blue twilight that arrives earlier every day — as the sky flakes and densens, as the first clear flakes float past the porch's wood to light on dirt of the driveway and on brown frozen grass or dry stalks of the flower border. They seem tentative and awkward at first, then in a hastening host a whole brief army falls, white militia paratrooping out of the close sky over various textures making them one. Snow is white and gray, part and whole, infinitely various yet infinitely repetitious, soft and hard, frozen and melting, a creaking underfoot and a soundlessness . . . But first of all it is the reversion of many into one. It is substance, almost the idea of substance, that turns grass, driveway, hay-field, old garden, log pile, Saab, watering trough, collapsed barn, and stonewall *into the one white.*

We finish early in November the task of preparing the house for snow — tacking poly over the low clapboards, raking leaves against the foundations as high as we can rake them. When the first real snow arrives, no dusting half inch but a solid foot, we complete the insulation, for it is snow that keeps us warm. After a neighbor's four-wheel-drive pickup, plow bolted in front, swoops clean our U-shaped driveway, and after we dig out the mailbox for Bert's rural delivery, it is time to heap the snow over leaves and against poly, around the house, on all sides of the house, against the granite foundation stones. Arctic winds halt before this white guard. When bright noon melts inches of snow away from the house, reflecting heat from the snowy clap-board, it leaves cracks of cold air for us to fill when new snow falls all winter long.

But November, although it begins winter, is only winter's approach, with little snow and with cold that announces itself only to increase. The calendar's winter begins at the solstice, Advent's event: the child's birth who rises from winter to die and rise again in spring. November is autumn's burial and the smoke of victims sacrificed is thanks for harvest and magic as we go into ourselves like maples for winter's bear-sleep. We make transition by way of feast and anticipatory snow, toward the long, white, hard hundred days of the true winter of our annual death. We wait for December to feel the *cold*, I mean COLD, like

thirty-five degrees below zero Fahrenheit. Seldom does it stay
cold, or COLD, for longer than a week, but we are ready now for
snow.

The first *big* snow accumulates one night. Kearsarge may disappear at noon, and darkness start early. In teatime twilight,
big flakes slowly, as if hesitant, reel past the empty trees like
small white leaves, star-shaped and infrequent. By bedtime,
driveway and lawn turn shaggy with the first cover. It is good to
go to bed early in winter, and tonight as we sleep our dreams
take punctuation from the thudding of snowplows as they roll
and bluster all night up and down Route 4, shaking the house
yet comforting our sleep: Someone takes care, the solitary cap-
tains in their great snowships breasting through vast whiteness,
fountaining it sideways into gutter drifts. If we stir as they
thump past, we watch revolving yellow lights flash through our
windows and reflect on the ceiling. We roll over and fall back
into protected sleep. In a house full of cats we sleep not alone,
for the snowplows that reassure us frighten our animals like
thunder or riflefire; they crawl between our warm bodies under
warmer electric blankets.

When we become aware, by the plows' repeated patrols, that
the first deep snow accumulates; when the first intense and
almost unbreakable sleep finishes and we enter the frangible
second half of the night's house, I pull myself out of bed at two
or three in the morning to inspect the true oncoming of winter's
work. I walk through the dark house from one vantage to another — parlor window that looks west toward pond, kitchen
from which I look toward Kearsarge, dining room that gives on
the north, and if I twist, back to the slope of Ragged Mountain
rising east above us. The night's flaking air breaks black sky into
white flecks, silent and pervasive, shuttering the day's vista. This
snow fills the air and the eyes, the way on spring nights peepers
fill the ears. Everywhere I look, limited by snow-limits, cold
dewy whiteness takes everything into itself. Beside the covered
woodshed, side by side, I see the shapes of two small cars
rounded and smooth like enormous loaves of dead-white bread.
Where the woodpile waits for final stacking in the shed, a round
mound rises with irregular sticks jagging out of it. Up on the
hill the great cowbarn labors under a two-foot layer of snow, its
unpainted vertical boards a dark upright shadow in all the

whiteness, like the hemlocks above it on Ragged's hill. Although snowplows keep Route 4 passable, they do not yet scrape to the macadam: In the darkness the highway is as white as the hayfields on either side. Down the road white cottage disappears against white field, green shutters a patch of vacancy in the whiteness. In the stillness of two A.M., in a silent unlit moment with no plows thudding, I regard a landscape reverted to other years by the same snow — and I might be my great-grandfather gazing from the same windows in 1885. Or it might be his mother's eyes I gaze from, born on a Wilmot hill in 1789. Or maybe I look, centuries earlier, from the eyes of a Penacook wintering over the pond. If I squint a little I cannot see that this depression is a road.

But now the snowplow's thunder signals itself, and I watch the revolving yellow light reflect upward into white prodigious air, and hear the great bruising barge roar and rumble past the house, 1985 and grateful, as a steel prow swooshes high waves of whiteness up and over the gutter almost to the front of the house, and buries the mailbox.

One year the first great snow came Christmas Eve after the family had struggled to bed. When we lit the tree in the morning, the day was thick and dark past the windows, and as we opened our presents the snow deepened in yard and hayfield outside, and on Christmas Day, all day, the great plows of state and town kept Route 4 clear. Snow stopped at three in the afternoon, and when Forrest rolled in to plow the driveway in the early blue twilight, Jane heaped slices of turkey between homemade bread to comfort him in his cab as he drove over the countryside digging people out.

The next morning was cold, thirty below, cold enough to notice. January is the coldest month, in fact, although many would argue for February. Usually our cold is dry, and it does not penetrate so much as damp cold. December of 1975, our first full winter here, I tried starting the Plymouth one morning with normal confidence in the old six and without cold-weather precautions; I flooded it. When I looked at the thermometer I was astonished to find it minus seventeen degrees, for my face and forehead had not warned me that it was *cold*. I had lived in Michigan where the winters were damp, and Ann Arbor's occasional zero felt harsher than New Hampshire's common

twenty below. Later that winter we did not complain of the
mildness. In January of 1976, morning after morning was thirty
below; one morning on the porch the thermometer read thirty-
eight degrees under — a temperature we did not equal again
until 1984. My grandmother had just died at ninety-seven, and
she had spent most of her late winters going south to Connecticut. The house had grown unaccustomed to winter, the old
heavy wooden storm windows broken, no central heat, and no
insulation. Jane and I had never lived without central heat. Now
we had a parlor Glenwood stove for heating, two kerosene
burners in the kitchen, and on occasion an electric oven with
the door left open. This twelve-room house, in January of 1976,
dwindled to a one-room house, with a kitchen sometimes habit-
able. Working at the dining room table, twenty feet from the
living room's Glenwood, I felt chilly. At the time, we were too
excited or triumphant to complain. We were camping out; we
were earning our stripes. The next summer we added alumi-
num combination storms and screens together with some insulation; we added two more small woodstoves, one for each study
so that we could each work despite the winter. My grandparents
survived with only two woodstoves because they bustled around
all day; in our work we sat on our duffs and required extra
stoves. When February came we learned we had passed our
initiation, for it had been the coldest January since New Hampshire started keeping records more than a hundred years earlier. In all my grandmother's ninety-seven Januarys she had not
known so cold a month.

My grandfather worked all day without any heat except for
the bodies of his cows. When he sat at morning and evening
between two great steaming black-and-white Holstein hulks,
pulling the pale thin tonnage of blue milk from their cud-
chewing bodies, he was warm. I can remember him, on my
winter visits to the farm as a boy, scurrying into the house for a
warm-up between his other daily chores, rubbing his hands together, opening the drafts of one of the woodstoves and looming over it for a moment. Early and late, he moved among cold
sheds and unheated barns. In the cowbarn, he fed the cattle
hay, grain, and ensilage, and provided his horse Riley with oats
and hay and water. He let the Holsteins loose to wander stiff-
legged to the old cement watering trough next to the milk room,

from which he first removed a layer of ice. Their pink muzzles dipped one by one into the near-freezing water. And he fed the sheep in sheepbarn and sheepyard. From the sheep's trough he dipped out water for the hens, who lived next door to the sheep, and carried feed for his hens from the grainshed beside the cowbarn.

He would start these chores early, most days of deep winter, rising at four-thirty, perhaps three hours before the sun, to do half the daily chores of feeding and watering, of milking and readying milk for the trucker, because the special daily chores of winter were the year's hardest. The pains of minus twenty were exacerbated by pains of hard labor. To chop wood for next year's stove the farmer stalked with his ax into his woodlot after chores and breakfast, and often marched far enough so that he carried with him his bread and butter, meat and pie, and thermos of coffee for dinner. Setting out with a great ax, usually working alone, the farmer chopped the tree down, trimmed branches, cut the trunk into four-foot sections, and stacked it. Later he would hitch oxen to the sledge and fetch the cordwood downhill for cutting in the barnyard to stove-length pieces, and for splitting. Maybe ten cord of a winter for the house — more for the sugaring in March.

In January he harvested another winter crop — the crop that people forget when they think of the needs of an old farm — which was the harvest of ice, cut in great oblongs two or three feet thick from Eagle Pond, ox-sledded up to the icehouse in back of the cowbarn's watering trough, packed against warm weather six months hence. Each winter the farmer waited for a cold stretch, augering through the pond ice to check its thickness. Then he cut checkerboard squares with his ice saws. He kept himself heavily mittened not only against cold and wind rattling over the open desert lake, but also against the inevitable clasp of near-frozen water. A crew of them — neighbors cooperated to fetch ice — sawed and grappled, lifted and hauled, hard work and cold work. In the icehouse they stacked layers of ice, thickly insulated with sawdust, to last from the earliest warmth of April through hot spells of June and the long summer hay days of July and August through autumn with its Indian summer until the ice froze again. In the hot months my grandfather brought one chunk a day downhill from the ice-

house, great square balanced with ice-tongs on his shoulder, to
the toolshed behind the kitchen where my grandmother kept
her icebox, drip drip. Most ice went to cool the milk, hot from
the udders of Holsteins, so that it would not spoil overnight in
the hot summer. July and August, I was amazed every time we
dug down through the wet sawdust in the cool shade of the
icehouse to find cold winter again — packed silvery slab of
Eagle Pond preserved against summer, just as we hayed to preserve for the winter-cattle summer's hay. On the hottest days
when we returned sweaty from haying, my grandfather cracked
off a little triangle of ice for me to suck on. Every January when
he dug down in the icehouse to bury his crop of new ice, he
found old ice underneath it. After all, you never wanted to find
yourself all out; some years, there might be hot days even in
November when you would require a touch of ice. One long hot
autumn, he found at the bottom of the ice shed, further than
he ever remembered digging, a small coffin-shaped remnant
from times past, ice that might have been five years old, he told
me; maybe older . . .

And my grandfather told me how, in the state of Maine especially, in the old days, clipper ships loaded up ice and sawdust, at the end of winter, and sailed this cargo — transient min-
eral, annual and reproducible reverse-coal tonnage — down the
East Coast to unload its cool for the South that never otherwise
saw a piece of ice: ice by the ton for coastal cities like Charleston, South Carolina. Sometimes they sailed all the way to the
West Indies with their perishable silvery cargo: Maine ice for
the juleps of Charleston, northern January cooling Jamaica's
rum.

By tradition the hard snow and heavy cold of January take a
vacation for the eldritch out-of-time phenomenon of January
thaw. Sometimes the January thaw comes in February, sometimes it never arrives at all, and on the rarest occasions it starts
early and lasts all winter . . . Mostly the January thaw lives up to
its name. Some strange day, after a week when we dress in the
black of twenty below, we notice that we do not back up to the
fire as we change our clothing. Extraordinary. Or at midday we
pick up the mail in our shirtsleeves, balmy at forty-two degrees.
(It is commonplace to observe that a temperature which felt
Arctic late in August feels tropical in mid-January.) Icicles drip,

snow slides off the south roof in midday sun, and mud season takes over the driveway. Snow melts deeply away from clapboard and poly. Or the January thaw comes with warm rain. ("If this was snow we'd have twelve feet . . .") And if warm rain pours for three January days, as I have known it to do, Ragged's melt floods our driveway, snow vanishes from all hayfields, and water drowns the black ice of Eagle Pond. Our small universe confuses itself with false spring. Bears wake perplexed and wander looking for deer-corpses or compost heaps, thinking that it's time to get on with it. I remember fetching the newspaper one morning at six o'clock (I pick up the *Globe* outside a store nearby that does not open for customers, slugabeds, until eight o'clock) on the third day of a warm rain. Chugging through deep mud in my outboard Nissan, I pulled up at the wet porch to see a huge white cat rooting about in perennials beside the walk, a white pussycat with black spots . . . Oh, no . . . Therefore I remained in the front seat, quietly reading the paper, careful not to make a startling sound or otherwise appear rude — until the skunk wandered away.

Until we replaced rotten sills three years ago, a family of skunks lived in our rootcellar every winter. We never *saw* them, but we found their scat; we found the holes by which they entered and exited; we confirmed their presence by another sense. In the spring they sometimes quarreled, possibly over the correct time and place for love, and we could hear them snapping at each other, and, alas, we discovered that skunks used on each other their special skunk-equipment: Once a year in February or March we threw our windows wide open. On one occasion, Ann Arbor friends visited in March, dear friends notable for the immaculateness of their house in a culture of unspotted houses. When we brought them home with their skis from the airport, and opened the door, we discovered that our rootcellar family had suffered a domestic disagreement; therefore we opened all downstairs windows, although it was of course fifteen below. As we prepared to take our friends upstairs to their bedroom, where the air would be purer, we opened the doorway upstairs to discover a dead rat on the carpet, courtesy of a guardian cat. Welcome to the country.

January thaw is dazzling, but it is a moment's respite. If this were January in England we would soon expect snowdrops;

here we know enough to expect replacement battalions of
snow's troopers following on coldness that freezes the melt,
covering it with foot upon foot of furry whiteness and moon-
coldness. We return to the satisfactions of winter, maybe even
to the deliverance and delirium of a full moon.

In New Hampshire the full moon is remarkable all year long,
because we suffer relatively little from garbage-air and even less
from background light. The great cloudless night of the full
moon is werewolf time, glory of silver-pale hauntedness whenever it happens — but in winter it is most beautiful. I set the
internal alarm, maybe three or four nights in a row, and wander, self-made ghost, through pale rooms in the pewter light
while the moon magnifies itself in bright hayfields and reflects
upward, a sun from middle earth, onto shadowy low ceilings.
High sailing above, higher than it has a right to, bigger, the
February full moon, huge disc of cold, rides and slides among
tatters of cloud. My breathing speeds, my pulse quickens; for
half an hour I wander, pulled like a tide through the still house
in the salty half-light, more asleep than awake, asleep not in
house or nightshirt in 1985 but in moon, moon, moon . . . What
old animal awakens and stretches inside the marrow of the
bones? What howls? What circles, sniffing for prey?

It's no winter without an ice storm. When Robert Frost gazed
at bent-over birch trees and tried to think that boys had bent
them playing, he knew better: "Ice storms do that." They do
that, and a lot more, trimming disease and weakness out of the
tree — the old tree's friend, as pneumonia used to be the old
man's. Some of us provide life-support systems for our precious
shrubs, boarding them over against the ice; for the ice storm
takes the young or unlucky branch or birch as well as the rotten
or feeble. One February morning we look out our windows over
yards and fields littered with kindling, small twigs and great
branches. We look out at a world turned into one diamond, ten
thousand karats in the line of sight, twice as many facets. What
a dazzle of spinning refracted light, spider webs of cold bril-
liance attacking our eyeballs! All winter we wear sunglasses to
drive, more than we do in summer, and never so much as after
an ice storm with its painful glaze reflecting from maple and
birch, granite boulder and stonewall, turning electric wires into
bright silver filaments. The snow itself takes on a crust of ice,

like the finish of a clay pot, that carries our weight and sends us
swooping and sliding. It is worth your life to go for the mail.
Until sand and salt redeem the highway, Route 4 is quiet; we
cancel the appointment with the dentist, stay home, and marvel
at the altered universe, knowing that midday sun will strip ice
from tree and roof and restore our ordinary white winter world.

Another inescapable attribute of winter, increasing in the
years of postwar affluence, is the ski people, cold counterpart
of the summer folks who have filled New Hampshire's Julys and
Augusts ever since the railroad came in the 1840s. Now the
roads north from Boston are as dense on a February Friday as
they are on a July; and late Sunday afternoon Interstate 93
backs up from the tollbooth. On twenty thousand Toyotas pairs
of skis ride north and south every weekend. At Christmas vacation and school holidays every hotel room fills all week with
families of flatlanders. They wait in line at the tows, resplendent
in the costumes of money, booted and coifed in bright petro-
chemical armor. They ride, they swoop, they fall, they drink
whiskey . . . and the bonesetter takes no holiday on a New
Hampshire February weekend, and the renter of crutches earns
time and a half. Now that cross-country rivals downhill, the ski
people grow older and more various; tourism, which rivals the
yard sale as major north country industry, brings Massachusetts
and New York money for the thin purses of the cold land. And
by the fashionable areas — much of Vermont, and the Water-
ville Valley in New Hampshire's White Mountains — restaurants and boutiques, cute-shops and quiche-cafés buzz like
winter's blackflies.

The snowmachine breaks trails for cross-country, and it is also
the countryman's ski outfit. Few natives ski, though some have
always done, and in our attic there are wide heavy wooden skis
from the time of the Great War on which my mother and her
sisters traipsed all winter, largely doing cross-country but perfectly willing to slide down a hill. Old-timers remember the
horse as ski-tow, pulling adventurers uphill.

The motorcycle roar of snowmachines, from a distance indistinguishable from chainsaws, interrupts the down-quiet of mid-
week evenings, as kids roar along disused railroad tracks and
over the surface of frozen lakes. Mostly kids. The older folks,
men mostly, park their bobhouses on thick ice of winter lakes,

saw holes in the ice, light a fire, warm themselves with a pint of whiskey, and fish for the wormless perch of winter. Like deer-hunting in November, of course, this fishing is not mere sport; it fills the freezers of ten thousand shacks, trailers, and extended farmhouses. On Eagle Pond just west of us we count six or a dozen bobhouses each winter, laboriously translated by pickup and pushed or slipped across the ice to a lucky spot. Most springs it seems one fisherman waits too late. How many little houses, some with tin stoves flaking away, raise a freshwater Davy Jones's condominium on the bottom of Eagle Pond?

After the labor of cordwood and ice in the old days, in March, as the winter ended, followed the great chore of maple sugaring. It still arrives, though without so much labor. Usually it comes in March, one stretch, but on occasion the conditions for sap turn right for two weeks in February, go wrong for twenty days, then right again — a split season of sugaring. Right conditions are warm days when the snow melts followed by cold nights when it freezes. Nowadays people suction sap from the sugarbush with miles of plastic tubing. In the old time, you pounded the spigot into the tree — several of them in a good-sized three-hundred-year-old maple — and hung a bucket from each for the sap to drip into. My grandfather trudged from tree to tree every day, wearing a wooden yoke across his shoulders; long pails hung from the ends of it, narrow on top and wide on bottom, for collecting sap from each bucket. He emptied these yoke-pails into a great receptacle sledged by an ox — oxen were especially useful in the winter, slow but unbothered by snow — and when he filled this great sledge-kettle, his ox pulled it to a funnel and pipe whence the sap flowed downhill to a storage tank behind the saphouse.

Gathering sap was a third of the work, or maybe a quarter. There was cordwood to cut and burn under the trays boiling the sap down. Someone had to tend the fire day and night, and to watch and test the sap on its delicate journey to syrup. In 1913 my grandfather corked five hundred gallons at a dollar a gallon, big money in 1913, with the help of his father-in-law Ben Keneston, cousin Freeman, and Ansel the hired man. When we remember that it takes about forty gallons of sap, boiled down, to make one gallon of syrup, we begin to assess the labor required.

But the sweetness of the task was not only the cash crop. With honey from the beehive next to the barn and the hollyhocks, my grandfather and grandmother grew and produced their own sweetening. With the cash from the syrup — sometimes from wool and baby lambs — they bought land and paid taxes. Often their tax was little or nothing, for in the old days many farmers paid their taxes by doing road work — scraping and rolling the dirt roads, filling in with hardpan, and in winter rolling down the snow on the road to make it fit for the runners of sleighs, taking on a mile of Wilmot's Grafton Turnpike.

March was always the month for blizzards. Still is. It is the time when we all tell ourselves: *We've had enough of winter.* Old folks come back from Florida and Hilton Head; younger ones, fed up, head off for a week where the weather performs like May or June in New Hampshire. Every morning the *Globe* measures a word from Florida: *baseball* . . . In New Hampshire, tantalizing melt is overwhelmed with four feet of snow, drifts to twelve feet . . . We comfort each other, when we use the form of complaint for our boasting, that even if we lost the old outhouse yesterday, or the '53 Buick that the chickens use for summer roosting, what comes quick in March goes quick in March, and three or four days from now it'll melt to reveal the lost Atlantis of the family barnyard. Of course three or four days later, we find another four feet.

Blizzards happen in March, like the great one of '88, which the old people still bragged about in the 1940s. My Connecticut grandfather and my New Hampshire one, who shared little, shared the blizzard of '88: a great watershed for bragging, or for telling lies about. And in the 1980s I still ask old people what they remember that *their* old people told them about '88, much as the '88ers themselves asked their old-timers about the Poverty Year of 1816. Great weather makes great stories. Paul Fenton told me a story he heard as a boy, not about '88 but just about "the big snows we used to have, back in the old days." It seems that a bunch went out after a heavy snow, dragging the roads with the help of oxen so that people could use their sleighs and sledges, when one of the oxen slipped and got stuck, couldn't move at all; got a hoof caught in something . . . Well, they dug down, dug around, trying to free the ox's hoof, and what do you know . . . That ox had stuck its foot into a chimney!

Now, the blue snow of 1933 is *not* a lie. I am sure of it, because of the way Ansel Powers tells me about it, because his wife Edna confirms it, because Les Ford from Potter Place, who has never been known to collaborate on a story, remembers it just as well and tells the same stories. It may be hard to believe: *but it was blue.* You stuck a shovel in it, and it was *blue,* blue as that sky, blue as a bachelor's button. It fell in April, a late snow, and it fell fast. Les remembers that he'd been to a dance at Danbury, and when he went to bed at midnight the sky was clear and full of stars; when he woke up in the morning, there was three feet of blue snow. The snowplows were disassembled for summer; the road agent had to start up the old dozer and go up and down the road with it, to clear a way for the Model T's — and a few shiny Model A's. Nobody *saw* it snow except Sam Duby, the same blacksmith who made the first snowplows in Andover. He woke up at two or three in the morning and had to do something, you know; well, the outhouse was across the road in the barn, and he came out on the porch and it was snowing to beat the band and he just dropped a load right there . . . He's the only one who saw it snow; the rest of us went to bed under stars, woke up to the sun shining in three feet of *blue snow.*

In *The Voyage of the Beagle* Charles Darwin wrote about finding red snow, *Protococcus nivalis,* on the Peuquenes Ridge in Chile in 1835. "A little rubbed on paper gives it a faint rose tinge mingled with a little brick-red." When he examined it later, Darwin found "microscopical plants." As far as I know, no one took our blue snow into a laboratory.

Of course it snows in April, every year, most often white, but you cannot call it winter anymore. Snow sticks around, in the north shade, most years until early in May, but it is ragged and dirty stuff, and we overlook it as we gaze in hopeful amazement at this year's crop of daffodils. Every year the earlier daffodils fill with snow, bright yellow spilling out white crystals, outraged optimism overcome by fact. And the worst storm I have driven through, after ten New Hampshire winters, occurred a few years back on the ninth day of May.

But annual aberration aside, March is the end of winter, and the transition to spring is April's melt. One year not long ago we had an open winter, with very little snow, *no* snow we all said; we exaggerated a little for we had an inch here and an inch there. The winter was not only dry but mild, which was a good thing, for an open winter with cold weather destroys flowers and bushes and even trees, since snow is our great insulator. As it was, in our open winter we suffered one cold patch — twenty below for a week — and in the spring that followed, and in the summer, we discovered winterkill: A few rose bushes and old lilacs, plants and bulbs that had survived for decades, didn't make it that year. When spring came without a melt, when mild days softened with buttery air and the protected daffodils rose blowing yellow trumpets, we felt uneasy; all of us knew: Lacking the pains of winter, we did not deserve the rapture and the respite of spring.

Our annual melt is the wild, messy, glorious loosening of everything tight. It is gravity's ecstasy as water seeks its own level on every level, and the noise of water running fills day and night. Down Ragged Mountain the streams rush, cutting through ice and snow, peeling away winter's cold layers. Rush, trickle, rush. Busy water moves all day and all night, never tired, cutting away the corrupt detritus of winter. Fingers of bare earth extend down hillsides. South sides of trees extend bare patches farther every day. Root-patterned rivulets melting gather downhill to form brief streams. Dirt roads slog, driveways turn swamps, cars smithereen transmissions. Rural delivery, which survives ten thousand blizzards, sticks in the mud of April.

Then it dries. Last snow melts. Trees bud green. Soft air turns. Who can believe in winter now?

All of us. We know that winter has only retreated, waiting. When the bear comes out of its winter sleep, winter itself goes into hibernation, sleeping off the balmy months of peeper-sing until the red leaf wakes it again and the white season returns with the New Hampshire by which we know ourselves.

PHILLIP LOPATE

Against Joie de Vivre

FROM PLOUGHSHARES

OVER THE YEARS I have developed a distaste for the spectacle of
joie de vivre, the knack of knowing how to live. Not that I disap-
prove of all hearty enjoyment of life. A flushed sense of happiness can overtake a person anywhere, and one is no more to
blame for it than the Asiatic flu or a sudden benevolent change
in the weather (which is often joy's immediate cause). No, what
rankles me is the stylization of this private condition into a bul-
lying social ritual.

The French, who have elevated the picnic to their highest
civilized rite, are probably most responsible for promoting this
smugly upbeat, flaunting style. It took the French genius for
formalizing the informal to bring sticky sacramental sanctity to
the baguette, wine, and cheese. A pure image of sleeveless *joie
de vivre* Sundays can also be found in Renoir's paintings. Weekend satyrs dance and wink; leisure takes on a bohemian stripe.
A decent writer, Henry Miller, caught the French malady and
ran back to tell us of *pissoirs* in the Paris streets (why this should
have impressed him so, I've never figured out).

But if you want a double dose of *joie de vivre*, you need to
consult a later, hence more stylized version of the French myth
of pagan happiness: those *Family of Man* photographs of end-
lessly kissing lovers, snapped by Doisneau and Boubat, not to
mention Cartier-Bresson's icon of the proud tyke carrying bottles of wine. If Cartier-Bresson and his disciples are excellent
photographers for all that, it is in spite of their rubbing our
noses in a tediously programmatic "affirmation of life."

Though it is traditionally the province of the French, the

whole Mediterranean is a hotbed of professional *joie de vivrism,* which they have gotten down to a routine like a crack *son et lumière* display. The Italians export *dolce far niente* as aggressively as tomato paste. For the Greeks, a Zorba dance to life has supplanted classical antiquities as their main touristic lure. Hard to imagine anything as stomach-turning as being forced to participate in such an oppressively robust, folknik effusion. Fortunately, the country has its share of thin, nervous, bitter types, but Greeks do exist who would clutch you to their joyfully stout bellies and crush you there. The *joie de vivrist* is an incorrigible missionary, who presumes that everyone wants to express pro-life feelings in the same stereotyped manner.

A warning: since I myself have a large store of nervous discontent (some would say hostility), I am apt to be harsh in my secret judgments of others, seeing them as defective because they are not enough like me. From moment to moment, the person I am with often seems too shrill, too bland, too something-or-other to allow my own expansiveness to swing into stage center. "Feeling no need to drink, you will promptly despise a drunkard" (Kenneth Burke). So it goes with me — which is why I am not a literary critic. I have no faith that my discriminations in taste are anything but the picky awareness of what will keep me stimulated, based on the peculiar family and class circumstances that formed me. But the knowledge that my discriminations are skewed and not always universally desirable doesn't stop me in the least from making them, just as one never gives up a negative first impression, no matter how many times it is contradicted. A believer in astrology (to cite another false system), having guessed that someone is a Sagittarius, and then told he is a Scorpio, says "Scorpio — yes, of course!" without missing a beat, or relinquishing confidence in his ability to tell people's signs, or in his idea that the person is somehow secretly Sagittarian.

1. The Houseboat

I remember the exact year when my dislike for *joie de vivre* began to crystallize. It was 1969. We had gone to visit an old Greek painter on his houseboat in Sausalito. Old Vartas's vitality was legendary and it was considered a spiritual honor to meet him, like getting an audience with the pope. Each Sunday he had a sort of open house, or open boat.

My "sponsor," Frank, had been many times to the houseboat, furnishing Vartas with record albums, since the old painter had a passion for San Francisco rock bands. Frank told me that Vartas had been a pal of Henry Miller's, and I, being a writer of Russian descent, would love him. I failed to grasp the syllogism, but, putting aside my instinct to dislike anybody I have been assured I will adore, I prepared myself to give the man a chance.

Greeting us on the gangplank was an old man with thick, lush white hair and snowy eyebrows, his face reddened from the sun. As he took us into the houseboat cabin he told me proudly that he was seventy-seven years old, and gestured toward the paintings that were spaced a few feet apart, leaning on the floor against the wall. They were celebrations of the blue Aegean, boats moored in ports, whitewashed houses on a hill, painted in primary colors and decorated with collaged materials: mirrors, burlap, Life Savers candies. These sunny little canvases with their talented innocence, third-generation spirit of Montmartre, bore testimony to a love of life so unbending as to leave an impression of rigid narrow-mindedness as extreme as any Savonarola. Their rejection of sorrow was total. They were the sort of festive paintings that sell at high-rent Madison Avenue galleries specializing in European schlock.

Then I became aware of three young, beautiful women, bare-shouldered, wearing white dhotis, each with long blond hair falling onto a sky-blue halter — unmistakably suggesting the Three Graces. They lived with him on the houseboat, I was told, giving no one knew what compensation for their lodgings. Perhaps their only payment was to feed his vanity in front of outsiders. The Greek painter smiled with the air of an old fox around the trio. For their part, they obligingly contributed their praises of Vartas's youthful zip, which of course was taken by some guests as double-entendre for undiminished sexual prowess. The Three Graces also gathered the food offerings of the visitors to make a midday meal.

Then the boat, equipped with a sail, was launched to sea. I must admit it gave me a spoilsport's pleasure when the winds turned becalmed. We could not move. Aboard were several members of the Bay Area's French colony, who dangled their feet over the sides, passed around bunches of grapes and sang what I imagined were Gallic camping songs. The French know boredom, so they would understand how to behave in such a situation. It has been my observation that many Frenchmen and women stationed in America have the attitude of taking it easy, slumming at a health resort, and nowhere more so than in California. The émigré crew included a securities analyst, an academic sociologist, a museum administrator and his wife, a modiste: on Vartas's boat they all got drunk and carried on like redskins, noble savages off Tahiti.

Joie de vivre requires a soupçon of the primitive. But since the illusion of the primitive soon palls and has nowhere to go, it becomes necessary to make new initiates. A good part of the day, in fact, was taken up with regulars interpreting to first-timers like myself certain mores pertaining to the houseboat, as well as offering tidbits about Vartas's Rabelaisian views of life. Here everyone was encouraged to do what he willed. (How much could you do on a becalmed boat surrounded by strangers?) No one had much solid information about the host's past, which only increased the privileged status of those who knew at least one fact. Useless to ask the object of this venerating speculation, since Vartas said next to nothing (adding to his impressiveness) when he was around, and disappeared below for long stretches of time.

In the evening, after a communal dinner, the new Grateful Dead record Frank had brought was put on the phonograph, and Vartas danced, first by himself, then with all three Graces, bending his arms in broad, hooking sweeps. He stomped his foot and looked around scampishly at the guests for appreciation, not unlike an organ grinder and his monkey. Imagine, if you will, a being whose generous bestowal of self-satisfaction invites and is willing to receive nothing but flattery in return, a person who has managed to make others buy his somewhat senile projection of indestructibility as a Hymn to Life. In no sense could he be called a charlatan; he delivered what he promised, an incarnation of *joie de vivre,* and if it was shallow, it was also effective, managing even to attract an enviable "harem" (which was what really burned me).

A few years passed.

Some Dutch TV crew, ever on the lookout for exotic bits of
Americana that would make good short subjects, planned to do
a documentary about Vartas as a sort of paean to eternal youth.
I later learned from Frank that Vartas died before the shooting
could be completed. A pity, in a way. The home movie I've run
off in my head of the old man is getting a little tattered, the
colors splotchy, and the scenario goes nowhere, lacks point. All
I have for sure is the title: The Man Who Gave *Joie de Vivre* a
Bad Name.

"Ah, what a twinkle in the eye the old man has! He'll outlive us
all." So we speak of old people who bore us, when we wish to
honor them. We often see projected onto old people this worship of the life-force. It is not the fault of the old if they then
turn around and try to exploit our misguided amazement at
their longevity as though it were a personal tour de force. The
elderly, when they are honest with themselves, realize they have
done nothing particularly to be proud of in lasting to a ripe old
age, and then carrying themselves through a thousand more
days. Yet you still hear an old woman or man telling a bus driver
with a chuckle, "Would you believe that I am eighty-four years
old!" As though they should be patted on the back for still
knowing how to talk, or as though they had pulled a practical
joke on the other riders by staying so spry and mobile. Such
insecure, wheedling behavior always embarrassed me. I will
look away rather than meet the speaker's eyes and be forced to
lie with a smile, "Yes, you are remarkable," which seems condescending on my part and humiliating to us both.

Like children forced to play the cute part adults expect of
them, some old people must get confused trying to adapt to a
social role of indeterminate standards, which is why they seem
to whine: "I'm doing all right, aren't I — for my age?" It is
interesting that society's two most powerless groups, children
and the elderly, have both been made into sentimental symbols.
In the child's little hungry hands grasping for life, joined to the
old person's frail slipping fingers hanging on to it, you have one
of the commonest advertising metaphors for intense appreciation. It is enough to show a young child sleeping in his or her
grandparent's lap to procure *joie de vivre* overload.

2. *The Dinner Party*

I am invited periodically to dinner parties and brunches — and
I go, because I like to be with people and oblige them, even if I
secretly cannot share their optimism about these events. I go,
not believing that I will have fun, but with the intent of observing people who think *a dinner party* a good time. I eat their fancy
food, drink the wine, make my share of entertaining conversation, and often leave having had a pleasant evening. Which does
not prevent me from anticipating the next invitation with the
same bleak lack of hope. To put it in a nutshell, I am an ingrate.

Although I have traveled a long way from my proletarian
origins and, like a perfect little bourgeois, talk, dress, act, and
spend money, I hold on to my poor-boy's outrage at the "deca-
dence" (meaning, dull entertainment style) of the middle and
upper-middle classes; or, like a model Soviet moviegoer watching scenes of prerevolutionary capitalists gorging caviar, I am
appalled, but I dig in with the rest.

Perhaps my uneasiness with dinner parties comes from the
simple fact that not a single dinner party was given by my soli-
tudinous parents the whole time I was growing up, and I had to
wait until my late twenties before learning the ritual. A spy in
the enemy camp, I have made myself a patient observer of
strange customs. For the benefit of other late-starting social
climbers, this is what I have observed:

As everyone should know, the ritual of the dinner party begins away from the table. Usually in the living room, hors
d'oeuvres and walnuts are set out, to start the digestive juices
flowing. Here introductions between strangers are also made.
Most dinner parties contain at least a few guests who have been
unknown to each other before that evening, but whom the host
and/or hostess envision would enjoy meeting. These novel pair-
ings and their interactions add spice to the postmortem: who
got along with whom? The lack of prior acquaintanceship also
ensures that the guests will have to rely on and go through the
only people known to everyone, the host and hostess, whose
absorption of this helplessly dependent attention is one of the
main reasons for throwing dinner parties.

Although an after-work "leisure activity," the dinner party is

in fact a celebration of professional identity. Each of the guests
has been preselected as in a floral bouquet; and in certain developed forms of this ritual there is usually a cunning mix of
professions. Yet the point is finally not so much diversity as
commonality: what remarkably shared attitudes and interests
these people from different vocations demonstrate by convers-
ing intelligently, or at least glibly, on the topics that arise. Naturally, a person cannot discourse too technically about one's line
of work, so he or she picks precisely those themes that invite
overlap. The psychiatrist laments the new breed of ego-less,
narcissistic patient who keeps turning up in his office — a beach
bum who lacks the work ethic; the college professor bemoans
the shoddy intellectual backgrounds and self-centered ignorance of his students; and the bookseller parodies the customer
who pronounced "Sophocles" to rhyme with "bifocles." The dinner party is thus an exercise in locating ignorance — elsewhere.
Whoever is present is ipso facto part of that beleaguered remnant of civilized folk fast disappearing from Earth.

Or think of a dinner party as a club of revolutionaries, a
technocratic elite whose social interactions that night are a dry
run for some future takeover of the State. These are the future
cabinet members (now only a shadow cabinet, alas) meeting to
practice for the first time. How well they get on! "The time will
soon be ripe, my friends . . ." If this is too fanciful for you, then
compare the dinner party to a utopian community, a Brook
Farm supper club, where only the best and most useful community members are chosen to participate. The smugness begins as soon as one enters the door, since one is already part of
the chosen few. And from then on, every mechanical step in
dinner party process is designed to augment the atmosphere of
group *amour-propre.* This is not to say that there won't be one or
two people in an absolute torment of exclusion, too shy to speak
up, or else suspecting that when they do, their contributions fail
to carry the same weight as the others'. The group's all-purpose
drone of self-contentment ignores these drowning people —
cruelly inattentive in one sense but benign in another: it invites
them to join the shared ethos of success any time they are ready.

The group is asked to repair to the table. Once again they
find themselves marveling at a shared perception of life. How
delicious the fish soup! How cute the stuffed tomatoes! What

did you use for this green sauce? Now comes much talk of ingredients, and credit is given where credit is due. It is Jacques who made the salad. It was Mamie who brought the homemade bread. Everyone pleads with the hostess to sit down, not to work so hard — an empty formula whose hypocrisy bothers no one. Who else is going to put the butter dish on the table? For a moment all become quiet, except for the sounds of eating. This corresponds to the part in a church service that calls for silent prayer.

I am saved from such culinary paganism by the fact that food is largely an indifferent matter to me. I rarely think much about what I am putting in my mouth. Though my savage, illiterate palate has inevitably been educated to some degree by the many meals I have shared with people who care enormously about such things, I resist going any further. I am superstitious that the day I send back a dish at a restaurant, or make a complicated journey to somewhere just for a meal, that day I will have sacrificed my freedom and traded in my soul for a lesser god.

I don't expect the reader to agree with me. That's not the point. Unlike the behavior called for at a dinner party, I am not obliged sitting at my typewriter to help procure consensus every moment. So I am at liberty to declare, to the friend who once told me that dinner parties were one of the only opportunities for intelligently convivial conversation to take place in this cold, fragmented city, that she is crazy. The conversation at dinner parties is of a mind-numbing caliber. No discussion of any clarifying rigor — be it political, spiritual, artistic, or financial — can take place in a context where fervent conviction of any kind is frowned upon, and the desire to follow through a sequence of ideas must give way every time to the impressionistic, breezy flitting from topic to topic. Talk must be bubbly but not penetrating. Illumination would only slow the flow. Some hit-and-run remark may accidentally jog an idea loose, but in such cases it is better to scribble a few words down on the napkin for later than attempt to "think" at a dinner party.

What do people talk about at such gatherings? The latest movies, the priciness of things, word processors, restaurants, muggings and burglaries, private versus public schools, the fool in the White House (there have been so many fools in a row that this subject is getting tired), the undeserved reputations of certain better-known professionals in one's field, the fashions in investments, the investments in fashion. What is traded at the dinner-party table is, of course, class information. You will learn whether you are in the avant-garde or rear guard of your social class, or, preferably, right in step.

As for Serious Subjects, dinner-party guests have the latest *New Yorker* in-depth piece to bring up. People who ordinarily would not spare a moment worrying about the treatment of schizophrenics in mental hospitals, the fate of Great Britain in the Common Market, or the disposal of nuclear wastes suddenly find their consciences orchestrated in unison about these problems, thanks to their favorite periodical — though a month later they have forgotten all about it and are on to something new.

The dinner party is a suburban form of entertainment. Its spread in our big cities represents an insidious fifth column suburbanization of the metropolis. In the suburbs it becomes necessary to be able to discourse knowledgeably about the heart of the city, but from the viewpoint of a day shopper. Dinner-party chatter is the communicative equivalent of roaming around shopping malls.

Much thought has gone into the ideal size for a dinner party — usually with the hostess arriving at the figure eight. Six would give each personality too much weight; ten would lead to splintering side discussions; eight is the largest number still able to force everyone into the same compulsively congenial conversation. My own strength as a conversationalist comes out less in groups of eight than one-to-one, which may explain my resistance to dinner parties. At the table, unfortunately, any engrossing *tête-à-tête* is frowned upon as antisocial. I often find myself in the frustrating situation of being drawn to several engaging people, in among the bores, and wishing I could have a private conversation with each, without being able to do more than signal across the table a wry recognition of that fact. "Some other time, perhaps," we seem to be saying with our eyes, all evening long.

Later, however — to give the devil his due — when guests and hosts retire from the table back to the living room, the strict demands of group participation may be relaxed, and individuals allowed to pair off in some form of conversational intimacy. But one must be ever on the lookout for the group's need to swoop everybody together again for one last demonstration of collective fealty.

The first to leave breaks the communal spell. There is a sudden rush to the coat closet, the bathroom, the bedroom, as others, under the protection of the first defector's original sin, quit the party apologetically. The utopian dream has collapsed: left behind are a few loyalists and insomniacs, swillers of a last cognac. "Don't leave yet," begs the host, knowing what a sense of letdown, pain, and self-recrimination awaits. Dirty dishes are, if anything, a comfort: the faucet's warm gush serves to stave off the moment of anesthetized stock taking — Was that really necessary? — in the sobering silence that follows a dinner party.

3. Joie's Doppelgänger

I have no desire to rail against the Me Generation. We all know that the current epicurean style of the Good Life, from light foods to Nike running shoes, is a result of market research techniques developed to sell "spot" markets, and, as such, is a natural outgrowth of consumer capitalism. I may not like it but I can't pretend that my objections are the result of a high-minded Laschian political analysis. Moreover, my own record of activism is not so noticeably impressive that I can lecture the Sunday brunchers to roll up their sleeves and start fighting social injustices instead of indulging themselves.

No, if I try to understand the reasons for my antihedonistic biases, they come from somewhere other than idealism. It's odd, because there seems to be a contradiction between this curmudgeonly feeling inside me and my periodically strong appetite for life. I am reminded of my hero, William Hazlitt, with his sarcastic, grumpy disposition on the one hand, and his capacity for "gusto" (his word, not Schlitz's) on the other. With Hazlitt, one senses a fanatically tenacious defense of his individuality and independence against some unnamed bully stalking him. He had trained himself to be a connoisseur of vitality, and got irritated when life was not filled to the brim. I am far less irritable — before others; I will laugh if there is the merest *anything* to laugh at. But it is a tense, pouncing pleasure, not one that will allow me to sink into undifferentiated relaxation. The prospect

of a long day at the beach makes me panic. There is no harder
work I can think of than taking myself off to somewhere pleasant, where I am forced to stay for hours and "have fun." Taking
it easy, watching my personality's borders loosen and dissolve,
arouses an unpleasantly floating giddiness. I don't even like
water beds. Fear of Freud's "oceanic feeling," I suppose . . . I
distrust anything that will make me pause long enough to be
put in touch with my helplessness.

The other repugnance I experience around *joie de vivrism* is
that I associate its rituals with depression. All these people sitting around a pool, drinking margaritas, they're not really
happy, they're depressed. Perhaps I am generalizing too much
from my own despair in such situations. Drunk, sunbaked,
stretched out in a beach chair, I am unable to ward off the
sensation of being utterly alone, unconnected, cut off from the
others.

An article on the Science page of the *Times* about depression
(they seem to run one every few months) described the illness
as a pattern of "learned helplessness." Dr. Martin Seligman of
the University of Pennsylvania described his series of experiments: "At first mild electrical shocks were given to dogs, from
which they were unable to escape. In a second set of experiments, dogs were given shocks from which they could escape —
but they didn't try. They just lay there, passively accepting the
pain. It seemed that the animals' inability to control their experiences had brought them to a state resembling clinical depression in humans."

Keep busy, I always say. At all costs avoid the trough of pas-
sivity, which leads to the Slough of Despond. Someone — a girlfriend, who else? — once accused me of being intolerant of the
depressed way of looking at the world, which had its own intelligence and moral integrity, both obviously unavailable to me.
It's true. I don't like the smell of depression (it has a smell, a
very distinct one, something fetid like morning odors), and I
stay away from depressed characters whenever possible. Except
when they happen to be my closest friends or family members.
It goes without saying that I am also, for all my squeamishness,
attracted to depressed people, since they seem to know something I don't. I wouldn't rule out the possibility that the brown-
gray logic of depression *is* the truth. In another experiment

(also reported on the Science page), pitting "optimists" against
clinically diagnosed "depressives" on their self-perceived abili-
ties to effect outcomes according to their wills, researchers tentatively concluded that depressed people may have a more
realistic, clear-sighted view of the world.

Nevertheless, what I don't like about depressives sometimes
is their chummy I-told-you-so smugness, like Woody Allen fans
who treat acedia as a vanguard position.

And for all that, depressives make the most rabid converts to
joie de vivre. The reason is, *joie de vivre* and depression are not
opposites but relatives of the same family, practically twins.
When I see *joie de vivre* rituals, I always notice, like a TV ghost,
depression right alongside it. I knew a man, dominated by a
powerful father, who thought he had come out of a long depression occasioned, in his mind, by his divorce. Whenever I met
him, he would say that his life was getting better and better.
Now he could long distances, he was putting healthy food
in his system, he was more physically fit at forty than he had
been at twenty-five, and now he had dates, he was going out
with three different women, he had a good therapist, he was
looking forward to renting a bungalow in better woods than the
previous summer . . . I don't know whether it was his tone of
voice when he said this, his sagging shoulders, or what, but I
always had an urge to burst into tears. If only he had admitted
he was miserable I could have consoled him outright instead of
being embarrassed to notice the deep hurt in him, like a swallowed razor cutting him from inside. And his pain still stunk up
the room like in the old days, that sour cabbage smell was in his
running suit, yet he wouldn't let on, he thought the smell was
gone. The therapist had told him to forgive himself, and he had
gone ahead and done it, the poor shlemiel. But tell me: why
would anyone need such a stylized, disciplined regimen of enjoyment if he were not depressed?

4. In the Here-and-Now

The argument of both the hedonist and the guru is that if we
were but to open ourselves to the richness of the moment, to

concentrate on the feast before us, we would be filled with bliss. I have lived in the present from time to time, and I can tell you that it is much overrated. Occasionally, as a holiday from stroking one's memories or brooding about future worries, I grant you, it can be a nice change of pace. But to "be here now" hour after hour would never work. I don't even approve of stories written in the present tense. As for poets who never use a past participle, they deserve the eternity they are striving for.

Besides, the present has a way of intruding whether you like it or not; why should I go out of my way to meet it? Let it splash on me from time to time, like a car going through a puddle, and I, on the sidewalk of my solitude, will salute it grimly like any other modern inconvenience.

If I attend a concert, obviously not to listen to the music but to find a brief breathing space in which to meditate on the past and future, I realize that there may be moments when the music invades my ears and I am forced to pay attention to it, note after note. I believe I take such intrusions gracefully. The present is not always an unwelcome guest, so long as it doesn't stay too long and cut into our time for remembering.

Even for survival, it's not necessary to focus one's full attention on the present. The instincts of a pedestrian crossing the street in a reverie will usually suffice. Alertness is all right as long as it is not treated as a promissory note on happiness. Anyone who recommends attention to the moment as a prescription for grateful wonder is only telling half the truth. To be happy one must pay attention, but to be unhappy one must also have paid attention.

Attention, at best, is a form of prayer. Conversely, as Simone Weil said, prayer is a way of focusing attention. All religions recognize this when they ask their worshipers to repeat the name of their God, a devotional practice that draws the practitioner into a trancelike awareness of the present and the objects around oneself. With a part of the soul one praises God, and with the other part one expresses a hunger, a dissatisfaction, a desire for more spiritual contact. Praise must never stray too far from longing, that longing which takes us implicitly beyond the present.

I was about to say that the very act of attention implies longing, but this is not necessarily true. Attention is not always infused with desire; it can settle on us most placidly once desire has been momentarily satisfied, like after the sex act. There are also periods following overwork, when the exhausted slavebody is freed and the eyes dilate to register with awe the lights of the city; one is too tired to desire anything else.

Such moments are rare. They form the basis for a poetic appreciation of the beauty of the world. However, there seems no reliable way to invoke or prolong them. The rest of the time, when we are not being edgy or impatient, we are often simply *disappointed,* which amounts to a confession that the present is not good enough. People often try to hide their disappointment — just as Berryman's mother told him not to let people see that he was bored, because it suggested that he had no "inner resources." But there is something to be said for disappointment.

This least respected form of suffering, downgraded to a kind of petulance, at least accurately measures the distance between hope and reality. And it has its own peculiar satisfactions: Why else do we return years later to places where we had been happy, if not to savor the bittersweet pleasure of disappointment?

Moreover, it is the other side of a strong, predictive feeling for beauty or appropriate civility or decency: only those with a sense of order and harmony can be disappointed.

We are told that to be disappointed is immature, in that it presupposes having unrealistic expectations, whereas the wise man meets each moment head-on without preconceptions, with freshness and detachment, grateful for anything it offers. However, this pernicious teaching ignores everything we know of the world. If we continue to expect what turns out to be not forthcoming, it is not because we are unworldly in our expectations, but because our very worldliness has taught us to demand of an unjust world that it behave a little more fairly. The least we can do, for instance, is to register the expectation that people in a stronger position be kind and not cruel to those in a weaker, knowing all the while that we will probably be disappointed.

The truth is, most wisdom is embittering. The task of the wise person cannot be to pretend with false naïveté that every moment is new and unprecedented, but to bear the burden of

bitterness that experience forces on us with as much uncom-
plaining dignity as strength will allow. Beyond that, all we can
ask of ourselves is that bitterness not cancel out our capacity still
to be surprised.

5. *Making Love*

If it is true that I have the tendency to withhold sympathy from
those pleasures or experiences that fall outside my capabilities,
the opposite is also true: I admire immoderately those things I
cannot do. I've always gone out with women who swam better
than I did. It's as if I were asking them to teach me how to make
love. Though I know how to make love (more or less), I have
never fully shaken that adolescent boy's insecurity that there
was more to it than I could ever imagine, and that I needed a
full-time instructress. For my first sexual experiences, in fact, I
chose older women. Later, when I slept with women my own
age and younger, I still tended to take the stylistic lead from
them, adapting myself to each one's rhythm and ardor, not only
because I wanted to be "responsive," but because I secretly
thought that women — any woman — understood lovemaking
in a way that I did not. In bed I came to them as a student; and
I have made them pay later, in other ways, for letting them see
me thus. Sex has always been so impromptu, so out of my control, so different each time, that even when I became the confident bull in bed, I was dismayed by this surprising sudden
power, itself a form of powerlessness because so unpredictable.
  Something Michel Leiris wrote in his book *Manhood* has always stuck with me: "It has been some time, in any case, since I
have ceased to consider the sexual act as a simple matter, but
rather as a relatively exceptional act, necessitating certain inner
accommodations that are either particularly tragic or particularly exalted, but very different, in either case, from what I
regard as my usual disposition."
  The transformation from a preoccupied urban intellectual to
a sexual animal involves, at times, an almost superhuman strain.
To find in one's bed a living, undulating woman of God knows
what capacities and secret desires may seem too high, too for-

mal, too ridiculous or blissful an occasion — not to mention the shock to an undernourished heart like mine of an injection of undiluted affection, if the woman proves loving as well.

Most often, I simply do what the flood allows me to, improvising here or there like a man tying a white flag to a raft that is being swiftly swept along, a plea for love or forgiveness. But as for artistry, control, enslavement through my penis, that's someone else. Which is not to say that there weren't women who were perfectly happy with me as a lover. In those cases, there was some love between us outside of bed: the intimacy was much more intense because we had something big to say to each other before we ever took off our clothes, but which could now be said only with our bodies.

With other women, whom I cared less about, I was sometimes a dud. I am not one of those men who can force himself to make love passionately or athletically when his affections are not engaged. From the perplexity of wide variations in my experiences I have been able to tell myself that I am neither a good nor a bad lover, but one who responds differently according to the emotions present. A banal conclusion; maybe a true one.

It does not do away, however, with some need to have my remaining insecurities about sexual ability laid to rest. I begin to suspect that all my fancy distrust of hedonism comes down to a fear of being judged in this one category: Do I make love well? Every brie and wine picnic, every tanned body relaxing on the beach, every celebration of *joie de vivre* carries a sly wink of some missed sexual enlightenment that may be too threatening to me. I am like the prudish old maid who blushes behind her packages when she sees sexy young people kissing.

When I was twenty I married. My wife was the second woman I had ever slept with. Our marriage was the recognition that we suited one another remarkably well as company — could walk and talk and share insights all day, work side by side like Chinese peasants, read silently together like graduate students, tease each other like brother and sister, and when at night we found our bodies tired, pull the covers over ourselves and become lovers. She was two years older than I, but I was good at faking maturity; and I found her so companionable and trustworthy and able to take care of me that I could not let such a gold mine go by.

Our love life was mild and regular. There was a sweetness to
sex, as befitted domesticity. Out of the surplus energy of late
afternoons I would find myself coming up behind her sometimes as she worked in the kitchen, taking her away from her
involvements, leading her by the hand into the bedroom. I
would unbutton her blouse. I would stroke her breasts, and she
would get a look in her eyes of quiet intermittent hunger, like a
German shepherd being petted; she would seem to listen far
off; absent-mindedly daydreaming, she would return my pet-
ting, stroke my arm with distracted patience like a mother who
has something on the stove, trying to calm her weeping child. I
would listen too to guess what she might be hearing, bird calls
or steam heat. The enlargement of her nipples under my fingers fascinated me. Goose bumps either rose on her skin where
I touched or didn't, I noted with scientific interest, a moment
before getting carried away by my own eagerness. Then we were
undressing, she was doing something in the bathroom, and I
was waiting on the bed, with all the consciousness of a sun mote.
I was large and ready. The proud husband, waiting to receive
my treasure . . .

I remember our favorite position was she on top, I on the
bottom, upthrusting and receiving. Distraction, absent-mind-
edness, return, calm exploration marked our sensual life. To be
forgetful seemed the highest grace. We often achieved perfection.

Then I became haunted with images of seductive, heartless
cunts. It was the era of the miniskirt, girl-women, Rudi Gern-
reich bikinis and Tiger Morse underwear, see-through blouses,
flashes of flesh that invited the hand to go creeping under and
into costumes. I wanted my wife to be more glamorous. We
would go shopping for dresses together, and she would complain that her legs were wrong for these new fashions. Or she
would come home proudly with a bargain pink and blue felt
minidress, bought for three dollars at a discount store, which
my aching heart would tell me missed the point completely.

She too became dissatisfied with the absence of furtive excitement in our marriage. She wanted to seduce me, like a stranger
on a plane. But I was too easy, so we ended up seducing others.
Then we turned back to each other and with one last desperate
attempt, before the marriage fell to pieces, sought in the other

a plasticity of sensual forms, like the statuary in an Indian temple. In our lovemaking I tried to believe that the body of one woman was the body of all women, and all I achieved was a groping to distance lovingly familiar forms into those of anonymous erotic succubi. The height of this insanity, I remember, was one evening in the park when I pounded my wife's lips with kisses in an effort to provoke something between us like "hot passion." My eyes closed, I practiced a repertoire of French tongue-kisses on her. I shall never forget her frightened silent appeal that I stop, because I had turned into someone she no longer recognized.

But we were young. And so, dependent on each other, like orphans. By the time I left, at twenty-five, I knew I had been a fool, and had ruined everything, but I had to continue being a fool because it had been my odd misfortune to have stumbled onto kindness and tranquility too quickly.

I moved to California in search of an earthly sexual paradise, and that year I tried hardest to make my peace with *joie de vivre*. I was sick but didn't know it — a diseased animal, Nietzsche would say. I hung around Berkeley's campus, stared up at the campanile tower, I sat on the grass watching coeds younger than I, and, pretending that I was still going to university (no deeper sense of being a fraud obtainable), I tried to grasp the rhythms of carefree youth; I blended in at rallies, I stood at the fringes of be-ins, watching new rituals of communal love, someone being passed through the air hand to hand. But I never "trusted the group" enough to let myself be the guinea pig; or if I did, it was only with the proud, stubborn conviction that nothing could change me — though I also wanted to change. Swearing I would never learn transcendence, I hitchhiked and climbed mountains. I went to wine-tasting festivals, and also accepted the wine jug from hippie gypsies in a circle around a beach campfire, without first wiping off the lip. I registered for a Free School course in human sexual response, just to get laid; and when that worked, I was shocked, and took up with someone else. There were many women in those years who got naked with me. I wish I could remember their names. I smoked grass with them, and as a sign of faith I took psychedelic drugs, and we made love in bushes and beach houses, as though hacking through jungles with machetes to stay in touch with our ecstatic genitals while our minds soared off into natural marvels. Such experiences taught me, I will admit, how much romantic feeling can transform the body whose nerve tendrils are receptive to it. Technicolor fantasies of one girlfriend as a señorita with flowers in her impossibly wavy hair would suddenly pitch and roll beneath me, and the bliss of touching her naked suntanned breast and the damp black pubic hairs was too unthinkably perfect to elicit anything but abject gratitude. At such moments I have held the world in my hands and *known* it. I was coming home to the body of Woman, those globes and grasses that had launched me. In the childish fantasy accompanying one sexual climax, under LSD, I was hitting a home run, and the Stars and Stripes flying in the background of my mind's eye as I "slid into home" acclaimed the patriotic rightness of my seminal release. For once I had no guilt about how or when I ejaculated.

If afterward, when we came down, there was often a sour air of disenchantment and mutual prostitution, that does not take away from the legacy, the rapture of those moments. If I no longer use drugs — in fact, have become antidrug — I think I still owe them something for showing me how to recognize the all-embracing reflex. At first I needed drugs to teach me about the stupendousness of sex. Later, without them, there would be situations — after a lovely talk or coming home from a party in a taxi — when I would be overcome by amorous tropism toward the woman with me. The appetite for flesh that comes over me at such moments, and the pleasure there is in finally satisfying it, seems so just that I always think I have stumbled into a state of blessed grace. That it can never last, that it is a trick of the mind and the blood, are rumors I push out of sight.

To know rapture is to have one's whole life poisoned. If you will forgive a ridiculous analogy, a tincture of rapture is like a red bandana in the laundry that runs and turns all the white wash pink. We should just as soon stay away from any future ecstatic experiences that spoil everyday living by comparison. Not that I have any intention of stopping. Still, if I will have nothing to do with religious mysticism, it is probably because I sense a susceptibility in that direction. Poetry is also dangerous. All quickening awakenings to Being extract a price later.

Are there people who live under such spells all the time? Was this the secret of the idiotic smile on the half-moon face of the

painter Vartas? The lovers of life, the robust Cellinis, the Casa-
novas? Is there a technique to hedonism that will allow the term
of rapture to be indefinitely extended? I don't believe it. The
hedonist's despair is still that he is forced to make do with the
present. Who knows about the success rate of religious mystics?
In any case, I could not bring myself to state that what I am
waiting for is God. Such a statement would sound too grandiose
and presumptuous, and make too great a rupture in my customary thinking. But I can identify with the pre- if not the post-
stage of what Simone Weil describes:

"The soul knows for certain only that it is hungry. The important thing is that it announces its hunger by crying. A child
does not stop crying if we suggest to it that perhaps there is no
bread. It goes on crying just the same. The danger is not lest
the soul should doubt whether there is any bread, but lest, by a
lie, it should persuade itself that it is not hungry."

So much for *joie de vivre*. It's too compensatory. I don't really
know what I'm waiting for. I know only that until I have gained
what I want from this life, my expressions of gratitude and joy
will be restricted to variations of a hunter's alertness. I give
thanks to a nip in the air that clarifies the scent. But I think it
hypocritical to pretend satisfaction while I am still hungry.

BARRY LOPEZ

The Stone Horse

FROM ANTAEUS

1

THE DESERTS OF southern California, the high, relatively cooler
and wetter Mojave and the hotter, dryer Sonoran to the south
of it, carry the signatures of many cultures. Prehistoric rock
drawings in the Mojave's Coso Range, probably the greatest
concentration of petroglyphs in North America, are at least
three thousand years old. Big-game-hunting cultures that flourished six or seven thousand years before that are known from
broken spear tips, choppers, and burins left scattered along the
shores of great Pleistocene lakes, long since evaporated. Weapons and tools discovered at China Lake may be thirty thousand
years old; and worked stone from a quarry in the Calico Mountains is, some argue, evidence that human beings were here
more than 200,000 years ago.

Because of the long-term stability of such arid environments,
much of this prehistoric stone evidence still lies exposed on the
ground, accessible to anyone who passes by — the studious, the
acquisitive, the indifferent, the merely curious. Archaeologists
do not agree on the sequence of cultural history beyond about
twelve thousand years ago, but it is clear that these broken bits
of chalcedony, chert, and obsidian, like the animal drawings and
geometric designs etched on walls of basalt throughout the desert, anchor the earliest threads of human history, the first record of human endeavor here.

Western man did not enter the California desert until the end
of the eighteenth century, 250 years after Coronado brought

his soldiers into the Zuni pueblos in a bewildered search for the cities of Cibola. The earliest appraisals of the land were cursory, hurried. People traveled *through* it, en route to Santa Fe or the California coastal settlements. Only miners tarried. In 1823 what had been Spain's became Mexico's, and in 1848 what had been Mexico's became America's; but the bare, jagged mountains and dry lake beds, the vast and uniform plains of creosote bush and yucca plants, remained as obscure as the northern Sudan until the end of the nineteenth century.

Before 1940 the tangible evidence of twentieth-century man's passage here consisted of very little — the hard tracery of travel corridors; the widely scattered, relatively insignificant evidence of mining operations; and the fair expanse of irrigated fields at the desert's periphery. In the space of a hundred years or so the wagon roads were paved, railroads were laid down, and canals and high-tension lines were built to bring water and electricity across the desert to Los Angeles from the Colorado River. The dark mouths of gold, talc, and tin mines yawned from the bony flanks of desert ranges. Dust-encrusted chemical plants stood at work on the lonely edges of dry lake beds. And crops of grapes, lettuce, dates, alfalfa, and cotton covered the Coachella and Imperial valleys, north and south of the Salton Sea, and the Palo Verde Valley along the Colorado.

These developments proceeded with little or no awareness of earlier human occupations by cultures that preceded those of the historic Indians — the Mohave, the Chemehuevi, the Quechan. (Extensive irrigation began actually to change the climate of the Sonoran Desert, and human settlements, the railroads, and farming introduced many new, successful plants into the region.)

During World War II, the American military moved into the desert in great force, to train troops and to test equipment. They found the clear weather conducive to year-round flying, the dry air and isolation very attractive. After the war, a complex of training grounds, storage facilities, and gunnery and test ranges was permanently settled on more than three million acres of military reservations. Few perceived the extent or significance of the destruction of the aboriginal sites that took place during tank maneuvers and bombing runs or in the laying out of highways, railroads, mining districts, and irrigated fields.

The few who intuited that something like an American Dordogne Valley lay exposed here were (only) amateur archaeologists; even they reasoned that the desert was too vast for any of this to matter.

After World War II, people began moving out of the crowded Los Angeles basin into homes in Lucerne, Apple, and Antelope valleys in the western Mojave. They emigrated as well to a stretch of resort land at the foot of the San Jacinto Mountains that included Palm Springs, and farther out to old railroad and military towns like Twentynine Palms and Barstow. People also began exploring the desert, at first in military-surplus jeeps and then with a variety of all-terrain and off-road vehicles that became available in the 1960s. By the mid-1970s, the number of people using such vehicles for desert recreation had increased exponentially. Most came and went in innocent curiosity; the few who didn't wreaked a havoc all out of proportion to their numbers. The disturbance of previously isolated archaeological sites increased by an order of magnitude. Many sites were vandalized before archaeologists, themselves late to the desert, had any firm grasp of the bounds of human history in the desert. It was as though in the same moment an Aztec library had been discovered intact various lacunae had begun to appear.

The vandalism was of three sorts: the general disturbance usually caused by souvenir hunters and by the curious and the oblivious; the wholesale stripping of a place by professional thieves for black-market sale and trade; and outright destruction, in which vehicles were actually used to ram and trench an area. By 1980, the Bureau of Land Management estimated that probably 35 percent of the archaeological sites in the desert had been vandalized. The destruction at some places by rifles and shotguns, or by power winches mounted on vehicles, was, if one cared for history, demoralizing to behold.

In spite of public education, land closures, and stricter law enforcement in recent years, the BLM estimates that, annually, about 1 percent of the archaeological record in the desert continues to be destroyed or stolen.

2

A BLM archaeologist told me, with understandable reluctance, where to find the intaglio. I spread my Automobile Club of Southern California map of Imperial County out on his desk, and he traced the route with a pink felt-tip pen. The line crossed Interstate 8 and then turned west along the Mexican border.

"You can't drive any farther than about here," he said, marking a small X. "There's boulders in the wash. You walk up past them."

On a separate piece of paper he drew a route in a smaller scale that would take me up the arroyo to a certain point where I was to cross back east, to another arroyo. At its head, on higher ground just to the north, I would find the horse.

"It's tough to spot unless you know it's there. Once you pick it up . . . " He shook his head slowly, in a gesture of wonder at its existence.

I waited until I held his eye. I assured him I would not tell anyone else how to get there. He looked at me with stoical despair, like a man who had been robbed twice, whose belief in human beings was offered without conviction.

I did not go until the following day because I wanted to see it at dawn. I ate breakfast at four A.M. in El Centro and then drove south. The route was easy to follow, though the last section of road proved difficult, broken and drifted over with sand in some spots. I came to the barricade of boulders and parked. It was light enough by then to find my way over the ground with little trouble. The contours of the landscape were stark, without any masking vegetation. I worried only about rattlesnakes.

I traversed the stone plain as directed, but, in spite of the frankness of the land, I came on the horse unawares. In the first moment of recognition I was without feeling. I recalled later being startled, and that I held my breath. It was laid out on the ground with its head to the east, three times life size. As I took in its outline I felt a growing concentration of all my senses, as though my attentiveness to the pale rose color of the morning sky and other peripheral images had now ceased to be important. I was aware that I was straining for sound in the windless air, and I felt the uneven pressure of the earth hard

against my feet. The horse, outlined in a standing profile on the
dark ground, was as vivid before me as a bed of tulips.

I've come upon animals suddenly before, and felt a similar
tension, a precipitate heightening of the senses. And I have felt
the inexplicable but sharply boosted intensity of a wild moment
in the bush, where it is not until some minutes later that you
discover the source of electricity — the warm remains of a
grizzly bear kill, or the still moist tracks of a wolverine.

But this was slightly different. I felt I had stepped into an
unoccupied corridor. I had no familiar sense of history, the
temporal structure in which to think: this horse was made by
Quechan people three hundred years ago. I felt instead a head-
long rush of images: people hunting wild horses with spears on
the Pleistocene veld of southern California; Cortés riding across
the causeway into Montezuma's Tenochtitlán; a short-legged
Comanche, astride his horse like some sort of ferret, slashing
through cavalry lines of young men who rode like farmers; a
hoof exploding past my face one morning in a corral in Wyoming. These images had the weight and silence of stone.

When I released my breath, the images softened. My initial
feeling, of facing a wild animal in a remote region, was replaced
with a calm sense of antiquity. It was then that I became conscious, like an ordinary tourist, of what was before me, and
thought: this horse was probably laid out by Quechan people.
But when? I wondered. The first horses they saw, I knew, might
have been those that came north from Mexico in 1692 with
Father Eusebio Kino. But Cocopa people, I recalled, also came
this far north on occasion, to fight with their neighbors, the
Quechan. And *they* could have seen horses with Melchior Díaz,
at the mouth of the Colorado River in the fall of 1540. So, it
could be four hundred years old. (No one in fact knows.)

I still had not moved. I took my eyes off the horse for a
moment to look south over the desert plain into Mexico, to look
east past its head at the brightening sunrise, to situate myself.
Then, finally, I brought my trailing foot slowly forward and
stood erect. Sunlight was running like a thin sheet of water over
the stony ground and it threw the horse into relief. It looked as
though no hand had ever disturbed the stones that gave it its
form.

The horse had been brought to life on ground called desert

pavement, a tight, flat matrix of small cobbles blasted smooth by sand-laden winds. The uniform, monochromatic blackness of the stones, a patina of iron and magnesium oxides called desert varnish, is caused by long-term exposure to the sun. To make this type of low-relief ground glyph, or intaglio, the artist either selectively turns individual stones over to their lighter side or removes areas of stone to expose the lighter soil underneath, creating a negative image. This horse, about eighteen feet from brow to rump and eight feet from withers to hoof, had been made in the latter way, and its outline was bermed at certain points with low ridges of stone a few inches high to enhance its three-dimensional qualities. (The left side of the horse was in full profile; each leg was extended at 90 degrees to the body and fully visible, as though seen in three-quarter profile.)

I was not eager to move. The moment I did I would be back in the flow of time, the horse no longer quivering in the same way before me. I did not want to feel again the sequence of quotidian events — to be drawn off into deliberation and analysis. A human being, a four-footed animal, the open land. That was all that was present — and a "thoughtless" understanding of the very old desires bearing on this particular animal: to hunt it, to render it, to fathom it, to subjugate it, to honor it, to take it as a companion.

What finally made me move was the light. The sun now filled the shallow basin of the horse's body. The weighted line of the stone berm created the illusion of a mane and the distinctive roundness of an equine belly. The change in definition impelled me. I moved to the left, circling past its rump, to see how the light might flesh the horse out from various points of view. I circled it completely before squatting on my haunches. Ten or fifteen minutes later I chose another view. The third time I moved, to a point near the rear hooves, I spotted a stone tool at my feet. I stared at it a long while, more in awe than disbelief, before reaching out to pick it up. I turned it over in my left palm and took it between my fingers to feel its cutting edge. It is always difficult, especially with something so portable, to re-channel the desire to steal.

I spent several hours with the horse. As I changed positions and as the angle of the light continued to change I noticed a number of things. The angle at which the pastern carried the hoof away from the ankle was perfect. Also, stones had been placed within the image to suggest at precisely the right spot the left shoulder above the foreleg. The line that joined thigh and hock was similarly accurate. The muzzle alone seemed distorted — but perhaps these stones had been moved by a later hand. It was an admirably accurate representation, but not what a breeder would call perfect conformation. There was the suggestion of a bowed neck and an undershot jaw, and the tail, as full as a winter coyote's, did not appear to be precisely to scale.

The more I thought about it, the more I felt I was looking at an individual horse, a unique combination of generic and specific detail. It was easy to imagine one of Kino's horses as a model, or a horse that ran off from one of Coronado's columns. What kind of horses would these have been? I wondered. In the sixteenth century the most sought-after horses in Europe were Spanish, the offspring of Arabian stock and Barbary horses that the Moors brought to Iberia and bred to the older, eastern European strains brought in by the Romans. The model for this horse, I speculated, could easily have been a palomino, or a descendant of horses trained for lion hunting in North Africa.

A few generations ago, cowboys, cavalry quartermasters, and draymen would have taken this horse before me under consideration and not let up their scrutiny until they had its heritage fixed to their satisfaction. Today, the distinction between draft and harness horses is arcane knowledge, and no image may come to mind for a blue roan or a claybank horse. The loss of such refinement in everyday conversation leaves me unsettled. People praise the Eskimo's ability to distinguish among forty types of snow but forget the skill of others who routinely differentiate between overo and tobiano pintos. Such distinctions are made for the same reason. You have to do it to be able to talk clearly about the world.

For parts of two years I worked as a horse wrangler and packer in Wyoming. It is dim knowledge now; I would have to think to remember if a buckskin was a kind of dun horse. And I couldn't throw a double-diamond hitch over a set of panniers — the packer's basic tie-down — without guidance. As I squatted there in the desert, however, these more personal memories seemed tenuous in comparison with the sweep of this animal in human time. My memories had no depth. I thought of the Hittite cavalry riding against the Syrians 3,500 years ago. And the first of the Chinese emperors, Ch'in Shih Huang, buried in Shensi Province in 210 B.C. with thousands of life-size horses and soldiers, a terra-cotta guardian army. What could I know of what was in the mind of whoever made this horse? Was there some racial memory of it as an animal that had once fed the artist's ancestors and then disappeared from North America? And then returned in this strange alliance with another race of men?

Certainly, whoever it was, the artist had observed the animal very closely. Certainly the animal's speed had impressed him. Among the first things the Quechan would have learned from an encounter with Kino's horses was that their own long-distance runners — men who could run down mule deer — were no match for this animal.

From where I squatted I could look far out over the Mexican plain. Juan Bautista de Anza passed this way in 1774, extending El Camino Real into Alta California from Sinaloa. He was followed by others, all of them astride the magical horse; *gente de razón,* the people of reason, coming into the country of *los primitivos.* The horse, like the stone animals of Egypt, urged these memories upon me. And as I drew them up from some forgotten corner of my mind — huge horses carved in the white chalk downs of southern England by an Iron Age people; Spanish horses rearing and wheeling in fear before alligators in Florida — the images seemed tethered before me. With this sense of proportion, a memory of my own — the morning I almost lost my face to a horse's hoof — now had somewhere to fit.

I rose up and began to walk slowly around the horse again. I had taken the first long measure of it and was now looking for a way to depart, a new angle of light, a fading of the image itself before the rising sun, that would break its hold on me. As I circled, feeling both heady and serene at the encounter, I realized again how strangely vivid it was. It had been created on a barren bajada between two arroyos, as nondescript a place as one could imagine. The only plant life here was a few wands of ocotillo cactus. The ground beneath my shoes was so hard it wouldn't take the print of a heavy animal even after a rain. The only sounds I heard here were the voices of quail.

The archaeologist had been correct. For all its forcefulness, the horse is inconspicuous. If you don't care to see it you can walk right past it. That pleases him, I think. Unmarked on this bleak shoulder of the plain, the site signals to no one; so he wants no protective fences here, no informative plaque, to act as beacons. He would rather take a chance that no motorcyclist, no aimless wanderer with a flair for violence and a depth of ignorance, will ever find his way here.

The archaeologist had given me something before I left his office that now seemed peculiar — an aerial photograph of the horse. It is widely believed that an aerial view of an intaglio provides a fair and accurate depiction. It does not. In the photograph the horse looks somewhat crudely constructed; from the ground it appears far more deftly rendered. The photograph is of a single moment, and in that split second the horse seems vaguely impotent. I watched light pool in the intaglio at dawn; I imagine you could watch it withdraw at dusk and sense the same animation I did. In those prolonged moments its shape and so, too, its general character changed — noticeably. The living quality of the image, its immediacy to the eye, was brought out by the light-in-time, not, at least here, in the camera's frozen instant.

Intaglios, I thought, were never meant to be seen by gods in the sky above. They were meant to be seen by people on the ground, over a long period of shifting light. This could even be true of the huge figures on the Plain of Nazca in Peru, where people could walk for the length of a day beside them. It is our own impatience that leads us to think otherwise.

This process of abstraction, almost unintentional, drew me gradually away from the horse. I came to a position of attention at the edge of the sphere of its influence. With a slight bow I paid my respects to the horse, its maker, and the history of us all, and departed.

3

A short distance away I stopped the car in the middle of the road to make a few notes. I could not write down what I was thinking when I was with the horse. It would have seemed disrespectful, and it would have required another kind of atten-

160

tion. So now I patiently drained my memory of the details it had fastened itself upon. The road I'd stopped on was adjacent to the All American Canal, the major source of water for the Imperial and Coachella valleys. The water flowed west placidly. A disjointed flock of coots, small, dark birds with white bills, was paddling against the current, foraging in the rushes.

I was peripherally aware of the birds as I wrote, the only movement in the desert, and of a series of sounds from a village a half-mile away. The first sounds from this collection of ramshackle houses in a grove of cottonwoods were the distracted dawn voices of dogs. I heard them intermingled with the cries of a rooster. Later, the high-pitched voices of children calling out to each other came disembodied through the dry desert air. Now, a little after seven, I could hear someone practicing on the trumpet, the same rough phrases played over and over. I suddenly remembered how as children we had tried to get the rhythm of a galloping horse with hands against our thighs, or by fluttering our tongues against the roofs of our mouths.

After the trumpet, the impatient calls of adults summoning children. Sunday morning. Wood smoke hung like a lens in the trees. The first car starts — a cold eight-cylinder engine, of Chrysler extraction perhaps, goosed to life, then throttled back to murmur through dual mufflers, the obbligato music of a shade-tree mechanic. The rote bark of mongrel dogs at dawn, the jagged outcries of men and women, an engine coming to life. Like a thousand villages from West Virginia to Guadalajara.

I finished my notes — where was I going to find a description of the horses that came north with the conquistadors? Did their manes come forward prominently over the brow, like this one's, like the forelocks of Blackfeet and Assiniboin men in nineteenth-century paintings? I set the notes on the seat beside me.

The road followed the canal for a while and then arced north, toward Interstate 8. It was slow driving and I fell to thinking how the desert had changed since Anza had come through. New plants and animals — the MacDougall cottonwood, the English house sparrow, the chukar from India — have about them now the air of the native born. Of the native species, some — no one knows how many — are extinct. The populations of many others, especially the animals, have been sharply reduced. The idea of a desert impoverished by agricultural poisons and varmint hunters, by off-road vehicles and military operations, did not seem as disturbing to me, however, as this other horror, now that I had been those hours with the horse. The vandals, the few who crowbar rock art off the desert's walls, who dig up graves, who punish the ground that holds intaglios, are people who devour history. Their self-centered scorn, their disrespect for ideas and images beyond their ken, create the awful atmosphere of loose ends in which totalitarianism thrives, in which the past is merely curious or wrong.

I thought about the horse sitting out there on the unprotected plain. I enumerated its qualities in my mind until a sense of its vulnerability receded and it became an anchor for something else. I remembered that history, a history like this one, which ran deeper than Mexico, deeper than the Spanish, was a kind of medicine. It permitted the great breadth of human expression to reverberate, and it did not urge you to locate its apotheosis in the present.

Each of us, individuals and civilizations, has been held upside down like Achilles in the River Styx. The artist mixing his colors in the dim light of Altamira; an Egyptian ruler lying still now, wrapped in his byssus, stored against time in a pyramid; the faded Dorset culture of the Arctic; the Hmong and Samburu and Walbiri of historic time; the modern nations. This great, imperfect stretch of human expression is the clarification and encouragement, the urging and the reminder, we call history. And it is inscribed everywhere in the face of the land, from the mountain passes of the Himalayas to a nameless bajada in the California desert.

Small birds rose up in the road ahead, startled, and flew off. I prayed no infidel would ever find that horse.

ELTING E. MORISON

The Master Builder

FROM AMERICAN HERITAGE OF INVENTION
& TECHNOLOGY

MY GREAT-UNCLE, George S. Morison, one of America's fore-
most bridge builders, died July 1, 1903, exactly (as he undoubt-
edly would have said) six years, five months, fourteen days, and
six hours before I was born. What follows begins with some
incidental intelligence that has nothing to do with his work;
these, listed in no order of relative importance, are just some of
the things I know about him:

He had, like Zeno, a conviction that time was a solid. If he
made an appointment to confer with a person at 3:15 P.M., or
as he always put it, at 1515 hours, that was when they met.
Those who arrived earlier waited; those who came at any time
after 1515 never conferred at all.

He read the *Anabasis* in Greek, the *Aeneid* in Latin, and the
dime novels of Archibald Clavering Gunter in English.

He had a substitute in the Civil War.

He invariably referred to Mexico as Pjacko.

He thought that people who were good with animals, particularly horses, were popular with their fellows and loose in their
morals. When he himself drove a horse, he brought it to a full
stop by saying, "Whoa, cow"; and at least once while trying to
turn a Concord buggy around, he turned it over in front of
White's Machine Shop.

He was rude to waiters.

One Sunday morning he walked out of church after telling
the minister, who was explaining to the congregation why he
thought silver should be coined at a ratio of 16 to 1, that he

should never try to deal with a subject he obviously didn't understand.

Of his neighbor Edward MacDowell, student of Liszt, composer of "To a Wild Rose" and the well-regarded Second Piano Concerto in D Minor, he said he was "a man with whom I had absolutely nothing in common."

A bachelor, he built a house in the years from 1893 to 1897 that had, by one way of counting, fifty-seven rooms, so that he would have a suitable place to eat Thanksgiving dinner and to watch the sun set over Mount Monadnock.

I could go on. Although I do not think that in themselves such items tell very much about the kind of man my great-uncle was, I cite them because, as the world goes, it is remarkable that I know them at all. That such supplementary biographical detritus should survive in such fullness and in such detail into a third, and now, I should say, into a fourth, generation, is remarkable.

There are, to be sure, some contributing circumstances. I spent a considerable part of my youth in the house George Morison built for Thanksgiving dinners and sunsets. Here, beyond those impalpable influences produced by the sense of being on the actual scene, there were more overt reminders of my great-uncle as a first cause. When, for instance, after a storm, moisture leaked through the northwest corner and ate away at the interior plaster, you knew it was because the novel arrangement of bricks and experimental cement that he had devised had not worked out — a rare exception. Or when, after going to bed, there were strange creaks and murmurs drifting through the halls and up the stairwell, you knew, or hoped you knew, that they were produced not by poltergeists or second-story men but by the contraction of his steel beams in the cooling night air.

But there was more to it than those visible and audible reminders. He was still around. The effect on those who came after was not the attenuated visitation of your run-of-the-mill family ghost; it was a one-on-one encounter with a continuing presence. When he died, his sister lived in that house in a rather grand manner for fourteen years, and then his younger brother, my grandfather, presided in distinctive style for eight more years. They were personages of considerable substance, and I knew them both. But when I came to live there as a boy of fifteen, I found that my great-uncle had set them to one side and was still occupying the place.

Of those who have written about him, one spoke of his ability to enforce a decision taken "with a tenacity and ruthlessness that bore down all opposition. . . . " Another called him "a bulwark." And a third said: "Force was the striking impression. When he entered a room, power came with him." They were all trying to explain the source of his remarkable works — he did in fact put a satisfying dent in oblivion by the things he made. But he bore down on the opposition of time in quite another and less obvious way. That ability to fill a room with power turned out to be sufficient to project the force of his character through three generations of his family.

In March 1902 George S. Morison appeared before the Senate Canal Committee. He explained at length why he believed that the best way to join the waters of the Atlantic and Pacific lay through the Isthmus of Panama. The only real difficulty was posed, he said, by the Culebra Cut. "It is a piece of work that reminds me of what a teacher said to me when I was in Exeter over forty years ago, that if he had five minutes in which to solve a problem he would spend three deciding the best way to do it." Because the Culebra Cut was a big problem, more time would be required. It would take two years to figure out what to do and how to do it.

There were many times when he was put in mind of his old teacher and quoted him on problem solving for the benefit of others. It was, said one associate, "one of the principal rules" of his life. He sought beforehand to take everything into account, analyze the evidence, determine the "best possible solution," and then reach the "inflexible, intractable decision." That, in fact, is the way be decided to become a civil engineer.

It took some time to do so. Born in New Bedford, Massachusetts, in 1842, the son of a Unitarian minister, he was educated, like his father before him, at Phillips Exeter Academy and Harvard College. From there he went south as the government superintendent of plantations on Saint Helena Island. The object was to bring some order out of the chaos produced by the Civil War among the resident whites and freedmen. After a year he returned to enter the Harvard Law School, in 1864, where he won the Bowdoin prize for the best dissertation. In 1866 he joined the great New York law firm of Evarts, Southmayd & Choate.

"Exactly one month later" he confronted the problem of what to do with himself — practice law, study the principles that lay beneath the practice and teach them at some university, or go west as a civil engineer. He set May 1 of the following year, seven months later, as the date to decide the matter. On that day he informed the firm of his intention to leave the law, and five months thereafter he went out to Kansas City, Missouri, to build a bridge with Octave Chanute. I have the distinct impression that he was turned in this direction by some work he did while in the law firm, on the bankruptcy of a small western railroad. I cannot verify this by the documents now available, but it has the support of a fairly reliable memory, and it suggests a link in the causality he always sought. When he started work "calculating the cubical contents of stone for the masonry piers," the "four years of doubt, vacillation and search" that had "formed the introduction to my life" were ended.

He could not have landed in a better place at a better time with a better man. The Missouri was a wild and willful river often disturbed by heavy floods and destructive ice jams. It constantly filled up old channels and cut out new ones. No serious bridge had ever been built across it, and the received judgment was that if a bridge were built, it could never be maintained. For someone who knew no engineering, it was a great place to begin.

There was also Octave Chanute, who had never built a big bridge before. But he had worked for a dozen years in various capacities constructing small western railroads, and he had learned a lot on the job. At a time when there was really no other way to learn, Chanute was, at thirty-four, near the top of his class. He was, as all his later career indicates, an "acute and accurate observer," an "inventive engineer," a "truly scientific spirit," and, withal, a man possessing the "Gallic power of clear and forceful expression." When in middle age he turned his attention to "aereal navigation," his experimental glider flights greatly expanded the knowledge of the field. To the success of the Wright brothers he contributed both useful principles and actual designs.

*

What it meant to start on such a job with such a man was made clear in a journal written in Kansas City on Thanksgiving Day, 1867. After laying out his daily work and study schedule from 0800 to 2130 hours "with not more than one evening a week being excepted," Morison went on to plot the move into the future. He was "ambitious, very ambitious." What he had set his sights on was not a financial fortune but "a good and useful life." With that as his purpose he would, when the Kansas City bridge was finished, "cross the Atlantic and devote a year to the study of French and German, and the acquirement of scientific knowledge; it being my wish to make the profession of engineering a truly liberal profession and through it to rise to science and philosophy, raising it with me rather than to prostitute it to mere money making. . . . " Not many of those who at the time were calculating the cubic contents of stones would have put it quite that way, and even now it must appear a very large and liberating definition of the possibilities in the field.

Given such attitudes and such a personal program, it is probably not surprising that he rose rapidly to the position of associate engineer on this first job and that, as soon as the bridge was finished, he went to work on a book that described the solutions to the problems encountered in the building of it. What followed — in a rare departure from his program — was not France and Germany but a six-year internship of steadily increasing responsibility in the design and construction of small, short western railroads with names like Leavenworth, Lawrence & Galveston or Detroit, Eel River & Illinois. Near the end of this period Chanute called him back to serve as his principal engineer on the Erie Canal.

On May 6, 1875, the bridge at Portageville, New York, said to be the largest wooden trestle in the world, was consumed by fire. Morison was put to work drawing up the design and specifications for an iron structure that would replace it. On May 10, four days later, the first building contract was let, and he assumed the direction of the construction. Eighty-two days after that the bridge was open for rail traffic. It was 818 feet 2 inches between abutments and it gave him, at age thirty-three, an "international prominence."

For the next seventeen years he devoted most of his time and

thought to building railroad bridges in the West. He built these
bridges across the Missouri, Mississippi, Ohio, Snake, Columbia,
and Willamette rivers. They all had certain common characteristics. Their specifications filled the requirements of the particular situations to a T, and in the building those specifications
were satisfied precisely. As at Plattsmouth, Nebraska, where the
"total deflection of the main span under the test load of 800,000
pounds was exactly" as previously calculated, so with all the
others. They were also on the grand scale. At Memphis, Tennessee, the main span was 790 feet, which made it the longest
truss in the country. At Cairo, Illinois, the metalwork was 10,560
feet — two miles — in length, the longest steel bridge in the
world. And they were all structures in which the function was
obviously made to determine the form, in studied austerity.

It was said that in this period he compiled a record that was
"unrivaled in the history of bridge construction." Whatever the
truth of this evaluation, it is certain he acquired a reputation
that made him sought after for many different kinds of services.
He joined the boards of four railroads. For fifteen years he
provided Baring Brothers of London with comprehensive anal-
yses of the physical condition, financial structure, and manage-
rial competence of American railroad companies. He played
a large part in the study that led to the reconstruction of the
Erie Canal. President Cleveland put him on one commission
that selected San Pedro as the deep-water port for Los Angeles
and on another that started the action that produced, nearly
forty years later, the George Washington Bridge across the
Hudson.

Then in 1899 he was appointed by President McKinley to the
Isthmian Canal Commission. For the next two and a half years
he devoted himself to an exhaustive examination of the political
difficulties and technical factors, past and present, that were
involved in the great enterprise. Twice he went to Europe; once
he made a four-month exploration of the isthmus itself; and he
attended all the fifty-one meetings of the commission in Washington. In November 1901 the members signed a report that,
reflecting a powerful combination of historical, political, and
technical pressures, recommended Nicaragua as the site for the
canal. Appended to this document was the dissenting opinion

of a minority of one. It recommended, with much careful explanation, the choice of the Isthmus of Panama as the preferred site; and it was signed by George S. Morison.

There followed weeks of argument within the commission, debates in Congress, discussion in the press, and earnest consideration in the White House. In January 1902 the commission rendered a supplementary report that unanimously concluded that the "feasible route for an Isthmian Canal to be under the control, management, and ownership of the United States is that known as the Panama Route."

In such a tangle of historical, political, international, and technical considerations and in such a concert of dominant personalities, it is hard to determine final causes. David McCullough, who has made the most recent and careful investigation of the situation, concludes as follows: "If one traces back through the chain of events . . . and if it is remembered that Morison . . . made no effort to glorify his contributions, at the time or later, then Morison emerges a bit like the butler at the end of the mystery — as the ever-present, frequently unobtrusive, highly instrumental figure around whom the entire plot turned." It is an image he would, beyond much doubt, never have chosen, but it makes a point he would never have made for himself.

Such, briefly, was the nature of his principal works. Before trying to establish a more coherent explanation of the man himself, it may be useful to say something about the man among his fellows. Was his record indeed "unrivaled," should he be called "the leading bridge engineer in America, perhaps in the world," did he deserve the title of Pontifex Maximus bestowed on him at one college commencement? That is a very doubtful kind of exercise that leads to no useful conclusion. What is far more to the point is that he was a contributing member of a remarkable company, some of whom held his achievements in a good deal higher respect than his person. And what is interesting is not what set the members apart but what they all had and did in common.

There were, of course, some distinguishing temperamental differences. John Roebling played the flute and allowed a caller to be five minutes late before canceling the appointment; Octave Chanute made witty remarks; James Eads interrupted a stun-

ning career for four years because he preferred the "happy
environment of his family"; Charles Latrobe liked to go about
in society and worked in watercolors; and so on. What really
matters is the shared experience of those who practiced civil
engineering in the last half of the last century and the effect of
that experience on themselves and those around them.

They came up, for the most part, the hard way. Leaving college and, more often, high school, they started out on the
ground floor, measuring stones, surveying lines, calculating
stresses. They did these things more often than not on a new
railroad, which for them, like the Erie Canal for the preceding
generation, was the only available institute of technology. Here
they learned from men who knew a little more than they did
because they had been a little longer on the job. Frequently they
followed these instructors into the engineering division of one
of the larger, more stable roads in the East. And from there,
after a time, they usually struck out on their own as "consulting
engineers," which meant they were ready to deal with whatever
propositions came to them.

Wherever they went, whatever they did, they found the subject matter was always changing. Larger loads, longer spans,
deeper excavations, new materials, novel procedures. In such
conditions the name of the game was figuring out sensible new
departures from what had been tried and true for centuries.
And if the figuring wasn't right, the cost of going wrong could
be measured out and the source of difficulty explicitly defined.
When, for instance, the bridge Amasa Stone had built at Ash-
tabula, Ohio, went down one stormy night, it took a train of
passengers with it. And after a jury found that the bridge had
been an experiment "which ought never to have been tried,"
Amasa Stone, "as exacting of himself as he had been of many
others," took his own life.

Those who started on the ground floor and worked their way
through to the top of such a calling were often said to be bold,
self-reliant, independent, secure, powerful, daring, resolute,
and, sometimes, arrogant and overbearing. At this distance it
may be seen that their most continuing collective contribution
was not the things they built but their way of going at things.
They gave a significant push to the developing new method of
solving certain kinds of problems that occur in life.

Over and over they demonstrated that the ingenious solution that worked was reached through accurate observation, exact knowledge of the strength of materials, precise calculation, due respect for the laws and forces of nature, and the resourceful ordering of evidence obtained by the unclouded intelligence. They could be daring when the findings from the hard data — subjected to the logical process — supported the bold conclusion, and they were resolute because, within their scheme of things, they could prove they were right. Faith might well have its uses, but they had found a surer way to remove a mountain. This method, increasingly refined, has put us wherever it is that we are today.

On this subject he had ideas that in his closing years he put down in a small book. It demonstrates the extent to which he had fulfilled his early intention to rise through his profession to philosophy, and it still speaks to our condition. Our ability to manufacture power in unlimited quantities, begun with Watt and the condenser, had opened up what Morison called a new epoch for mankind. Carried to its logical conclusions, it would in time give men the capacity to create all the essential conditions for their living and to determine their own fate. He foresaw a future when "material developments will come to a gradual pause," when "an immense population will live comfortably and happily, and the qualities which make the good citizen and the contented man will be more in demand than those which make leaders in periods as we are familiar with."

But he also believed that the new epoch, before it reached this possible end, would "destroy many of the conditions which give most interest to the history of the past, and many of the traditions which people hold most dear." Among other things it would "destroy ignorance, as the entire world will be educated, and one of the greatest dangers must come from this very source, when the number of half-educated people is greatest, when the world is full of people who do not know enough to recognize their limitations. . . . "

How do we assemble the bits and pieces of Morison's personality and character in a more intelligible mosaic? If the design is supposed to fulfill a familiar expectation, this is a hard question. Remember that until he built the great brick house, at the age of fifty-five, he had no place to call his own, and during the remaining years of his life his accumulated occupancy of that house came to little more than forty-nine days. Though he had apartments in Chicago and New York, he didn't use them much, and then only for bed and sometimes breakfast. For the most part he stayed in hotels and sleeping cars, and ate in clubs and restaurants. Considered as a social being, he seems a programmed nomad.

There are some family letters, but for the most part they have to do with the arrangement for a proposed visit or the details of some small errand he wished a member to perform. There is also the daily diary he kept throughout his life. In the entries are faithfully reported temperatures, rainfalls, and the number of minutes the train he was riding on was behind schedule.

In such conditions one must respect the dead air spaces, accept the fact that what you see is all you're going to get, and recognize that he planned it that way. If you look back to the journal entry for Thanksgiving Day, 1867, you will find his program for a good and useful life. What he did with himself from those first calculations of cubic quantities to his closing consideration of engineering as the source of a new epoch satisfied the terms of that program — not less, not more, but exactly.

WILLIAM PFAFF

The Lay Intellectual
(Apologia Pro Vita Sua)

FROM SALMAGUNDI

THE PRIVATE SCHOLAR has all but vanished, the emperor of
Japan possibly the last of this distinguished line. The private or
lay intellectual was to be found in the United States fifty years
ago, usually but not always making his living in the serious journalism of the time — the intellectual weeklies and monthlies,
such newspapers as the *World,* the *Herald Tribune,* the *Baltimore
Sun,* the *Chicago Daily News,* where value was placed on general
cultivation and good writing. Such newspapers no longer exist
in the United States. The monthlies no longer have their old
authority, or the audience they once possessed. We have, thank-
fully, *The New York Review of Books* and a few general quarterlies
such as the present one, but contributors are mostly academic,
and in the case of *The New York Review* largely British, which
itself is significant.

The lay intellectual survives in numbers in Britain, France,
and elsewhere in Western Europe, where serious general jour-
nals and newspapers do survive (the latter precariously) and
state broadcasting systems also support an intellectually and ar-
tistically serious output of drama, music, talk, and public affairs
programming.

By "intellectual," of course, I mean the person who deals in
ideas primarily for their own sake, for the pleasure they give,
and only then for their practical effect and application. There
are plenty of intelligent professional people, officials, business
and organizational executives, journalists and broadcasters, sci-

entists, engineers, who are not intellectuals. There are people in the university who are not intellectuals; but the university is nonetheless the intellectuals' institution, the community of learned men and women, the center of speculation. Why then are there some of us whose lives revolve about ideas but who avoid the university, lack its credentials and certification, and find only a qualified pleasure in the company of university intellectuals or presence in the university community? The alternatives, for persons without independent incomes, have grievous disadvantages.

The intellectual life and teaching have always been connected, but never more so than in the United States today; and they are not, of course, the same vocation, as everyone knows. Their present degree of amalgamation has not been particularly good for either, as everyone also knows, requiring teachers to perform scholarly research for which they may not be particularly gifted — prejudicing the career of teachers of merit, even genius, who lack this certification or resist it. Natural scholars, speculative intelligences, on the other hand, are compelled to teach, which they sometimes do gracelessly, grudgingly, and badly. The church did these things better, offering Jesuit and Carthusian fundamentally different ways to live essentially the same life, which was, is, a form of the intellectual life.

The life of the intellectual outside the university is, first of all, as such, insecure. He is a free lance in a world only passingly interested in what he professionally provides. He is nearly always pressed to make his living in some compromising manner. This is the inevitable consequence of renouncing the only institution in contemporary society interested, in principle at least, in ideas for their own sake. The lay intellectual has to sell his thought if he and his family are to eat, or alternatively, he must support them and himself, and his ideas as well, by work that is apart from his vocation. Either way is difficult. The choice of nonintellectual work — to keep a shop, manage a business, practice a trade or profession — is the least corrupting, but also the most distracting and difficult. It is, I would argue, a more satisfactory solution for artists than for intellectuals. Even among artists, it seems to work best for poets, for whom the actual output is very limited and intensely concentrated, the product of a distillation that may in fact benefit from the distraction of lay life. Thus Eliot the publisher, Claudel and Perse the diplomats, Williams the Rutherford physician, Stevens the Hartford insurance executive. It seems to work less well as a permanent arrangement for novelists or playwrights, although there are the cases of Celine, and Maugham at the start of his career, physicians, and the odd diplomat, the spy. The novelist seems very much at home as a spy, inventing lives being his trade in both cases.

The novelist, like the intellectual, seems more often drawn to journalism, broadcasting, films, public relations or advertising, creative or quasi-creative ways of making a living. A profession tolerant of the intellectual life has, in the past at least, been the army, particularly European armies, where the intellectual soldier, or the soldier who is also an artist, has not been uncommon. In the ranks, in most armies — as in the printing trades, and in the old days, telegraphy — a tradition of autodidact intellectualism exists, not to be despised.

The intelligence services have been good to lay scholars and lay intellectuals, perhaps better than anyone else since 1940, offering a provisional professional engagement, often an interesting one, and, usually, eccentric and sympathetic colleagues. They have supported the generalist intellectual (and the specialist in eccentric or academically unfashionable subjects) to an extent largely overlooked, or deliberately obscured, in the United States since Vietnam. A significant part of the knowledge we possess on Soviet society, China, the Eastern European states, Southeast Asia, obviously, but other and more exotic subjects as well, is owed to work done within the intelligence agencies, or more or less patiently funded by the CIA, the British SIS, the French, German, Italian, and other secret services, in outside institutions, or supported by them at places like Saint Anthony's College, Oxford, and MIT.

The research institute, the so-called think tank, largely an American phenomenon, has been less important to intellectuals because it is less interested in speculative and scholarly work than in a form of bureaucratic analysis. Even as scientific institutions these have declined since the war, as first-rate scientists, reasonably enough, prefer university circumstances. Rand was an interesting place in the 1950s, and even in the 1960s, a place where the odd, exotic, autodidact, or unclassifiable brain could be housed, people — as Herman Kahn once remarked of his staff at Hudson Institute — "otherwise unemployable." The impression I have of Rand and its counterparts today is that they are made up of people who would rather be at the university, if one would take them, or in the government bureaucracy, which they usually are actively working to join. The atmosphere at Hudson Institute in New York in the 1960s, despite the efforts of some, was more that of an adjunct to the bureaucracy, and later of a business consultancy, than of a speculative center. At best, life is not very satisfying professionally at these institutions, although they may free time for one's own work. Even the most serious policy analysis, "soft" research on government-funded projects, can expect to do no more than shift the direction of bureaucratic thinking by a hair's breadth, and that rarely, except on those occasions when it provides a felicitous rationalization for something the government already wants to do but has not found a way to justify. Every effort that seriously diverges from the client's interests risks being characterized as "theology."

One reflects that they did these things better in the past — or somewhere else. The intellectual, though, did not exist in the past. Jefferson was not an intellectual but an educated man. The size of his world is noteworthy, and I think that scale is the critical factor in the survival of the lay intellectual in Britain and France (the other countries I know most about), at the same time that his kind declines in the United States. In France, for example, where I have lived for the last fifteen years, an interested observer of these matters, the following would be a perfectly normal career for an ambitious young intellectual today, after making his or her mark at *normale sup* (philosophy and literature — science too, but I am not talking about scientists here) or *sciences-po* (economics and politics), plus taking an *agrégation* or other advanced theoretical degree somewhere else. (The *École Nationale d'Administration*, although ordinarily considered at the summit of the *grandes écoles* system, prepares for the higher civil service rather than the intellectual life as such. The *grandes écoles* provide the great audiences for the great poets.)

There is, to begin with, a limited and coherent community for the young intellectual to enter. There is a capital city, a limited number of intellectual institutions, interaction and dialogue among them. Europeans who come to the United States often feel tremendous relief at how open and anarchically, creatively free it all is in the United States. The American, on the other hand, is likely to be astounded and gratified to find that in Paris or London people actually talk to one another and, sometimes, listen; that government officials, politicians, professors, journalists, professional men, and intelligent business people all know one another, read and write for the same publications, meet one another at dinner parties, argue, and may actually pay attention to what the others say.

The young intellectual enters this community with connections already made because of the schools from which he has come. Meritocracy it is (not that social qualifications are a disadvantage, but they are not decisive), and the selection/admission processes have already taken place in the awful examination struggles of *baccalauréats,* Oxbridge examinations and interviews, the grueling admission competitions of the *grandes écoles* — and the examinations that enable you to stay in them. By the time a young man or woman in France or Britain is ready to head for his Big Apple (if Mayor Koch will allow me), his or her success there, and role to be played in this larger world, has already largely been decided.

The following is caricatural, but only mildly: our young French intellectual, launching himself or herself in Paris, can expect to build up a career in which simultaneously he or she may (with a few friends) turn out a "little" literary or political magazine or irregular paper; edit, for one of the publishing houses, a "collection" built around their circle of friends or some theme of interest; write a column or regular articles for one of the weeklies or for the daily press; and find a broadcasting niche on "France Culture" or "France Music" — the state radio — or as a commentator or documentary producer on commercial radio. One can make a film. State or quasi-official subsidy is easy to find for projects with cultural pretensions. Regularly, one must produce a "brilliant" book, not very heavily researched or documented (no time for that). To write a novel, at least one, is expected even of political and economic intellectuals; the artist's and intellectual's are seen as overlapping careers. One possibly will also keep an academic connection, teaching a single course or giving an annual seminar at one of the *grandes écoles* or at the university.

This is a path leading normally, even inevitably, toward public appointments in state cultural institutions, executive posts in publishing or broadcasting, possibly an embassy, a call to government, innumerable invitations to smart dinners where one will be afforded a quarter hour in which to dazzle ("étonnez-moi!"), and eventual membership in the *Institut,* even the *Collège de France* (not the *Academie* — no intellectuals there).

Government and intellectual careers are compatible. The *grandes écoles,* at the summit of the French educational system, are all fundamentally professional schools preparing candidates for the state service. The unique advantage of a French civil service career — after admission into one of the *grandes corps* of the civil service, the inspection of finance, diplomatic service, *Conseil d'État* (judicial supervision of the administration), etc. — is that the member can take leave at any time for projects in private life, literature, business, and industry, or to run for political office, knowing that at any time he or she can be reintegrated into the *corps* with standing and seniority intact.

In Britain, too, as everyone knows, it is common to be broadcaster, politician, diarist, and author, all in the same career, and perhaps Oxford don as well. Harvard at its most worldly has never come near to the matter-of-fact political-governmental involvements of Oxford. While England (not Scotland) distrusts "over-cleverness," and France esteems it, in both countries the intellectual life is taken seriously and is at the center of public life.

An American, puritan and heir to German academic seriousness, looks with astonishment and suspicion at this kind of thing. It seems irredeemably lightweight to have so versatile a career, which it often is. But a man like Raymond Aron, for example, was certainly as serious and creative an intellectual figure as the century has seen, and he was a journalist all his life, writing on questions of the moment in *Combat, Le Figaro,* and *L'Express,* dealing with economics as well as politics, while at the same time producing major works on philosophy, the philosophy of history, strategy and war, and sociology. He began as a university intellectual but the war turned him to journalism (editor of the Free French paper in London), where he remained. He took up teaching again only in the mid-1950s but remained a journalistic commentator and essentially a man of the larger world.

Camus was a journalist, publisher, editor, dramatist, and theatrical director. Malraux was a publisher, publicist, adventurer. Saint-Exupéry was an air mail pilot. Orwell, their British contemporary, was never really a systematic thinker at all but rather an artist and critic, a dystopian visionary (and, of course, a wrong-headed one: 1984 occurred in 1948 — we have subsequently moved away from it, not toward it). Virtually every non-university intellectual in Britain since the First World War has been mixed up at one time or another with the BBC, the British Council, diplomacy, or the intelligence service. Lippmann, who springs to mind as the American equivalent, never had the intellectual weight of an Aron or Camus, although he too produced works on general questions of politics. Mencken does not survive as much of a heavyweight, rather as a superlative and erudite polemical journalist. Edmund Wilson is the most notable modern American intellectual (artist *manqué*) who successfully conducted a career of the utmost seriousness and integrity outside the academy, and this was perhaps only feasible because of some private means and, in his later years, because of the existence of that peculiar and unique American phenomenon, *The New Yorker* magazine, which by a fluke of fortune became, from its comic-paper origins, at the same time the most serious of American general publications and a highly successful vehicle of consumer advertising (of often the most grotesque and transparent snobbishness; one wonders who the advertisers think the readers really are, or alternatively, a more disturbing thought, who the readers really are that such advertisements are addressed to them).

The professional problem of the lay intellectual is a function of his choice to renounce the university. He has to find another buyer. If he can find a large enough audience for his books or articles to provide him with an independent livelihood, fair enough; but one needs scarcely say that in the United States this is rare, rarer probably than those cases when serious artists find an audience big enough to support them. Otherwise he sells a part of his talent to those who will buy, the politicians, the government agency, the business corporation, the research institute, the broadcasting network or newspaper or public relations agency. This may not be very good for his talent in the short run, forcing compromises upon it, although in another respect it may prove valuable in providing a range of experience, a worldliness, the academic intellectual does not ordinarily possess.

Why follow the irregular's career? At the heart of it, I think, are two factors: the rejection of specialization and the dislike of the cloister, which may also be considered worldliness. We who do this are often synthesizers, generalists, speculators — butterflies, gypsies, irresponsibles. Some want power and public appointment or office. This is very common, obviously, among people in think tanks and journalism, but is an ambition usually more easily obtained from the starting point of the university. Some are cosmopolitans, travelers, the curious, café dwellers, for whom the constrained life, the introversion and intrigue of the academic community, are repellent. Some are incorrigible free-lancers, movers-on, independent souls. Some simply don't like and don't want to teach.

The late J. P. Nettle, the biographer of Rosa Luxemburg, drew a distinction between ideas of "scope" and those of "quality," the former being proper to the university, involving the transmission of the cultural patrimony. Ideas of "quality" address some form of preferential restructuring and qualitative dissent in the culture, and thus are in a degree political and ideological. These, he argued, usually are the product of the non-university intellectual world. Nettle, indeed, calls the non-university dealer in ideas *the* intellectual, remarking that it is, of course, only fairly recently that intellectuals have entered the university. As David Schalk observes, Nettle thus identifies the intellectual with political engagement, which may certainly be challenged. Nonetheless there unquestionably is a form of the intellectual vocation that does not belong in the university and to which the university is hostile. But more and more, in the United States at least, there is little room for intellectuals anywhere else.

When I left the University of Notre Dame in 1949, I did not think of myself as an intellectual. What I was sure of was that I was not an academic. The majority of my friends intended to go to graduate school and expected to teach. This seemed to me a deeply depressing prospect — to stay longer in school, good God! I knew that I had to go to the city, some city, the only way, it seemed to me, finally to become an adult. To work at what? I didn't know. My degree was in English, but at Notre Dame at that time English scarcely meant English at all, but was two senior years studying the Greeks, aesthetics, Dante, Shakespeare, Kierkegaard, Rimbaud and Baudelaire, Maritain, Bernanos, Mauriac, Hermann Broch, Romano Guardini . . . This is not the place to go into why this was so; and it was not a bad education to offer provincial boys from the Catholic immigration; but it was not exactly an education calculated for success in the American Dream.

I thought sketchily of the State Department or the CIA — international politics increasingly interested me, and that was a time when Stalinism seemed to present a kind of historical challenge to justify a public career. Then circumstances drew me into intellectual journalism, *The Commonweal,* and from there to the Army, travel, political warfare, policy research, and eventually, possibly wiser, back to free-lance journalism. I cannot say that I am sorry, haphazard and hazardous as all this has so far been, and God only knows where it will end. Possibly it will end in a trailer park in Arizona like everybody else, or in a room without a view in Antibes with all those books we've accumulated. Possibly it will be at a university nonetheless, as happens to aged journalists, to become — I believe I have the right expression — a "resource person," whom I take to be an elderly mariner or retired explorer propped up with a gin to tell repetitive tales of the cannibals and kookaburras of the uncloistered world. Thus may the circle close and the irreconcilable be reconciled. I cannot say that I really look forward to it.

SAMUEL PICKERING, JR.

Pictures

FROM THE SOUTHERN REVIEW

I LIKED THE PICTURE on our Christmas card this year. Vicki took it one October morning after I had been raking leaves. She brought a kitchen table into the yard, and while Francis, Edward, and I sat in a big pile of leaves, she put the camera on the table, and after setting it on automatic, ran over and dropped down beside us. "How did you like the card?" I said while visiting my parents in Nashville during the holidays. "Well," Mother answered, "at least you can't see the garbage cans." Last year Vicki took the picture in the side yard near the garage. Although she didn't notice them at the time, our garbage cans were in the background. When the picture came back from the developer, Vicki saw the cans and asked me if we should use it on the card. I said yes, arguing that the cans were "us." Instead of being plastic tubs that hardly made a sound when trundled out to the road, they were metal and behaved like real garbage cans. Whenever a wind overturned them, their tops blew into neighbors' yards, and their bottoms clattered down the driveway and crashed into the woodpile. I usually heard them tumbling about and, feeling comfortable, invariably said, "Listen to that wind; there's going to be a storm."

My idea that the cans somehow revealed a real "us" did not impress Mother. "If it is honesty you are looking for," she said, "take the next picture in the bathtub." Mother had a point, and this year we made sure that there were no cans in the background. Of course, putting a family picture on a Christmas card is hokey. Not many people we know do it. The literary folk among our acquaintance send cards depicting nativity scenes taken from medieval psalters, while businessmen and doctors send cards with illustrations of spare Scandinavian Christmas trees or Santa Claus hurrying about in a Mercedes loaded with smoked salmon and Johnny Walker. Still, I thought Mother would like this year's card, and when she did not, I examined all the cards she received. She kept them in a silver, shell-shaped nut dish in the living room. Our card wasn't among them, and it wasn't there, I decided, because it was too informal for the room. In the few cards with family photographs, people wore their best clothes. Mothers and fathers dressed in grays and dark blues with touches of red and green here and there. Little girls wore pink dresses and white leather shoes, while little boys wore short pants suits and shirts with Peter Pan collars. Deep in the leaves the overalls our boys wore were not noticeable, and, wearing an orange and yellow sweater, Vicki looked like autumn itself. The trouble with the card was me. I wore a blue and white T-shirt. On the front was a profile of an Indian with three feathers in his hair; above his head was printed "Tarzan Brown Mystic River Run."

What a good race it had been, I recalled as I thought about the card, a sunny day along a road near the tall ships at Mystic, and I had run well. For my parents the shirt evoked no memories and, seeing only unseasonable and indecorous dress, they longed for the formality traditionally associated with holidays. That formality, however, is often as posed as holiday snapshots. Life is frayed around the collar, wears T-shirts, and rakes leaves. By bringing things into ordered perspective photographs distort living. Not long ago Vicki and I received a packet of pictures from a relative with whom we spent Thanksgiving. The scenes in the pictures were arranged. On the dining room table were a linen tablecloth and napkins, ornate nineteenth-century candelabra, silver goblets, and plates with blue and gold bands running around the edges. Wild rice, turkey, beans with mushrooms, sweet potatoes, and a score of cut-glass dishes containing brightly colored condiments rested on the sideboard. Beside it stood our hostess, knife and fork in hand, ready to serve the meal. The people sitting around the table were smiling and seemed happy and relaxed. The smiles, however, were just clothes put on for the occasion; beneath them was tension. Our hostess was an alcoholic; barely able to stand for the picture, she collapsed and had to be carried to bed halfway through the meal. Most people had left when she reappeared four hours later, explaining, "That was the worst sinus attack I have ever had."

As clear photographs blur truth, so correspondingly, and perhaps fittingly, an individual's perspective distorts clarity. When looked at through the long lens of living, no event is ever what it first seems. In one of the simplest photographs we received, our little boys and their cousins sat on a couch. In his hand each child held a toy pilgrim or turkey. The photograph was balanced; the five children were evenly spaced out; on each side of the couch was an end table; on top of each was an arrangement of yellow and white chrysanthemums. On the back of the photograph, our hostess drew a smiling face and wrote, "HOW CUTE!!!" Cute the children may have been, but when I first looked at the photograph I did not see them. Instead I noticed a small green and gold china pelican on one of the tables. It was Herend china; for some time I had given Herend figurines to close relatives for Christmas. "It was funny how that began," I thought as I held the picture. Years ago in London I had gone to Asprey to buy a leather satchel to hang over my shoulder. Many men in London wore them, and I thought one would make a good carrying case. Asprey is an expensive store; a footman in top hat and tails opens the door for customers, and the saleswomen look like rich aunts from the right part of the country. I was ill at ease, and when a woman asked if she could help me, I found it difficult to describe what I wanted. "I'm looking for a pocketbook to throw over my shoulder," I said. When the woman did not respond immediately, I hurried forward, adding, "You know, the kind homosexuals carry." "They are not," the woman answered after a pause, "all homosexual. Some are French." "Oh," I said, feeling and probably sounding like a punctured balloon, "I guess I don't want one." Then glancing quickly around in hopes of finding something else to talk about so I would seem less foolish, I asked, "I need to buy my mother a present. Do you have any suggestions?" "Ah," the woman answered, "we have just received a shipment of Herend china; the figurines make very nice presents."

After putting my parents' Christmas cards back on the dish, I stood up and, glancing around, noticed that there were no

photographs in the room. On the walls were paintings and portraits and an occasional print; photographs were in the back, private part of the house: on chests and night tables in bedrooms
and on shelves in dressing rooms. Unlike the portraits, which
seemed permanent and had hung in the same places as far back
as I could remember, photographs appeared ephemeral. Whenever Mother received new pictures of Edward and Francis, she
forced them into frames in front of old pictures. When the
frames became filled and started to bow, she took the old pictures out and stuffed them carelessly into a box at the top of
her closet. Throughout the house were boxes like this, out of
sight and cluttered with photographs and remnants of time
past.

In my old bedroom was a sugar chest filled with scrapbooks.
The first part of each scrapbook was organized with pictures
and papers arranged neatly. Like life, though, the scrapbooks
soon got out of hand, and at the end of each book pictures were
pushed in haphazardly, the bindings of the books split, and, like
stones eroded from the face of a cliff by wind and water, negatives had slipped loose and rolled through layers of memories
to litter the bottom of the chest. My scrapbooks were on top,
and I wanted to hurry through them. Pictures of myself usually
make me uneasy. When Vicki brings a group back from the
developer, I look at them once, then consign them to the attic.
Returning to them months and even years later embarrasses me
and makes me feel guilty. As I age and my world constricts, I
do not want to confront my past and be compelled to judge it
and then regret life missed. This time, however, I went slowly
through the scrapbooks and looked at each picture. I am not
really sure why. Because I had examined the photographs on
my parents' Christmas cards almost dispassionately, maybe I
started out interested in the photographs simply as photographs. Whatever my motivation, however, I soon left the world
of the abstract and entered that of the personal.

In scrapbooks, pictures are not isolated; letters, newspapers,
cards, written materials of all kinds frame them. In one book, I
found a letter addressed to "3rd Lt. Sammy." Mailed to me from
El Paso in October 1945, it was from Jack Spore, who lived with
his relatives in an apartment on the same landing as ours. Jack
was about to be discharged from the Army, and he wrote, "Tell

Tigue and Kaka I may be home sooner than they expect — and to have plenty of coffee on hand so you and I can drink our coffee together." I have always been a poor athlete, but in school I tried hard and played just about everything, in the process suffering untold anxiety. As I read Jack's letter and looked at pictures of me holding cars, football helmets, tennis rackets, and baseball bats, I remembered a football game my junior year in high school. The game was important, and since I was a rarely used substitute, I did not expect to play. At the end of the third quarter we led by two points, but the other team made a first down on our eight-yard line and appeared certain to score. The evening was cool, and despite the excitement I was dreaming blissfully and safely in the middle of the bench when I heard, "Pickering, get in there at left tackle." The coach made a mistake, and when the other team came out of its huddle, I prayed they would run the ball the other way. Just before the ball was snapped, though, the referee blew his whistle and approached me. It was Jack Spore. I had not seen him for eight years; at the end of the third grade, my parents and I moved into a house in the suburbs. "Sammy," Jack said loudly, "if you hurt any of these boys, I am going to tell your mommy and daddy." Then blowing his whistle again, he shouted, "Play ball." And that we did, after everybody on the field stared at me.

Although scrapbooks are filled with tokens of success, looking through one brings failure sharply to mind. "He has achieved what I predicted for him when he came here," a dean of my college wrote to my parents twenty-five years ago. "He's our finest type, and we are grooming him for a Rhodes Scholar candidate — I hope you'll encourage him in this." My parents followed the dean's suggestion, but as this year's Christmas card illustrated, grooming has never done much for me. On the same page as the letter was a photograph of a friend and me going rabbit hunting in 1960. I still have the jacket I wore in the picture. Although it has more tears than buttons, I wear it everywhere in the fall. "Did you make that coat?" a university administrator asked me when I walked into his office. "No," I answered. "Well, you sure fooled me," he said, "because it looks like you made it — in the garage with a hammer and nails."

I fell in love for the first time in nursery school, but love didn't become a nuisance until the sixth grade. That year Santa Claus

brought me a book entitled *for BOYS only*. In it a Dr. Richardson
lectured schoolboys on proper behavior with girls. "There are
lots of ways of having good times with girls. Let's not choose the
wrong ones," he urged. In the sixth grade following the good
doctor's advice was easy. Sadly, that happy state of simplicity
lasted only a few years. In the scrapbooks were pictures of
Irene, Alice, Becky, Pam, Charisse, and a classroom of others.
Times always seemed to start out "good," but inevitably they
ended wrong; smiles turned into frowns, and bright interest
became boredom. Among my old loves was a picture of Vicki.
Her hair hung over her shoulders, and she wore jeans, a green
cashmere sweater, and a double string of pearls. Her right hand
rested jauntily on her hip, her eyes were laughing, and her
mind was on love. Now Vicki's hair is short like a boy's. She
wears support hose to shore up veins broken down by three
quick pregnancies, and when she travels, it is not with love on
her mind but earaches, antibiotics, and cough syrup.

People sentimentalize while looking through scrapbooks and
often imagine meeting old loves and friends. Characters in photographs are not real and can be controlled: buried deep for
years, then dug up and molded to suit a whim. Actual people
do not behave so conveniently, and if faced with the choice of
renewing a long-interrupted friendship or looking at a picture
and creating a past and a future, I suspect most people would
choose the photograph. As a boy I spent summers on my grandfather's dairy farm in Virginia; during those years my closest
friends were the Cutter boys, five country children with whom
I lived days of building, catching, and exploring. In the scrapbooks were several photographs of us together. Looking at the
boys, I wondered where they were and imagined our meeting.
What a lot we had to talk about. Would they remember the
sliding hill, the bamboo woods, and the mud turtles we fished
out of a swamp near the Tappahannock and turned loose in the
spring? Would they know what finally happened to the crazy
man who broke into the dairy, telephoned the house, and
threatened to cut my throat? For two days he roamed through
the woods eluding the sheriff and a posse of searchers. Even as
I drifted along in the comfortable shade of memory, I knew I
was only indulging myself. My life had diverged sharply from
those of the Cutters, and I had become part of a safe formality.

Although my clothes are tattered and formless, at the core I am acutely sensitive to propriety and knew I did not want to entertain the Cutters. Two of them had been in prison, and I realized little good would come from our meeting. Two years ago James Cutter called Mother in Nashville and asked for my address, saying he wanted to visit me. Mother told him I was out of the country and would not be back for at least four years. When Mother told me what she had done, I wanted to cry, "Oh, Mother, how could you? We were best friends." Instead I said, "Thank you, you did the right thing."

Outside Nashville on the road to Chattanooga, there used to be a modest white clapboard church. In front of the church was a sign reading, "Founded on Calvary in 33 A.D." Nashville has grown, and the Chattanooga highway has become an interstate, too busy and expensive for little churches and bordered instead by shopping centers, condominiums, motels, and restaurants. Like my memory of the Chattanooga road, scrapbooks always contain pictures of places long gone. With stalls for horses and cars, the garage of Grandfather Ratcliffe's house outside Richmond was larger than the house in which I now live. After the house burned, Grandfather bought Cabin Hill, a farm deep in Hanover County. Redoing the house was a labor of love, and near its completion, when I was four and a half, Grandfather wrote me. "This beautiful picture on the back of your letter," he said, "I will hang up in my new house that I am having fixed, and I do not want any little boys to pull any of the paper off of the wall, and if they do, it is no telling what will happen to them. I am fixing everything as nice as I know how," he continued. "I am working my finger nails to the bone to get food for you and your Mother when you get here." With magnolias throughout the grounds, long rows of pink and white dogwood along the drive, and a forest of boxwood about the house, Cabin Hill bloomed like spring in an album of pictures. The reality now resembles autumn. The farm has been divided and the gardens plowed under for a housing development. Even worse was the fate of Grandfather Pickering's home in Carthage, Tennessee. In one picture my father and his brother Coleman, aged six and four, stood in front of a two-story Victorian house. A porch wrapped around two sides of the house; on it were a swing, rocking chairs, and a child's hobbyhorse. Behind the house long, gray fields sloped down toward the Cumberland River. The house doesn't exist now; a decade ago it was torn down to make room for a Ben Franklin variety store. Since my memories of Cabin Hill and Carthage are clear, the photographs frightened me. Instead of eliciting sweet reveries, they made me aware of the evanescence of things and my mortality, built not upon stone and wood but upon soft flesh and brittle bone.

In the sugar chest were many items from my parents' pasts. Two of my father's baby teeth were in an envelope labeled, "Samuel's First Teeth Shed, June 1915, Age 6 Years, 11 Months." In another envelope, supplied by "The City Barber Shop. Sam King, Proprietor. North Side Public Square. Carthage, Tennessee Box 201," was a lock of Father's hair. The color was a kind of fawn blond, just the same as Edward's, and I showed it to Vicki and Mother and Father. Although the childhood mementos of people whose lives were quickly gathering toward an end were endowed with pathos, finding them pleased me. The similarity between Father's and Edward's hair linked generations and seemed a sign of continuation. In contrast to those of childhood, I hurried through the photographs and keepsakes of my parents' adolescence and young, unmarried years. In a jewelry case in the attic, I found the love letters Father wrote Mother before they were married. When I saw the handwriting and read the postmark on the first envelope, I knew what the letters were, and I quickly closed the jewelry box. My children and their children could read them, not me. The only photographs I paused over that showed my parents as young adults were those in which I appeared. After my birth, their worlds were mine. Before I was born, their lives seemed private. Mother was lovely, and when I found pictures of her at dances at Princeton and Washington and Lee, showing Dalmatians at the Orange Lawn Tennis Club, and shooting trap on Long Island, I felt like a voyeur. Pictures of distant relatives did not affect me the same way. A photograph of a great-grandmother with lace billowing up to a buttonlike gold earring in one ear and then rolling in rich curves over her shoulders and chest reminded me of Annie, an old love rounded and warm as the dark summer earth.

Not all the pictures of Mother as a young woman bothered me. Occasionally something on the edge of a photograph caught my attention. On the way to the Maryland Cup Race, Mother, her date, and another couple stopped for a picnic. In the background of the picture was their car, a wonderfully boxy Rolls-Royce, a car I now associate with the pampered rich but one I would like to travel in just once. I want to feel special and imagine myself beyond the ordinary; a single ride, though, would be enough; more might make me believe I was different and thus corrupt me. Mother's date for the race was Ernest. Although Ernest had been her best beau for a time, I did not mind looking at him. His expression was bland and had none of the seductive power of the bold, appraising glance that marked photographs of Father in the 1930s. Ernest was certain to be disappointed in love, and I traced his courtship up to the telegram he sent on the eve of Mother's wedding, apologizing for not attending. "Terribly Disappointed," it read. "Business Engagements Prevent Being There Stop My Sincerest Best Wishes Ernest."

In the library were several family albums. Bound in leather, they resembled books from the back; across the front ornate metal buckles clasped them shut. Inside were pictures taken from the 1860s through the 1880s. Unlike the people in the scrapbooks, few of these people were immediately identifiable. There were women with heavy stovepipe curls, in dark dresses bound at the neck by brooches, or with roses in their hair; little girls in high-topped button boots and bloomers; boys wearing new hats and checkered vests out of which hung watch chains; and soldiers — three young men in Confederate uniforms, then a Union captain with his hair slicked down and who signed his picture, "Yours Truly Tom Waters." Exchanging pictures was fashionable in the last part of the nineteenth century, and every town had a photographic studio. On the back of a picture was the photographer's name and address: B. W. Rose, Corner, Main & Broadway, Paris, Kentucky; J. H. Van Stavoren's Metropolitan Gallery, 53 College Street, Nashville, Tennessee; A. D. Lytle, Main Street, Baton Rouge, Louisiana. My great-grandfather came from Ohio, and the albums contained photographs taken in Athens, Cincinnati, Portsmouth, and Springfield. Unlike this year's Christmas card, which turned my thoughts inward to Mystic and memory, the photographs thrust me outward as I tried to identify people in the pictures.

I started leafing through old books in the library. The going was slow, and soon what I searched for was less important than what I found. In a family Bible was a copy of *The Athens Messenger* for January 12, 1899. My great-great-grandfather's obituary was on the front page. "During the last week," the article stated, "he grew gradually more infirm, and early Sunday morning, after he had journeyed long and journeyed far, there came for him the twilight and the dusk, the mist gathered over the mirror of memory, the pulse throbbed faint and low, and finally ceased to beat on earth forever." Like catacombs into which individuals disappear to become part of great heaps of bones, the yellow, spotted pages of the Bibles reeked of death and families gone from memory. Unlike the death that stalks through my days making me tremble at the names of diseases, death in the Bibles was not terrifying. The saddest losses were often adorned with poetry. When two young sisters, Elizabeth and Mary Perkins, died on September 12, 1829, their father wrote, "They were lovely and pleasant in their lives, and in their death were not divided. Departed ones," he continued, quoting verse, "I do not wish you here, / But though ye are in a lovelier land, / Among a sacred and a holy band, / For you is yet shed many a bitter tear." Unlike the accounts one hears of friends who are dying, the comments and remembrances in the Bibles were reassuring. My grandfather Pickering died when I was small, and although I have often heard he was a gentle, kindly man, I remember little about him except that he grew marvelous strawberries. He sold insurance and his office was above the bank. Eight years after his death, a note appeared on the editorial page of the *Carthage Courier*. I found the note in a Bible, and it made me happy, not bringing cold and disorder to mind, but long neat rows of shining strawberries. "An unprepossessing, probably little noticed metal sign, its enamel chipped with age," the note said, "is fastened to the stairway entrance of a business building here, proclaiming to his friends in life, the destiny of a man in eternity. The sign reads:

SAM PICKERING
UPSTAIRS.''

Rummaging through the old books enabled me to identify some people. A little girl about eight years old and dressed completely in white, from high-buttoned shoes and stockings to the ribbon in her hair, was Alice Garthright, my great-grandmother. During the Battle of Cold Harbor, her home was turned into a Union hospital. The blood, so the family story goes, dripped from floor to floor and gathered in pools in the basement. Stories about the Civil War abound in my family, and I found much that touched on the conflict. When fighting broke out, my great-grandfather joined the Ohio Volunteer Infantry and fought in Kentucky and Tennessee. An older brother Levi was killed at Perryville, and an obituary of a younger brother Joseph recalled that "a memory of war days was his capture by General Stonewall Jackson at Harpers Ferry, when Jackson was storming through the Shenandoah Valley." Great-grandfather became adjutant of the Fifth Tennessee Cavalry. At the end of the war he was stationed at Carthage, where he married and settled. After the war, people collected photographs of generals, much like children collect baseball cards today. Many of the albums must have come from the Pickerings. Although one contained pictures of Robert E. Lee and Jefferson Davis, in most a headquarters of Union generals appeared: Grant, Sherman, Thomas, O. M. Mitchell, Hooker, Rosecrans, McPherson, Butler, Crook, and Rousseau, all taken from negatives in Brady's National Portrait Gallery and published by E. & H. T. Anthony, 501 Broadway, New York.

I did not linger over the generals. Even pictures of great-grandfather in uniform and what must have been members of his troop did not attract my attention so much as photographs of unknown Confederates. Not only does success gradually fade into the ordinary and thus become uninteresting, but the elation of triumph so overwhelms other feelings that celebratory photographs rarely appeal to the imagination. Instead of reflecting a tapestry of emotions, such photographs only capture the simple brightness of success. Rarely do they hint at the dark complexity of life and provoke wonder. In wonder is the stuff, perhaps not of thought but of sentiment — sentiment that smoothes the edges of time and turns loss into gain, making the defeated more human and more appealing than the victorious. As deaths, not births, in family Bibles attracted me, so the losers drew me, and I searched for glimpses of their lives. Little things turned up: from a desk in the attic first a bit with "7TH VA CAV CSA" stamped on it and then a single letter dated February 16,

1864. "My Dearest Maggie," Mollie began. "I have intended replying to your welcome affectionate letter ever since its reception but have company staying with me all the time & parties &c engrossing all time. I had rather have had a quiet time all my own in which I could have written long letters to loved friends, yet we owe certain duties to society & when there is any gayety we generally are constantly occupied. We have had a great many parties dinners &c," she continued. "I am becoming I very much fear too dissipated. We have 8 or 10 companies of Cavalry in the county. The Regiment to which my Brother is attached is now at home, & he is with us. I was at a large dancing party, given by the Signal Corps, which is stationed a short distance from us. My Brother, a Capt. friend from one of the R–D [Richmond] Howitzers & my sister accompanied me. I danced until 4½ o'clock & got home just before day."

The dancing would not last. In less than a month Grant would take command of the Union forces. Leading the Army of the Potomac through the Wilderness, Spotsylvania Court House, Cold Harbor, and Petersburg, he drove Lee to Appomattox and surrender in April 1865. In February 1864, though, the Army of the Potomac had not crossed the Rapidan, and the dancers played. "The Capt.," Mollie wrote, "staid with us ten days & we had many invitations out. Then I had a young lady staying here. One Saturday we went up to see a Tournament. There were eleven Knights, dressed in pretty & very becoming costumes. The cavalry had a dinner & dance on the same day & all passed pleasingly. I was invited to another party a few days since & two nice beaux came to take me but I declined. Thursday I am invited to a 'grand Military Ball,' given by the soldiers, several hundred invitations issued. I expect to go. Most of the girls will dress in silks. They expect a fine time. A Cousin of mine will dress in black velvet & pearls. She is a beauty & will look superbly. I will accompany her. I see some of Col. Robbins Command some times," she added. "They are stationed about 20 miles from us & have amusing dances some times. Mr. Tomkins looks so well. The Sargt has not yet returned & when asked by Mr. T– when he would do so, his reply was by singing 'When the Spring time comes gentle Annie.'"

Major Robinson, Millie wrote, "is the general heart-breaker of this community. I hope I will pass unscathed." There were breaks between dances and after songs and tournaments, and Mollie was not unmarked. "Maggie dear," she concluded, "is there any appearance of peace in R–d? Do they express any hopes as to the termination of this most evil & unnatural struggle? Oh! when will we be at peace. It seems so long to look forward to — perhaps years — long weary years may escape & those most cherished will find a soldiers grave. Oh! Maggie what an awful thought! & is such a time a season for gayety — I feel condemned."

The life my great-grandfather lived in Carthage, a small town on the edge of the Cumberland Plateau, was far different from that of northern Virginia. The wife he married there was the daughter of a blacksmith, James McClarin, who after emigrating from Ireland had made his way south from Pennsylvania and who, as someone wrote beside his name in a family Bible, was known as Pittsburg Jim. His daughter Eliza Jane was not beautiful. Because she wore a brooch containing a photograph of great-grandfather, I identified her. Her lips were narrow, and her mouth cut straight across her face. Her cheeks were thin, and, twisted in small curls, her hair was plastered down over her forehead. Her nose, too big for her mouth and cheeks, was masculine and domineering. There were no pearls or velvet, just the brooch, a white collar, and a plain checked dress. Named William Blackstone after the legal scholar, perhaps my great-grandfather wasn't interested in gaiety. When the music stopped in 1865, he was on the winning, and the right, side. Among the old books in the library was the "Memorial Record" of his funeral in 1919. The "Good Samaritans–Colored Society" sent flowers. "These flowers," the accompanying card stated, "are sent in grateful remembrance by the descendants of Slaves you helped to free. They will ever remember that through all the intervening years you have been their faithful guide and friend. May thy slumbers be peaceful and thy awakening pleasant in the arms of a liberty loving God."

The scrapbooks contained many photographs of the descendants of slaves: Bessie, Wilna, Mealy, Lizzie, Marie, and John Derrycote, bigger than a barn and carrying me on his shoulders. Writing about these photographs is difficult, and I would like to turn from them as I did Father's love letters. Would that I could always see the springtime of my life through a haze. Age and its consort knowledge have, however, burned off the mist, and although I want to remember the hours spent with servants as forever golden, I have learned better and feel sick at heart when I think of seventy-year-old men calling a six-year-old boy "Mister Sammy." Among family papers was the will of Philip Claud, a distant cousin. Claud's will was made out in Williamson County, Tennessee, in April 1845. Claud left much property. To his daughter Matilda, he bequeathed "the following negroes, to wit Wiley and Evaline"; to his son Eldridge, he left Amy; to William, another son, "a negro boy named Joe"; and to Frances, a daughter, "a negro boy Anthony and a negro girl Phillis." Caroline, William, Mary, Clarissa, Sandra, Sarah, Martha, and Felise were left to other members of the family. "It is also my will and desire," Claud added, "that any increase of the above named slaves may have hereafter shall be considered and taken as bequeathed with their mothers."

In 1885 a relative in Kentucky discussed the Civil War in a letter. "It may be that Providence," he wrote, "was working out a great problem, the freedom of the negro race — which no doubt in the End, will be the best thing for us, both as a People & as a Nation!" When I was a child, the end was not in sight. Even now when I read about velvet and pearls, hear stories about my grandmother's grandmother playing the piano while field hands stood outside the parlor window singing hymns, when I recall plucking chickens in a tub of steaming hot water with Mealy, walking with Lizzie to her home in Frogtown, and driving with Grandfather to the Voo-Doo Man to get a hex removed from the dairy — when such things come to me, liberty and right are far out of mind.

In a family Bible published in 1726, just the book of Luke was marked. A thin black line ran down the margin alongside selected verses, but only verse twenty from chapter fifteen, recounting the history of the prodigal son, was underlined. For someone the verse was important because two thick lines underscored it. "But when he was a great way off," Luke recounted, "his father saw him, and had compassion, and ran, and fell on his neck, and kissed him." My memory is prodigal reveling in recollections of childhood spent with the descendants of the people for whom Great-grandfather fought but who still needed, if not a guide, at least a hand toward greater freedom.

Unlike the prodigal son who turned his back on faraway places and returned home to lead a good life of right deeds, I left home. Memories that should have made me struggle for decency, if not justice, became artifacts, stripped of meaning and posed like holiday photographs.

Like a print sliced from an ancient folio, then framed in gold leaf and hung in an airy reception room above green plants and an Empire table, servants have appeared in my writings as part of a decorous and soothingly smooth whole. Maybe I am too hard on myself. Like photographs, memories are packed away in sugar chests and brought out, for the most part, when it is convenient. Memories that make people uncomfortable or threaten propriety are discarded or buried deep in an attic of the mind. Days filled with uncomfortable memories become unlivable; people struggle to order and dignify their lives. Perhaps they are wise to banish indecorous Christmas cards, indeed indecorous and disturbing thoughts. After the war William Blackstone became county court clerk, chief clerk of the Tennessee legislature, and then postmaster. "He filled all these positions," his obituary noted, "with unusual accuracy, care, and neatness, and wrote a splendid hand." For me, feeling vulnerable and thinking more about death and its effect upon my young children, neatness occasionally seems all important.

Tucked in among the Bibles was *Familiar Scenes; or, The Scientific Explanation of Common Things*. "I began this book in Mr. Morris School," my grandfather wrote and on the back binding listed nine students attending the school: himself, Ada Salter, Josie Myers, Charles McClarin, three Sanders children, and Ernest and Julia Fisher. At the top of page five he wrote, "If how to be rich, / you wish to find, / look on page 109." Immediately I turned to that page and read, "*Mind your business.*" The advice was good, but no Pickering, so far as I know, has ever followed it closely. At least none has been wealthy. Maybe one of my boys will, but I doubt it. If they resemble me, they will spend too much time rummaging through the past and other people's lives to mind any business. I have brought all the old family photographs, letters, books, and Bibles to Connecticut. Those that are not framed or on my bookshelves are packed in trunks in the attic. On top of the material in one trunk is an envelope that slipped out of a scrapbook and fell to the bottom of the sugar chest. Stamped on it is the return address of Grandfather's business: "Pickering & Highers Insurance, Carthage, Tennessee." Inside are copies of the Christmas cards Vicki and I had sent. To please Mother I have decided to pose in a coat and tie next year. In the future some member of the family will look at the cards. I wonder if he will notice differences in dress. I hope so, because I am going to wear the coat and tie more for him than for Mother.

GREGOR VON REZZORI

A Stranger in Lolitaland

FROM VANITY FAIR

In 1958 my German publisher asked another writer and me to give him a hand in translating Vladimir Nabokov's *Lolita* into German. Since a first draft had already been produced by a crew of venerable literati so numerous that in a group photograph they would have resembled the Don Cossack Choir, our little team was unprepared for the difficulties still lurking under Nabokov's demonic artistry.

At one point a heated discussion arose over the possible interpretation of *Lolita* as a grandiose metaphor of the classic European's hopeless love for young, seductive, barbaric America. In his afterword to the novel Nabokov himself mentions this as the naïve theory of one of the publishers who turned the book down. And although there can't be the slightest doubt that Nabokov did not mean to limit *Lolita* to that interpretation, there is no reason to exclude it as one of the novel's many dimensions. The point, I felt, became obvious when one drew the line between *Lolita* as a delightfully frivolous story on the verge of pornography and *Lolita* as a literary masterpiece, the only convincing love story of our century. If one accepted it as the latter, there was no longer a question of whether to read it as "old Europe debauching young America" or as "young America debauching old Europe." It simply stood as one of the great examples of passion in literature, a deeply touching story of unfulfillable longing, of suffering through love, love of such ardor that though it concentrated on its subject monomaniacally, it actually aimed beyond it, until it flowed back into the great Eros that had called it into being. Every passionate love

can find its image in Humbert Humbert's boundless love for
Lolita, I said; why should it not also reflect the longing of us
Europeans for the fulfillment of our childhood dreams about
America? As for myself, that longing had become irresistible
from the moment, in our translation, when we arrived at Lolita
and Humbert's crisscrossing of the United States. I vowed then
that someday humble humble me would follow in their tracks.

From the time I first became aware of the existence of America — part of a continent colored beige, yellow, orange, brown,
and lime green and stuck like a decalcomania of some prehistoric bird on the cerulean cardboard globe in my sister's and my
nursery — I had been filled with the desire to go there and
roam over its boundless spaces, occupied, I imagined, by buffalo
and skyscrapers, redskins on mustangs, gangsters with their
molls, black men playing jazz on saxophones, and Buster Kea-
ton. That was in the early 1920s, in a Europe battered by the
First World War, and many Europeans saw America as the
promise of a bright future. It took another war to make us
realize that what had seemed like a bright future had become a
rather tedious present, one we hadn't had to go around the
globe to seek. What was left of Europe after World War II was
not European any longer. Most of it had been transformed into
a secondhand America. The rest of it was joined to Russia.
Nabokov's birthplace.

I can well imagine Nabokov's sardonic giggle at the thought
of anyone's wishing to visit the real places of a fictitious story.
Nabokov, who said that the word "reality" should never be used
except in quotation marks, could not have been more amused
than by such a confusion of the factual and fictional. But I am
used to his sardonic giggles. I hear them every time my writing
evokes his image within me, for I was once told that we have
certain similarities as writers, and though I am not so conceited
as not to see all our differences in genus as well as in quality, yet
every now and then my vanity seduces me into thinking there
may be some truth in the remark.

Certainly we are both *déracinés:* uprooted from the soil of a
beloved birthplace. But already the disparity gapes. Nabokov
was a Russian; I am an Austrian from central Europe (and
Nabokov loathed everything Austrian to such a degree that he
refused even to take notice of the great writer Robert Musil; the

only thing he loathed almost as much was central Europeans).
Furthermore, the cultural climate of St. Petersburg in the first
two decades of this century was very different from that of
Czernowitz in Bukovina between the two great wars. Nabokov's
father was a fervent liberal politician closely linked to the intellectuals and artists of his day; mine spent most of his time hunting, and thought of intellectuals as the gravediggers of the
monarchy, whose downfall he deplored. Nabokov's governess
came from Cambridge, mine from Smyrna. Yet in our writing
we share a certain lifelong homesickness, and we both lament a
loss far greater than any given spot on the globe. The modern
world was never genuinely our "reality."

Why, then, after helping to translate *Lolita,* did I not attempt
to meet the author? It would not, after all, have been too difficult, particularly in the late sixties, when he was living in Switzerland. But I did not want to go to Montreux and have tea with
Professor Vladimir Vladimirovich under the surveying eyes of
his wife, Véra. I have always been against visiting celebrities as
if they were exotic birds in a zoo. Had we met through Humbert
Humbert's great foe (and every writer's best ally), Mr. McFate,
I would have been delighted and certainly enriched. But I hated
the idea of imposing myself on someone whose self-esteem as a
Nabokov was tripled by his consciousness of being a great
writer, a fascinating teacher, and a distinguished lepidopterist.

Just as I had avoided ever making the personal acquaintance
of Nabokov, I decided to avoid any attempt to reconstruct the
precise route Humbert had taken on his inverted odyssey with
Lolita. There is no better evidence of Nabokov's art than in his
summing up a country as huge and multiform as the United
States with such perspicacity that everyone who has ever read
the description of it in *Lolita* feels that it corresponds precisely
with his own impressions and experiences. I wonder how many
of those readers who are still haunted by Humbert and Lolita's
wanderings from motel to motel, and who believe that the whole
book is concerned with that trip, are aware that only a few more
than a dozen of the three hundred pages of the novel are devoted to it.

There lay the main trap for me, and it had not been laid by
Nabokov without the help of McFate, one of whose most effi-
cient weapons is the flow of time. Between the publication of

our German translation of *Lolita* and the day I slipped into the role of Quilty and set out in pursuit of the ever eloping couple, another quarter of a century had passed. I could not follow my prey under the conditions their creator had set for them. In no way could I identify myself with Humbert Humbert, the total European, and find in a sloppy, gum-chewing, and utterly desirable teenager the personification of the world she belonged to. For in the twenty-five years that had elapsed, my world and I had undergone a pretty thorough, if secondhand, Americanization. It was as if Humbert had been married to Lolita for a quarter of a century and *then* decided to have a look at where she came from.

I knew it would be dishonest of me, after having seen the sun rise out of the Atlantic and sink into the Pacific, to wind up declaring that Americans today are not like the ones Frederic Remington sculpted or Norman Rockwell painted, but rather like those tourists we see on the Champs-Élysées, at Saint Peter's and Saint Mark's, in the Tivoli gardens and on the Acropolis — men in plaid slacks or Bermuda shorts, women with spiderweb nets holding the violet confectionery of their hair in place, buying junk souvenirs, innocent, ignorant, kindhearted, and loud. I realized, therefore, that like Nabokov I would have to "invent" America, and that my invention would have to correspond to the "reality."

Of the 27,000 miles Humbert traveled with Lolita in a year, I did about half, 13,400, in less than three months, so I had to cheat a little and take planes a few times. Still, I honestly covered 13,400 miles on rubber tires. I lived more in all those swift, silent, comfortable rented cars than in the infamous motels of *Lolita,* for since I had no pliant teenage captive with me, I spent my nights sleeping. By putting the geography of the United States into motion, I changed from a simple European rooted in the past into a modern nomad, and so discovered Lolitaland.

A vast blue sky and flaming red hills, billowy, immense, through which the road cuts as tidily as in a park, every now and then bending into the red, gold, and purple foliage, vanishing in the thicket, then reappearing miles ahead, running straight up to the crest of one of the huge gold-red waves that rise and sink and rise and sink while high above them a tiny sun, glistening like a golden coin, moves steadily along a cosmic semicircle — that is the image printed on my mind since that October morning when I finally set out across New York State in hot pursuit of Humbert Humbert and Lolita. This was America as I had envisioned it long ago: endless forests in autumnal glow, and on a silver river a canoe paddled by a trapper in fringed deerskin, an Indian standing in the stern of the boat, a freshly killed deer laid across the bow.

The river, of course, flowed some fifty miles to the east, and at its mouth embraced the island of Manhattan. There were no canoes on it, only outboard motorboats, and neither trappers nor Indians; as for the deer, it would be tied to the fender of a fast-moving car. To be honest, even the forests lacked the grandeur I had imagined. They were rather scrubby, with none of those "Chateaubriandesque" trees Humbert Humbert purports to see all over the United States (of course, that was forty years ago). Nevertheless, they covered the huge hills so densely that the landscape seemed to be a waving sea of molten copper, thoroughly American in its immensity.

Space: I had come from a jam-packed Europe hungering for space, and the vastness of the American sky appeared unique to me. I saw the landscape as if through special field glasses — with everything seeming far, far away even when it was near, and utterly precise in outline, single, solitary, sharply isolated, in a halo, as if its contours had been drawn with a thin line borrowed from a rainbow. I got drunk on that space.

I spent my first night in a place called Climax, in the Catskills (where Lolita once went on a three-day hike). The whole area could have been invented by Nabokov: Sodom Road, Surprise Road, Tranquillity Road, and nearby a village called Coxsackie.

I was heading for Ithaca. Instead of concentrating on my fugitives, I was first going to have a look at the place where their creator gave them life. There, on the campus of Cornell University, where Professor V. Nabokov used to scare the wits out his pupils by asking them what color the gloves were that Anna Karenina wore on such and such an occasion, I expected some sort of epiphany or benediction for my audacious enterprise, which was to match my observations with one of the masterpieces of our century.

*

My companion on this first part of my trip was no Lolita but a young man of cool discretion combined with a sharp wit. Every traveler needs an interpreter. Even if you speak the language of the country (you'll soon find out how badly), you will never really get into it without the help of a native guide. Mine — Mark by name — though not a redskin, was as American as a descendant of Polish Jews can be, and as proud of his country as the fiercest Reaganite. We would ride for hours without exchanging a word, but his very presence assured me of a genuine, honest confrontation with this huge nation.

And huge indeed it seemed to my space-hungry eyes, in fact to all my senses. I heard, I smelled, I tasted its vastness. I even got the sense of what it must feel like to be an American and bear this monstrous continent within you, consciously or subconsciously having its immensity in your mind. I could feel its tremendous centrifugal force. I could tell that, as a native of this mighty mass of land, you don't carry in your soul a *Heimat*, a small idyllic homeland such as every European cradles in his sentiments. You may be born in Kansas, or Virginia, or Wyoming, and love your birthplace in the kitschiest way, but deep down you know it is only one tiny spot in the vast crazy quilt of the United States. You can leave it without regret for another state, and another, and still be home. No wonder nomadism is such an American phenomenon.

I was pondering this while I watched the horizon recede as quickly as we sped to reach it. A newly born American, I already felt sad for Europeans. They had no space around them, poor things. And where there is no space, there is no future, I said to Mark. And where there is no future, the present is disoriented. That explains our — the Europeans' — uncritical acceptance and thoughtless aping of everything American.

We arrived in Ithaca in the fading turquoise light of evening and spent the night in a semirustic motel called the Collegetown Motor Lodge. The next day we roamed over the Cornell campus. *Nous connûmes* (to use a Nabokovian intonation borrowed from Flaubert) the Slavic-studies librarian, a stern young lady stiff with mistrust of anyone who dared to poke his nose into the august halls of academic research for the frivolous purpose of tailing Professor Vladimir Vladimirovich's most dubious fancies. *Nous connûmes* charming Professor Emeritus John Francle-

mont, a specialist in moths, and his grumpy old terrier at Com-
stock Hall, where the professor showed us some pale-azure-
blue, silver-dotted butterflies discovered and named by Nabokov.
Professor Franclemont and his dog were friends of Nabokov's; they used to go specimen hunting together. *Nous connûmes*
crowds of those hairy-legged, lanky lads so thoroughly hated
by Humbert Humbert as potential rivals for Lolita's favors, and
swarms of those deadly serious, buxom female students who, in
the eyes of V.N., were an offense to womanhood as well as to
scholarship. By the time this day, too, faded into a perfectly
turquoise evening, I thought I had found the key to a few of
Humbert Humbert's most characteristic views and attitudes. I
thought it significant, for instance, that his creator was a bit
nomadic himself; in the eleven years between 1948, when Nabokov arrived in Ithaca, and 1959, when he left his post there
as professor of Russian literature, he never made the feeblest
attempt to settle in a home of his own, or to stay put in a rented
one, but moved from one house to another for a total of eleven
addresses.

I must confess that, before I saw Ithaca, Nabokov's solemn
isolation in the world of nineteenth-century literature (and lep-
idopterology), from which he looked haughtily down on contemporary "reality" and pretended to ignore it, sometimes
irritated me to the point of exasperation, especially since I
couldn't help admiring the acuteness of his observations. Together with his playing games with the reader — Setting traps
based on literary knowledge and an understanding of other
languages, as well as veiling meanings behind the subtlest allusions to classical literature — All his pretentious magnificence
and esotericism seemed to me unbearably vain.

But you have to imagine Nabokov, the Russian immigrant,
burying his eternal homesickness in scholarship, a professor
among other professors with all their pompousness and jealousy
and vanity and petit bourgeois pettiness (so subtly described in
Pnin). While feeling very much at home in this world of erudi-
tion, at the same time this ironical man must have been driven
to outbursts of biting sarcasm. He was well aware of being privileged to share in the very best America has to offer: its academic life. On the other hand, this well of spiritual ambrosia,
with its rich libraries and stimulating research, always had to be

carefully screened from the generally dumb, rowdy student body.

Isn't it wonderful, I said to Mark, how all this finds its sublime image in *Lolita*? Think of Lolita Haze's beauty while she is still a child — a naughty child, admittedly, but still in her prepubescent nymphet innocence — and her metamorphosis into plump, vulgar, ugly Dolly Schiller when she comes to the age of procreation. And think of Humbert's monomania, his existence totally bound up in hers, his blindness to what is going on in the rest of the world. Don't tell me this cannot be read as the perfect metaphor for passionate scholarship. I added that with little doubt, and except for Van Veen in *Ada*, Humbert Humbert was the Nabokovian invention most animated by his author's own traits, features, and perhaps even experiences. As for the nymphet, Nabokov once said, "For Lolita I took one arm of a little girl that came to see my son Dmitri, and a kneecap from another."

There is still another meaning in Professor Nabokov's (or his hero's) imperious ignoring of certain "realities" outside his own. Imagine: during the year Humbert Humbert and Lolita were traveling over this continent, two other great travelers were "on the road," roaming about the crazy quilt of the United States. At some point our two fugitives must have come across Sal Paradise and Dean Moriarty or some of their ilk — the new Beat dropouts, who were offenders of bourgeois taboos and totems just like they were, only they were spontaneous, deliberate sinners against convention. Compared with Humbert and Lolita, the hippies of the forties and fifties seem such free, careless barbarians. I asked Mark if he didn't believe that we owed them a great deal for having taught us to shake off some of our dusty Victorianism. Didn't he think they were bold conquerors of new dimensions of life, of a new "reality," a new world? Even as I said this to my young friend, I felt as old and decrepit as the father Dean Moriarty had lost and never found again, the father he blamed for his forlornness in this vast waste world.

Next morning we drove off at an early hour, with twenty miles of blue lake on one side of us and on the other woods and pastures with deep-eyed, deep-chested cows, phallic silos, and white toy churches. In the grass at the side of the road were tiny flowers of the same pale azure as those butterflies which, since primeval times, had lived so merrily and anonymously until Professor Vladimir Nabokov came along and defined them as a subspecies:

> I found it and I named it, being versed
> in taxonomic Latin; thus became
> godfather to an insect and its first
> describer — And I want no other fame.

High up in the sky, silver-winged sea gulls were the dots on this blue butterfly of a perfect autumn day. There were white gingerbread houses sitting on the green velvet produced by the sweat of the brow of a subspecies of the American husband whom I now thought to name after me: *Herbataglians domesticus Americanus Rezz.* (Rezzori's American Sunday lawn mower). Not a single specimen was to be seen. There were no people at all in this lovely country, and very few cars. By studying some pamphlets we had picked up at the motor lodge, we learned that we were driving through the Finger Lakes region, "a land full of enchantment and charm, of natural and man-made wonders."

Like Lolita, we paid close attention to all food ads. When, as foretold in the brochure, "the dream came true," we found ourselves engulfed in the voluptuous depths of the chintz easy chairs in the lounge of the Inn at Belhurst Castle. Since its construction in 1885, mostly of materials imported from Europe, Belhurst, "a splendid example of the style known as Richardson Romanesque," had served variously as a home, a speakeasy, a casino, and a restaurant. In the spectral light of the late afternoon, filtered through stained-glass windows, as we ordered from the menu's "rich choice of authentic Continental food" (only to declare later, "They call these fries *French? Grand Dieu!*"), it suddenly occurred to us that this place could have been the model for the Enchanted Hunters, the hotel in which tenderhearted, morbidly sensitive Humbert Humbert's calvaries began. In any case, it was exactly the "palace of gracious living" Lolita dreamed about, and so we explored its "luxurious bedrooms," furnished with Victorian antiques and Oriental rugs, and its two-room suites with a working fireplace or a Jacuzzi, "plenty of old-fashioned closet and cupboard space," air conditioning, and a smoke alarm in each room. Then we drove to Canandaigua, dined at Mary Mac's Fish Shanty, and stayed overnight in the Seaview Motel for exactly a tenth of what we would have had to spend at the Belhurst Castle inn.

We crossed an Indian reservation without seeing a single Indian. Then, slowly, mange appeared on the land — the mange that spreads around big cities: prosperity's dumps, the destruction that results from the progress that devours man. But the city we were nearing was not big, and the mangy girdle did not enclose a teeming downtown center. It surrounded one of the most renowned wonders of nature, which turned out to be one of the biggest disappointments of my long life.

In those prehistoric times when I was a boy and dreamed of the day when I would stand before the marvel of Niagara Falls watching, perhaps, a daredevil shooting the boiling waters in a barrel, I could not foresee how such natural beauty might be commercialized. I saw myself standing there like a watcher of the moon reflected in the sea around the Isle of Rügen in the painting by Caspar David Friedrich, not on the top of a ghastly thirty-floor tower overlooking cement embankments, a cement parking lot, cement cafeterias and hot-dog stands, cement souvenir shops, and a network of cement paths surrounding the spectacle of a million megatons of (probably polluted) water streaming down a cliff like the hair of an aging platinum blonde in a shampoo ad and dissolving in a cloud of iridescent mist. It was not the vastness of the land around that made the huge falls appear small and ugly; it was their degradation, their spoliation. I believe that Lolita, licking her ice cream cone, would have stared at them unimpressed too, without uttering the slightest *Wow!* or *Gee!*

The falls had attracted crowds of tourists, mainly, it seemed, from Japan, but also from the remotest parts of the United States. And still the huge cement wasteland looked deserted. For the most part, the visitors were just like the ordinary Pan-Americans we would meet everywhere else in the course of 13,400 miles. They could have been from Wisconsin or Virginia, from Arkansas or Montana, and they were essentially indistinguishable in appearance from the people one would meet in Holstein, Bavaria, Lombardy, Scandinavia, Australia, or Canada. They looked like the crowd in any airport anywhere in the so-called Western (i.e., American) zone of our globe, and they were dressed the way 99 percent of today's population dress — the same T-shirts and Levi's or polo shirts and polyester slacks, the same synthetic Windbreakers, the same sneakers or loafers, the same baseball caps. The motley of ethnic particularities never completely canceled out the prototype: the Ideal American, designed by Norman Rockwell for the cover of *The Saturday Evening Post,* yet generally lacking in what Nabokov would have called *poshlust* — a certain coy, coquettish, corny quality that should go with the type.

Of course, it's difficult to live up to any ideal. But as we traveled on, we were bound to run into some honest-to-goodness Rockwellian Americans. They were nearly always standing in front of a natural or man-made wonder, like Old Faithful or the Grand Canyon or Mount Rushmore. These were the only places where we saw many people at all, once we had been pulled into the gigantic void in the middle of America, and we stared at them with the same awe and curiosity with which they stared at the spectacles.

Every single one of them bore some of the characteristic signs of the Rockwellian types. Some of them bore them to the point of monstrosity. There was the unavoidable specimen of American obesity: the male or female mountain of wobbling fat, walking laboriously on barrel thighs, swinging short, cone-shaped arms. There was the juvenile giant: the six-foot-seven sixteen-year-old with the body of a mammoth child. There was the typical example of puritan dehydration: the person composed of bones, sinews, and loose skin in loose clothes, with a dancing Adam's apple and fanatical eyes. There was the muscle man, bursting his sleeveless T-shirt with colossal bulges of beef. And last but not least, there were all the stereotypes of female beauty: the Mae West blonde, all frills and milky dimples; the fox-haired witch, freckled like a partridge's egg and smelling vaguely of seaweed; the bowlegged, globular-calved pocket edition of Carmen, on red stiletto heels, with a lacquered cap of black curls glued onto chalky cheeks. But there was no Lolita.

We finally spotted a specimen of the precious nymphet deep in Ohio, after we had fled Niagara Falls and were heading west along Lake Erie. We had touched the tip of Pennsylvania, where the houses are made of brick and look much uglier than the

white wooden ones in New York, and where Polish wine grow-
ers produce a beverage with nearly all the criteria of wine. We
had got sick on turkey in a country club near Erie and had
stopped briefly for tea in Art Deco Cleveland. Then we swung
south. And there we met up with our prey.

It was in a small town whose name I shall not give away for
fear it would attract too many child-molesting lepidopterists.
Off the highway, on what seemed to be the town's main road, a
fair was going on: dinky, pathetic, a handful of booths full of
plastic dolls and similar junk, hamburger wagons, and games of
chance. A small crowd in T-shirts and blue jeans and sneakers
idled in the pale sunshine of the autumn day, while three or
four loudspeakers filled the dusty air with rock 'n' roll. And
there, in a group of children craving to be out of childhood's
blissful spell and into the desolation of maturity, *she* stood, looking at the bustle around her with the lost expression of a woman
listening to an enigmatic message coming from the very core of
herself. I say "woman" because she was a woman in a child's
pupation, and she didn't know it, and at the same time knew it.
That made even looking at her an ambiguous, if not a down-
right obscene, act, as if you were trying to make her aware
of her erotic attraction. She was not the original Lolita type,
auburn-maned and tanned, but a pale, long-limbed blonde with
tiny budding breasts, a kitten's face, enormous, wide-set, pike-
gray eyes, and a delicate chin gracefully balanced on the thin
stem of her neck.

Behaving as discreetly as possible, we tried not to stare, or to
loiter too long within the range of her chemical message, or to
make the slightest attempt to talk to her or pick her up, even
for an ice cream cone. For purposes of research, of course, we
wanted to take her picture; so Mark pretended he was taking
mine, just accidentally standing near her. But as if something in
the opposite direction had attracted her attention, she turned
her head away; then, with the same artificial aloofness as ours,
she stepped aside, shot a stern glance over her shoulder at us,
and demonstratively joined her hopelessly ordinary friends. We
now realized the difficulties of nymphet hunting. And since our
purposeful idling had become obvious not only to her but to
everybody around, we strolled casually to the other end of the
row of stands and pretended to look at the junk exhibited there,

all the while trying not to lose sight of the group of girls she was with. When we slowly strolled back, she wasn't any longer among them.

A good many things had changed in the forty years that separated us from bad old Humbert Humbert and the evil Quilty. For one thing, true Lolitas had become rare. They were lately being absorbed into a whole new species, which, by recognizing the precarious phase between childhood and maturity as a state of existence in its own right, and as a social group distinct from any other by virtue of its independence and tremendous buying power, has lost the charm of its inherent ambiguity. It takes more than a sexy teenager to be a Lolita. Only once more, near the end of my trip, in Santa Fe, did I meet another. She was six.

I traversed the 13,400 miles at random, in ever larger loops, not all of them with Mark, but with different partners, depending on who was ready at any given time to join me in so vaguely definable a quest as meandering over a continent in order to follow the presumable itinerary of a mythical couple. I could actually have been more precise. In one of the many interviews Nabokov gave to awestruck literary enthusiasts, he said that anyone who wanted to know what real places had served him for his description of Humbert Humbert's travels with Lolita need only go to the Museum of Comparative Zoology at Harvard and note down the locations where he had caught the butterflies that he contributed to the collection of lepidoptera there. But I felt that for me to do so and then go to all those places and try to redescribe what had already been put into sublime literary form would be just a bit pedantic. Moreover, I was hunting my own butterfly. Like the one that gave immortal fame to Professor Nabokov when he finally caught it, mine too had been in my mind since childhood. And whereas his was tiny and of a delicately silver-spotted pale blue, mine was huge and of dazzling colors: the rich green of impenetrable forests, the white of an eagle feather stuck in the shiny black hair of an Indian brave, the powerful brown of the buffalo's coat, the purple of rocky mesas, the red of blood, and the blue of a vast sky against which gray puffs of smoke announced breathtaking adventures. When, at the end of my trip, I had caught my butterfly, it turned out to be much paler than that. Its colors were the same as those on the globe in my sister's and my nursery: beige, yellow, orange, brown, and lime green, swimming in cerulean blue — the color scheme of nature as well as of all the rooms in the numberless motels I stayed in. Each one combined these chromatic elements in its own nauseating way: yellow walls, lime-green curtains and bedspread, orange-brown carpet, beige easy chair; or lime-green walls, orange curtains and bedspread, yellow carpet, beige-brown easy chair — a mathematician could tell you how many possible combinations there are. Except for some poisonously bright Jell-Os, these were also the colors of the food we had to endure.

The motels and hotels were, for the most part, all right. The plumbing functioned without those sudden gushes of ice-cold and scalding-hot water in the showers so vividly described by Humbert Humbert; and the feared acoustic effects of banging radiator pipes, roaring transistors and TV sets, and coughing, quarreling, and fornicating neighbors were discreetly muffled. There is great comfort in the anonymity, the total lack of sentimentality, with which one gets in and out of these places and then forgets about them the moment he starts the car to leave.

In *Lolita*, Nabokov does not use a single obscene word to describe the highly erotic situations and scenes. I shall likewise refrain from the terms commonly employed to describe the sort of alimentation my various companions and I had to choke down. With very few — always triumphantly celebrated — exceptions during the journey, it was impossible to divine why these vomitive victuals, desperately trying to look like the lacquered perfection in the advertisements, should be supposed for human consumption at all. Ethnic cuisine offered no escape, as anyone who has tasted the Chinese egg rolls in Flagstaff, Arizona, or the Bavarian *Knödel* in Abbeville, South Carolina, knows. It is common knowledge that some of the worst food on this globe is eaten in Greece; so why, in God's name, does every Greek who comes to America and is not as rich as Onassis or Niarchos immediately open a Greek restaurant? And how come the American public has not yet realized that bad Italian food has done more damage to this country than Cosa Nostra ever did? In Florence, Oregon, I definitely turned anti-pasta!

After weeks of traveling, I really began to miss people, for the more I penetrated into the middle of the continent, the fewer

of them I saw. I saw hundreds of square miles of waving grass-
land divided into lots by barbed-wire fences, but no people. Not
even cattle. Just the empty fields, for one day, two days, three
days at a time. The center of America seemed to me a huge void
between the parentheses of the two populous coasts.

Of course we went through towns and cities. But they were
empty. Rarely was there a single individual walking in the
streets. The only things that moved in them were cars. Night
dipped these towns in a desperate blackness, even when the sky
was studded with stars. They lay motionless, with not a single
bright light on in any window.

Yet where the highways encircled the towns or crossed
through them, they glowed and sprayed multicolored lights into
the black sky. Geysers of light, flaming rainbows, cataracts of
poisonously candy-colored beams promised a megalopolis in
these godforsaken holes. The fairy palaces sketched out in
azure, emerald, and ruby contours — they were just gas stations
and hotels and motels and drive-ins, all with their names written
in flaming letters on the blackboard of the sky; the cupolas and
pagodas and turreted castles and mushroom-capped cottages
were eateries and snack bars and cafeterias, all ablaze in a full
spectrum of psychedelic tints.

But they were empty. Just a few forlorn vagrants like us
around, looking for food and a room, certainly not company.
This hell that opened its gates in the heart of the night was an
abstract hell of fires that did not burn, a cold hell that inflicted
no punishment, a void, an empty promise. When we came to
the end of a day's driving, enclosed in the capsule of our car, in
a state of unreality, isolated from the world that streamed in
through the car windows, we felt ourselves slip into another
unreality. There ahead, out of the dense darkness, over an invisible line that might be the lost horizon, crept the glow and
then the glare of one of those stretches on the highway where it
touched a sleeping town, and the abstract life in it — the silent
drivers in the capsules of their cars — seemed to be creating
sparks. We knew it was a fata morgana, an abstraction of life's
glorious possibilities, shamming them and at the same time
withholding them, like the erotic promise of a striptease.

I also realized that these stretches of light and promised life
along the interminable roads were truly Lolita's America.

Where else could she have found such an accumulation of her life's great expectations: mniam-mniam eateries, soda fountains, souvenir shops, jukeboxes, and pinball machines? What could correspond more closely to her own ambiguous state between childhood and a never fully achieved maturity than that garish mixture of illusion and crude reality? Actually, we never saw a single specimen of the precious nymphet in any of these places. Perhaps the Humbert Humberts and Quiltys had them too well hidden. No matter — for 13,400 miles they were out of sight. Still, we gave the parallel lines of fireworks that sprang out of the nights where the highways touched the sleeping cities the name Lolitaland. For thousands of miles we traveled from one such place to another, until in the end they merged into one big neutral and abstract hell, what seemed to be the core of the United States. We felt its tremendous growing power, as it developed into shining megalopolises, the ultimate unencumbered perversion of the small town's dream to become a great city. And we knew that, when we went home to Tuscany or the Black Forest, to the Scottish Lowlands or the Île-de-France, we would soon be in Lolitaland again. Just as we would be there in Nairobi, or Ankara, or Novosibirsk, or anywhere else on our globe, especially Tokyo and Hong Kong. It is the land of the future.

I found it also as I headed south in search of the natural ambiance of another mythical American female, Lolita's spiritual great-grandmother, Scarlett O'Hara. The idea of a link between Lolita the nymphet and Scarlett the voracious dragonfly I owed to Marianne, the person who accompanied me on this part of my journey, and who was no Lolita either, but rather a twenty-nine-year-old vintage virgin of my acquaintance. Blushing a faint pink, she had confessed to me how deeply *Gone with the Wind* had impressed her as a girl of fourteen; and it occurred to me that Lolita too might have been influenced by the flippant, wanton, tough, steadfast daughter of Tara — provided, of course, that she ever read anything besides comic books and movie magazines. I therefore willingly gave in to Marianne's wish to visit Scarlett O'Haraland.

Naturally, this was no longer aimless roaming of the sort I had enjoyed with Mark. A female had taken over, and instead of carelessly letting ourselves drift along in the hands of McFate, we were now driven by a will. In order to avoid states I had crossed through already, we took a plane from New York to St. Louis. It was evening, and we drove our rented car to the river in order to have a look at the boats on the Mississippi and to take in the arch, which looked as if McDonald's had set up only halı of its logo over the town. As for the riverboats, they were permanently anchored, and turned into the most vulgar, *poshlust* restaurants I've ever come across in my long life. We checked into a motel with a Spanish-colonial façade behind which two somber Kafkaesque corridors led to the rooms (orange bedspread, brown carpet, yellow-and-lime-green-striped sofa, beige curtains). When we asked for two rooms, the clerk at the desk gave my vintage virgin an ironic look, which, since the difference in our ages was considerably greater than that between Humbert and Lolita, made her the morally questionable character in our situation. He was silently telling her that her obvious gerontophilia was nothing to worry about in this day and age.

In the South even nature's color scheme was inverted. Grass was yellow and rivers were lime green, mountains were brown, and the horizon did not fade into pale blue but burned a vivid orange even at noon. Before we got there, McFate played another of his tricks, and we drove out of an intricate cloverleaf in the wrong direction. After a detour of several hundred miles to Jefferson City (which we admired because of a decent meal we had in a Chinese restaurant there), we ended up at one of the shrines of American history.

For Europeans, with three millennia behind them, history is so remote in time that it has lost any sense of "reality." It is recounted as drama, abstracted to the high level of saga. The blood of American history is so shockingly fresh that it is the color of real human blood. When I stood on the top of the tower overlooking the site of the Battle of Gettysburg and the slaughter of 51,000 men, I felt the shock of identification with history as never before. It was as if I had been there, at the battle. I forgot about the ghastly technical effects: the tower turning 360 degrees, a narrator on a record conjuring up the scene, and a glitzy sound track evoking the blare of trumpets, the thunder of cannons, and the roar of attacking troops. I felt I was there, only three generations earlier, in the days of our great-grand-fathers, watching brothers shoot at brothers.

I felt the same immediacy at the site of Custer's last stand, and the same shock at Harpers Ferry. What frightened me was that all these places evoked my compassion not only for the victims but also for the assassins. The cruel face of history is very seductive. When you feel it so near that you can smell the fresh blood, it charges you with aggression and violence. I felt very much an American at the historical sites across America — much more than I feel a European when visiting the rubble history has left us Europeans with.

Of course, battlefields and the sites of smaller shoot-outs were hardly the places shrewd Humbert Humbert would have taken his nymphet to. They could not possibly have interested her, or improved her mood, much less increased her willingness to yield to her abductor's vicious whims. Therefore, I had to visit them more or less on the sly, so to speak, usually with Mark. I took the vintage virgin to a peaceful historical monument — Daniel Boone's log cabin in Fort Boonesborough, Kentucky. While a very proper white-haired lady showed us the rooms that surely conveyed the taste of the preservation committee rather than of Mr. and Mrs. Boone, I said in a low voice to Marianne that it was amazing how the American character — like American movies — was at its best when it showed signs of violence, and that it invariably descended to kitsch when it attempted to display its better qualities — courage, generosity, justice. But she hardly heard me, so moved was she by the woman telling how Boone's daughter was kidnapped by Indians.

I expected my fill of kitsch in the South, where we now descended in a wide zigzag. But I was luckily disappointed. In Kentucky, Tennessee, Arkansas, Mississippi, Georgia, and Alabama, we looked in vain for white houses with Greek-columned porticoes set in emerald lawns, where ladies in crinolines fed peacocks while black workers picked cotton and sang spirituals. Dixieland turned out to be as somber and empty as the rest of the United States, except that the stretches of Lolitaland here, where the roads met the towns on their outskirts, were shorter and shabbier than in the North. There was no cotton either.

Scarlett O'Haraland is covered with ivy. There are some very beautiful parts. In the Ozarks, we passed through areas that would have made Switzerland and Austria green with envy. But like all the other really beautiful spots in America, the areas along the mountain lakes had been turned into a tourist's paradise, with one tacky row after another of Candy Kitchens, Ozark Maids, Able Marines, and Yankee Peddlers.

Marianne had to face a severe disenchantment some hundred miles farther southeast, in Jonesboro, where she had expected to find traces of the "real" Scarlett O'Hara; for, according to the book, Jonesboro was Scarlett's home town. But the people there — the few we could find: a senile shopkeeper, a farmer on a tractor wearing a straw hat that could have belonged to Uncle Tom, a yawning waitress in a snack bar at the end of a particularly dismal stretch of Lolitaland — didn't know what we were talking about. A book about a Jonesboro girl? Never heard of it. The woman who was the real Scarlett O'Hara? Never heard of her either. Feeling that these folks might sooner be moviegoers than readers, Marianne asked if they knew where *Gone with the Wind* had been shot. Nobody had any idea.

Nashville, too, was a disappointment. We spent one whole night and the next morning there without seeing a single country-and-western or rock musician. We couldn't reconcile this legendary place with the ordinary-looking people we saw in the supermarkets and bars. And when we got to Memphis, the holiest shrine of American schmaltz — Elvis Presley's mausolomuseum — happened to be closed.

Charleston brought out my wickedness. It is such a pretty place, and the effort to preserve not only all of its former charm but also all the horrors that put an end to it makes it uncanny. I started to tease poor Marianne (who, of course, was enchanted with the place) by telling her that I could not think of a better way to illustrate the subtle difference between sickening schlock and healthy kitsch than by comparing this carefully preserved token of the past with the square out of the Old South in Disneyland.

Seeing that such observations made my vintage virgin suffer acutely, I shut my mouth and drove her through dusty Alabama and misty Mississippi straight down to New Orleans, hoping that the horrors of Bourbon Street (which is for Americans on

moral leave what Bangkok is for Germans) would do more to
cure her of an all too romantic conception of the South than my
eloquence could ever achieve. I hoped in vain. When we were
back in New York, she told me that the most beautiful drive she
had ever taken was down the alley that leads to Middleton Place.
All the way, she said, she had made believe that Clark Gable was
at her side. I am convinced that Lolita (much more my mental
contemporary than the vintage virgin) would have agreed with
me in preferring Disneyland to Dixieland.

I went west in the company of my beloved wife, Beatrice, feeling
very respectable, as Nabokov felt when he went off butterfly
hunting in the care of his never failing consort, Véra. Actually,
I was much closer in spirit to Kerouac's Sal Paradise on the trail
of his friend Dean Moriarty. I could not resist the call of the
West, that wonderful young world of the decidedly uncivil-
ized, where history is just an element of decoration, like the His-
panic and Chinese architecture; where the real remnants of the
past — the Indian pueblos, the adobe fortresses, and the ghost
towns — sit in happy conjunction with all the cheap turquoise
bracelets, beaded Mexican booties, kachina dolls, and mass-pro-
duced ponchos; where the bleached skeleton of a horse and a
wall-sized mosaic of Leonardo's *Last Supper* blend with Tarzan
at a heart-shaped swimming pool, the late Miss Monroe's boobs,
and Silicon Valley into a very definite style, one that is even
more unmistakably American than the Pan-Americanism of
Norman Rockwell. Westward ho!

We set out on a circular tour of Arizona, New Mexico, Colorado, Utah, and Nevada — Professor V.N.'s favorite hunting
grounds — from Los Angeles, a city I venerate for many reasons but mainly because it symbolizes total liberation from the
dictates of good taste. Beatrice was studying the map so assidu-
ously that she forgot to give me directions in time, and I missed
a whole series of exits. Instead of driving out of the city, we
went around it and ended up in Hollywood, where — just like
Humbert Humbert and Lolita — we had a horrendous row.
Suddenly I longed for Mark, with whom there was no such
thing as missing a turn; any old road was fine with Mark, and
fine for our pursuit of, well, not the mythical nymphet (she was
just the pretext), but rather the butterfly I had been dreaming

about since childhood and had been tracking down now for some ten thousand miles. My Lolita was, indeed, America. And I found the very essence of her in the West, the only part of the country or the world where Disneyland could have been invented and realized.

Beatrice likes things to be precise and sensible. Why, she asked me, did I imagine California was any more American than, say, Ohio? Because of its promise, I said; America is the land of promise, in fact the Promised Land, not only for the Pilgrim fathers but for all of us Pan-Americans everywhere. And there is more promise in Disneyland than, say, in Cincinnati. Would I please define what I meant by Disneyland? Oh, not the place, naturally, not the amusement park, but the spirit that created it. The playfulness. The fancy. The fun. It shows how magnificently childlike Americans are. It's a nation of poets. A nation of enthusiasts. Even the rat race after success and wealth is engaged in with an almost religious ardor, which makes it seem somehow poetic. Look at Citizen Kane . . . I went on in this vein until my beloved spouse declared that my ideas were not just incorrect, they were incomprehensible.

I couldn't have chosen a better place to be told that I am a fool. We were driving through Death Valley. In Los Angeles, David Hockney had told us that we should take a tape cassette of Handel's *Messiah* with us and listen to it in that primordial landscape. It was truly impressive. Just by accident, though, we found an even more striking way to experience the thrill of Death Valley. It was toward evening, and the growing dusk made me aware that a tiny red light on the dashboard had been on for quite a while — the light that meant we were running out of gas. The map — and now *I* was studying it anxiously — indicated that we were about fifty miles from the next filling station. There was no way of knowing if we had enough fuel to get us there. We were in the hands of the Almighty. We turned the Handel off and kept very silent, listening intently for the slightest sputter of the engine. And finally we made it. Our dear little car did it. Just as we were down to our very last drop of fuel, we arrived at a lodge, filled the tank with gas and ourselves with bourbon and chili, and felt as if we had escaped the worst agony imaginable.

It was a good thing that, before our journey ended, we had

this taste of the menacing side of nature in America, and a sense
of her sublime disregard of the individual. Up to then we had
wallowed in the pleasantness of the country. Now it was time
that we understood the potential threat in the vast horizons that
merged so magnificently with the peach-colored skies at the end
of golden days. We could now see that they hatched not only
star-filled nights but also blizzards, tornadoes, and droughts. In
short, we began to see the land with American eyes. A European
sees any landscape as a potential garden. An American sees it as
an object of enterprise, a building site for some bold undertaking that might be blown or washed away at any moment. There
is a ruthless give-and-take in Americans' relationship with nature. In fact, the few places where nature is regarded for its
own sake, as nature — the Grand Canyon, Niagara Falls, Kings
Canyon, Yosemite, Yellowstone — are kept in cages, like animals in a zoo.

Beatrice was studying the map. I was wondering whether I
should do the same in order to be able to give an accurate
account of my 13,400-mile trip across the crazy quilt of America.
But that would not tell how I saw things, or certainly how I
remembered them. Geography is an abstract discipline: our
image of the world is not a clear or comprehensible one. Did we
emerge originally from the waters? Probably, for in our inner
world, things are still floating. In every traveler's mind, his journey is a loose accumulation of impressions, swimming mysteri-
ously between memory gaps. Thinking back, he has to ask
himself over and over again the same question: Where was it?
Where was it that I saw that beautiful blond girl standing under
a maple tree in all its autumnal glory, its leaves showering down
on her like the gold on Danaë? Where was that garage sale that
told one family's whole history, their likes and dislikes, their
whims and ambitions, all laid out in a heap of dishes, frying
pans, roller skates, books, pictures, and miscellaneous junk?
Where was it that black-bonneted ladies looked out of horse-
drawn carriages shaped like European beach chairs, and the
man had those archaic short beards under their chins and
plowed with oxen, meanwhile keeping their tractors hidden in
the barn? Where was that awful joint with the pretty topless
dancers who acted sexy to get the country yokels drinking beer

and gawking at them to stick ten-dollar bills into their
G-strings; who, when they finished their numbers, went and sat
in a group in the corner and knitted? And that road that went
downhill for a whole day, only downhill, till night fell — where
was that? And the big bar with all the saddles and cattle horns
and silver dollars nailed to the counter? And the funny graffiti
in the men's room: WE AIM TO PLEASE. YOU AIM TOO, PLEASE?
And the face of that blind woman with the white hair standing
in a wind that rolled the shrubs of the desert like bowling balls?
And the unbelievably fresh, clean, rosy gums of those black
children playing in the dust and giggling at us, and that frosty
morning when it snowed and the rows of orange trees with the
ripe fruit hanging on them looked like a Grandma Moses painting — where was all that? The beige, yellow, orange, brown,
and lime-green country I, as a child, had dreamily looked at on
the globe in my sister's and my nursery in faraway Bukovina
had become a jigsaw puzzle of bits and pieces, a patchwork of
quick impressions, an album of casual snapshots taken at random in different states of mind. "Do you remember that Diane
Arbus photograph of the middle-aged parents looking up helplessly at their giant of a son, who seems ready to grow out of the
ceiling of their apartment?" I asked Beatrice. "The more I've
seen of the United States, the more it grows out of my compre-
hension."

It was the end of a long day on the road. We were driving
toward the peach-colored brim of one of those infinitely clear
skies on which invisible jet planes were drawing white lines. Like
blotting paper, it swallowed up the ink of night and soon was
drowned by it; and there ahead, where the last cold fire of the
evening had just died, another, even colder gleam arose and
slowly grew to a glare. We recognized it as a strip of Lolitaland
at the edge of a town. But this was more than just a strip. It was
a whole city aflame with multicolored light, and the closer we
got to it, the more intensely the cold fire of this hell burned.
G. K. Chesterton once said of Times Square at night that a
person who couldn't read might think it was Paradise. But this
was ten times, a hundred times, Times Square. And it was totally
devoid of people. There were thousands of cars, though, but
their soft cores had left them and had swarmed into the ephem-
eral-looking buildings whose outsides glowed so enchantingly in

the star-spangled night. Inside those buildings, at hundreds of gambling tables and thousands of slot machines, they were busily trying to make money. We knew that in the morning these places would be deserted, and that all the splendor before us would have been extinguished, and that there would be nothing left but a tremendous void with a cluster of flimsy buildings on it. And I thought to myself, What a tale Sinbad the Sailor would have to tell about Las Vegas, this splendid place that looked like Paradise at night and a desert during the day, and was populated by rubber-tired steel creatures whose soft cores left them to go and make money. And then I realized that the tremendous dam and power plant we had passed hours earlier existed expressly to re-create, night in, night out, the cold hell of this desert paradise; and that the soft cores of the steel creatures had to destroy nature in order to create their own, artificial nature. Here I had in its essence, the new world of the terrible poetic children: Lolitaland in Disneylandish perfection. The Promised Land's New Jerusalem. Finally I had caught it, *my* butterfly.

PHYLLIS ROSE

Tools of Torture:
An Essay on Beauty and Pain

FROM THE ATLANTIC

IN A GALLERY off the rue Dauphine, near the *parfumerie* where I
get my massage, I happened upon an exhibit of medieval torture instruments. It made me think that pain must be as great a
challenge to the human imagination as pleasure. Otherwise
there's no accounting for the number of torture instruments.
One would be quite enough. The simple pincer, let's say, which
rips out flesh. Or the head crusher, which breaks first your tooth
sockets, then your skull. But in addition I saw tongs, thumb-
screws, a rack, a ladder, ropes and pulleys, a grill, a garrote, a
Spanish horse, a Judas cradle, an iron maiden, a cage, a gag, a
strappado, a stretching table, a saw, a wheel, a twisting stork, an
inquisitor's chair, a breast breaker, and a scourge. You don't
need complicated machinery to cause incredible pain. If you
want to saw your victim down the middle, for example, all you
need is a slightly bigger than usual saw. If you hold the victim
upside down so the blood stays in his head, hold his legs apart,
and start sawing at the groin, you can get as far as the navel
before he loses consciousness.

Even in the Middle Ages, before electricity, there were many
things you could do to torment a person. You could tie him up
in an iron belt that held the arms and legs up to the chest and
left no point of rest, so that all his muscles went into spasm
within minutes and he was driven mad within hours. This was
the twisting stork, a benign-looking object. You could stretch
him out backward over a thin piece of wood so that his whole

body weight rested on his spine, which pressed against the sharp wood. Then you could stop up his nostrils and force water into his stomach through his mouth. Then, if you wanted to finish him off, you and your helper could jump on his stomach, causing internal hemorrhage. This torture was called the rack. If you wanted to burn someone to death without hearing him scream, you could use a tongue lock, a metal rod between the jaw and collarbone that prevented him from opening his mouth. You could put a person in a chair with spikes on the seat and arms, tie him down against the spikes, and beat him, so that every time he flinched from the beating he drove his own flesh deeper onto the spikes. This was the inquisitor's chair. If you wanted to make it worse, you could heat the spikes. You could suspend a person over a pointed wooden pyramid and whenever he started to fall asleep, you could drop him onto the point. If you were Ippolito Marsili, the inventor of this torture, known as the Judas cradle, you could tell yourself you had invented something humane, a torture that worked without burning flesh or breaking bones. For the torture here was supposed to be sleep deprivation.

The secret of torture, like the secret of French cuisine, is that nothing is unthinkable. The human body is like a foodstuff, to be grilled, pounded, filleted. Every opening exists to be stuffed, all flesh to be carved off the bone. You take an ordinary wheel, a heavy wooden wheel with spokes. You lay the victim on the ground with blocks of wood at strategic points under his shoulders, legs, and arms. You use the wheel to break every bone in his body. Next you tie his body onto the wheel. With all its bones broken, it will be pliable. However, the victim will not be dead. If you want to kill him, you hoist the wheel aloft on the end of a pole and leave him to starve. Who would have thought to do this with a man and a wheel? But, then, who would have thought to take the disgusting snail, force it to render its ooze, stuff it in its own shell with garlic butter, bake it, and eat it?

Not long ago I had a facial — only in part because I thought I needed one. It was research into the nature and function of pleasure. In a dark booth at the back of the beauty salon, the aesthetician put me on a table and applied a series of ointments to my face, some cool, some warmed. After a while she put something into my hand, cold and metallic. "Don't be afraid, madame," she said. "It is an electrode. It will not hurt you. The other end is attached to two metal cylinders, which I roll over your face. They break down the electricity barrier on your skin and allow the moisturizers to penetrate deeply." I didn't believe this hocus-pocus. I didn't believe in the electricity barrier or in the ability of these rollers to break it down. But it all felt very good. The cold metal on my face was a pleasant change from the soft warmth of the aesthetician's fingers. Still, since Algeria it's hard to hear the word "electrode" without fear. So when she left me for a few minutes with a moist, refreshing cheesecloth over my face, I thought, What if the goal of her expertise had been pain, not moisture? What if the electrodes had been electrodes in the Algerian sense? What if the cheesecloth mask were dipped in acid?

In Paris, where the body is so pampered, torture seems particularly sinister, not because it's hard to understand but because — as the dark side of sensuality — it seems so easy. Beauty care is among the glories of Paris. *Soins esthétiques* include makeup, facials, massages (both relaxing and reducing), depilations (partial and complete), manicures, pedicures, and tanning, in addition to the usual run of *soins* for the hair: cutting, brushing, setting, waving, styling, blowing, coloring, and streaking. In Paris the state of your skin, hair, and nerves is taken seriously, and there is little of the puritanical thinking that tries to pursuade us that beauty comes from within. Nor do the French think, as Americans do, that beauty should be offhand and low-maintenance. Spending time and money on *soins esthétiques* is appropriate and necessary, not self-indulgent. Should that loving attention to the body turn malevolent, you have torture. You have the procedure — the aesthetic, as it were — of torture, the explanation for the rich diversity of torture instruments, but you do not have the cause.

Historically torture has been a tool of legal systems, used to get information needed for a trial or, more directly, to determine guilt or innocence. In the Middle Ages confession was considered the best of all proofs, and torture was the way to produce a confession. In other words, torture didn't come into existence to give vent to human sadism. It is not always private and perverse but sometimes social and institutional, vetted by the government and, of course, the Church. (There have been few bigger fans of torture than Christianity and Islam.) Righteousness, as much as viciousness, produces torture. There aren't squads of sadists beating down the doors to the torture chambers begging for jobs. Rather, as a recent book on torture by Edward Peters says, the institution of torture creates sadists; the weight of a culture, Peters suggests, is necessary to recruit torturers. You have to convince people that they are working for a great goal in order to get them to overcome their repugnance to the task of causing physical pain to another person. Usually the great goal is the preservation of society, and the victim is presented to the torturer as being in some way out to destroy it.

From another point of view, what's horrifying is how easily you can persuade someone that he is working for the common good. Perhaps the most appalling psychological experiment of modern times, by Stanley Milgram, showed that ordinary, decent people in New Haven, Connecticut, could be brought to the point of inflicting (as they thought) severe electric shocks on other people in obedience to an authority and in pursuit of a goal, the advancement of knowledge, of which they approved. Milgram used — some would say abused — the prestige of science and the university to make his point, but his point is chilling nonetheless. We can cluck over torture, but the evidence at least suggests that with intelligent handling most of us could be brought to do it ourselves.

In the Middle Ages, Milgram's experiment would have had no point. It would have shocked no one that people were capable of cruelty in the interest of something they believed in. That was as it should be. Only recently in the history of human thought has the avoidance of cruelty moved to the forefront of ethics. "Putting cruelty first," as Judith Shklar says in *Ordinary Vices,* is comparatively new. The belief that the "pursuit of happiness" is one of man's inalienable rights, the idea that "cruel and unusual punishment" is an evil in itself, the Benthamite notion that behavior should be guided by what will produce the greatest happiness for the greatest number — all these principles are only two centuries old. They were born with the eighteenth-century democratic revolutions. And in two hundred years they have not been universally accepted. Wherever people believe strongly in some cause, they will justify torture — not just the Nazis, but the French in Algeria.

Many people who wouldn't hurt a fly have annexed to fashion the imagery of torture — the thongs and spikes and metal studs — hence reducing it to the frivolous and transitory. Because torture has been in the mainstream and not on the margins of history, nothing could be healthier. For torture to be merely kinky would be a big advance. Exhibitions like the one I saw in Paris, which presented itself as educational, may be guilty of pandering to the tastes they deplore. Solemnity may be the wrong tone. If taking one's goals too seriously is the danger, the best discouragement of torture may be a radical hedonism that denies that any goal is worth the means, that refuses to allow the nobly abstract to seduce us from the sweetness of the concrete. Give people a good croissant and a good cup of coffee in the morning. Give them an occasional facial and a plate of escargots. Marie Antoinette picked a bad moment to say "Let them eat cake," but I've often thought she was on the right track.

All of which brings me back to Paris, for Paris exists in the imagination of much of the world as the capital of pleasure — of fun, food, art, folly, seduction, gallantry, and beauty. Paris is civilization's reminder to itself that nothing leads you less wrong than your awareness of your own pleasure and a genial desire to spread it around. In that sense the myth of Paris constitutes a moral touchstone, standing for the selfish frivolity that helps keep priorities straight.

SCOTT RUSSELL SANDERS

The Inheritance of Tools

FROM THE NORTH AMERICAN REVIEW

AT JUST ABOUT the hour when my father died, soon after dawn one February morning when ice coated the windows like cataracts, I banged my thumb with a hammer. Naturally I swore at the hammer, the reckless thing, and in the moment of swearing I thought of what my father would say: "If you'd try hitting the nail it would go in a whole lot faster. Don't you know your thumb's not as hard as that hammer?" We both were doing carpentry that day, but far apart. He was building cupboards at my brother's place in Oklahoma; I was at home in Indiana, putting up a wall in the basement to make a bedroom for my daughter. By the time my mother called with news of his death — the long distance wires whittling her voice until it seemed too thin to bear the weight of what she had to say — my thumb was swollen. A week or so later a white scar in the shape of a crescent moon began to show above the cuticle, and month by month it rose across the pink sky of my thumbnail. It took the better part of a year for the scar to disappear, and every time I noticed it I thought of my father.

The hammer had belonged to him, and to his father before him. The three of us have used it to build houses and barns and chicken coops, to upholster chairs and crack walnuts, to make doll furniture and bookshelves and jewelry boxes. The head is scratched and pockmarked, like an old plowshare that has been working rocky fields, and it gives off the sort of dull sheen you see on fast creek water in the shade. It is a finishing hammer, about the weight of a bread loaf, too light, really, for framing walls, too heavy for cabinet work, with a curved claw for pulling nails, a rounded head for pounding, a fluted neck for looks, and a hickory handle for strength.

The present handle is my third one, bought from a lumber-yard in Tennessee, down the road from where by brother and I were helping my father build his retirement house. I broke the previous one by trying to pull sixteen-penny nails out of floor joists — a foolish thing to do with a finishing hammer, as my father pointed out. "You ever hear of a crowbar?" he said. No telling how many handles he and my grandfather had gone through before me. My grandfather used to cut down hickory trees on his farm, saw them into slabs, cure the planks in his hayloft, and carve handles with a drawknife. The grain in hickory is crooked and knotty, and therefore tough, hard to split, like the grain in the two men who owned this hammer before me.

After proposing marriage to a neighbor girl, my grandfather used this hammer to build a house for his bride on a stretch of river bottom in northern Mississippi. The lumber for the place, like the hickory for the handle, was cut on his own land. By the day of the wedding he had not quite finished the house, and so right after the ceremony he took his wife home and put her to work. My grandmother had worn her Sunday dress for the wedding, with a fringe of lace tacked on around the hem in honor of the occasion. She removed this lace and folded it away before going out to help my grandfather nail siding on the house. "There she was in her good dress," he told me some fifty-odd years after that wedding day, "holding up them long pieces of clapboard while I hammered, and together we got the place covered up before dark." As the family grew to four, six, eight, and eventually thirteen, my grandfather used this hammer to enlarge his house room by room, like a chambered nautilus expanding its shell.

By and by the hammer was passed along to my father. One day he was up on the roof of our pony barn nailing shingles with it, when I stepped out the kitchen door to call him for supper. Before I could yell, something about the sight of him straddling the spine of that roof and swinging the hammer caught my eye and made me hold my tongue. I was five or six years old, and the world's commonplaces were still news to me. He would pull a nail from the pouch at his waist, bring the hammer down, and a moment later the *thunk* of the blow would reach my ears. And that is what had stopped me in my tracks and stilled my tongue, that momentary gap between seeing and hearing the blow. Instead of yelling from the kitchen door, I ran to the barn and climbed two rungs up the ladder — as far as I was allowed to go — and spoke quietly to my father. On our walk to the house he explained that sound takes time to make its way through air. Suddenly the world seemed larger, the air more dense, if sound could be held back like any ordinary traveler.

By the time I started using this hammer, at about the age when I discovered the speed of sound, it already contained houses and mysteries for me. The smooth handle was one my grandfather had made. In those days I needed both hands to swing it. My father would start a nail in a scrap of wood, and I would pound away until I bent it over.

"Looks like you got ahold of some of those rubber nails," he would tell me. "Here, let me see if I can find you some stiff ones." And he would rummage in a drawer until he came up with a fistful of more cooperative nails. "Look at the head," he would tell me. "Don't look at your hands, don't look at the hammer. Just look at the head of that nail and pretty soon you'll learn to hit it square."

Pretty soon I did learn. While he worked in the garage cutting dovetail joints for a drawer or skinning a deer or tuning an engine, I would hammer nails. I made innocent blocks of wood look like porcupines. He did not talk much in the midst of his tools, but he kept up a nearly ceaseless humming, slipping in and out of a dozen tunes in an afternoon, often running back over the same stretch of melody again and again, as if searching for a way out. When the humming did cease, I knew he was faced with a task requiring great delicacy or concentration, and I took care not to distract him.

He kept scraps of wood in a cardboard box — the ends of two-by-fours, slabs of shelving and plywood, odd pieces of molding — and everything in it was fair game. I nailed scraps together to fashion what I called boats or houses, but the results usually bore only faint resemblance to the visions I carried in my head. I would hold up these constructions to show my father, and he would turn them over in his hands admiringly, speculating about what they might be. My cobbled-together guitars might have been alien spaceships, my barns might have been models of Aztec temples, each wooden contraption might have been anything but what I had set out to make.

Now and again I would feel the need to have a chunk of wood shaped or shortened before I riddled it with nails, and I would clamp it in a vise and scrape at it with a handsaw. My father would let me lacerate the board until my arm gave out, and then he would wrap his hand around mine and help me finish the cut, showing me how to use my thumb to guide the blade, how to pull back on the saw to keep it from binding, how to let my shoulder do the work.

"Don't force it," he would say, "just drag it easy and give the teeth a chance to bite."

As the saw teeth bit down, the wood released its smell, each kind with its own fragrance, oak or walnut or cherry or pine — usually pine because it was the softest, easiest for a child to work. No matter how weathered and gray the board, no matter how warped and cracked, inside there was this smell waiting, as of something freshly baked. I gathered every smidgen of sawdust and stored it away in coffee cans, which I kept in a drawer of the workbench. When I did not feel like hammering nails, I would dump my sawdust on the concrete floor of the garage and landscape it into highways and farms and towns, running miniature cars and trucks along miniature roads. Looming as huge as a colossus, my father worked over and around me, now and again bending down to inspect my work, careful not to trample my creations. It was a landscape that smelled dizzyingly of wood. Even after a bath my skin would carry the smell, and so would my father's hair, when he lifted me for a bedtime hug.

I tell these things not only from memory but also from recent observation, because my own son now turns blocks of wood into nailed porcupines, dumps cans full of sawdust at my feet and sculpts highways on the floor. He learns how to swing a hammer from the elbow instead of the wrist, how to lay his thumb beside the blade to guide a saw, how to tap a chisel with a wooden mallet, how to mark a hole with an awl before starting a drill bit. My daughter did the same before him, and even now, on the brink of teenage aloofness, she will occasionally drag out my box of wood scraps and carpenter something. So I have seen my apprenticeship to wood and tools re-enacted in each of my children, as my father saw his own apprenticeship renewed in me.

The saw I use belonged to him, as did my level and both of my squares, and all four tools had belonged to his father. The blade of the saw is the bluish color of gun barrels, and the maple handle, dark from the sweat of hands, is inscribed with curving leaf designs. The level is a shaft of walnut two feet long, edged with brass and pierced by three round windows in which air bubbles float in oil-filled tubes of glass. The middle window serves for testing if a surface is horizontal, the others for testing if a surface is plumb or vertical. My grandfather used to carry this level on the gun rack behind the seat in his pickup, and when I rode with him I would turn around to watch the bubbles dance. The larger of the two squares is called a framing square, a flat steel elbow, so beat up and tarnished you can barely make out the rows of numbers that show how to figure the cuts on rafters. The smaller one is called a try square, for marking right angles, with a blued steel blade for the shank and a brass-faced block of cherry for the head.

I was taught early on that a saw is not to be used apart from a square: "If you're going to cut a piece of wood," my father insisted, "you owe it to the tree to cut it straight."

Long before studying geometry, I learned there is a mystical virtue in right angles. There is an unspoken morality in seeking the level and the plumb. A house will stand, a table will bear weight, the sides of a box will hold together, only if the joints are square and the members upright. When the bubble is lined up between two marks etched in the glass tube of a level, you have aligned yourself with the forces that hold the universe together. When you miter the corners of a picture frame, each angle must be exactly forty-five degrees, as they are in the perfect triangles of Pythagoras, not a degree more or less. Otherwise the frame will hang crookedly, as if ashamed of itself and of its maker. No matter if the joints you are cutting do not show.

Even if you are butting two pieces of wood together inside a cabinet, where no one except a wrecking crew will ever see them, you must take pains to ensure that the ends are square and the studs are plumb.

I took pains over the wall I was building on the day my father died. Not long after that wall was finished — paneled with tongue-and-groove boards of yellow pine, the nail holes filled with putty and the wood all stained and sealed — I came close to wrecking it one afternoon when my daughter ran howling up the stairs to announce that her gerbils had escaped from their cage and were hiding in my brand new wall. She could hear them scratching and squeaking behind her bed. Impossible! I said. How on earth could they get inside my drum-tight wall? Through the heating vent, she answered. I went downstairs, pressed my ear to the honey-colored wood, and heard the *scritch scritch* of tiny feet.

"What can we do?" my daughter wailed. "They'll starve to death, they'll die of thirst, they'll suffocate."

"Hold on," I soothed. "I'll think of something."

While I thought and she fretted, the radio on her bedside table delivered us the headlines: Several thousand people had died in a city in India from a poisonous cloud that had leaked overnight from a chemical plant. A nuclear-powered submarine had been launched. Rioting continued in South Africa. An airplane had been hijacked in the Mediterranean. Authorities calculated that several thousand homeless people slept on the streets within sight of the Washington Monument. I felt my usual helplessness in the face of all these calamities. But here was my daughter, weeping because her gerbils were holed up in a wall. This calamity I could handle.

"Don't worry," I told her. "We'll set food and water by the heating vent and lure them out. And if that doesn't do the trick, I'll tear the wall apart until we find them."

She stopped crying and gazed at me. "You'd really tear it apart? Just for my gerbils? The *wall?*" Astonishment slowed her down only for a second, however, before she ran to the workbench and began tugging at drawers, saying, "Let's see, what'll we need? Crowbar. Hammer. Chisels. I hope we don't have to use them — but just in case."

We didn't need the wrecking tools. I never had to assault my handsome wall, because the gerbils eventually came out to nibble at a dish of popcorn. But for several hours I studied the tongue-and-groove skin I had nailed up on the day of my father's death, considering where to begin prying. There were no gaps in that wall, no crooked joints.

I had botched a great many pieces of wood before I mastered the right angle with a saw, botched even more before I learned to miter a joint. The knowledge of these things resides in my hands and eyes and the webwork of muscles, not in the tools. There are machines for sale — powered miter boxes and radial-arm saws, for instance — that will enable any casual soul to cut proper angles in boards. The skill is invested in the gadget instead of the person who uses it, and this is what distinguishes a machine from a tool. If I had to earn my keep by making furniture or building houses, I suppose I would buy powered saws and pneumatic nailers; the need for speed would drive me to it. But since I carpenter only for my own pleasure or to help neighbors or to remake the house around the ears of my family, I stick with hand tools. Most of the ones I own were given to me by my father, who also taught me how to wield them. The tools in my workbench are a double inheritance, for each hammer and level and saw is wrapped in a cloud of knowing.

All of these tools are a pleasure to look at and to hold. Merchants would never paste NEW NEW NEW! signs on them in stores. Their designs are old because they work, because they serve their purpose well. Like folk songs and aphorisms and the grainy bits of language, these tools have been pared down to essentials. I look at my claw hammer, the distillation of a hundred generations of carpenters, and consider that it holds up well beside those other classics — Greek vases, Gregorian chants, *Don Quixote,* barbed fish hooks, candles, spoons. Knowledge of hammering stretches back to the earliest humans who squatted beside fires, chipping flints. Anthropologists have a lovely name for those unworked rocks that served as the earliest hammers. "Dawn stones," they are called. Their only qualification for the work, aside from hardness, is that they fit the hand. Our ancestors used them for grinding corn, tapping awls, smashing bones. From dawn stones to this claw hammer is a great leap in time, but no great distance in design or imagination.

On that iced-over February morning when I smashed my thumb with the hammer, I was down in the basement framing the wall that my daughter's gerbils would later hide in. I was thinking of my father, as I always did whenever I built anything, thinking how he would have gone about the work, hearing in memory what he would have said about the wisdom of hitting the nail instead of my thumb. I had the studs and plates nailed together all square and trim, and was lifting the wall into place when the phone rang upstairs. My wife answered, and in a moment she came to the basement door and called down softly to me. The stillness in her voice made me drop the framed wall and hurry upstairs. She told me my father was dead. Then I heard the details over the phone from my mother. Building a set of cupboards for my brother in Oklahoma, he had knocked off work early the previous afternoon because of cramps in his stomach. Early this morning, on his way into the kitchen of my brother's trailer, maybe going for a glass of water, so early that no one else was awake, he slumped down on the linoleum and his heart quit.

For several hours I paced around inside my house, upstairs and down, in and out of every room, looking for the right door to open and knowing there was no such door. My wife and children followed me and wrapped me in arms and backed away again, circling and staring as if I were on fire. Where was the door, the door, the door? I kept wondering. My smashed thumb turned purple and throbbed, making me furious. I wanted to cut it off and rush outside and scrape away the snow and hack a hole in the frozen earth and bury the shameful thing.

I went down into the basement, opened a drawer in my workbench, and stared at the ranks of chisels and knives. Oiled and sharp, as my father would have kept them, they gleamed at me like teeth. I took up a clasp knife, pried out the longest blade, and tested the edge on the hair of my forearm. A tuft came away cleanly, and I saw my father testing the sharpness of tools on his own skin, the blades of axes and knives and gouges and hoes, saw the red hair shaved off in patches from his arms and the backs of his hands. "That will cut bear," he would say. He never cut a bear with his blades, now my blades, but he cut deer, dirt, wood. I closed the knife and put it away. Then I took up the hammer and went back to work on my daughter's wall, snugging the bottom plate against a chalk line on the floor, shimming the top plate against the joists overhead, plumbing the studs with my level, making sure before I drove the first nail that every line was square and true.

ROBERT STONE

A Higher Horror of the Whiteness: Cocaine's Coloring of the American Psyche

FROM HARPER'S MAGAZINE

ONE DAY in New York last summer I had a vision near Saint Paul's Chapel of Trinity Church. I had walked a lot of the length of Manhattan, and it seemed to me that a large part of my time had been spent stepping around men who stood in the gutter snapping imaginary whips. Strangers had approached me trying to sell Elavil, an antidepressant. As I stood on Broadway I reflected that although I had grown to middle age seeing strange sights, I had never thought to see people selling Elavil on the street. Street Elavil, I would have exclaimed, that must be a joke!

I looked across the street from Saint Paul's and the daylight seemed strange. I had gotten used to thinking of the Wall Street area as a part of New York where people looked healthy and wholesome. But from where I stood half the men waiting for the light to change looked like Bartleby the Scrivener. Everybody seemed to be listening in dread to his own heartbeat. They're all loaded, I thought. That was my vision. Everybody was loaded on cocaine.

In the morning, driving into Manhattan, the traffic had seemed particularly demonic. I'd had a peculiar exchange with a bridge toll taker who seemed to have one half of a joke I was expected to have the other half of. I didn't. Walking on Fourteenth Street, I passed a man in an imitation leopard-skin hat

who was crying as though his heart would break. At Fourth
Avenue I was offered the Elavil. Elavil relieves the depression
attendant on the deprivation of re-refined cocaine — "crack" —
which is what the men cracking the imaginary whips were selling. Moreover, I'd been reading the papers. I began to think
that I was seeing stoned cops, stoned grocery shoppers, and
stoned boomers. So it went, and by the time I got to lower
Broadway I was concerned. I felt as though I were about to
confront the primary process of hundreds of thousands of un-
sound minds. What I was seeing in my vision of New York as
super-stoned Super City was cocaine in its role of success drug.

Not many years ago, people who didn't use cocaine didn't have
to know much about it. Now, however, it's intruding on the
national perception rather vigorously. The National Institute
on Drug Abuse reported almost six million current users in
1985, defining a current user as one who took cocaine at least
once in the course of the month preceding the survey. The same
source in the same year reckoned that more than twenty-two
million people had tried cocaine at least once during their lives.

So much is being heard about cocaine, principally through
television, that even people who live away from the urban centers are beginning to experience it as a factor in their lives.
Something of the same thing happened during the sixties, when
Americans in quiet parts of the country began to feel they were
being subjected to civil insurrection day in and day out.

One aspect that even people who don't want to know anything
about cocaine have been compelled to recognize is that people
get unpleasantly weird under its influence. The term "dope
fiend" was coined for cocaine users. You can actually seem unpleasantly weird to yourself on coke, which is one of its greatest
drawbacks.

In several ways the ubiquity of cocaine and its derivative crack
have helped the American city to carry on its iconographic function as Vision of Hell. Over the past few years some of the street
choreography of Manhattan has changed slightly. There seems
to be less marijuana in the air. At the freight doors of garment
factories and around construction sites people cluster smoking
something odorless. At night in the ghettos and at the borders
of ghettos, near the tunnels and at downtown intersections, an

enormous ugly argument seems to be in progress. Small, con-
tentious groups of people drift across the avenues, sometimes
squaring off at each other, moving from one corner to the next,
the conformations breaking up and re-forming. The purchase
of illegal drugs was always a sordid process, but users and
dealers (pretty much interchangeable creatures) used to attempt
adherence to an idealized vision of the traffic in which smoothie
dealt with smoothie in a confraternity of the hip. Crack sales
tend to start with a death threat and deteriorate rapidly. The
words "die" and "motherfucker" are among the most often
heard. Petty race riots between white suburban buyers and minority urban sellers break out several times an hour. Every half
block stand people in various states of fury, mindless exhilara-
tion, and utter despair — all of it dreadfully authentic yet all of
it essentially artificial.

On the day of my visionary walk through the city I felt beset
by a drug I hadn't even been in the same room with for a year.
New York always seems to tremble on the brink of entropy —
that's why we love her even though she doesn't love us back.
But that afternoon it felt as though white crystal had seeped
through the plates and fouled the very frame of reference.
There was an invisible whiteness deep down things, not just the
glistening mounds in their little tricorn Pyramid papers tucked
into compacts and under pocket handkerchiefs but, I thought,
a metaphysical whiteness. It seemed a little out of place at first.
I was not in California. I was among cathedrals of commerce
in the midst of a city hard at work. I wondered why the sense
of the drug should strike most vividly on Wall Street. It might
be the shade of Bartleby, I thought, and the proximity of the
harbor. The whiteness was Melvillean, like the whiteness of the
Whale.

In the celebrated chapter on whiteness in *Moby-Dick,* Melville
frequently mentions the Andes — not Bolivia, as it happens, but
Lima, "the strangest saddest city thou canst see. . . . There is a
higher horror in the whiteness of her woe." Higher horror
seemed right. I had found a Lima of the mind.

"But not yet," Melville writes, "have we solved the incantation
of this whiteness and learned why it appeals with such power to
the soul . . . and yet should be as it is, the intensifying agent in
things the most appalling to mankind . . . a dumb blankness full

of meaning in a wide landscape of snows — a colorless all-color of atheism from which we shrink."

I was in the city to do business with some people who tend toward enthusiasms, toward ardor and mild obsession. Behind every enthusiasm, every outburst of ardor, every mildly obsessive response, I kept scouring the leprous white hand of narcosis. It's a mess when you think everybody's high. I liked it a lot better when the weirdest thing around was me.

We old-time pot smokers used to think we were cute with our instant redefinitions and homespun minimalism. Our attention had been caught by a sensibility a lot of us associated with black people. We weren't as cute as we thought, but for a while we were able to indulge the notion that a small community of minds was being nurtured through marijuana. In a very limited way, in terms of art and music, we were right. In the early days we divided into two camps. Some of us were elitists who thought we had the right to get high because we were artists and musicians and consciousness was our profession and the rest of the world, the "squares," could go to hell. Others of us hoped the insights we got from using drugs like pot could somehow change the world for the better. To people in the latter camp, it was vaguely heartening when a walker in the city could smell marijuana everywhere. The present coke-deluded cityscape is another story.

Cocaine was never much to look at. All drugs have their coarse practicalities, so in the use of narcotics and their paraphernalia, dexterity and savoir-faire are prized. Coke, however, is difficult to handle gracefully. For one thing, once-refined cocaine works only in solution with blood, mucus, or saliva, a handicap to éclat that speaks for itself.

I remember watching an elegant and beautiful woman who was trying cocaine for the first time. The lady, serving herself liberally, had a minor indelicate accident. For a long time she simply sat there contentedly with her nose running, licking her lips. This woman was a person of such imposing presence that watching her get high was like watching an angel turn into an ape; she hung there at a balancing point somewhere midway along the anthropoid spectrum.

The first person I ever saw use cocaine was a poet I haven't seen for twenty-five years. It was on the Lower East Side, one night during the fifties, in an age that's as dead now as Agamemnon. Coltrane's "My Favorite Things" was on the record player. The poet was tall and thin and pale and self-destructive, and we all thought that was a great way to be. After he'd done up, his nose started to bleed. The bathtub was in the kitchen, and he sat down on the kitchen floor and leaned his head back against it. You had to be there.

Let me tell you, I honor that man. I honor him for his lonely independence and his hard outcast's road. I think he was one of the people who, in the fifties, helped to make this country a lot freer. Maybe that's the trouble. Ultimately, nothing is free, in the sense that you have to pay up somewhere along the line.

My friend the poet thought cocaine lived someplace around midnight that he was trying to find. He would not have expected it to become a commonplace drug. He would not have expected over 17 percent of American high school students to have tried it, even thirty years later, any more than he would have expected that one quarter of America's high school students would use marijuana. He was the wild one. In hindsight, we should have known how many of the kids to come would want to be the wild ones too.

A few weeks after my difficult day in the city I was sitting in my car in a New England coastal village leafing through my mail when for some reason I became aware of the car parked beside mine. In the front seat were two teenage girls whose tan summer faces seemed aglow with that combination of apparent innocence and apparent wantonness adolescence inflicts. I glanced across the space between our cars and saw that they were doing cocaine. The car windows were rolled up against the bay breeze. The drug itself was out of sight, on the car seat between them. By turns they descended to sniff. Then both of them sat upright, *bolt upright* might be the way to put it, staring straight ahead of them. They licked their fingers. The girl in the driver's seat ran her tongue over a pocket mirror. The girl beside her looked over at me, utterly untroubled by my presence; there was a six-inch length of peppermint-striped soda straw in her mouth. There are people I know who cannot re-move a cigarette from its pack with someone standing behind them, who between opening the seal and lighting up perform the most elaborate pantomimes of guilty depravity. Neither of these children betrayed the slightest cautious reflex, although we couldn't have been more than a few hundred yards from the village police station. The girl with the straw between her teeth and I looked at each other for an instant and I saw something in her eyes, but I don't know what it was. It wasn't guilty plea-sure or defiance or flirtatiousness. Its intellectual aspect was crazy and its emotional valence was cold.

A moment later, the driver threw the car into reverse and straight into the path of an oncoming postal truck, which for-tunately braked in time. Then they were off down the road, headed wherever they thought their state of mind might make things better. One wondered where.

Watching their car disappear, I could still see the moment of their highs. Surfacing, they had looked frosted, their faces streaked with a cotton-candied, snotty sugary excitement, a pair of little girls having their afternoon at the fair, their carnival goodies, and all the rides in a few seconds flat. Five minutes from the parking lot, the fairy lights would be burned out. Their parents would find them testy, sarcastic, and tantrum prone. Unless, of course, they had more.

The destructiveness of cocaine today is a cause for concern. What form is our concern to take?

American politicians offer a not untypical American political response. The Democrats say they want to hang the dealers. The Republicans say they want to hang them and throw their bones to the dogs. Several individuals suggest that the military be used in these endeavors. Maybe all the partisan competition for dramatic solutions will produce results. Surely some of our politically inspired plans must work some of the time.

I was talking with a friend of mine who's a lawyer recently. Like many lawyers, she once used a lot of cocaine, although she doesn't anymore. She and I were discussing the satisfactions of cocaine abuse and the lack thereof, and she recounted the story of a stock-trading associate of hers who was sometimes guided in his decisions by stimulants. One day, all of his clients received telephone calls informing them that the world was coming to an end and that he was supervising their portfolios with that in mind. The world would end by water, said the financier, but the right people would turn into birds and escape. He and some of his clients were already growing feathers and wattles.

"Some gonna fly and some gonna die," the broker intoned darkly to his startled customers.

We agreed that while this might be the kind of message you'd be glad to get from your Yaqui soothsayer, it hardly qualified as sound investment strategy. (Although, God knows, the market can be that way!)

"But sometimes," she said, "you feel this illusion of lucidity. Of excellence."

I think it's more that you feel like you're *about* to feel an illusion of lucidity and excellence. But lucidity and excellence are pretty hot stuff, even in a potential state, even as illusion. Those are very contemporary goals and quite different from the electric twilight that people were pursuing in the sixties.

"I thought of cocaine as a success drug," one addict is reported saying in a recent newspaper story. Can you blame him? It certainly looks like a success drug, all white and shiny like an artificial Christmas morning. It glows and it shines just as success must. And success is back! The faint sound you hear at the edges of perception is the snap, crackle, and pop of winners winning and losers losing.

You can tell the losers by their downcast eyes bespeaking unseemly scruple and self-doubt. You can tell the winners by their winning ways and natty strut; look at them stepping out there, all confidence and hard-edged realism. It's a new age of vim and vigor, piss and vinegar and cocaine. If we work hard enough and live long enough, we'll all be as young as the President.

Meanwhile, behold restored as lord of creation, pinnacle of evolution and progress, alpha and omega of the rationalized universe, Mr. Success, together with his new partner and pal, Ms. Success. These two have what it takes; they've got heart, they've got drive, they've got aggression. It's a no-fault world of military options and no draft. Hey, they got it all.

Sometimes, though, it gets scary. Some days it's hard to know whether you're winning or not. You're on the go but so's the next guy. You're moving fast but so is she. Sometimes you're afraid you'd think awful thoughts if you had time to think. That's why you're almost glad there isn't time. How can you be sure you're on the right track? You might be on the wrong one. Everybody can't be a winner or there wouldn't be a game. "Some gonna fly and some gonna die."

Predestinarian religion generated a lot of useful energy in this republic. It cast a long December shadow, a certain slant of light on winter afternoons. Things were grim with everybody wondering whether he was chosen, whether he was good enough, really, truly good enough and not just faking. Finally, it stopped being useful. We got rid of it.

It's funny how the old due bills come up for presentation. We had Faith and not Works. Now we've got all kinds of works and no faith. And people still wonder if they've got what it takes.

When you're wondering if you've got what it takes, wondering whether you're on the right track and whether you're going to fly, do you sometimes want a little pick-me-up? Something upbeat and cool with nice lines, something that shines like success and snaps you to, so you can step out there feeling aggressive, like a million-dollar Mr. or Ms.? And after that, would you like to be your very own poet and see fear — yes, I said fear — in a handful of dust? Have we got something for you! Something white.

On the New York morning of which I've spoken I beheld its whiteness. How white it really is, and what it does, was further described about 130 years ago by America's God-bestowed prophet, who delineated the great American success story with the story of two great American losers, Bartleby and Ahab. From *Moby-Dick:*

> And when we consider that . . . theory of the natural philosophers, that all other earthly hues — every stately or lovely emblazoning — the sweet tinges of sunset skies and woods; yea, and the gilded velvets of butterflies, and the butterfly cheeks of young girls; all these are but the subtle deceits, not actually inherent in substance, but only

laid on from without; and when we proceed further, and consider that the mystical cosmetic which produces every one of her hues, the great principle of light, for ever remains white or colorless in itself, and if operating without medium upon matter, would touch all objects, even tulips and roses, with its own blank tinge — pondering all this, the palsied universe lies before us a leper; and like wilful travellers in Lapland, who refuse to wear colored and coloring glasses upon their eyes, so the wretched infidel gazes himself blind at the monumental white shroud that wraps all the prospect around him.

All over America at this moment pleasurable surges of self-esteem are fading. People are discovering that the principal thing one does with cocaine is run out of it.

If cocaine is the great "success drug," is there a contradiction in that it brings such ruin not only to the bankers and the lawyers but to so many of the youngest, poorest Americans? I think not. The poor and the children have always received American obsessions as shadow and parody. They too can be relied on to "go for it."

"Just say no!" we tell them and each other when we talk about crack and cocaine. It is necessary that we say this because liberation starts from there.

But we live in a society based overwhelmingly on appetite and self-regard. We train our young to be consumers and to think most highly of their own pleasure. In this we face a contradiction that no act of Congress can resolve.

In our debates on the subject of dealing with drug abuse, one of the recurring phrases has been "the moral equivalent of war." Not many of those who use it, I suspect, know its origin.

In 1910, the philosopher William James wrote an essay discussing the absence of values, the "moral weightlessness" that seemed to characterize modern times. James was a pacifist. Yet he conceded that the demands of battle were capable of bringing forth virtues like courage, loyalty, community, and mutual concern that seemed in increasingly short supply as the new century unfolded. As a pacifist and a moralist, James found himself in a dilemma. How, he wondered, can we nourish those virtues without having to pay the dreadful price that war demands? We must foster courage, loyalty, and the rest, but we must not have war. Very well, he reasoned, we must find the *moral equivalent of war.*

Against these drugs can we ever, rhetoric aside, bring any kind of real heroism to bear? When they've said no to crack, can we someday give them something to say yes to?

CALVIN TRILLIN

Rumors Around Town

FROM THE NEW YORKER

THE FIRST HEADLINE in the *Junction City Daily Union* — "EMPORIA MAN FATALLY SHOT" — seemed to describe one of those incidents that can cause a peaceful citizen to shake his head and mumble something about how it's getting so nobody is safe anywhere. The Emporia man was Martin Anderson, a peaceful citizen who had a responsible job and a commission in the Army Reserve and a wife and four little girls. Early on a November evening in 1983, he was murdered by the side of State Highway 177, which cuts south from Manhattan through the rolling cattle-grazing land that people in Kansas call the Flint Hills. According to the newspaper story, the authorities had been told that Anderson was killed during a struggle with an unidentified robber. At the time of the murder, Anderson was on his way back to Emporia from Fort Riley, the infantry base that lies between Junction City and Manhattan. Apparently, the trip had been meant to combine some errands at the fort with an autumn drive through the Flint Hills. His wife was with him, and so were the little girls.

There is a special jolt to the headline "EMPORIA MAN FATALLY SHOT." For many Americans, Emporia, Kansas, conjures up the vision of a typical American town in the era when people didn't have to think about violent men bent on robbery — a town where neighbors drank lemonade on the front porch and kidded one another about their performances in the Fourth of July softball game. The vision grew out of the writings of William Allen White, the Sage of Emporia, who, as owner and editor of the *Emporia Gazette,* was widely thought of during the first forty years of this century as the national spokesman for the unadorned values of the American Midwest. The residents of Emporia in those days may have thought of their town as even more tranquil than its national reputation. What White had been looking for when he set out to buy a small-town newspaper, in 1895, was not a typical town but a college town — a place where his editorials could be understood and appreciated by "a considerable dependable minority of intelligent people, intellectually upper-middle class." Emporia, the seat of Lyon County and a division point for the Santa Fe Railway and a trading center for the surrounding farmland, had two colleges — the Kansas State Normal School and a small Presbyterian liberal arts school called the College of Emporia. During the years that people across the country thought of Emporia as a typical midwestern town, its boosters sometimes spoke of it as the Educational Center of the West, or even the Athens of Kansas.

In some ways, Emporia didn't change much after William Allen White passed from the scene. The White family continued to own the *Gazette.* Even now, Mrs. William L. White — the widow of the Sage's son, who was an author and a foreign correspondent known into his seventies around Emporia as Young Bill — comes in every day. Commercial Street still has the look of the main trading street in a Kansas farm town — two-story buildings separated by a slab of asphalt wide enough to accommodate angle parking on both sides and four lanes of traffic. The College of Emporia folded some years ago, though; its campus is now owned by a religious cult called The Way. Although the Santa Fe's operation has been shrinking in recent years, Emporia has, on the whole, become more of what was called in White's day a lunch-bucket town. The construction of the Wolf Creek nuclear power plant, forty miles to the southeast, brought a few thousand construction workers to the area, and some of them remained after the plant was completed. Although Kansas State Normal expanded as it evolved first into Kansas State Teachers' College and then into Emporia Kansas State College and then into Emporia State University, the largest employer in town these days is not a college but a big meatpacking plant, most of whose employees are not the sort of citizens who spend a lot of their time perusing the editorial page. There is less talk than there once was about Emporia's being the Athens of Kansas.

Still, a lot of people in Emporia lead an updated version of
the peaceful front-porch life that White portrayed, a life revolving around family and church and school and service club and
neighbors. The Andersons seemed to lead that sort of life.
When they walked into Faith Lutheran Church every Sunday,
the little girls wearing immaculate dresses that Lorna Anderson
had made herself, they presented the picture of a wholesome,
attractive American family that a lot of people still have in mind
when they think of Emporia. Marty Anderson, a medical tech-
nologist, ran the laboratory at Newman Memorial County Hospital. He was on the board of directors of the Optimist Club.
His wife was working part time as secretary of Faith Lutheran.
She was a member of a social and service sorority called Beta
Sigma Phi, which used its annual Valentine's Day dance as a
benefit for the local hospitals. The Andersons were among the
young couples who saw one another at Optimist basketball
games or church-fellowship meetings or Beta Sigma Phi socials
— people who tended to recall dates by saying something like,
"Let's see, that was the year Jenny started nursery school" or "I
remember I was pregnant with Bobby."

Faith Lutheran Church is dominated by such families. It's a
young church, in a former Assembly of God building on the
West Side of Emporia, an area filled with split-level houses
along blocks so recently developed that most of the trees are
still not much higher than the basketball goals. Faith Lutheran
was founded in 1982, when the one Missouri Synod Lutheran
church in Emporia, Messiah Lutheran, decided that the way to
expand was to ask for volunteers to form what was thought of
as a "daughter congregation" on the West Side. Faith Lutheran
grew so quickly that in October of 1982, just eight months after
its founding, it was chartered as a separate congregation. The
church — a pale brick building on a corner lot across the street
from a school — turned out to have been well placed, but the
congregation had other advantages besides a fortunate location.
The people who had volunteered to move from Messiah tended
to be active young families with a strong interest in a range of
church activities — what was sometimes called at Messiah "the
early-service crowd." Thomas Bird, the minister who had been
called from Arkansas to Messiah to lead the new undertaking,
turned out to be a dynamic young pastor who fitted right in

with his congregation. Tom Bird had been a long-distance run-
ner at the University of Arkansas. He was married to his high
school sweetheart, an astonishingly energetic young woman who
had a master's degree in mathematics and managed to combine
the responsibilities of a pastor's wife with some teaching at Emporia State. Like a lot of couples in the congregation, they had
three small children and a small split-level and a swing set in
the back yard.

The Missouri Synod is a particularly conservative branch of
American Lutheranism. Tom Bird thought of himself as conservative in doctrinal and liturgical matters but flexible in dealing with the concerns of his congregation. Distinguishing Faith
Lutheran from Missouri Synod churches more set in their
ways — Messiah, for instance — he has said that he wanted his
church to be more interested in people than in policies. Faith
Lutheran lacked the stern, Germanic atmosphere sometimes
associated with Missouri Synod churches. The attachment of
some of the young West Side couples who soon joined the
founders from Messiah was more demographic than liturgical.
A lot of them were attracted by a friendly, almost familial bond
among contemporaries who tended to be interested in the
church volleyball team as well as the Bible classes. The Andersons, who had been active at First Presbyterian, were introduced
to Faith when Lorna Anderson decided that its preschool, the
Lord's Lambs, might be a convenient place for their two youngest children, twin girls. Eventually, Martin and Lorna Anderson
found Faith Lutheran a comfortable place for the entire family.
Lorna Anderson went to work half days as the church secretary.
Marty Anderson put the pastor up for the Optimists.

A memorial service for Marty Anderson was held at Faith
Lutheran. Tom Bird, Lorna Anderson's boss and friend as well
as her pastor, was by her side. He could have been assumed to
have sad cause for empathy. Only four months before, his own
wife had died — killed, from what the authorities could ascer-
tain by reconstructing the event, when her car missed a nasty
curve next to the Rocky Ford Bridge, southeast of town, and
plunged over an embankment into the Cottonwood River. On
the day of Martin Anderson's memorial service, the sanctuary
of Faith Lutheran Church was full. Tom Bird delivered the
eulogy. The Optimists sat in the front rows.

The day before the memorial service, Susan Ewert, a friend of Lorna Anderson's from the Andersons' days at First Presbyterian, walked into the office of the *Emporia Gazette* first thing in the morning with an angry complaint. She said that the *Gazette* article reporting Martin Anderson's murder — a short Saturday-afternoon item that had been written near deadline on the strength of telephone conversations — implied that Lorna Anderson wasn't telling the truth about what had happened. The *Gazette's* implication, according to Mrs. Ewert, had so disturbed Mrs. Anderson that her pastor, who was trying to console her, had found her nearly suicidal. The managing editor of the *Gazette*, Ray Call, said that the paper would be happy to give Mrs. Anderson the opportunity to tell her story in detail, and when the *Gazette* came out that afternoon, it carried a story headlined "MURDERED EMPORIAN'S WIFE RECALLS TERROR ON HIGHWAY."

Lorna Anderson's story was this: She was at the wheel of the family's van as it headed down 177 from Manhattan toward Emporia that evening. Apparently having eaten something in Manhattan that disagreed with her, she felt that she was about to be ill, so she stopped the car. As she got out, she took the keys with her — her husband had always insisted that she remove the keys any time she left the van — and then accidentally dropped them in the field at the side of the road. When her husband came out to help her look for them, he told her to return to the van and shine the headlights in his direction. While she was doing that, she heard someone say, "Where's your wallet?" She turned to see her husband hand his wallet to a masked man, who started shooting. Her husband fell to the ground. Then the man grabbed her, held the gun to her head, and pulled the trigger. The gun failed to fire. He fled into the darkness.

The story presented some problems. Would someone who was about to be ill really pull the keys out of a car parked on a deserted stretch of highway when her husband was sitting right in the front seat? What were the odds against a bandit's being on that stretch of highway when the Anderson's van stopped? The original item in the *Gazette* — an item that followed Lorna Anderson's account with the sentence "Officers are investigating the story" — had, in fact, reflected the skepticism of the Geary County officers who listened to the account the night of the murder. The implication of that skepticism was clear in a headline run by the *Junction City Daily Union* the next day: "VICTIM'S WIFE AMONG SUSPECTS IN KILLING." The *Emporia Gazette* was not as blunt, but that didn't mean an absence of suspicion in Emporia. There were a lot of rumors around town.

Emporia, with a population of twenty-five thousand, is about the right size for rumors. In a tiny town, people are likely to know firsthand what is true and what isn't. In a large city, most of the population won't have any connection at all with the people under discussion. In a place the size of Emporia, though, people tend to have an uncle who knows the cousin of someone through the Kiwanis, or a next-door neighbor who has the word through a lawyer who has a kid in the same Boy Scout troop. The Andersons had been in Emporia for only seven years — Marty Anderson was from a small town south of Wichita, and his wife had grown up in Hutchinson — but a lot of people knew someone who knew them. Just about everybody had something to say about them.

Marty Anderson sounded like a person who had been both easy to like and easy not to like. "He could be very aggravating, and the next minute he could get you laughing," a fellow Optimist has said. The way Anderson tried to get people laughing was usually through needling or practical jokes, and in both forms he occasionally passed over the line from funny to mean. Sometimes the object of the needling was his wife. He was a big man, more than six feet tall, and not the sort of big man who slowed up coming into second base for fear of bowling over a smaller player. At Newman Hospital, he sometimes employed an army-sergeant manner that irritated people in other departments, but the technologists who worked for him considered him an essentially fair man who tried to run a meticulous laboratory. Basically, they liked him. Outside the hospital, he was known as a man who after quite a bit too much to drink at a party might decide to play a prank that turned out not to have been such a good idea after all. His wife was given to tearful recitals of how miserable life with Martin Anderson could be, and some of the people who tried to be of comfort were told that he beat her.

"Everybody was always comforting Lorna," a female associate

of Martin Anderson's said not long ago, putting a little twist on
the word "comforting." Lorna Anderson cried easily. Until a
couple of years before her husband's death, she had often
phoned him at the lab, distraught and tearful, but she was better
known for seeking her comfort elsewhere. The Emporians of
William Allen White's day could have described her with one
sentence: She had a reputation. A trim, dark-haired, pleasant-
looking woman of about thirty, she did not have the appearance
of the town bombshell. But there were women in Emporia —
women who worked at the hospital or were members of Beta
Sigma Phi — who said that they avoided parties where the Andersons were likely to be present because they knew that before
the evening was out Lorna Anderson would make a play for
their husband. There were people in Emporia who said that a
police investigation that included scrutiny of the Anderson's
marriage had the potential of embarrassing any number of
prominent business and professional men — men who had met
Lorna Anderson when she worked at one of the banks or men
who knew her through her work as local fund raiser for the
American Heart Association or men who had simply run into
her late in the evening at a place like the Continental Club of
the Ramada Inn. Some people in Emporia — people who, say,
worked with someone who knew someone connected with Faith
Lutheran Church — were saying that Lorna Anderson's latest
catch was Pastor Tom Bird. "Just after we got home from Marty's funeral, the phone rang," a colleague of Martin Anderson's
recalled not long ago. "The person calling said there was a
rumor that Lorna and Tom Bird had something to do with
Marty's death."

Pastor Bird had been one of the people who were always
comforting Lorna. Almost from the time she began working for
the church, in early 1983, there were whispers in the congregation about the possibility that the pastor and his secretary had
grown too close. After Sandra Bird's death, in July of 1983,
Lorna Anderson was just one of a number of women from the
congregation who concentrated on providing whatever support
they could for the young pastor, but she was the only one whose
relationship with Tom Bird continued to cause uneasiness in
the congregation. The pastor of Messiah had spoken confiden-
tially to Bird about what people were saying, and so had Faith's

lay ministers — the equivalent of church elders in some Lutheran congregations. At one point, the lay ministers, intent on avoiding even the appearance of impropriety by the pastor, considered Lorna Anderson's resignation. Finally, it was agreed that she would remain church secretary but would limit her presence at the church to the hours that her job called for. Bird had assured the lay ministers that there was in fact no impropriety in his relationship with his secretary. She had a troubled marriage and a tendency to "spiral down," he told them, and he was only doing his best to counsel and support her. He continued to stand by her after Martin Anderson's death, and after suspicion was cast on her. He continued to stand by her when, only a couple of weeks after Anderson's death, Daniel Carter, an Emporia man who had been picked up by the Geary County authorities on a tip, said she had given him five thousand dollars to see that her husband was killed. Pastor Bird's support did not waver even when, shortly after Carter's arrest, Lorna Anderson herself was arrested for conspiracy to commit first-degree murder.

Lorna Anderson said she was innocent. Daniel Carter said he was guilty. He agreed to cooperate with the authorities investigating the role of Lorna Anderson and others in the plot.

"Do you recall when it was you first had occasion to meet her?" Steven Opat, the Geary County attorney, asked during one of the times Carter testified in court.

"Yes," Carter said. "I used to cut her hair."

That was at Mr. & Ms., on Commercial Street, in 1981. The relationship was strictly business for about a year, Carter testified, and then there was an affair, which lasted a few months, and then, in August of 1983, Lorna Anderson asked him to find someone to get rid of her husband. By that time, Carter was working on the construction crew at Wolf Creek, where he presumably had a better chance of finding a hit man among his co-workers than he would have had at the hairdresser's. The Geary County authorities didn't claim that Carter had concocted a scheme that actually resulted in the death of Martin Anderson. As they pieced the story together, Carter took five thousand dollars from Lorna Anderson and passed it on to Gregory Curry, his supervisor at Wolf Creek, who passed it on to a third

man, in Mississippi, who, perhaps realizing that nobody was in
a position to make a stink about having the money returned if
services weren't rendered, didn't do anything.

That left the mystery of who killed Martin Anderson, which
meant that a number of investigators from the Geary County
Sheriff's Office and the Lyon County Sheriff's Office and the
Kansas Bureau of Investigation were still asking questions
around Emporia — scaring up a covey of rumors with each interview. When the next arrest came, though, it was not for murder but for another plot, which nobody claimed had gone any
further than talk. On March 21, 1984, four and a half months
after Martin Anderson's death, the Lyon County attorney, Rodney H. Symmonds, filed charges against Thomas Bird for criminal solicitation to commit first-degree murder. In an affidavit
filed at the same time, a KBI agent said that the prosecution was
acting largely on information it had received from an Emporia
house builder named Darrel Carter, Daniel Carter's older
brother. Shortly after the arrest of Daniel Carter, the affidavit
said, Darrel Carter had gone to the authorities to inform them
that in May of 1983, three months before the plot his brother
had described, he, too, had been asked to help get rid of Martin
Anderson. According to the affidavit, Darrel Carter had gone
to Faith Lutheran Church one weekday morning at Lorna Anderson's request, and there had been asked by Tom Bird if he
would help in a murder scheme that was already worked out.
After Martin Anderson's death, the affidavit said, Darrel Carter
had got word that Tom Bird wanted to meet with him again in
order to "reaffirm their trust," but this time Carter had shown
up wearing a hidden transmitter provided by the Kansas Bureau of Investigation.

"Who would have thought that little old Emporia would have
two hit men?" a professor at Emporia State University has said.
Even to people in Emporia who had spent the months since
Martin Anderson's death savoring the ironies or embellishing
the rumors, though, the idea of a minister plotting a murder
scheme right in his own church was shocking. There was an
accompanying shock in what the affidavit said about one of the
possible murder plans that Bird was accused of presenting to
Darrel Carter: "Bird told Carter he found a place with a bend
in a road and a bridge outside of Emporia, which had an ap-

proximately fifty-foot drop-off to the river and that a person could just miss the curve, especially if the person were drunk, and go off down the embankment. Bird told Carter they were going to drug Marty, take him out there, and run the car off into the river."

Anyone who might have missed the implication of that could see it spelled out in the *Gazette*'s coverage of Bird's arrest. "On July 17, Sandra Bird, Mr. Bird's wife, was found dead near the wreckage of her car that went off the road at the Rocky Ford Bridge southeast of Emporia," the *Gazette* said. "According to the accident report, Mrs. Bird had been driving northbound on the county road when the car apparently went off the roadway at the approach to the bridge and down a 65-foot embankment.

"An autopsy concluded that Mrs. Bird's death was accidental, caused by severe abdominal and chest injuries.

"Mr. Symmonds declined to comment on whether he considered Mrs. Bird's death to be accidental.

" 'Whenever a person dies, it's always subject to further investigation,' he said."

Members of Faith Lutheran offered to post Tom Bird's bond. The church's attitude was summed up by the *Wichita Eagle* with the headline "CONGREGATION RALLIES AROUND PASTOR." There were people in the congregation who had been put out at Tom Bird at one time or another — he was known as someone who could be strong-willed about having things done his own way — but in general he was a popular figure. To people who might have expected a Missouri Synod Lutheran pastor to be a severe man on the lookout for sin, Tom Bird had always seemed accessible and informal and concerned. "We're going to stand behind him all the way," one young woman in the congregation told the reporter from Wichita. Faith Lutheran people spoke of Christian love and the American principle that a man is innocent until proved guilty. A lot of them considered the charge against Tom Bird a horrible mistake that would be straightened out at his first hearing. There were some people in the congregation, however, who believed that it would be inappropriate for Bird to continue in his pastoral duties as if nothing had happened, and there were a few who thought he should resign. Bird said that he had no intention of resigning or asking for a leave of absence. In a congregational meeting, a compromise was reached: it was decided that as a way of easing the pressure on Pastor Bird while he dealt with his defense, he could be relieved of preparing and delivering sermons while retaining his other pastoral duties. That arrangement was supposed to last until Bird's preliminary hearing. When the hearing was postponed for some weeks, Bird said that he would prefer to take the pulpit again, and the lay ministers, to the irritation of a few members who were outspokenly opposed to Pastor Bird's continued presence, agreed. On the Sunday that he preached his first sermon after his arrest, the worshipers emerging from the church after the service were greeted not only by their pastor but also by a couple of television crews and some out-of-town reporters.

In Bird's view, the presence of the press that Sunday effectively ended his ministry at Faith Lutheran by making it clear that the church would be no sanctuary from temporal concerns as long as Thomas Bird was its pastor. With or without television cameras at Sunday services, it was a hard time for Faith Lutheran. The atmosphere of relaxed fellowship that had attracted so many young families had turned tense. The effort of most members to withhold judgment meant that no one was quite certain of where anyone else stood A few families had dropped out of the congregation, and some people came to church less often. "I didn't feel comfortable going to church," a member who was a strong supporter of Pastor Bird has said. "I felt people judging us as well as judging Tom." Faith members also felt some pressure from outside the church. The questions and remarks they heard from outsiders often seemed to carry the implication that the attitude of the congregation toward its pastor was naïve or silly. In the view of one Faith Lutheran member, "It got to be socially unacceptable to go to our church." In the days after Bird's return to the pulpit, it was clear from the pressure within the church not simply that he would no longer deliver sermons on Sundays but that he would have to resign. He delayed the announcement by several weeks in order to avoid going into his preliminary hearing carrying the burden of having resigned under pressure.

Bird had often expressed gratitude for the congregation's support, but even before his arrest he had written in a church newsletter that his reputation was being "sullied by the local

gossips." Some of the people who thought the congregation had
not been strong enough in its support believed that in the
strained atmosphere that followed his arrest the pastor had reason to feel "unwelcome and unloved" in his own church. When
he finally resigned, two months after his arrest, his farewell
speech to the congregation was partly about such subjects as
authentic Christian love and the purposes of the church, but it
also included some rather bitter remarks about his treatment.
"When I remained silent, I was judged to be unfair for not
informing people; when I have spoken, I was judged to be
defensive," he said. "When I looked depressed, I was judged to
be full of self-pity; when I smiled and looked strong, I was
judged to be failing to take matters seriously. When I acted
timid, I was judged to be weak; when I acted boldly, I was
judged to be manipulating. When I was indecisive, I was judged
to have lost my leadership capacity; when I acted decisively, I
was judged to be using my position to railroad matters. To
multiply the anguish of my predicament, I only hear these judgments second or third hand, so that I cannot share directly what
is in my heart and my intentions to my accusers within the
congregation."

By the time of Tom Bird's resignation, a folklorist at Emporia
State who is interested in the sort of jokes people tell was collecting Tom-and-Lorna jokes. The folklorist, Thomas Isern, believes that the range of humor in the mass media these days has
forced folk humor to be scurrilous in order to remain folk
humor, and scurrilous jokes flowed easily from a situation that
included a couple of stock folklore characters — the preacher
and the loose woman. The relationship between Tom Bird and
Lorna Anderson was not the only subject of intense speculation
in Emporia. A lot of people were talking about whether Sandra
Bird's death had really been an accident. A couple of months
after Bird's arrest, the *Gazette* reported that Sandra Bird's family, in Arkansas, had asked a Little Rock lawyer to supervise an
investigation into the circumstances of her death. Once some
doubt about the incident was made public, it became apparent
that a number of people had at the time entertained doubts
about whether Sandra Bird had simply missed a curve. A lot of
people — neighbors, for instance, and people at Emporia State

— had driven out to the Rocky Ford Bridge to have a look at the scene. What had given them pause was not any suspicion of Tom Bird but a feeling that the physical evidence didn't make sense. If Sandra Bird liked to take late-night drives by herself to unwind, as her husband had reported, why would she drive on the distinctly unrelaxing gravel road that approached the Rocky Ford Bridge? If the car was going so fast that it missed the curve at the bridge, which is the second half of an S curve, how did it negotiate the first half? If the car was going that fast, how come it wasn't more seriously damaged? It turned out that there had been people in Emporia who for months had not actually believed the official version of how Sandra Bird died. They thought that she might have committed suicide or that she might have been abducted in the parking lot at Emporia State, where she sometimes went late at night to use the computers, and murdered by her abductor.

By far the most popular topic for speculation, though, was what people in Emporia began to call simply the list. The prosecution, it was said, had a list of Emporia men who had been involved with Lorna Anderson. In some versions of the story, the *Gazette* had the list. In some versions, it was not a list but a black book. In some versions, the men who were on a list of potential witnesses for Lorna Anderson's trial had been informed of that by the prosecution so that they could break the news to their families themselves. The version of the list story some of the reporters on the *Gazette* liked best turned into one of the jokes that could be collected by Tom Isern:

A prominent businessman calls an acquaintance on the *Gazette* news staff and says nervously, "I have to know — does the *Gazette* have a list?"

"No," the *Gazette* reporter says in a soothing voice. "But we're compiling one."

Those people in Emporia who were counting on Lorna Anderson's trial to end the suspense were in for a long wait. The case against her got tangled in any number of delays and legal complications. As it turned out, the first person to come to trial for plotting to murder Martin Anderson was Tom Bird. The defense asked for a change of venue, providing the court with the results of a survey indicating that the overwhelming majority of

Emporia residents were familiar with the case. The motion was denied. In Kansas, there is a strong tradition against granting changes of venue even when there is wide community awareness of a case, and, as it happened, the survey indicated that a relatively small percentage of those who were familiar with the charges and the rumors had already made up their minds. But among the ones who had there was a strong indication of how Emporia opinion was running: out of thirty-nine people with firm opinions, thirty-two thought Tom Bird was guilty.

Bird's mother and his father, who is also a Lutheran minister, came up from Arkansas for the trial. So did Sandra Bird's father and mother and stepfather — who, it was noted around town, seemed to keep their distance from their former son-in-law during the proceedings. Reporters and television crews from Wichita and Topeka were in town; despite objections from the defense, a fixed television camera was permitted in the courtroom for the first time in Lyon County. There were members of Faith Lutheran who had come to testify for the defense and members who had come to testify for the prosecution and members who had come merely because, like most residents of Emporia, they were attracted by the prospect of seeing witnesses under oath clear up — or perhaps improve on — the rumors that had been going around town for eight months. The courtroom was jammed every day. "I've never been to anything like this before," one of the spectators told the *Gazette*. "I feel like I know them all; I've heard their names so many times."

The prosecution's case was based on the assumption that Tom Bird and Lorna Anderson had been lovers. According to the prosecutor, they wanted Marty Anderson out of the way, and they weren't interested in a less violent means of accomplishing that — divorce, for instance — because they also wanted the $400,000 in insurance money his death would bring. The prosecution's witnesses included the Anderson's insurance agent — he turned out to be the president of the Optimist Club — and a babysitter, who said that she once heard Lorna Anderson say on the telephone, "I cannot wait for Marty to die; I can't wait to count the green stuff." There was testimony from Faith Lutheran people who had been concerned that the pastor and his secretary were growing too close. "I saw a sparkle in their eyes when they talked to each other," said the preschool teacher, a young woman who under cross-examination acknowledged that she herself had wrestled with a crush on the pastor. "I felt electricity in the air." There was testimony from a development director of the Heart Association, who reduced the talk of electricity and eye-sparkling to more direct language; according to her testimony, Lorna Anderson had told her about having an affair with the pastor and had said that she was using Heart Association business as a cover for trysts in out-of-town motels. The Anderson's nine-year-old daughter, Lori, testified that she had seen her mother and Tom Bird hugging; Marty Anderson's brother and a KBI agent both testified that what Lori had said when she was first questioned was that she had seen her mother and Tom Bird kissing.

The prosecution's star witness was, of course, Darrel Carter. He testified that the meeting at the church in the spring of 1983 was not the first time Lorna Anderson had asked his help in killing her husband. She had first asked him a year or so before that, he said, at a time when the Andersons and the Carters knew each other casually from Beta Sigma Phi functions. "I was really kind of shocked to think that she would ask me that," Carter testified, " 'cause Martin Anderson was a friend of mine." According to Carter's testimony, that friendship hadn't prevented him from having his own fling with Lorna some months later. To back up Carter's story of the meeting at Faith Lutheran, the prosecution called a couple of people he had mentioned the scheme to at the time. "I was doing a little work there one evening in my garage on an old Corvette that I'm restoring," one of them, a neighbor of Carter's, said in testimony that summoned up the traditional vision of summertime Emporia. "We visited about several things, which I can't tell you all they were, but the one that sticks in my mind right now is that he told me that someone had contacted him about killing someone."

What the defense asked the jury to do was to view Darrel Carter's testimony not as a story he had finally come forward with after his brother's arrest but as a story he had concocted in order to win some leniency for his brother — who had, in fact, been given probation, while Gregory Curry, his confederate in the scheme, was sentenced to prison. From that angle, the details that Darrel Carter knew could be seen as coming from police reports available to the defense in his brother's case. The similarity of the murder plan to the circumstances of Sandra Bird's death could be explained by the fact that when Carter concocted the story, he knew how Sandra Bird had died. The meeting at Faith Lutheran had indeed taken place, the defense said; its purpose was not to plot murder, though, but to explore the possibility of Faith youth-group members' working at Carter's fireworks stand in order to raise money for a trip to see the Passion Play in Eureka Springs, Arkansas. After Marty Anderson's death, Bird had indeed let it be known that he wanted to talk to Carter, the defense said, but that was because Susan Ewert, Lorna Anderson's friend, had told Bird that Carter was spreading rumors about him, and Bird wanted to put a stop to that. "I've heard enough rumors for sure," Bird could be heard saying on the tape. "Rumors are rampant."

During that conversation with Carter, in a bowling-alley parking lot, Bird made what the prosecution presented as incriminating remarks about the meeting at his church ("I just wanted to touch the bases and make sure that we just talked about possibly my youth group sellin' firecrackers for you") and about the murder of Martin Anderson ("Well, maybe we ought to be glad that we didn't follow through") and about how he felt about Anderson's death ("I ain't celebratin', but I ain't mournin', either"). Still, nothing on the tape was absolutely explicit, and Bird took the stand to provide a benign explanation for every remark — mostly based on the contention that what he and Carter hadn't followed through on was a plan to refer Lorna Anderson to an agency that assists battered wives. When the prosecution managed to bring into evidence two notes from Tom Bird that the police said they had found in Lorna Anderson's lingerie drawer, Bird said that they were meant simply to buck up Lorna's spirits and that such sentiments as "I love you so very much and that's forever" were expressions not of romantic attachment but of "authentic Christian love."

In describing his efforts to counsel Lorna Anderson, Bird admitted that, emotionally drained by his wife's death, he might have used bad judgment in providing the gossips with even the appearance of something worth gossiping about. In explaining why he had arranged the parking-lot meeting through a go-between, a woman he knew from an inquiry she had made about the Lord's Lambs preschool, he admitted a pressure tactic that some jurors might have considered un-Christian: he happened to know that the woman and Darrel Carter were having an affair, he testified, and he figured that making Carter aware of that knowledge might send "the message that everybody is capable of being a victim of rumors." But that was about all he admitted. Bird said that people who saw him hugging Lorna Anderson while comforting her might not have understood that standing across the room with consoling words would not have been "full communication." She had a "self-esteem problem" that required a lot of comforting, he said, and he had provided it as her pastor and her employer and her friend but not as her lover.

"If only he had admitted the affair," a remarkable number of people in Emporia said when talking about Tom Bird's trial for criminal solicitation. The defense had insisted that the case amounted to a simple choice of whether to believe Tom Bird or Darrel Carter. In some ways, it was an unequal contest. Darrel Carter was nobody's idea of a model citizen. He did not claim that his response to having been asked to help murder a friend of his had included outrage or a telephone call to the authorities. He acknowledged — boasted about, the defense might have said — two affairs with married women while he was married himself. Someone who had hired him to build a house took the stand to say that he was "the biggest liar in ten counties." In contrast, several character witnesses testified that Tom Bird was a trustworthy, God-fearing man. "He is very conscious of the Word of God," the chairman of Faith Lutheran's board of lay ministers said, "and he is very deliberate in his close attention and following of the Word of God."

But practically nobody in Emporia believed Tom Bird when he said he had not had an affair with Lorna Anderson. If only he had admitted the affair, people in Emporia said, the jury might have believed the rest of the story — or might at least have been understanding about what passion could have led him to do. The defense that Emporia people thought might have worked for Tom Bird amounted to a sort of Garden of Eden defense — a tragic twist on the jokes about the preacher and the loose woman. To some people in Emporia, it seemed that Tom Bird could have been presented as a vulnerable man who, at a particularly stressful time in his life, had been led by his passion for a temptress to do some things he came to regret, but who would never have conspired to break God's commandment against murder. A lot of people in Emporia, in other words, thought that Tom Bird's only hope was to repent. The people from Faith Lutheran who continued to believe in Pastor Bird right through the trial found that approach enraging. He could not repent, they said, for the simple reason that he had done nothing that required repentance. That, apparently, was not the view of the jury. Bird was found guilty of soliciting murder. He was sentenced to a term of two and a half to seven years in the Kansas State Penitentiary.

"Like most Emporians, we love a bit of juicy gossip now and then," an editorial in the *Gazette* said a month or so after Tom Bird's conviction. "But in recent weeks here, the saturation point for rumors has been reached and innocent people are being hurt." The *Gazette* mentioned some rumors about the possibility that "the defendant in a recent sensational trial had remarried." There were also further rumors about Lorna Anderson, who had moved back to Hutchinson, and about what might be revealed in her trial. Time had swollen accounts of the list. "At first the list was said to contain 20 names," the *Gazette* said. "Now the number has grown to 110 and includes 'bankers, lawyers and other professional men.' This is a case of gross exaggeration." The *Gazette* thought it necessary to inform its readers that a professional man who had recently left town had not in fact fled because he was on the list and feared exposure.

The *Gazette* had begun a campaign to have the rumors surrounding Sandra Bird's death tested in a court of law. "Was it only coincidence that Mr. Bird's wife died in the manner and in the place that the minister had suggested for the murder of Mr. Anderson?" its editorial on the verdict in Tom Bird's trial asked. Two *Gazette* reporters, Roberta Birk and Nancy Horst, pounded away at the Sandra Bird case with stories carrying headlines like "CIRCUMSTANCES OF DEATH RAISE SUSPICIONS" and "TROOPER THOUGHT DEATH NOT ACCIDENT." The *Gazette* made a reward fund available for information on the case, and ran a series of stories about contributions to the fund from Sandra Bird's friends and family. In a sheriff's election that November, the

Gazette editorialized against the incumbent partly on the ground that he had bungled the original investigation of Sandra Bird's death, and he was defeated. Eventually, Sandra Bird's body was exhumed, a second autopsy was performed, and a grand jury began investigating the case. In February of 1985, the grand jury handed up an indictment against Tom Bird for the murder of his wife.

The *Gazette*'s campaign angered the people in Emporia who continued to believe in Bird's innocence. In the months since the headline "CONGREGATION RALLIES AROUND PASTOR," of course, their ranks had suffered serious attrition. Some supporters had dropped away as they heard more and more about the relationship between Tom Bird and Lorna Anderson. A lot more had defected after the revelations of the trial or after the guilty verdict. But there remained people in the Faith Lutheran congregation who believed that the verdict was just wrong — a result of Darrel Carter's perfidy and the judge's perverse refusal to move the trial out of a community that had convicted Tom Bird before any witnesses took the stand. The Bird supporters who remained could point out inconsistencies in prosecution testimony. But basically they believed Bird was innocent partly because they thought he was incapable of the deeds he was accused of and partly because he said he was innocent. "He told me that he swears before God he's innocent," one of the lay ministers has said. "I have to believe him. I don't think he would say that if he were guilty."

Almost everybody else in Emporia tended to believe that Bird was guilty not only of plotting to kill Martin Anderson but also of murdering his own wife. According to a survey taken for Bird's lawyer to support a motion to move his murder trial out of Emporia, virtually everyone in town was familiar with the case, and more than 90 percent of those who had made up their minds about it believed that he was guilty. The motion was denied. Last July, the familiar cast of characters gathered once again in Lyon County District Court — Tom Bird and his parents, the family of Sandy Bird, the small band of Faith Lutheran members who remained loyal to Bird, County Attorney Rodney H. Symmonds, Darrel Carter, the TV crews from Topeka and Wichita. As the trial got under way, though, what most Emporia residents seemed to be discussing was not any revelation from the witness stand but news from Hutchinson that Lorna Anderson, whose trial was finally scheduled to begin later in the summer, had remarried. The bridegroom was a Hutchinson man named Randy Eldridge, someone she had known for years. In answer to reporters' questions, Eldridge said he believed that his new wife was innocent. She said that he was "a wonderful, Christian person" — someone who, it turned out, in his spare time was a member of a gospel-singing sextet. That fact and the rumors that both Eldridges were quite active in an Assembly of God church in Hutchinson had some people in Emporia concerned. It looked as if Lorna Anderson Eldridge might be planning to come to court as an upstanding Christian wife and mother who couldn't have had anything to do with plotting murder — and presumably the prosecution might attempt to destroy that picture of probity by calling to the stand any number of men from the list.

In Tom Bird's trial for murder, there was even more testimony about his relationship with his secretary than there had been in the previous trial. The prosecution called witnesses — Sandra Bird's mother among them — who testified that the pastor's wife had been so distraught over the relationship that she had been unable to eat. But a lot of the testimony was rather technical — testimony from pathologists and accident-reconstruction specialists — and there were days when finding a seat in the spectators' section was no problem. The prosecution called expert witnesses to testify that neither the injuries to Sandra Bird nor the damage to the car was consistent with an accident; the defense called expert witnesses to testify the opposite. By pointing out inconsistencies in Tom Bird's account of that evening and presenting some physical evidence, such as the presence of bloodstains on the bridge, the prosecutor suggested that Bird had beaten his wife, thrown her off the Rocky Ford Bridge, run their car off the embankment, and dragged her body over to it in order to create the appearance of an accident. The defense argued that inconsistencies were to be expected from a man who had been up half the night worrying about where his wife was and had had to start the day by telling his children that their mother was dead. Tom Bird was on trial not for how he ran his personal life, his lawyer said, but for the crime of murder, and "there's no evidence that a crime of any kind was committed." The testimony required twelve days. After that, the jury deliberated for six hours and found Tom Bird guilty of first-degree murder. He was sentenced to life in prison.

"Even a lot of people who thought he was guilty didn't think the trial proved it," a supporter of Bird's said not long ago. It is true, at least, that the prosecutor was not able to provide an eyewitness, as he had done in the criminal-solicitation case. It is also true that he went into the trial holding the advantage of Bird's conviction for plotting Martin Anderson's murder. Among people familiar with the case, it is taken for granted that without the earlier conviction Bird would never have been brought to trial for his wife's murder. Discussing the astonishing chain of events that transformed Tom Bird from a popular young minister to a lifer convicted of killing his wife, a lot of people in Emporia continue to say, "If only he had admitted the affair."

A month after Bird's second conviction, Lorna Anderson Eldridge sat in the same courtroom — neatly dressed, composed, almost cheerful — and said, "I believe it was in June 1983, Thomas Bird and I met with Darrel Carter at the Faith Lutheran Church. During that meeting we discussed various ways of murdering my husband, Martin Anderson." In a last-minute plea bargain, she had agreed to plead guilty to two counts of criminal solicitation to commit first-degree murder and to tell the authorities anything she knew about a case that had presumably already been decided — the death of Sandra Bird. In her plea, she said that Tom Bird had also been involved later in trying to hire a hit man through Danny Carter, and had, in fact, furnished the five thousand dollars. Lorna Eldridge's lawyer said she wanted to purge her soul. A month later, she was sentenced to a term of five and a half to eighteen years in state prison.

Her plea was a blow to those who had continued to believe in Tom Bird, but it did not significantly reduce their ranks. At one point, one of them said not long ago, Bird had told his supporters, "There are very few left. They are falling away. And sooner or later you, too, will be gone." As it turned out, the people who had stuck with Tom Bird even through the murder trial did not

fall away just because Lorna Anderson stated in open court that
what the prosecution said about Tom Bird was true. They figured that she might be lying because she thought a plea bargain
was in her best interest, or that she might be lying simply because she liked to lie. They continue to believe that someday
something — a large criminal operation like a drug ring, perhaps — will come to light to explain events that the state has
explained with accusations against Tom Bird. At times, they
sound like early Christians who manage to shake off constant
challenges to their faith. "Questions come up," one of them has
said. "And I stop and think. But I always work it out." Tom
Bird, when asked by a recent visitor to the Kansas State Penitentiary about the loyalty of his supporters, also explained their
support in religious terms — as the action of Christians who
understand that we are all sinners and that it is not our role to
judge others. "They've grown in their faith," he said.

It is possible that the challenges to their faith in Tom Bird are
not at an end. It is not known yet precisely what, if anything,
Lorna Anderson Eldridge had to tell the prosecutors about the
death of Sandra Bird. So far, nobody has been charged with the
murder of Martin Anderson. In Geary County, though, investigators believe that they have made considerable progress. Presumably acting on information provided by Lorna Anderson
Eldridge, the Geary County Sheriff's Office drained several
farm ponds this fall and eventually found the gun it believes
was used in the killing. It is said that the gun belonged to Martin
Anderson. Shortly after the sheriff began draining farm ponds,
Tom Bird was taken to Junction City from prison to answer
questions. Each step in the investigation in Geary County set off
ripples of speculation in Lyon County. Will Tom Bird be
charged with another murder? Had one of the murder schemes
already uncovered by the authorities resulted in Anderson's
death after all? Or could it be that little old Emporia had *three*
hit men?

To some extent, Lorna Anderson Eldridge's guilty plea meant
that William Allen White's home town could get back to normal.
Faith Lutheran Church, which had absorbed a fearful blow, has
begun to recover. Nobody claims that it has regained the mo-
mentum of its early days, but the new pastor — another athletic

and personable man with several children — believes that the church has come through its crisis into a period of consolidation. The Lord's Lambs preschool is back to its routine. So are the Optimist basketball games and the laboratory at Newman Hospital and the front page of the *Gazette*. Presumably, Mrs. Eldridge's guilty pleas brought a great sense of relief to those residents of Emporia who had reason to look with some trepidation on the prospect of her coming to trial. There was now less danger that what the *Gazette* called "the most sordid case in Emporia's history" would extend to sworn testimony about the sexual escapades of prominent citizens.

One change in Emporia is that two families are no longer there. The adults are dead or imprisoned, the children living in other cities. (The Anderson children have been adopted by Randy Eldridge; the Bird children are living in Arkansas with Tom Bird's parents, who are in the midst of a custody suit brought by the family of Sandra Bird.) Also, there are some people who believe that what happened to the Birds and the Andersons has to have changed what Emporians think of their town and their neighbors. People who have long taken the guilt of Tom Bird and Lorna Anderson for granted are still left with questions about how they could have brought themselves to do such awful deeds. Was Lorna Anderson a temptress who merely used Tom Bird to help get rid of her husband? Or did the death of Sandra Bird — perhaps caused by her husband in some fit of rage — lead inevitably to the death of Martin Anderson? If Tom Bird and Lorna Anderson were bound together, were they bound together by love or by guilty knowledge? Lately, there has been more talk in Emporia about the possibility that what happened can be explained through some sort of mental illness. In a 1984 story about the background of the Birds, Dana Mullin of the *Topeka Capital-Journal* reported that Tom Bird was once hospitalized with a severe heat stroke after a six-mile run in Arkansas and that such heat strokes have been known to cause brain damage. Putting that information together with some of the bizarre behavior attributed to Lorna Anderson even before her husband's death, some people in Emporia have theorized that perhaps Tom Bird and his secretary, who seemed so much like their neighbors, had mental difficulties that somehow meshed to result in deeds their neighbors consider unthinkable.

What was sordid about Emporia's most sordid case, of course, was not simply the crimes but the lives they revealed — lives full of hatred and maybe wife beating and certainly casual, apparently joyless liaisons. (When Daniel Carter testified that his affair with Lorna Anderson had ended because she seemed to want more from him than he was willing to offer, the prosecutor asked what he had been willing to offer. "Nothing," Carter said.) Although the *Gazette* may have criticized rumors about a 110-man list as "a gross exaggeration," the prosecutors have never denied that a list, perhaps of more modest size, existed — assembled, it is assumed, in case the state of the Andersons' marriage became an issue. A jury had concluded that an Emporia minister beat his wife until she was unconscious or dead and threw her body off a bridge. A church secretary acknowledged involvement in plans to get rid of her husband, who was murdered virtually in front of their own children. What now seems remarkable about the outrageous rumors that gripped Emporia for so long is that so many of them turned out to be true.

GEOFFREY C. WARD

Tiger in the Road!

FROM AUDUBON

THE DUST IS the same as it was thirty years ago on the old Jaipur road
that leads from Delhi to the Indian desert state of Rajasthan. It hangs
in the hot still air above the field where a farmer and his haggard bullock
scratch at the flat, beaten earth; swirls up from the sharp hooves of a
herd of goats nibbling their way along the roadside; filters, gritty, between a traveler's teeth. But much else has changed since, as a boy, I
last drove along this road to hunt.

Indian wildlife had seemed inexhaustible then. "Game" was all we
ever called it. Partridges and peacocks bustled along the shoulders of
the road back then, and the bright-green plots of wheat and mustard
were home to blackbuck antelope, so many and so buoyantly curious that,
at the sight of our Jeep rolling along a track then still traveled mostly by
bullock carts, they sometimes left off their grazing to race in front of us,
scores of them leaping over the road until the dust they kicked up made
it impossible to see.

Now, blaring, overloaded trucks fill that same road, day and night,
and the great bounding herds are gone. I wondered, as the familiar
landscape flashed by, what remained of the animals I had once pursued
here with such heedless enthusiasm.

I. Game

The Sariska Tiger Reserve, where I was headed and where I
had often hunted three decades ago, was still a game sanctuary
in those days; until very recently it had been the exclusive hunting reserve of the maharajas of Alwar, rulers of one of hun-

dreds of small princely states and best remembered for the lavish tiger hunts they once organized for visitors from abroad.

In 1954, when my family and I arrived in India, where my father was to serve as consultant to a large foundation, I was just fourteen. I had not much wanted to come. City-bred and slowed down by polio that had been contracted two years earlier, I thought India simply sounded strange and impossibly far from my friends. But on the long shipboard journey I discovered *Jungle Lore* and several other books by Colonel Jim Corbett, the intrepid British dispatcher of man eaters. His accounts of growing up in the Indian forests were irresistible, and I secretly resolved that I would somehow experience as much of it as I could myself.

Perhaps my resolve was not so secret, for shortly after we moved into our house on what were then the outskirts of New Delhi, my father gave me a pellet gun. I began to prowl our compound and the scrub jungle that surrounded it, shooting at the doves that settled on the telephone wires and the little gray lizards that skittered along the red-brick garden wall. It was not the killing itself that drew me — though I can't deny that I enjoyed it — so much as the excitement of seeing how close I could get, and the extraordinary sense of power that shooting then represented. It was an activity well outside the tranquil world in which my parents had sought to raise my brother and sister and me, and perhaps more important, it provided me with vivid proof that even after polio I could affect things directly — even brutally — on my own.

In any case, two of my father's American friends took me on my first real hunt just a few miles outside the city one Sunday morning. They were after antelope. None was to be seen that day, but they lent me an old over-and-under, a combination .22 rifle and .410 shotgun, with which to shoot at anything else that turned up as we drove. I shot a fox, a rabbit, an owl, and a lynx with tufted ears, then took the whole furry haul home and had myself photographed with it spread out around me on the lawn.

I don't remember my mother's reaction — I suspect she was appalled — but my father seemed delighted. "The boy is a crack shot," he wrote home to my grandparents. "Who would have thought it?" And he paid to have the owl and the lynx stuffed by a local taxidermist; the cat's snarling head hung in my upstairs bedroom for years, dust settling on its bright pink tongue.

My parents bought the over-and-under for me, and when it proved too light and too slow to reload, they gave me a fine old Belgian twelve-gauge shotgun, purchased from two white-bearded Sikhs, proprietors of a gun shop in Connaught Circus that had served the shikar needs of several generations of British sahibs. I loved to visit their shop, partly just to admire the polished weapons and boxes of bright red shotgun shells ranked in glass cases around its walls, but also because of the grave courtesy with which its owners pretended that this fourteen-year-old with round glasses was to be treated as a mighty hunter.

No gun was ever better cared for than mine: its walnut stock always slippery with oil, its twin barrels gleaming inside and out. I studied up on wing shooting, doing my best to memorize how-to photo sequences featuring elderly Britons in plaid knickers, then stood in the garden taking pantomime aim at the taunting crows that flapped in and out of our trees.

Despite all my earnest backyard practice, I was never any good at shooting birds. I spent a number of frosty mornings crouched in blinds built in the midst of flooded fields, banging away without success at the ducks and geese that muttered overhead. A slender boy of twelve or so watched me most of one especially discouraging morning, drawn by all the noise my friends and I were making and by the rare spectacle of seeing a wet foreigner so near his home.

"What are you doing, sahib?" he finally asked after the last birds had moved too far off for us to scare into taking off again. "Do you want ducks? *I* will get them for you. Five rupees." How many did we want?

"Five," I said for no special reason; one number seemed as unlikely as another.

"Wait here," he said. The boy slipped into the water, which just covered his shoulders, and began walking slowly toward the sitting birds. Big clay water pots bobbed here and there, trapped in the fields when the rains came. He paused to break the neck off one of these, placed its round bottom over his head with just room enough to see, and resumed his slow, steady progress toward the ducks. It took him almost half an hour to reach them. But then, one by one and with only the slightest disturbance of the surface, he yanked five birds under, holding each there by its feet until it had stopped struggling. The hardest part was bringing them back; his thin legs trembled when he emerged, grinning, from the water, and it took both hands to carry his limp burden. We paid him double what he'd asked. I think that may have been my first faint inkling that there was something inherently foolish about shooting.

The four friends who watched with me as the boy drowned ducks that morning were my hunting companions throughout my three and a half years in India. All were much older than I. Bhagat and Harbans Singh were Sikh brothers, descended from a family of hunters, and fine shots. R. V. Raman was an airline executive for whom Bhagat Singh worked; he was an able, fast-talking, self-made man who seemed to have a hospitable friend or grateful client living near every likely forest and fishing stream in northern India. The last was my family's Christian driver, Mathew. (Those are not their real names; since these old friends are still living, and I am unclear about the Indian statute of limitations, I have thought it wise to invent new ones.) I suspect that these grown-ups were initially willing to take me hunting mostly because I had access to a Jeep, then still a relatively rare thing in India. But after a time they seemed to take a genuinely avuncular interest in my having as good a time as they.

One of Raman's many friends was Vikram Singh, the Rao Raja of Alwar, and it was with him that we first hunted in the Sariska forest. He was a chunky little man, soft-spoken and round-faced and almost perpetually melancholy. He was the illegitimate son of the late maharaja — his title, Rao Raja, was itself a courtly euphemism for "bastard" — and there was a good deal of hard feeling between him and the half-brother then on the throne.

Because the boy could never rule, his father had decided when his son was still an infant that something else must be found for him to do with his time. Hunting was the answer, and although the Rao Raja grew wonderfully good at it, I don't think he ever liked it much. From early boyhood on he had been made to stand hip-deep in a nearby lake for hours at a time, firing at wildfowl. When the surface of the lake was at last empty, the birds driven elsewhere, he was still expected to continue shooting — hundreds, sometimes thousands of shells a day — until his ears rang and his cheek and shoulder were blackened. To teach his son how to bag bigger game on the run, the maharaja ordered a railroad track built especially for him up one of the slopes in his state forest and had a flatcar fitted out with stuffed animals — tigers, leopards, an assortment of glass-eyed deer. A bullet-proof cab was constructed for the steam engine that pulled it so that the fireman and engineer could tow the targets up and down the hillside in relative safety. The young Rao Raja fired from a rocky perch across the valley, and when he had riddled all the beasts so that they sagged and spilled out most of their stuffing, replacements were nailed to the flatcar floor and the oversized shooting gallery hauled up the slope again.

The Rao Raja became a superb marksman. Without seeming even to aim, he could plink copper anna pieces from the sky with a .22 rifle, and by the time I knew him in his mid-thirties, he had accounted for scores of tigers and leopards, hundreds of deer, thousands of birds from his family's preserve. His bravery was celebrated, too: Villagers like to tell of the time he entered a cave alone to track a wounded panther.

It had all bored him. "Too easy," he told me once. "Just bang, bang, bang." Still, he seemed to enjoy driving us into the forest. As he inched the Jeep through the bazaars of his battered old city or slowed to weave his way through one of the many villages that had once belonged to his father, it was clear that some things had not changed since the old days. Aged men called out greetings to the prince, bowing almost to the ground; at intersections they reached out to touch his feet. Women smiled shyly from behind the corners of their saris. Naked children waved. The Rao Raja acknowledged their greetings by lifting one hand slightly from the wheel. At first all this obeisance seemed disturbing, but before long I was doing my best to mimic his princely nonchalance.

In British times, only members of the royal family had been permitted to shoot at Sariska; the muzzle of anyone else's weapon carried through their land was sealed with wax. By the

time I first saw it, the forest was at least officially off limits even
to the Rao Raja — though neither he nor the forest officers in
charge seemed willing to admit it. He did not so much as slow
the Jeep at the gatehouse, and the game wardens in khaki all
saluted as we roared past.

The Rao Raja knew every parched hillside and stony ravine.

"Now," he said, slowing the Jeep as we approached a forest
curve one afternoon. "Around the corner, in the clearing on
your left, you will find seven partridge." We stopped. "Get out,
shoot just one, then come right back." I got down and walked
up the road, aware that he was watching, knowing I was supposed to hold up my end, but knowing also that no one, not
even the Rao Raja of Alwar, could possibly know how many
birds there would be in an unseen clearing. I saw nothing at
first; the clearing seemed empty. But as I stared I began to see
them; seven brown-gray birds almost invisible against the
brown-gray earth.

I stamped my foot, and when the startled partridges whirred
into the air I fired both barrels. Not a feather fell.

"Bad shooting," the prince said as we drove off again.

Most of our hunting at Sariska was done at night, however,
and the Rao Raja usually found something else to do just as we
were about to set out. I suspect he thought night shooting un-
sporting but was too polite to say so to his guests. Instead, we
were sometimes driven into the dark forest by a local friend of
his, a raffish Parsi liquor distributor from Bombay, who owned
a sprawling bungalow, a herd of polo ponies, and a bright red
roofless Buick built in the 1930s and equipped with twin spot-
lights powerful enough to transfix any animal we passed. (The
car looked a good deal more impressive than it was. Late one
afternoon, as we rolled down a steep road, I was startled to see
something big and black bounding along ahead of us on the
left. It was the rear wheel. Seconds later, we fetched up against
the hillside and had to be towed back to town.) One night, from
that Buick's leather-covered back seat I fired at a pair of anonymous eyes and killed a chousingha, or four-horned antelope,
the smallest and rarest of all Indian antelope. Since this dainty
animal was even then officially protected, I had to leave its small
broken body where it had fallen, for fear someone would turn
us in.

Most of my contacts with the Sariska forest were like that — urgent, ignorant, aimed only at ending lives I did not remotely understand. One favorite road twisted up a stony hillside past several natural pools. A cold mist hung perpetually in this valley on winter nights, and whenever we drove through it, we wrapped ourselves in blankets and put up the Jeep's windscreen to keep off the chill. A big sambar stag suddenly appeared on the right side of the road one night, his shaggy neck and impressive antlers hung with branches torn from the brush through which he had just come. We stopped. He began to step slowly across the road, head back, one rolling eye glittering in the headlights. I struggled to get to my feet, clawing at the blankets so that I could take aim over the windscreen. My shotgun caught. I fell back. Behind me my friends tried to hold me upright, whispering, "Shoot! Shoot!" Before I could, the stag disappeared down the hillside on our left. I dreamed of him for years.

Another night, not far from there, our spotlight picked out a whole constellation of gleaming eyes. Unable to tell stags from does — or even for sure what sort of animals these were — I jumped down to creep closer, careful to keep from being silhouetted in the paralyzing beam. My friends waited in the Jeep. I had moved twenty yards or so into the forest when I saw in the topmost branches of the trees the faint shifting glow that meant another car was coming. "Game wardens," I heard Raman say. "Come back!" Mathew called to me: "Hurry up. The patrol is coming." He started the motor. The lights were coming closer, the car's whine now unmistakable. Thorn bushes clawed at my legs. An unseen hole sent me sprawling. "Stay there," Mathew shouted. "We'll come back for you."

The Jeep sped away. Alone now in the black forest, I could hear the herd moving off through the thickets as the sound of the second car drew nearer. Its lights swung around a curve and the car slid to a stop perhaps twenty feet from where I lay on top of my shotgun; I was certain I was about to be seen, arrested, imprisoned. A spotlight's beam swung over my head, lighting up the thorn bush beneath which I was huddled. A gun barrel slid through the car's front window; two more muzzles appeared at the back. Not game wardens. Poachers. Now I would be shot. I held my breath.

"Nothing. I told you, *nothing*," a voice said from inside the car. "Why don't you listen to me?"

"I'm telling you, something moved in there. I saw it."

More lights appeared in the trees; another motor could be heard. The guns were withdrawn and the car pulled away, spattering me with gravel. I stayed where I was. Moments later my friends drove up. They had circled back for me, and it was their lights that had driven off the strangers.

We spent hour upon hour on those dark roads, peering along the spotlight's beam as it probed and poked its way between the trees and through the grass. Here and there it picked out a remnant of the sanctuary's royal past: gateposts carved with the Alwar coat of arms; stone shooting towers; the huge abandoned palace that had once served as the maharaja's hunting lodge, looming white above the undergrowth that choked its abandoned garden.

By three or four in the morning, when every stump in the forest seemed a crouching tiger to our exhausted eyes, we returned to the little Canal Department rest house, where we stayed when we were not the Rao Raja's guests. There, the resident cook would prepare dinner for us — curried venison if we'd been lucky; chicken otherwise — while we sat on string beds around the fire, talking over the night's hunting. I rarely managed to stay awake long enough to eat, drifting off beneath the stars, surrounded by the fire's warmth and the smell of woodsmoke, listening to the distant gunfire that meant other poachers were still out on the road, and to the sleepy voices of my friends, chuckling at jokes in Hindi I only half understood.

Sometimes the far-off shooting continued all night. It was echoing all over the subcontinent then. Understandably enough, free India's first priority was the growing of enough food to feed her restless, fast-growing population. In the face of that overwhelming need, old forestry practices introduced by the British came to seem somehow undemocratic. Forests were systematically ravaged for timber and fuel, thrown open to grazers, leveled to provide farmers with more land. Gun licenses were issued wholesale for crop protection, an invitation to massive poaching; animals not shot were trapped or poisoned. The export of skins and hides became a major source of foreign exchange. Shikar outfitters brought in wealthy foreign sportsmen to mop up what the villagers had overlooked. Demoralized and underpaid officials could earn more by looking the other way than by enforcing wildlife statutes no one bothered about much anymore.

Forest cover shrank steadily; wildlife vanished. Even the once ubiquitous jackals, whose weird cackling yowls had kept us awake in New Delhi itself, were all but annihilated for their skins. The tiger provided the most dramatic evidence of what was happening everywhere. At the turn of the twentieth century, there were at least 40,000 tigers in India (some authorities put the figure at 50,000). By 1972 there were just over 1,800, concentrated largely in a few pockets of forest that had once been the exclusive preserves of the Indian princes.

These rulers were implausible conservationists. Their preserves were after all intended primarily to assure them of a steady supply of birds and animals at which to shoot. The sheer volume of game a prince could parade past his guests' guns provided vivid evidence of his wealth and hospitality. The Maharaja of Bharatpur, a small state not far from Sariska, for example, was host to an annual wildlife shoot; on a single deafening morning in 1938, he and thirty-seven guests (including the British viceroy, Lord Linlithgow) accounted for 4,327 ducks and geese. Tigers were the top trophy, of course, and the princes vied with one another to see who could run up the highest tally; the hands-down winner was the last Maharaja of Surguja, who claimed 1,150. No other prince ever managed to overtake him — not even when some of the overeager among them took to including in their lifetime totals every fetus found in pregnant tigresses.

Still, the royal preserves offered wildlife a kind of qualified but genuine sanctuary rarely found elsewhere. In the early 1970s, concerned citizens finally forced the Indian government to realize what it had allowed to happen, to ban shooting and the export of wild animal skins, and to launch Project Tiger as a last-minute effort to rescue the tiger and something of the complex ecosystem upon which it depended. Several of the nine sanctuaries it set aside were former royal preserves. Sariska was not initially one of them. Poaching continued there unabated until 1978, when it was at last added to the roster of tiger reserves that now numbers fifteen.

Since I knew it as a boy, the city of Alwar has become an industrial center, ringed with smokestacks. A billboard on the main road reads WELCOME TO KELVINATOR COUNTRY. Its feudal past has largely been forgotten, though tourists sometimes visit the florid city palace and an old bronze cannon still guards a traffic island around which oblivious trucks and motor scooters now flow without a break. The Rao Raja died several years ago, a local man told me; during his last years he had been forced to take a relatively minor bureaucratic job with the democratic government he had despised.

But Sariska itself at first seemed unchanged. It remains a parched, inhospitable place, a cluster of sharp quartzite hills and valleys thinly covered with drab forest, relieved only here and there by bursts of brilliant green that signal the presence of a spring or streambed. There is very little rain, and most of what there is of it falls between July and September; much of the rest of the year the dry leaves of the dhok trees that cover all but the steepest slopes are more or less the same dispiriting color as the fine dust that is thrown into the air at the slightest movement of man or animal. Were the terrain more congenial, the Sariska forest would long ago have been cut and farmed and grazed into oblivion.

The old royal hunting lodge that had been deserted and overgrown in my day has recently been reopened as the Sariska Palace, a luxury hotel, and painted a gaudy yellow, blue, and pink. A bright banner flies again from the central flagstaff: green, red, black, and saffron stripes (Alwar's princely colors, the manager told me, "but rearranged, so no one will accuse us of monarchism"). Inside, the public rooms are oddly gloomy — high-ceilinged, and lit by bare bulbs so feeble that I could see every detail of the glowing filaments. The green walls are hung with white skulls of deer. Tigers in glass cases crouch in the corners; the one next to my table in the dining room was undersized, its stripes faded to tan, its claws rotted away, its tail only recently reattached with plaster.

The lodge is a monument to the turn-of-the-century pretensions of Maharaja Jay Singh of Alwar, one of India's most bizarre and sinister princes. Jay Singh believed himself the earthly incarnation of the god Rama and was therefore especially rigorous in his orthodoxy: He wore black silk gloves even when shaking hands with the English king. He had two vast towered kitchens, three stories tall, built on either side of his hunting lodge, one for his own food, the other for the preparation of the unclean things his foreign guests insisted upon eating. And he was fiercely proud. Visiting the Rolls Royce showroom in London sometime during the 1920s, he asked how much a certain model cost. The salesman smiled; no Indian could possibly afford such a vehicle, he said. Jay Singh ordered ten on the spot, had them shipped home and their roofs torn off; then, to the distress of the Rolls Royce company and the delight of his fellow princes, sent them out from his city palace each morning to collect his subjects' garbage.

He privately loathed the British, but always treated those Britons who visited his preserve with distant but elaborate courtesy. Goats were tied near the fountain in the center of the garden; the gate was left open so that leopards would get used to padding past the lawn furniture in search of easy meals. The after-dinner kills in the moonlit garden are said to have delighted the ladies seated on the veranda. His entire state army was routinely marshaled to beat the Sariska forests for his guests, squads of infantry and cavalry and an elephant corps driving before them everything that walked or flew. The shooting towers I had seen as a boy were his, too; tall, thick-walled, and provided with cushions and gun slits so that visitors could safely sit and sip their whiskey sodas while waiting for a tiger to kill the plaintive buffalo calf tethered to an iron ring just a few steps away.

When no visitors were about, Jay Singh's private life was filled with cruelty. It amused him to stake out elderly widows and small children as tiger bait. He was said to be given to sexual excesses with boys as well as with the young women his agents routinely kidnapped off the streets of his city. Evenings in his private chambers sometimes ended in murder. More than half his state's revenues went to pay for his personal extravagances. The British did nothing about any of this. Sir Edwin Montague, the secretary of state for India, is said to have particularly ad-

mired Jay Singh's unfailing good manners. But in 1933 the
maharaja went too far: After his polo pony threw him during a
hotly contested game, he doused it with gasoline and set it
ablaze. At that, the animal-loving British exiled him forever
from his state.

Under Project Tiger, access to Jay Singh's forests is now rigor-
ously controlled. No visitor can enter the reserve on foot or
without a forest guard to serve as guide. Mine was named Ramchandran Singh, a slender young man with a waxed mustache
and white teeth. Beyond the gate, the scrub forest still spread
out on either side of the narrow tarmac road that ran between
the brown hills, just as I remembered. Within a hundred yards
I spotted two nilgai moving through the roadside brush on our
left. My friends and I had shot a good many of these big antelope, whose fancied resemblance to cattle makes some Hindus
revere them as sacred; their meat was in fact a fair substitute
for the beef that for obvious reasons was rarely available in
India. They are ungainly, even ludicrous animals — the slate-
gray males have white-striped ankles and a ragged goatee and
are built on a sort of slant — but it was wonderful to see them
again, and so close to the road. What good luck, I thought, and
clapped Ramchandran on the shoulder.

He seemed a little startled at my enthusiasm. We would see
many more, he assured me. I thought he was being overly opti-
mistic. I knew this place, after all; one or two brief glimpses like
this were all one could expect. But within half a mile or so, we
were surrounded by hundreds of antelope and deer grazing in
the feathery grass or filing to one or another of the seven artificial water holes that now line the road.

There were nilgai and sambar in groups of five and six. Chital, the red-dappled deer that must be among the most beautiful
on earth, could be seen in herds of ten to twenty. There had
been no chital at all when I hunted at Sariska. Now they seemed
to be everywhere — some eight thousand of them, if the official
figures are correct — all descended from three or four terrified
animals chased here by village dogs when a royal deer park
nearby was obliterated not long after I left India in 1957. And
I had never before seen sambar in the daytime; there are now
six thousand of them.

For someone who remembered this place as dark and mysterious, its animals as furtive, even ghostly, Sariska was now a revelation. It was the end of the mating season, Ramchandran told me. Chital fawns minced through the grass. A sambar stag, still larger than the one of which I sometimes still dreamed, lowered his great head and horns and sprayed himself spectacularly with urine. The smell, Ramchandran assured me, would make him irresistible to the does that waited a few yards away. Here and there among the trees, young chital stags clashed with elaborate ceremony. Heads down, antlers locked, feet braced, they strained back and forth, whining with the effort like big angry babies. Then they simultaneously lifted their heads, froze to glare into one another's eyes from a distance of perhaps two feet, and went back at it.

It was almost too much. I had a sense after a while that I was in some sort of safari park, that the herds must be only half wild. This feeling intensified when the animals did not even flinch as a brightly painted tour bus hurled past us, its passengers leaning out the windows to hoot at them.

An afternoon in a small cinder-block blind on the edge of a water hole changed my mind. Lying on a mattress in the dark cool interior of the hide, just thirty feet from the farthest edge of the muddy pool, I found myself in the midst of a steady, slow-moving procession of thirsty animals whose every waking moment was obviously spent in terror — not of the people passing by in vehicles, who no longer represent a menace to them, but of the unseen tigers that can lie hidden anywhere. The deer and antelope approach the water with infinite wariness, nostrils flaring to catch the faintest scent, ears alert for telltale sounds, big eyes wide and staring, placing their hooves gingerly, as if they feared the earth itself might suddenly move beneath them.

The delicate four-horned antelope that drink near noon seemed most skittish. It took each one two or three tries to work up the courage to actually approach the pool; once each had swallowed its precious mouthful of water, it raced back to the woods in frenzied bounds. But the larger animals were only slightly less tentative. Later that afternoon, ten chital were bunched along one side of the pool and a big sambar stag was approaching slowly, ready to join a pair of does already at the water. Suddenly two baby wild boar ran into the clearing, kick-

ing up a tiny cloud of dust with their frantic trotters. The stag
bellowed as if two tigers were charging and galloped toward the
forest; his does beat him to the tree line. The chital had already
vanished. With the big clearing to themselves, the piglets raced
back and forth in perfect tandem for perhaps three minutes
before rushing off again.

I witnessed more forest life in that single afternoon than I'd
seen during three and a half years of hunting. A big nilgai
stalked down to the water, the insides of his twitching ears glowing pink before he dipped his head. A chital stag slipped up
behind him and, although there was plenty of room, jolted him
hard in the backside with his antlers. The startled nilgai, far
larger than his tormentor but equipped with horns no longer
than my index finger, trotted heavily away. The deer's antlers
reach extraordinary size now that hunting has been ended. One
old chital, his blunt muzzle gray with age, bore horns so huge
and heavy that it seemed miraculous he could hold them upright, let alone move through the forest without help.

The sounds of the forest were new to me, too. One after
another all afternoon, the far-off chital stags challenged one
another, their horny wheezes echoing from the slopes. When a
herd of perhaps twenty nervous young chital shouldered their
way to the edge of the pool, they kept up a high-pitched running commentary of squeals and whines, as if to reassure one
another that it was really all right to take a moment out from
their eternal vigilance to drink. A few moments later, five pea-
fowl waddled down to the water. While the hens drank, the lone
male began his courting dance, his huge fan spread out above
him. When that iridescent spectacle failed to impress one thirsty
hen, he stood stock still behind her and began literally to vibrate
with yearning, his clashing feathers producing an astonishingly
loud chatter. It certainly impressed me, but the hen for which it
was intended remained unmoved.

No tiger came to the pool while I was there. I had never seen
one at Sariska in the old days, either. (Once I thought I had, at
night; I took aim at its striped haunch, then held my fire, hoping
the half-hidden animal would move and offer me a clearer shot.
It did; it was a hyena.) After dark that first evening, and for
three evenings after that, Ramchandran tried very hard to show
me a tiger. He drove with me up and down the dark roads I

remembered so well, holding a spotlight out the window and swinging its white beam furiously from one side of the road to the other so as not to leave a yard of forest unexamined.

"Sambar," he would whisper, able instantly to see the whole outline of an animal whose gleaming eyes were all I had time to glimpse, then whirled to catch a chital as it faded into the brush on the opposite side. Several porcupines rattled across the road. A civet tumbled after one of them, a white ball in the headlights, its striped tail stretched out behind it.

But no tiger ever appeared. "One thing," Ramchandran muttered to the driver. "VIPs *never* see a tiger."

Before heading back to the hotel for the last time, we stopped at a guard post deep in the sanctuary. It was cold, and the five forest guards who lived there made room for us around their fire; one poured me a cup of spiced tea. I was sorry at having failed again to see a tiger where I had always hoped to see one. Perhaps I would do better at the Ranthambhore Tiger Reserve, the next stop on my trip. But as I sipped the tea, my disappointment was swept away by memory. Everything came back to me from thirty years before: the velvet black of the surrounding hills against the star-filled sky; the low voices of my companions; the smell and welcome warmth of the fire. There was no distant shooting now; it had been replaced by a new and comforting sound: From just beyond the firelight came the strenuous clacking of two chital stags, contesting to ensure the future of their herd.

II. Tigers

When I told Ramchandran that I was on my way to Ranthambhore with an introduction to its field director, Fateh Singh Rathore, he was clearly impressed. "A *very* dangerous man," he said, by which I think he meant that Fateh Singh was brave and resolute. He is in fact a legend among Indian conservationists. No wildlife official has worked harder or sacrificed more to protect the land and animals under his care; none has seen his hard work crowned with greater success. Under his implacable protection, the number of tigers flourishing at Ranthambhore has grown from fourteen to forty in just thir-

teen years. "You will see a tiger at Ranthambhore," Ramchandran assured me as I left Sariska. "Fateh Singh can *always* show
you one."

Ranthambhore is no more lush than Sariska; neon para-
keets and iridescent bee-eaters provide the brightest spots of
green among its seared hillsides. But it is far more beautiful.
The towers and sprawling battlements of an abandoned tenth-
century fortress cover the top of its highest hill. For centuries,
Ranthambhore was the hunting preserve of the princes of Jaipur. Scattered all through its forests are crumbling walls, fallen
temples, and carved *chatris* — domed monuments, each marking the spot where some long-forgotten man of consequence
was cremated.

A chain of three small, bright blue lakes runs down the center
of the preserve, and I stayed for several days on the shore of
the largest of these, in a restored pavilion called the Jogi Mahal.
From its cool veranda I watched crocodiles and soft-shelled turtles sun themselves and herds of chital browse along the shore.
Sambar came down to the water, too, and splashed right in to
stay for hours, immersed among succulent lotus pads, their
broad backs becoming islands for snowy egrets.

This extraordinary place is Fateh Singh's domain. He is a
Rathore, a member of the ancient clan whose chief is the former
Maharajah of Jodphur. He has none of his ancestors' bloody-
mindedness, but he has inherited their fascination with the forest and their sense of proprietorship over everything that lives
within it. He speaks of Ranthambhore as "my park," its tigers as
"my tigers."

Fateh Singh is forty-five years old, short, and chesty, with a
steel-gray mustache. He is given to sporty hats, sunglasses, and
dapper green safari clothes. There is little of the ascetic about
him: He savors a bawdy joke and a stiff drink on the rooftop of
his forest home after dark, and he lets nothing interfere with
his favorite situation comedy in Hindi, which he watches on a
small black-and-white set powered by a car battery.

But his animals come first, always. Even his marriage was
allowed to founder on that premise.

"There's your music!" he shouted as we drank a cup of tea
shortly after dawn on my first morning at Ranthambhore. We
were listening to the steady *poot-poot-poot* of the coppersmith,

which, he said, meant that summer was coming fast. The forest
chorus grew more complex. The shrill triple-noted call of the
gray partridge blended discordantly with the contralto *peeoar* of
the peacocks, the insistent *Did-you-do-it? Did-you-do-it?* of the
lapwings, and finally, the deep solemn hooting of the gray langur
monkeys. "They're telling each other 'I'm O.K., you're O.K.,' "
Fateh said. "Glad they got through another night."

Suddenly, the langurs' mellow choruses turned to angry,
hawking coughs. We put down our cups and raced for Fateh's
Jeep. From their perches in the tops of trees, langurs are often
the first to announce the presence of a prowling tiger. We would
spend the next four days like firefighters, careening over the
stony landscape to answer every alarm. As we drove, Fateh sat
ramrod stiff in the back, humming to himself at the sheer pleasure of being in his forest and occasionally pointing out one or
another of the 275 species of birds seen there.

The deer and antelope at Ranthambhore are no less serene
in the presence of human beings in vehicles than they are at
Sariska, but they are less thickly concentrated and are more
often screened by the trees and grass and thorny undergrowth
that now grows everywhere. Part of the reason that Sariska had
seemed initially so like a zoo was that buffalo and cattle are still
permitted to browse along its roadsides during the day, chewing
away the foliage and opening up broad, artificial vistas. Local
politics has prevented Sariska's field director from pressing forward with plans to shift several cattle camps out of the reserve.
There had always been a certain tension between the Sariska
herdsmen and the forests their voracious animals steadily de-
voured. One night thirty years ago, we encountered a very old
man walking all alone along a dark forest road, his only weapon
the long-handled ax with which he cut fodder from the trees
when his buffalo had eaten everything else within reach. What
was he doing there at such an hour? we asked. "Sahib, last week
I owned two buffalo," he said. "A tiger has killed one. Now I
will kill the tiger before he can get the other one." We took him
home to his village. Such people are not easily persuaded to
change their ways and so far, in Sariska at least, it has been
thought best to leave the squatters alone.

At Ranthambhore, however, Fateh Singh had felt differently.
There had been sixteen villages in his preserve, a thousand

villagers, perhaps ten thousand head of livestock. The life they led there was meager and marginal — their herds were scrawny; the land they farmed was stony and exhausted — but for more than two centuries it was all their ancestors had known and no one had wanted to leave. Fateh Singh could have resorted to force. (When herdsmen were barred from the Kaladeo Bird Sanctuary that now occupies the broad artificial lake where the maharajas of Bharatpur once organized their annual slaughter of wildfowl, there was an angry confrontation with the local police that left five villagers dead and thirty-five more wounded.) Instead, he used patience and persuasion, concentrating on the younger and better-educated headmen. He was authorized to offer them additional land if they agreed to move to a new site twenty kilometers outside the sanctuary on far better land than they had ever known. Two new temples would be built there for each old one left behind. There would be a new school, access to a post office, improved breeding stock, a modern well, and electricity with which to pump its precious water. If they were wary of government promises, he told them, they should hold him personally responsible for making good on all of them. Like his princely ancestors he would provide for them.

But mixed in with these material incentives was a spiritual message as well. The forest and all its creatures were the creation of the gods, he argued over the village fires: Did not the great goddess Durga herself ride a tiger? No man had a right to disturb that divine creation; the forests must be left to grow back, to become again what their creator had intended. To continue to live in the forest was to commit a kind of blasphemy.

When the day finally came and trucks drew up to carry the villagers' few belongings to their new homes, many of them wept. One old man hugged a gnarled tree, crying that his father and grandfather had rested in its shade, that such fine shade could never be obtained elsewhere. Fateh Singh cried with them. But he made sure they went.

The lands their herds had ravaged are thickly overgrown now, but some of their crumbling huts still stand, and one day not long ago, Fateh Singh took the headman of one of the old villages back to see its transformed site. A tiger was sleeping in one of the ruined houses. The headman was delighted. "Now we are happy," he said. "The goddess has come."

Despite Ramchandran's confidence in him and Fateh Singh's intimate knowledge of the Ranthambhore tigers (half of which he knows by name and can identify at a glance), even he cannot summon up a tiger at will to show to visitors. We drove through his preserve for four days, off and on, listening for the alarm calls of deer and monkeys and leaning down from time to time to examine the pug marks of tigers that seemed always to have just preceded us on the twisting forest track.

In the late afternoons we parked overlooking one or another of the lakes, hoping to see a tiger charge out of the grass to kill one of the hundreds of deer feeding there. One evening as we sat watching in the fading golden light, we spotted two figures strolling along the path toward us, a tall Englishman hung with binoculars and wearing khaki shorts, arm in arm with an eighty-year-old Dutch woman whom I recognized as a fellow guest at the Jogi Mahal. The two had dawdled along obliviously for hundreds of yards between high yellow walls of dhok grass whose soft sibilance in even a faint breeze can disguise the movements of the clumsiest tiger. Fateh was apoplectic. "Stupid! Stupid! Bloody idiots!" he shouted at the startled visitors, pulling them into his Jeep. "I should throw you out of this park. You will get my tigers killed."

People, not animals, remain his most vexing problem. In the heart of the Ranthambhore fortress is a temple dedicated to Ganesa, the fat, amiable, elephant-headed god who blesses all new ventures, including marriage and childbearing. Small groups of worshipers seeking his favor climb the hill every morning, and on one annual festival day some ten thousand pilgrims troop along the main sanctuary road to converge on the temple. Even Fateh Singh does not dare interfere with the rights of the faithful to worship where they please, but he does worry about what might happen if one of his tigers should someday attack a pilgrim. Then, too, scattered among the deepest ravines, live a handful of solitary sadhus. These ascetic hermits have vowed to end their days there, praying in the wilderness. Fateh isn't sure how many there are — perhaps five, he says — and so far the animals have left them alone. The sadhus attribute this to the power of their belief; Fateh credits "damned good luck."

Fateh does the best he can to control the rest of those who seek admission to his sanctuary. No one is allowed to walk in the forest. Tourists must be driven by trained guards, and a good deal of his time is spent allocating seats for them among the small fleet of spavined vehicles at his disposal. One evening I counted thirty-one spectators packed into five parked Jeeps, all of us watching to see if a single, noisy sambar calf would find its missing mother before a hungry predator found it. (It did.)

The most serious trouble still comes from local people. A dozen villages have been successfully shifted out of the park, but thirty more ring its perimeter. The trees have always provided fuel for their cook fires; its grass and undergrowth have fed their herds. The villagers are only bewildered and angered by the notion that their ancient forest should suddenly be off limits to them. Women slip into the park through hidden ravines to cut grass, carrying out great heaps of it on their heads. Troops of wood cutters enter, too, and so do herdsmen with their grazing animals and tribal hunters with packs of trained dogs.

Fateh Singh and his forest guards do their best to fend them all off, but it is not easy. He has too few men to patrol the entire border of the park. The grass cutters hide their curved blades beneath their skirts, then charge the guards with molestation when they are searched. When disputes arise local politicians often favor the villagers — who can vote — over animals that cannot. Three years ago, Fateh Singh himself was set upon by some fifty angry herdsmen. They beat him unconscious, broke his arm, shattered his kneecap, and left him for dead. (He spent three months in a hospital, then was awarded India's highest civilian medal for valor.)

One morning during my visit, a forest guard staggered into the field director's office, the side of his face bruised and badly swollen. He had been beaten by four wood cutters. Fateh Singh instantly dispatched a party of his own men to retaliate in kind. "We can't treat these people the way you do in America," he said. "No psychiatrists here. We don't ask, '*Why* do you do this?' We just give them a good bashing."

He is a stern sovereign, but he tries hard to be fair. When, not long ago, the former Maharani of Jaipur visited her family's old hunting lodge just outside the park and ordered that several partridges be shot for her guests' luncheon, Fateh Singh took her to court. "There must be the same law for rich and for poor," he told me. The Maharani's case is just one of some three hundred he still has pending in the Indian courts.

His is an intensely personal struggle. Here and there across India other determined individuals have also managed to save patches of forest and the wildlife that lives within them, at least for the moment. But their achievements, like Fateh Singh's, will remain fragile, tenuous, until the ordinary people who live nearby come to see their value. So far they do not. Whenever Fateh leaves his stronghold, even for a few days, interlopers stream across its borders and have to be driven out again when he gets back. "It's an endless war," he told me as we drove through the forest on my last morning at Ranthambhore, and it is one he would prefer not to have to fight. Despite almost daily threats and his own near-fatal beating, he refuses to carry a gun and won't let his men carry them either. "I'm too hot-tempered," he told me. "If I had a gun I know I would shoot someone."

"We want to be friendly," he said, "to work *with* the people, not against them. What we need is a 'Project People for Project Tiger.' " He has called for teams of conservation workers to move from village to village, explaining the long-term benefits of keeping the forests intact; a program to recruit tribal hunters into the forest service so that their forest skills can be used to save animals rather than slaughter them. The periphery of the park should be replanted with improved grasses for harvesting, he says, but only to nourish stall-fed livestock — and funds must be found to encourage traditional herdsmen to abandon their inferior, wasteful animals in favor of improved breeds. All of this will take time and money and coordinated planning.

In the meantime, the tigers of Ranthambhore have only Fateh Singh. He has worked within the sanctuary for twenty of his twenty-five years in the forest service, and his success has several times led his superiors at Delhi to try to promote him to a desk job. He always turns them down. He plans to stay in one place — and in charge — until he retires. "I know this place," he explained, rising in his seat to peer over the tops of the thorn bushes. "I'm not happy anywhere else. I've bought myself a farm at the edge of the forest so that every day until I die I can drive over and visit my park."

He clutched my shoulder. "Tiger in the road," he said. Perhaps forty feet ahead of us a tiger sat in the middle of the track. It filled the track, in fact, and seemed somehow to fill the forest that stretched away on either side as well. Nothing had prepared me for its size or for the palpable sense of menace and power that emanated from it. "His name is Akbar," Fateh whispered, beginning softly to hum with pleasure at the sight of him. "About five hundred pounds."

The tiger rose slowly to his feet. Everything about him seemed outsized: his big round ruffed face; his massive shoulders and blazing coat; his empty belly that hung in folds and had finally forced him into the open to hunt; his long twitching tail. It seemed inconceivable that such a big, vivid animal could have stayed hidden in this drab open forest for so long.

We sat very still in the open Jeep as the tiger stared at us. "He's a good boy," Fateh said, still humming. I devoutly hoped so. The tiger turned and cocked his huge head to listen as a sambar called from a clearing off to our left; then, after fixing us with one more steady glance, he slipped silently into the grass. Neither his smiling protector nor his protector's wary guest had been worth so much as a growl.

III. Blackbuck

I had only dreamed of tigers as a boy. What I really hunted were blackbuck — fleet, delicate antelope whose spiraling horns and richly patterned skins made handsome trophies. They had been scattered nearly everywhere across the northern Indian plains then, and my friends and I had traveled nearly everywhere in search of them.

I knew them then only as targets, of course. Sometimes Bhagat Singh shot them with his old rifle from what always seemed to me to be fantastic distances. Much more often we pursued them in our Jeep, Mathew at the wheel, careening around thorn bushes at forty miles an hour, slamming across rutted fields, flying over the tamped mud walls that separated one man's crop from the next, while my friends and I struggled both to stay in our seats and to fire buckshot into the frantic animals zigzagging ahead of us. Once, our Jeep turned entirely over, though with such merciful slowness that we were all able to step safely out into the soft dust. An amused old farmer and his bullocks came along and helped us right ourselves. At harvest time we had to be particularly careful not to hit the village women who were hidden, kneeling in the billowing wheat.

I must have shot thirty blackbuck during my years in India. At the end of one especially busy day my friends and I drove home with thirteen of them heaped beneath a flapping tarpaulin in the back of our Jeep, enough to fill our freezer and those of our friends for several months. I could sense always that my parents were of two minds about my shooting. They liked having the fresh meat (a rare thing then in Delhi), and they thought it good that I had a hobby that got me out of the house and into the outdoors. But I think they also found the apparently gleeful killing a little alarming, and I was always vague about the dangers of our hunts for fear my parents might have second thoughts about letting me go. I know my mother worried anyway and sometimes took to her bed until I got back safely. Once or twice my father asked to accompany me, not because he had any interest in shooting, I suspect, but because he thought my mother would feel better if he came along.

Two American agricultural advisers took my father and me out with them one morning. They were country boys, one thin, the other fat, and they couldn't get over their good luck in having been stationed in a land where hunting was so easy and hunting laws so lax. We drove out to a series of stony, broken hills just a few miles from the city. I had my shotgun. The fat hunter lent my father a spare rifle, a .30-06 with a telescopic sight. We shot a partridge or two shortly after sunup, but saw nothing else worth shooting until midmorning when a placid nilgai appeared at the foot of a scrub-covered hill just off the road. The two hunters urged my father to take a shot at him. He was barely fifty yards away, a big animal, and standing

broadside to us. Hard to miss. But my father was as nearsighted
then as I am now and could not make him out against the
hillside. The watery, magnified image in the scope did not help.
"Shoot before he runs," the fat hunter urged. The muzzle
moved helplessly over the hill. Finally, just to please the rest of
us, I think, my father pulled the trigger. Dust exploded from
the slope, yards above the nilgai but close enough to send him
lumbering out of sight. I was embarrassed by my father: How
could he not even have *seen* him?

A little later, we saw a blackbuck feeding in a mustard field.
It was the fat man's turn. He turned off the engine, cradled the
rifle on his knee, and took a long time aiming. At the sound of
the rifle, the buck staggered and fell. We drove close and got
down, my father still carrying the rifle.

The buck was trying to get up, to get away. Its back legs
scrabbled for purchase, but its front legs were useless. The fat
man's bullet had smashed through both his shoulders.

The thin man offered his congratulations. The fat one
thanked him. They agreed the horns weren't bad. Not great,
but not bad. The buck watched us, mouth open, snorting flecks
of blood. More blood was pooling in the dust. Maybe he'd be
worth taking to the taxidermist, the thin one suggested. The
buck began a low, shuddering bawling, its eyes rolling. It tossed
its head and horns from side to side. But which taxidermist?
There were two in Delhi, one a good deal more expensive than
the other, but also more artistic.

Gripping the barrel of the borrowed rifle with both hands,
my father brought the stock down onto the buck's skull. The
animal kicked more urgently. He swung the rifle again, high
above his head this time, then down as hard as he could. The
buck stiffened, then relaxed. The terrible bawling stopped, but
the rifle stock had splintered.

The hunters were polite, but full of scorn. The buck had
really been dead, they said; it couldn't feel anything. They
would have got around to cutting its throat. Besides, the stock
had been expensive and would be hard to replace.

As we picked up the dead buck and swung it by its frail legs
into the back of the Jeep, my father offered to pay whatever it
took to have the rifle repaired. I didn't know what to say to him

on the long drive home, but I knew inside myself that he had done what I should have done, that what my friends and I had been doing was wrong.

Not long after that trip, in 1957, I left India. The killing of the blackbuck continued. By 1970 only a few scattered herds survived outside sanctuaries.

The largest concentration of blackbuck — some twelve thousand animals, I was told upon my return to India last year — now lived near Jodhpur, not under the protection of the forest department but as the fiercely defended charges of a small Hindu sect called the Bishnois, whose fields and villages encircle that medieval desert city. The Bishnois follow the teachings of a fifteenth-century Hindu guru whom they call Jambaji. There were twenty-nine principles to his creed — the sect's name derives from the Hindi words for twenty and nine, *bis* and *no* — and they included tenets common to ascetics everywhere: no tobacco or alcohol, no cursing or lies, no impure foods. But two of his teachings were unique: all animals were to be considered sacred, but the blackbuck was the most sacred of all; anyone who dared hunt them on Bishnoi lands did so at his own peril. And because green trees offered the antelope shelter from the searing sun, they must never be cut down.

The Bishnois' devotion has rarely been found wanting. When an eighteenth-century ruler of Jodhpur sent his army to cut down a number of feathery khedaji trees to make way for a royal thoroughfare into his city, the Bishnoi women are said to have barred its way, embracing the trees and warning that they were willing to die rather than have them destroyed. Three hundred and sixty-three Bishnois, most of them women, were killed along with the trees to which they clung.

The women still sacrifice for the welfare of the herds. Tradition requires that for every four pots of water they carry home to their families, a fifth must be brought to fill the communal trough from which the antelope drink on summer evenings. And it is the women who make sure that each village maintains its store of hoarded grain, which sustains the antelope in lean times. But at the sound of a shot fired, it is the men who come running. Suspected poachers are seized, bound to trees, and beaten senseless. Some years back, an unwitting wildlife photographer had to be rescued from them after he was found aiming what seemed to the Bishnois to be a suspiciously long telephoto lens.

At Jodhpur I was told to call upon a prince of the former ruling family, a hunter-turned-conservationist, my informant assured me, who would be eager to introduce me to the Bishnois and to show me the herds that thrive under their protection. He turned out to be a bald, sinewy little man with a flaring Rajput mustache. His brisk hauteur perfectly suited his new status as a hotel keeper. He seemed remarkably uninterested in my plans to write about the wildlife of his district until I suggested that I would be happy to pay him for his trouble. At that he brightened a little. Although he was preparing for the wedding of his daughter, he told me, he would be willing to take the time to drive me out into the countryside for the equivalent in rupees of fifty dollars. And he knew where there was a rare white buck. If he managed to show it to me I was to give him an additional "present." I agreed.

The prince — I think it best not to give his name, in light of what happened later — picked me up in his Jeep the following morning. He was a taciturn, even sullen guide at first, answering my questions in grunts and monosyllables as he gripped the wheel. No admiring words I could summon up to say about the flat, shriveled landscape around his city seemed to make him brighten. After twenty mostly silent minutes we turned off the main road and onto the first of a series of rutted, dusty village tracks. Neither they nor his Jeep had improved over the years, and conversation grew still more difficult as I tried to stay in my seat.

I did manage to ask about the Bishnois. Was it true that they still protected the herds? "Yes, yes, of course they do," he said, scowling, "though the women are too lazy to bring as much water for them as they once did." But the old story that his royal ancestors had "cut down the bloody trees and the bloody girls with them" was a lie, he said, invented by Congress Party politicians who wanted to make princes look bad in retrospect. He knew politicians, he added. He had himself represented the district in the legislative assembly: "My people love me." Certainly they seemed deferential. When we stopped for a cup of tea, the villagers crowded around our Jeep. The men wore big loose turbans and locket portraits of Guru Jambaji; the women dressed in burnished reds and oranges, their thin wrists and ankles heavy with hammered silver. When I asked what they would do if they saw someone with a gun near their village, the men all laughed and chopped at their necks with their right hands.

We began to see animals as soon as we left their village. Nilgai trotted heavily away as we clanked through an arid, unplanted area. Delicate chinkara gazelles stopped nibbling at isolated thorn bushes to watch us pass, their edginess betrayed only by the agitated waggling of their downturned tails. When we came out into the green open fields again, I felt as if I were back in the midst of some boyhood dream. Blackbuck were everywhere, hundreds of them, chasing one another through the crops, jousting with their spiral horns, dancing right up to the mud walls of the Bishnoi villages. Farmers on camels moved placidly among them; so did bullock carts heaped with fodder and village women carrying water on their heads.

The prince barely slowed. There was no sense in stopping, he said. There were always plenty more animals to see as we circled his city, and he wanted to find the rare white buck that would earn him his additional payment.

I was astonished, and in my astonishment began to tell him of my past: of how many of these animals I had killed, of how wonderful it was to see them again.

"*See* them? What's the use of seeing them?" he said, suddenly alert and enthusiastic. "You're a hunter, you say. So am I. Don't you want to *shoot* them?"

Surely shooting was impossible, a thing of the past, I said.

"Difficult, but not impossible," the prince said, taking my surprise for encouragement and warming to his topic. Laws were made to be broken. True, it would be hard to shoot here. Too open, he said. He could hit a buck with the Jeep if I liked: "No noise." Of course it would cost me. He could arrange a hunt in one of his family's old sanctuaries some distance from Jodhpur, he said, gesturing vaguely toward the faint blue hills that lined the horizon. A relation lived there who was in charge of such things.

What would I like to shoot? A crocodile? A sloth bear? A panther? Sadly there were no tigers in his lands anymore, but anything else was possible for the right price. We would shoot with a spotlight at night, of course. Five hundred dollars and a few bottles of imported liquor would cover everything, including something for his relative and payments to the local villagers for their silence. For a little more he could even have the skins and heads prepared for me, though I would have to have them smuggled out of India on my own. That should not be a problem, he added. His friends at the Dehli embassies used their diplomatic pouches.

A chinkara buck gazed at us from behind a bush just off the road. The prince stopped the Jeep. "He wouldn't dare stick his head up like that if I had a two-two," he said, taking imaginary aim. "When you come, you must bring me one, and plenty of ammunition. And maybe a silencer as well." All I needed to do — his words tumbling now as we drove on — was to send him a telegram saying I was arriving for "the party." We would both know what that meant, and he would have everything ready when he met me at the Jodhpur airport.

It was hot and still now, nearing noon, and the antelope had begun to cluster in the shade of the scattered trees. "There he is," the prince said, wrenching the Jeep off the track and into the fields. The white buck lay alongside two normally colored ones beneath a khedaji tree. His fragile legs were folded decorously beneath him and his horns seemed unusually long. We picked up speed as we rattled through the newly planted mustard. All three animals rose to their feet, staring at the oncoming Jeep. Then they began to skip forward, to run, finally to bound, racing across the fields at right angles to us, making for a high mud wall overgrown with thorns.

We swerved to follow and drove faster. I held on with both hands. The white buck lagged a little behind the others. His left hind leg seemed to have been injured.

"Some village dog's been at him," the prince shouted as the Jeep rose in the air and slammed down again. "Damn it. I knew I should have shot him when I last had the chance. Now someone else will get him." He gunned the motor.

The other two bucks did not even pause at the wall, soaring over it in the sure knowledge that we could never follow. The white buck slowed, then scrambled to his left, head down, horns held flat along his back, running along the wall looking for an opening. We roared closer.

He stumbled, then gathered himself and leaped over the wall, white against the blue sky, floating, already almost like a ghost.

TOM WOLFE

Land of Wizards

FROM POPULAR MECHANICS

THE THREAT WAS DELIVERED to Lemelson's lawyer. "Tell your client we're gonna bury him under a ton of paper." Lemelson wasn't too worried. He thought it was a figure of speech.

So the next day, Lemelson is in the courtroom, sitting at the plaintiff's table with his lawyer, waiting for the proceedings to begin. Lemelson is an inventor. He invented the automated warehouse, the automated machine shop, one of the first two industrial robots, several robot-vision machines, the drive mechanism of the audio cassette player, and 380 other things. He holds more patents than anybody except the great Edison himself and Edwin Land, inventor of the Polaroid camera. This causes him to be in courtrooms a great deal.

Many corporations manufacture his inventions, but not many mention it to him beforehand.

So it is on this particular day Jerome H. Lemelson is in a court of law under the usual circumstances, charging a manufacturer with patent infringement. The lawyers for the manufacturer are right across from him at the defendant's table. Between the two tables and the judge's bench is a fifteen-foot stretch of floor.

The next thing Lemelson knows, the door to the courtroom opens, and here comes a trucker's helper pushing a hand truck with archive boxes piled from the fender on the bottom to the curve of the handles at the top.

An archive box is a box made of heavy cardboard with oak-grain patterns printed on it to make it look like wood. On one end of the box is a little metal frame that holds a card describing the contents. The box has a lid, like a shoe box. Inside, there is room for a dozen reams of documents, usually arranged in file folders with little tabs sticking up. However you want to arrange it, you can get about forty pounds of paper into each box.

Fascinated, the way the chickadee is fascinated by the snake, Lemelson watches as the trucker's helper begins unloading the boxes. He puts them right on the floor between the tables and the judge's bench. One of the lawyers is out there like a field commander, pointing to spots on the floor. This one goes here. That one goes there. No sooner is that load arranged than the courtroom door opens again, and here comes another teamster, puffing and pushing a fresh load of archive boxes on a hand truck. Now he's lugging his stack off the hand truck and putting it on the floor. The door opens again. Here comes another yobbo pushing a hand truck with archive boxes piled as tall as he is. You can hear the floor groaning from the weight of the load as the wheels roll over the hardwood.

The field commander is out there, and the archive boxes are lining up in rows like a tank formation. Lemelson's pale gray-blue eyes are the size of radar dishes. He's speechless. The cargo humpers keep coming. Pretty soon seventy or eighty square feet of floor is occupied by this squat battalion of archive boxes. You don't have to be an engineering genius like Lemelson to figure out that there is now a ton of paper sitting there. More than a ton, perhaps a ton and a half.

"Well," Lemelson says to his lawyer, "at least it's not on top of me."

Neither of them laughed. They both had the feeling it was only a matter of time. There was a judge but no jury. Apparently the ton of paper was supposed to impress the judge and intimidate Lemelson.

Something impressed the judge; no question about that. Lemelson lost. It wasn't even close.

He gritted his teeth and announced he was going to appeal. The next message said: "O.K., go ahead. We'll search for evidence in Europe."

That meant they would send a lawyer to Europe to take depositions from anybody they could find who had dealings with Jerome H. Lemelson or his invention. Here you have the greatest device for generating paper ever thought up by the legal profession: the deposition. All successful inventors know about

depositions. They learn to live with them the way one learns to
live with arthritis.

A deposition is a pretrial maneuver in which lawyers take
sworn testimony from people out of court, usually in somebody's office. A court reporter records the testimony on a sten-
otype machine and then types up a transcript. The number of
pages of testimony that can come out of an hour of this is fabu-
lous, and some depositions go on for a week. What might actually be divulged about Jerome H. Lemelson or his works on
any of these thousands of pieces of paper was beside the point.
The point was that Lemelson would have to hire a lawyer to
represent his interests during each deposition, day after day,
city after city, across the map of Europe. The sheets of paper
would go into archive boxes, and every sheet meant another
little hemorrhage in Lemelson's net worth.

This case began in the 1970s. It grinds on still. So far it has
cost Lemelson $250,000 in lawyers' fees, and the meter is still
ticking. It sounds like something from out of *Bleak House*, which
Charles Dickens wrote in 1852 and 1853, but it is merely a
typical episode in the life of an American inventor in the 1980s.
Which is to say, it is the story of a man trying to dig his way out
from under a ton of paper.

Is there any more feverish dream of glory in the world, outside
of Islam, than the dream of being an inventor? Certainly not in
the United States, and probably not in Japan or in any other
industrial country. An invention is one of those superstrokes,
like discovering a platinum deposit or a gas field or writing a
novel, through which an individual, the hungriest loner, can
transform his life, overnight, and light up the sky. The inventor
needs only one thing, which is as free as the air: a terrific idea.

He doesn't need connections. The great American inventors
of the past hundred years, the so-called age of technology, have
not come from prominent families. They have not had money.
They have not been part of the highly touted, highly financed
research teams of industry and the universities. They have not
been adept politically or socially. Many have been breathtak-
ingly deficient in charm.

Thomas Edison was scarcely educated at all; three years in
public school, and that was it. Alexander Graham Bell was a

teacher who began his experiments, leading to the telephone, in the cellar of a house in Boston, where he rented a room. Steven Jobs and Steven Wozniak, of Apple Computer fame, were a pair of public high school A-V types. A-V types are audio-visual nerds who wear windbreakers, carry a lot of keys, and wire up directional mikes for the drama club. The Silicon Valley of California, center of the most spectacular new industry of the second half of the twentieth century, computers and semiconductors, is known as the Land of Nerd, the Planet of the Nerds, and the Emerald City of Nerdz. The centimillionaires of the Silicon Valley want nothing to do with the traditional Society of nearby San Francisco. They can't get into Trader Vic's wearing their nerd shirts, which are short-sleeved white sport shirts with pencil guards on the pockets.

Wilbur and Orville Wright were regarded as two wet smacks who ran a bicycle repair shop in Dayton, Ohio, when they arrived at Kitty Hawk for their airplane experiment in 1903. Neither had graduated from high school. But theirs was the invention that dazzled Jerome H. Lemelson and thousands of other boys who were born in the early 1920s.

As a teenager, Lemelson was typical of the airplane "hobbyists," as they were known, quiet boys who built gasoline-powered model airplanes, took them out in the fields, and flew them by wire or remote control. There were still a lot of open fields on Staten Island, where he grew up. His father was a doctor, a general practitioner, but Lemelson's passion was airplanes. During the Second World War he found his way into the engineering department of the Army Air Corps. After the war he earned a bachelor's degree in aeronautical engineering at New York University, then went to work at NYU for the Office of Naval Research's Project Squid. Project Squid was supposed to develop rocket and pulse jet engines.

One day in 1951, Lemelson took the subway over to the Arma factory in Brooklyn, which made control mechanisms for aircraft, to see a demonstration of a fully automatic, feedback-controlled metal lathe. "Feedback" was a hot new word in engineering circles. Nobody there on the work way at Arma took a second look at Jerome H. Lemelson. He was twenty-eight years old, neither fat nor thin, neither very tall nor very short, not bad looking and not Tyrone Power, either. He had a broad forehead, light brown curly hair, large eyes, and a long, straight nose. He was quiet, polite, reserved, and a typical hard-working young engineer, by the looks of him, if you looked at all.

Lemelson took more than a second look at the metal lathe, however. An ordinary metal lathe turned a metal rod while an operator shaved it down to whatever diameter or shape he wanted by adjusting a tool bit. In the case of the feedback-controlled lathe, the bit was controlled automatically by punch cards. The crowd murmured a lot as the bit rose and fell to unseen commands.

Lemelson began wondering how far you could take this idea of a programmed factory machine. Over the next three years he developed the designs for a "universal robot." The robot would have an arm with joints. It would rivet, weld, drill, measure, pick things up and move them. He drew up a 150-page patent application and submitted it to the U.S. Patent Office in Washington, D.C., on Christmas Eve, 1954. Unbeknownst to Lemelson, an inventor named George Devol had filed an application for a robot two weeks earlier. Theirs were the first industrial robots. As it turned out, both men had a long wait ahead of them.

In the meantime, Lemelson was already working on a second application for an offshoot of the universal robot, a "flexible manufacturing system," which was the automated machine shop.

That same year, 1954, Lemelson married an interior decorator named Dolly Ginsberg. The first stop on their honeymoon was Bermuda. The second stop was the Willard Hotel in Washington because it happened to be across the street from the Search Room of the Patent Office. Lemelson was already deep in the grip of The Dream.

The Search Room was an enormous archive the size of Uline Arena, where the Washington Capitols, the professional basketball team, played their games. It was full of ancient wooden shelves and boxes, known as shoes, containing nearly 150 years' worth of patent documents. The spaces between the stacks of shelves were so narrow that the clerks had to shimmy past each other to fetch the shoes for people doing patent searches. This led to a lot of waiting and sighing. Dolly heard one patent lawyer complaining to another: "There ought to be some way to mechanize this place."

She happened to mention this to Lemelson. That started him off on another track, resulting in his "video filing system." The documents would be recorded on reels of videotape or magnetic tape. The average patent application was ten pages long. You could store 100,000 applications on just four reels of tape. You would look at them on a television screen in stop-frame pictures. (His conception of the stop-frame picture would lead, during the 1960s, to filmless photography, still pictures created from video images.)

Instead of having GS-8 civil servants shimmying between stacks of shelves, you would press a few buttons and send a playback device along a track to a slot where the tape was. But how could the device connect with the tape and enable you to play it and wind it back and forth? Lemelson thought about that awhile and conceived of the mechanism that eventually became the core of the audio cassette player. He presented video filing and its components in a sixty-page patent application in 1955.

And he waited some more. Several years went by, and the Patent Office still had not issued any patents for all these brilliant ideas. Lemelson was now learning one of the facts of life about being an inventor in America. The first flash of genius lights up only a few yards of the road. The road is long and uphill.

More than once, he and Dolly had to fall back on her earnings as an interior decorator. There was only one way an inventor could make money rapidly without waiting for the patent process to go its course, and that was to design toys. In the case of a toy, you prudently filed for a patent but went ahead and sold the design immediately, if you could. Lemelson had an idea for a face-mask kit for children that would be printed on a cereal box. A child could cut out the pieces, assemble them in different combinations and put on the mask. He filed for a patent and took his drawings to one of the cereal manufacturers. The company said it wasn't interested, and so he put the drawings away and forgot about them.

One day, three years later, he is in the grocery store, and there on the shelf is a cereal box with a face-mask kit on it. It's put out by the very people he showed his drawings to. He can't believe it. The way he sees it, he's staring at as blatant a case of patent infringement as you could imagine. He files suit. So now he's in court. It's a jury trial. The judge comes in, and he gives Lemelson and the lawyers a long look down his nose.

"This is a patent case," he says. He lets the term "patent case" hang in the air for a moment, like a bad smell. "I have better things to do with my time than listen to patent cases. It is now ten-fifteen. You have until three o'clock this afternoon to complete your arguments."

Sure enough, at three o'clock on the dot he looks at his watch, stands up, and, without saying a word, walks out. Lemelson has an expert witness testifying for him at the time, and the fellow is sitting there on the stand with his mouth hanging open.

Then the judge pops back in. "Ladies and gentlemen of the jury, my apologies. I neglected to dismiss you. You are dismissed."

It turns out the case has been dismissed, too. Lemelson appeals, and a new trial is called — before the same judge, who summarily dismisses the suit, this time for good.

When Lemelson spoke of these things to other inventors, they smiled without joy. He was just getting the picture. First, many American corporations, including many of the most respected, ignored patent rights without batting an eye. They didn't give you so much as a sporting wink. Second, the courts couldn't be bothered. Practically none of the judges who heard patent cases had any background in patent law, much less engineering. It was unfamiliar terrain, which seemed to make them irritable. On the one hand, they couldn't stand all these obsessive small-fry inventors, these parasites on the hide of Science, with their endless theories and their transducers and capacitive-sensitive relays and the rest of that paralyzing jargon. But on the other hand, if they, the judges, could understand an invention, then it must not be much of an invention. They had developed "the doctrine of obviousness." If an invention looked obvious, they declared the patent invalid.

The inventors kept ratings of the chances of having their patent rights upheld in the various federal jurisdictions. Back when Lemelson was starting out, your chances ran from zero in the Eighth Circuit, which covered most of the Midwest, to 45 percent in the South. The Second Circuit, covering New York, was rated about average, one chance in four.

But what about the corporations? How could they get away with flouting the patent system and patent law? It was simple, the inventors told Lemelson. All that the corporations needed to overcome was their scruples, if any. In the United States, unlike Japan and parts of Europe, patent infringement was not considered a form of theft, so there were no criminal penalties. There were not even punitive damages in patent cases unless the inventor could prove "willful infringement." To avoid that, a manufacturer merely had to take the precaution of going to its own lawyer and having him write an opinion saying that such and such a product did not infringe upon any existing patents for such and such reasons. It didn't matter how cockeyed the reasons were. That was what lawyers were for.

Once the manufacturer had that document in hand, the worst that could have happened, even if the firm had been found guilty in court, was that the manufacturer would have had to pay the inventor the royalties he would have received if a license had been obtained. There were lawyers who would actually advise their corporate clients to ignore patents, calling it a no-risk strategy.

Just in case the inventor was new at this game, the manufacturer would let him know the odds, discreetly, or, if he looked a little thick, bluntly. To get a case as far as the trial stage was going to cost $40,000. Was he ready for that? To get a case through the trial and all the appeal stages — was he ready for $250,000? For good measure, the manufacturer usually added some variation of the theme, "We're gonna bury you under a ton of paper." If a corporation was big enough, it would threaten anybody, not merely little lone-wolf inventors but even another, smaller corporation. When J. Reid Anderson, the chief executive officer of Verbatim, a company specializing in computer storage devices, went to a big manufacturer complaining of patent infringement, he was told: "We have more patent attorneys than you have people in your company, and they are just sitting back waiting for someone to start a patent fight like this."

Lemelson's saving grace was that he was not a cynic. He didn't have a cynical or even a morbidly pessimistic bone in his body. Despite everything, he believed that it wasn't a bad world. His most important inventions had disappeared somewhere in the papyraphagous mew of the Patent Office. A manufacturer had just walked right over him, without stopping, and the court he had gone to for help hadn't even been able to hide its contempt for Jerome H. Lemelson. Moreover, he had just learned that this was the customary state of affairs for small-fries of his vocation.

But that was just what it was — a vocation, a calling. By now, Lemelson derived an aesthetic or spiritual — or some kind of — satisfaction that went beyond the money he wasn't making from inventing. He was irrepressible. He was thinking up new inventions at the rate of one a month, a pace that he managed to keep up for the next thirty years.

Once Lemelson had designed robots that did every imaginable industrial chore, he designed a robot that inspected what the other robots had done. He invented robot-vision or "image analysis" machines that could, among other things, detect diseased blood or tissue cells, such as cancer cells. He invented the "computer-controlled coordinate measuring machine," which would later be used to measure and align the tiles on the exterior of the space shuttles. He invented a computerized tourniquet that would allow a surgeon to perform an operation without stopping to turn valves to alter the flow of a patient's blood. He designed several systems for transfer of information between computers. He designed two laser-powered recording and reproduction systems, Lasercard and Videocard, to perform the computer functions now performed by floppy disks. He invented a widely used "automated teller machine" that scans credit cards and checks out their credit status. He invented both a cordless telephone and a cordless videophone.

At the same time, he was turning out toy and novelty designs. He designed the "watchpen," a ballpoint pen with a watch built into it. He invented the flexible-track car toy — one of the biggest-selling toys of all time — manufactured by at least five companies under different names, Hot Wheels being the best known. He invented the Velcro dart game, in which you throw a Velcro-covered ball, instead of a steel-tipped dart, at a Velcro-

covered dart board. He invented the "printing putty toy," best
known under the brand name Monster Print Putty, with which
you can remove words and pictures from a newspaper and re-
print them on another piece of paper. Lemelson was thinking
up these things, doing the drawings, writing the descriptions,
and dispatching them to the Patent Office so fast, his two sons
called him The Blur.

During the early 1960s, when Lemelson was pushing forty, the
patents finally started rolling in. First was his video filing system
in 1961. Then the automated warehouse in 1962. In 1966, almost twelve years after he had submitted the application, his
universal robot patent was issued. Devol's had come through
five years earlier.

Lemelson closed his first major deal in 1964, selling an exclusive license for his automated warehouse system to a firm called
Triax, but almost immediately he was up to his neck in lawsuits.
Other firms, he and Triax charged, had already begun pirating
the invention in violation of Triax's license. That litigation continues today, twenty-two years later.

In 1967, he sold an exclusive license to an English company,
Molins, for the automated machine shop. In 1973, he made the
best deal of his career, selling an exclusive license for his cassette
drive mechanism to Sony. Sony sublicensed it to more than a
hundred Japanese firms. Today, practically every audio cassette
player on the market operates with the Lemelson drive.

None of this brought any dramatic improvement in Lemelson's style of living. In 1959, after the birth of their second son,
he and Dolly moved from a garden apartment in Metuchen,
New Jersey, looking out not onto a garden but U.S. Route 1, to
an eight-room house in Metuchen on a quarter of an acre. It
wasn't until 1985 that they moved to greener, grander scenery
in Princeton. No small part of the picture was the hundreds of
thousands of dollars that Lemelson was spending on legal fees,
trying to deal with American firms.

From the first, there were cases of what he regarded as the
most arrant infringement. It absolutely stupefied him. The re-
tort of "go ahead and sue" (. . . "and we'll bury you under a ton
of paper") was standard practice. Some firms were bluffing. If
you brought suit, they would settle. But there was only one way

to find out, which was to sue. Other firms were not bluffing. They would spend half a million dollars in legal fees to keep from taking a license and paying royalties they knew wouldn't run over $150,000. Lemelson couldn't figure these people out. He didn't know whether they were trying to teach a lesson to other small-fry inventors — the lesson being that Lemelson's legal bills were running well over $150,000 — or whether these were displays of sheer competitive ego.

Sometimes the lawsuits sprang up on so many fronts, it was hard to keep track of them. Lemelson found himself suing all the major manufacturers of the flexible-track car toy. These cases live on today. Some of the suits turned ludicrous, but the laughs never came cheaply.

In one case, Lemelson was suing the U.S. government and two private manufacturers over the same invention. He decided to abandon the case against the government and grant it a license free of charge. The private firms sought to block this move, apparently on the grounds that the government's acceptance of the license implied recognition of Lemelson's patent rights.

He ended up spending $18,000 in lawyers' fees to give the license away.

Lemelson was in noble, but expensive, company. Robert Goddard, now called — officially, by the U.S. government — the father of American rocketry, ran a lone-wolf rocket program west of nowhere in the New Mexico desert in no small part to try to put an end to the pirating of his patented inventions — chiefly by the U.S. government.

Fifteen years after his death, the government gave his wife $1 million to settle his many claims of infringement. There was something melancholy about this refrain of the widow and the million dollars.

One day Lemelson met a lawyer who had been in on the Armstrong case. Edwin Armstrong was the inventor of FM, frequency modulation, the greatest advance in broadcasting since the invention of the radio itself. In 1940, the Radio Corporation of America offered Armstrong a flat fee of $1 million for his FM patents. The lawyer had been in the room when Armstrong was handed the check. Armstrong looked at it and then, with great deliberation, tore it up and dropped the pieces on the floor.

In 1948, Armstrong sued RCA, Motorola, and several other corporations for patent infringement. The lawyers rubbed their hands and licked their chops and started manufacturing a ton of paper. By the early 1950s, Armstrong was lamenting, "They will stall this along until I am dead or broke." It was the former. On the night of January 31, 1954, he jumped out the window of his Manhattan apartment ten stories above the East River. For some reason, he put on his overcoat, scarf, hat, and gloves before he jumped. Late that year, his widow accepted a million-dollar settlement. It was the merest fraction of what his invention had come to be worth.

Then there was the case of another loner, Gordon Gould, one of the three main holders of patents on the laser. Gould and Lemelson were about the same age. They had hit upon their major concepts at about the same time, the mid-1950s. Gould had been a thirty-six-year-old graduate student at Columbia University when what he called "the fire" first possessed him. He was the one who thought up the acronym LASER (for Light Amplification by Stimulated Emission of Radiation). For twenty-seven years he was embroiled in legal battles on two fronts, with the Patent Office and with laser manufacturers.

By the time a court ordered the Patent Office to grant him his key patents, Gould had retired. He was spending his golden years with his lawyers. He had twelve lawsuits going in the United States and Canada. His legal bills had come to $2.5 million, much of it paid for by a firm that would get 64 percent of his income — down the road — if he won the suits.

As for himself, Gould indicated in an interview, he was long past the stage of life in which the big money would interest him, even if it ever came.

Lemelson's problems were still more complicated, because he had so many patents. He lived like a chess player who takes on forty opponents at once, walking from board to board, trying to keep straight in his mind what threats are coming up where.

Well, at least Lemelson had had enough victories to be able to

Land of Wizards

keep breathing in the avalanche of paper and lawyers' bills. Very few independent inventors had the money even to get in the game.

In the late 1970s, it began to dawn on government statisticians that the United States was no longer the great world center of technological innovation. Over a single five-year stretch, 1971 to 1976, the number of American citizens receiving U.S. patents declined by 21 percent. The number of foreign citizens receiving U.S. patents increased by 16 percent. By 1979, about four of every ten new U.S. patents were going to foreigners. That year, the subject began to break out in the press. *Newsweek* ran a cover story titled "Innovation: Has America Lost Its Edge?" The conclusion was that it had lost it, or was losing it, to the Japanese. That was not news to Lemelson. The underlying problem, as he saw it, was the sad fate of the independent inventor.

By the late 1970s, the corporations had managed to create the impression that in the twentieth century the greatest technological innovations were no longer coming from the loners but from the corporate and university research teams. But this had never been true. Innovation and corporate research were very nearly a contradiction in terms; at bottom, the corporations were interested only in improvements in existing product lines. As for the universities, they actually looked down upon invention as an amateur pastime, despite the fact that much scientific study, especially in the area of electronics, was nothing more than the analysis of discoveries made by inventors.

In 1975, Lemelson was appointed to the Patent and Trademark Office Advisory Committee. In July 1979, he testified at Senate hearings investigating what was beginning to be called "the innovation crisis." In a prepared statement, he said that corporations and the courts had combined to create an "antipatent philosophy" in the United States. "Company managers know that the odds of an inventor being able to afford the costly litigation are less than one in ten; and even if the suit is brought, four times out of five the courts will hold the patent invalid. When the royalties are expected to exceed the legal expense, it makes good business sense to attack the patent."

He contrasted this with the situation in Japan, where patent law was taken seriously, both morally and legally. "Although the majority of my income is derived from foreign licenses, I have *never* had to enforce a patent against a foreign infringer. I leave it to you to conclude the reason as to why the attitude is so different. My licensees have told me that they recognize the clear value of invention from an economic point of view. They feel that the United States has lived off the fat of its own technology for so long that we don't recognize that the consequence of the legal destruction of patents is a decline in innovation, a situation that is not within anyone's economic interest.

"What all this means to the inventor is that he either quits inventing or he licenses foreign."

One fine day a few months ago, Lemelson was in his New York office on Park Avenue, near Grand Central Terminal, talking to a reporter from a magazine. The two of them were sitting on a couch across from Lemelson's desk. The reporter had on a checked suit and a shirt collar like Herbert Hoover's. It looked about four inches high. Underneath his necktie you could see a brass-plated collar button of the sort that went out forty-six years ago. Lemelson's office, on the other hand, had a cool, immaculate, low-slung, modern look in tones of beige, gray, taupe, and teak. Lemelson himself was just as neatly composed. He was wearing a navy blazer, dark gray pants, a blue shirt, and a sincere necktie. He was now sixty-two years old and what remained of his curly hair was turning gray. But he was as trim as a digital watch. That morning, as usual, he had run a mile and a half and done forty push-ups, fifty sit-ups, and a hundred sidesaddle hops. His face had the gaunt athletic look of those who stare daily down the bony gullet of the great god Aerobics.

The reporter with the collar was wrapping his eyebrows around his nose as he tried to think of the technical terms concerning Lemelson's inventions. Lemelson listened patiently and sipped a glass of orange juice. Every now and then, one of the two telephones on the desk would ring. Lemelson would excuse himself and walk to the desk. One telephone had an ordinary ring, and he would answer that one by saying hello. The other one rang with an electronic burble. That one he would answer by saying, "Licensing Management." Licensing Management Corp. was a firm he had created chiefly to sell licenses for his own inventions to manufacturers.

"Licensing Management . . . Yes . . . This is Jerry Lemelson . . . Oh, hi . . . No, I can't do it this week. I have three days of depositions coming up."

The other telephone rings.

"Hello? . . . Oh, hi . . . Thursday of next week? I can't make it. I have to be in Cleveland . . . What for? For a deposition."

It goes on like that.

"Hello? . . . Yes . . . Oh, hi . . . This afternoon? . . . I won't be here that late. I have an appointment with my lawyer in half an hour."

Lemelson walks back to the couch. The reporter with the trick collar says, "If you don't mind my asking, when do you . . . *invent?*"

"On the train."

"On the train?"

"On the train out to Princeton, where I live."

"On the train," the fellow with the collar repeats it, all the while staring at him, apparently wondering if Lemelson is putting him on. But Lemelson isn't the type.

Then the fellow says, "Your opponents say, or they imply, that you make your money by filing lawsuits."

Not much ruffles Jerome H. Lemelson, but this gets under his skin.

"Who said that?"

"One of the lawyers."

Lemelson shakes his head. "Oh, sure. They accuse me of being litigious. But I've *lost* money on litigation. I've spent more than a million dollars on it, and I don't even like to think about the time."

"Then why get involved in it?"

"*Why?* To protect my rights. What do you do when your rights are being violated? Lie down? Walk away? You show me a successful inventor who hasn't been a scrapper."

Then his expression changes. "I don't know if I should even stress this side of it. It all sounds so negative. I don't want to discourage inventors. I want to encourage them. I think we ought to have something like the National Inventors Council

that we had during World War II. The government called upon
our people for inventions to help win the war. They received
four hundred thousand ideas during World War II alone, and
over four thousand of them actually went into production, and
they helped win the war. I'd like to see this type of thing revived
to see if we can win the technological battle with the rest of the
world."

He thinks a moment. "There's nothing wrong with our patent
system itself. We just need to protect patents. And actually
things are getting a little better. There's a new federal court for
handling patent cases now, the court of appeals for the federal
circuit, and the judges know patent law. Your chances are much
better now. They're about fifty-fifty."

"If every opponent in every piece of litigation you have going
right now decided to settle in your favor, how much money
would you receive?"

The thought of the corporations suffering this sudden mass
attack of equity makes Lemelson laugh. "Millions. It won't turn
out that way, of course.

"But I don't have any regrets. This has been a good life. I've
been independent, and I've done exactly what I wanted to do."

The train to Princeton was fifteen or twenty minutes out of
Penn Station, and everybody was settling into the dim blue haze
of the car and the jouncing and bouncing. The roadbed was in
a little better shape than it used to be. They were starting to
replace the old wooden ties with concrete. It would be easy
enough to invent better rail systems, and no doubt plenty of
people had, but they would never be built, and so it wasn't worth
thinking about.

A little more of the lurching there in the haze, a few more
metal shrieks from between the cars, and — bango! — it came
to Lemelson, just like that. The drug delivery system, the whole
thing — it all came to him while he was sitting there. For a long
time he had been trying to think of a way to use drugs to treat
a diseased area of the body without having to diffuse the chem-
icals and subject the entire body to their effects, as happens in
chemotherapy. For people with certain forms of cancer, it
would be a godsend. And now he had it! The time-release thing!
The insertion system! All the parts were in place!

Lemelson reached into his briefcase and pulled out the pad he always kept on hand for such moments as these. He was aware for the first time of the man sitting next to him. The man looked like nothing more than a dead-average New Jersey commuter, but you never knew. You just never knew. Lemelson began writing it all down in a shorthand he had created for himself. The drug delivery. The time release. He was no longer aware of the haze and the motion of the car. He was soaring. It was like the beginning, once more, of a dream come true.

Biographical Notes

JOHN BARTH is the author of *The Floating Opera; The End of the Road; The Sot-Weed Factor; Giles Goat-Boy; Letters; Sabbatical: A Romance; Lost in the Fun House,* a series of short fictions; *The Friday Book: Essays and Other Nonfiction;* and *Chimera,* a volume of novellas that won the National Book Award for fiction in 1973. He was elected in 1974 to both the National Institute of Arts and Letters and the American Academy of Arts and Sciences, and is currently the Alumni Centennial Professor of English and Creative Writing at Johns Hopkins University. His latest book is *The Tidewater Tales: A Novel.*

RICHARD BEN CRAMER has been a magazine writer for several years and was formerly Middle East correspondent for the *Philadelphia Inquirer.* His work has appeared in *Esquire* and *Rolling Stone,* and he has written on a variety of public figures. He is currently writing a book on the 1988 presidential campaigns. He lives in San Francisco and Washington, D.C.

JOHN GREGORY DUNNE is the author of *Delano; The Studio; Vegas; True Confessions; Quintana and Friends; Dutch Shea, Jr.;* and *The Red, White and Blue.* With his wife, Joan Didion, he has co-authored several screenplays, including *Panic in Needle Park, A Star Is Born,* and *True Confessions.* He has contributed articles and essays to many magazines.

GRETEL EHRLICH is the author of *The Solace of Open Spaces* and *Wyoming Stories.* Her essays have appeared in *Harper's, The Atlantic, Time,* the *New York Times, New Age Journal,* and *Antaeus.* Her novel, *Heart Mountain,* and a new collection of essays are forthcoming from Houghton Mifflin in spring 1988. She lives with her husband on a ranch in Shell, Wyoming.

DANIEL MARK EPSTEIN is the author of five books of poetry, the most recent of which is *Spirits,* two plays, textbooks, and a collection of memoirs and essays, *Star of Wonder,* in which "The Case of Harry Houdini" appears. In 1977 he received the Prix de Rome in literature from the American Academy and Institute of Arts and Letters, and in 1983 a Guggenheim Fellowship. He is writer-in-residence at Towson State University in Baltimore.

JOSEPH EPSTEIN is the editor of *The American Scholar.* His essays and stories have appeared in *Commentary, The New Criterion, Harper's, The Hudson Review,* and *The New Yorker.* His most recent book, a collection of familiar essays, is *Once More Around the Block,* published by W. W. Norton. His new collection of literary essays, to be entitled *A Better Class of Goods,* will appear sometime next year.

GARY GIDDINS, a staff writer for *The Village Voice,* is the author of three books on music, *Riding on a Blue Note, Rhythm-a-ning,* and *Celebrating Bird: The Triumph of Charlie Parker,* which won an American Book Award and has been adapted by Giddins as a documentary film. In 1985 he founded the American Jazz Orchestra, an eighteen-piece repertory ensemble that resides at Cooper Union. He is at work on a two-volume history of recorded jazz, an illustrated study of Louis Armstrong, and a collection of essays on musical and literary subjects.

DONALD HALL'S eighth book of poems, *The Happy Man,* appeared in 1986. He lives on a family farm in New Hampshire where he makes his living by free-lance writing. In 1987 he published his first book of short stories, *The Ideal Bakery,* a play in verse called *The Bone Ring,* and a book of essays, *Seasons at Eagle Pond,* which includes "Winter."

PHILLIP LOPATE is the author of two novels, *The Rug Merchant* and *Confessions of Summer,* two poetry books, *The Daily Round* and *The Eyes Don't Always Want to Stay Open,* a collection of personal essays, *Bachelorhood,* and a nonfiction book, *Being with Children.* He is currently writing a new volume of essays, tentatively titled *Against Joie de Vivre.* He teaches one semester at the University of Houston and lives the rest of the year in New York City.

BARRY LOPEZ has published several collections of short stories and is the author of *Arctic Dreams,* which won an American Book Award in 1986, and *Of Wolves and Men,* which won the John Burroughs Medal in 1979. A contributing editor to *Harper's* and *North American Review,* he has received an Award in Literature from the American Academy and Institute of Arts and Letters. His new book, *Crossing Open Ground*, will be published next year.

ELTING E. MORISON is Killian Professor of Humanities Emeritus at the Massachusetts Institute of Technology. He is the author of *Men, Machines and Modern Times* and *From Know-How to Nowhere* and editor of the eight-volume *Letters of Theodore Roosevelt*. He is at present a contributor to *American Heritage*.

WILLIAM PFAFF writes political essays for *The New Yorker* and a column for the *International Herald Tribune* and the Los Angeles Times Syndicate. Until 1978, he was deputy director of the European affiliate of Hudson Institute. Earlier, he had been a political warfare officer, a soldier, and an editor, as well as the author or co-author of four books on contemporary history and politics.

SAMUEL PICKERING, JR., teaches English at the University of Connecticut. He is the author of critical books on evangelical religion and the novel and on John Locke and eighteenth-century children's books. Two books of his familiar essays have been published, *A Continuing Education* and *The Right Distance*, recently published by the University of Georgia Press. He is now completing another collection of essays called *May Days*.

GREGOR VON REZZORI is an Austro-Italian born in Rumania. Of his novels written in German, two have been published in English translations, *Memoirs of an Anti-Semite* and *The Death of My Brother Abel*. In 1958 he translated Vladimir Nabokov's *Lolita* into German. Rezzori, who wrote his report on Lolitaland in English, lives in Tuscany and New York.

PHYLLIS ROSE is the author of two biographical works, *Woman of Letters: A Life of Virginia Woolf* and *Parallel Lives: Five Victorian Marriages*. She has written about literature and life for *The Atlantic*, *Vogue*, the *Washington Post Book World*, the *New York Times Book Review*, and *The Nation*, and did the "Hers" column for the *New York Times* for ten weeks. Some of her reviews and literary essays appeared in her collection, *Writing of Women*. A professor of English at Wesleyan University, she is currently working on a book about Josephine Baker, the black American dancer who went to Paris in 1925 and never came back.

SCOTT RUSSELL SANDERS teaches literature and intellectual history at Indiana University. He is the author of ten books, including *The*

Paradise of Bombs, which appeared earlier this year and won the Associated Writing Programs Award for creative nonfiction. Two of his novels, *The Invisible Company* and *The Engineer of Beasts,* will appear in 1988. "Quarriers" and "Stone Towns and the Country Between," both of which were listed among "Notable Essays of 1985," have been collected in *Stone Country,* a book about southern Indiana's limestone region.

ROBERT STONE is the author of *A Hall of Mirrors,* which won the Faulkner Award in 1967; *Dog Soldiers,* which received the National Book Award in 1975; *A Flag for Sunrise* in 1981; and *Children of Light* in 1986. His articles and short stories have appeared in many publications, and he has received the John Dos Passos Prize for literature and an award from the American Academy and Institute of Arts and Letters. He taught creative writing for many years at Amherst College and recently at the University of California at San Diego.

CALVIN TRILLIN wrote a column for *The Nation* from 1978 to 1985 and is currently a syndicated columnist. He is the author of many books, including *U.S. Journal, American Fried, Runestruck, Floater, Uncivil Liberties, Killings, With All Disrespect,* and *If You Can't Say Something Nice.* He has been a staff writer with *The New Yorker* since 1963, where "Rumors Around Town" appeared as part of his "U.S. Journal" series. Mr. Trillin lives in New York with his wife and their two daughters.

GEOFFREY C. WARD is the author of *Before the Trumpet: Young Franklin Roosevelt 1882–1905* and is currently at work on three books: a second volume on FDR, a brief history of the Civil War, and *Return Passage,* a personal look at India as he knew it thirty years ago and as it is today, in which an expanded version of "Tiger in the Road!" will eventually appear. He is a former editor of *American Heritage,* for which he does a regular column, "Matters of Fact," and he also writes historical documentaries for Florentine Films.

TOM WOLFE holds a Ph.D. in American studies from Yale University and is the author of many books, including *The Kandy-Kolored Tangerine-Flake Streamline Baby, The Electric Kool-Aid Acid Test, Radical Chic & Mau-Mauing the Flak Catchers, The Painted Word,* and *From Bauhaus to Our House. The Right Stuff* won the American Book Award for general nonfiction in 1980. He received the Columbia Journalism Award in 1980 and the John Dos Passos Award in 1984. His first novel, *The Bonfire of the Vanities,* is being published this year.

Notable Essays of 1986

Selected by Robert Atwan

EDWARD ABBEY
Even the Bad Guys Wear White Hats.
  Harper's, January.

JOSEPH ALSOP
Art into Money. *The New York Review
  of Books,* July 17.

ANTHONY BAILEY
Coracles. *The New Yorker,* June 2.

ROY BARRETTE
A Neighbor's Farewell. *Yankee,*
  February.

CONGER BEASLEY, JR.
The Return of Beavers to the
  Missouri River. *Antaeus,* Autumn.

JACK BEATTY
Along the Western Front. *The
  Atlantic,* November.

RALPH BEER
Wind upon the Waters. *Antaeus,*
  Autumn.

SAUL BELLOW
Chicago: The City That Was, The
  City That Is. *Life,* October.

JOHN BERGER
Her Secrets. *Threepenny Review,*
  Summer.

MARTHA BERGLAND
Salt Creek, Truly Toothacher, and
  Stringtown Lane. *New England
  Review and Bread Loaf Quarterly,*
  Summer.

SVEN BIKERTS
The Rage of Caliban. *Pequod,* No. 22.

JOHN BRENTLINGER
A Nicaraguan Journal. *Massachusetts
  Review,* Fall/Winter.

HAROLD BRODKEY
A Partisan's View of World Peace.
  Partisan Review, No. 4.

FRANKLIN BURROUGHS
A Pastoral Occasion. *Kenyon Review,*
  Fall.

WILLIAM BURROUGHS
The Cat Inside. *Conjunctions,* No. 9.

PHILIP CAPUTO
Styron's Choice. *Esquire,* December.

CALVIN TRILLIN
The Life and Times of Joe Bob
  Briggs, So Far. *The New Yorker,*
  December 22.

ALICE WALKER
Redemption Day. *Mother Jones,*
  December.

PHILIP WEISS
Forbidden Pleasures. *Harper's,* March.

MAX WESTBROOK
An Apology for the Non-Traveler.
  North Dakota Quarterly, Fall.

ROBERT WEXELBLATT
Complaining Before and After 1984.
  Iowa Review, Vol. 16, No. 2.

Interested readers will also find many
essays in the following special
magazine issues that appeared in
1986:

Antaeus: "On Nature," edited by
Daniel Halpern (Autumn); *North
Dakota Quarterly:* "Travel/Travail,"
edited by Robert W. Lewis (Fall);
Salmagundi: "Intellectuals," edited by
Robert Boyers (Spring-Summer);
TriQuarterly: "The Writer in Our
World," edited by Reginald Gibbons.

CORRECTION
In *The Best American Essays 1986* the
title of the essay by Alexander
Cockburn was incorrect. It should
have been: "Heatherdown: A Late
Imperial Memoir."